Southern Living®

2021 Annual Recipes

COCONUT-LIME
CUPCAKES
(PAGE 155)

ERIKA KWEE'S CARROT SPICE CAKE WITH CANDIED PECANS AND BROWN SUGAR CARAMEL SAUCE (PAGE 206)

STICKY-SWEET
KOREAN
BARBECUE RIBS
(PAGE 224)

SPOON BREAD
WITH MUSHROOMS
AND HERBS
(PAGE 88)

RASPBERRY-WHITE
CHOCOLATE
MERINGUE SANDWICHES
(PAGE 71)

CHRISTMAS CRAB CAKES
(PAGE 333)

Cooking Our Way Through

Dear Friends,

Cooking is often a communal activity, and that's especially true of the work we do in the *Southern Living* Test Kitchens. There are groceries to buy, pots and pans to get ready, ingredients to prep, and recipes to taste until we get them right. If you visit the fifth floor of our Birmingham offices on a normal day, it can look like a bunch of folks getting ready for a giant church potluck. Of course, the last year has been anything but normal. Our Test Kitchen staffers have had to find new ways of working—wearing masks, socially distancing, and sometimes working from their home kitchens—even as they create hundreds of new recipes for the readers of *Southern Living*.

The book you're holding represents the creative work of these talented cooks, as well as the editors, photographers, food stylists, and prop stylists who bring the recipes to life in our pages. As we've done for the last 55 years, our Test Kitchen pros methodically test and fine-tune every recipe until it meets our very high standards, even when challenged with the curveballs thrown by COVID-19. If you find a recipe in the pages of *Southern Living*, you can cook with confidence that it's worth making and sharing. Despite all the disruptions of 2021, that promise has not changed.

Perhaps now more than ever, we believe in inspiring and guiding our readers to cook together, eat together, and create lasting memories around the dinner table. Our "Quick Fix" recipes are easy weeknight dishes that never skimp on flavor. Our "Southern Classic" recipes are beloved regional favorites that always come with a story. And we never forget dessert. Whether you're an experienced baker or an eager amateur, you'll find sweet delights that you'll always be proud to serve.

We're excited to share our year with you, and we hope this collection brings you some comfort, inspiration, and joy.

Sid Evans
Editor-in-Chief
Southern Living magazine

Contents

Top-Rated Recipes

We cook, we taste, we refine, we rate—and at the end of each year, our Test Kitchen shares the highest-rated recipes from each issue exclusively with *Southern Living Annual Recipes* readers.

January–February

- Mashed Potatoes and Rutabaga with Collards (page 22) We combined three of our favorite vegetables into one irresistible side dish. Serve alongside beef roast, pork tenderloin, or baked chicken for a delicious dinner.
- German Chocolate Cake (page 25) Our version of this beloved cake has a special surprise in the frosting and whips up in no time. You'll never turn to a boxed cake mix again.
- Spicy Spaghetti Squash with Shrimp (page 29) Once you master the art of spaghetti squash, you'll use it for all your pasta recipes. This delicious recipe is one of our all-time favorites.
- Red Rice (page 33) This classic Lowcountry favorite calls for ham, but you can leave it out for a vegetarian dish or substitute chicken or sausage. The sky is the limit!
- Slow-Cooker Chipotle Brisket Sliders (page 35) We love these sandwiches for game-day tailgating—the perfect combination of spicy and sweet.

SLOW-COOKER CHIPOTLE
BRISKET SLIDERS

March

- Raspberry Snack Cake with Salted Milk Chocolate Frosting (page 45) Single-layer snack cakes have a heartier texture than multilayer cakes and can be prepared on a whim. They are just as easy to throw together as a boxed cake mix, and this beautiful and tasty cake will soon be a family favorite.
- Chocolate-Banana Custard Pie (page 49) You'll go bananas for this pie! The secret to success is all in the bananas. For best results, use bright yellow bananas with no brown spots.
- Slow-Cooker French Onion Soup (page 52) Once you make this blissfully delicious bistro classic in the slow cooker, you'll never go back to stovetop.
- Sunshine Smoothie (page 60) This creamy smoothie is packed with vitamins A and C, thanks to mangoes and orange juice, and is a refreshing way to start your day.

April

- Spicy Strawberry-Goat-Cheese Crostini (page 65) Sweet strawberries and tangy goat cheese complement each other perfectly in this easy-to-prepare appetizer that's as pretty as it is delicious.
- Basic Meringue (page 67) Sweet and light, this basic meringue recipe include tips and step-by-step instructions to ensure your meringue is glossy, stiff, and beautiful each and every time. Then enjoy five recipes to show off your new skills.
- Flourless Pecan-Fudge Cake (page 77) You won't miss the flour in this beautiful and delicious dessert. Make it ahead for Easter or Passover celebration, then enjoy serving it to your guests.
- Simple Seared Fish with Pea Salad (page 78) This quick and easy meal is on the table in about 30 minutes—a boon for busy weeknights. Prepare with fillets one time, then meaty scallops or shrimp the next.
- Shrimp Cake Sandwiches (page 81) The next time you crave a burger, try these hearty shrimp patty sandwiches, topped with creamy mayo-sriracha sauce, crunchy red onion, juicy tomato slices, and tender Bibb lettuce. They're a mouthwatering swap from traditional burgers.

May

- Cucumber-Mint Mojitos (page 105) Get ready for refreshment and relaxation. This vibrant, garden-fresh green mojito will be a new summertime staple, perfect for cooling off by the pool or sipping during happy hour on the porch. You'll want to keep a batch in your fridge all summer.
- Blueberry-Citrus Rolls with Orange Glaze (page 110) If you're pressed for time, use purchased dough in place of making dough from scratch. The typical brown-sugar-and-cinnamon filling is replaced with jammy berries and orange zest, plus a sweet citrus glaze.
- Brown Butter Blondies (page 115) Similar in flavor to chocolate chip cookies but more dense in texture, this hybrid bar will please all ages. Because these blondies hold up well, they're a good choice for make-ahead desserts.

HASH BROWN FRITTATA

- Seared Steak and Field Pea Salad (page 117) A flawlessly seared flank steak is the star of this impressive meal. The marinade—composed of brown sugar, white balsamic vinegar, and olive oil—tenderizes the meat. A bright field pea salad is the ideal companion to a simple cut of steak.
- Hash Brown Frittata (page 121) Two timeless breakfast foods—eggs and hash browns—are transformed into a brunch showstopper. Once you learn the simple technique of how to make a frittata, the flavor possibilities are endless.

June

- Chicken with 40 Leaves of Basil (page 135) Inspired by the famous Chicken with 40 Cloves of Garlic recipe, this basil-filled bird is just as aromatic. Serve alongside crusty bread or roasted potatoes to enjoy every last bit of the herb oil.
- Fresh Mint-Chocolate Pie (page 138) This pie's decadent dark chocolate custard filling is infused with fresh mint for an intense flavor that you just can't get from an extract. Thanks to the dynamic duo of chocolate and mint, our Fresh Mint-Chocolate Pie strikes a perfect balance between fresh and rich.
- Turkey Cheeseburgers with Grilled Vidalia Onion Rings (page 143) Turkey burgers have a reputation for being dry and lacking flavor, but this burger is moist and tastes like a holiday roasted turkey.

- Sweet-and-Spicy Corn Soup (page 148) This fresh corn soup doesn't have to cook all day to develop serious flavor. Serve as part of a light lunch or as a starter to a family dinner.

July

- Lemon-Lime Poke Cake (page 155) The tangy combination of citrus-spiked sweetened condensed milk and buttermilk adds a double dose of moisture to a white cake mix.
- Creamed New Potatoes (page 163) We've tested hundreds of potato recipes over the years, and this creamy dish stands out. Somewhere between mashed potatoes and potato salad, it can be served hot or cold.
- Spiced Chicken and Veggie Kebabs with Grilled Pita Bread (page 168) Celebrate summertime with a backyard barbecue, and make this recipe the star of the show. Reminiscent of chicken shawarma with a light char and juicy interior, these kebabs have big flavor.
- Chorizo Breakfast Tacos (page 171) We packed these breakfast tacos with scrambled eggs and Mexican chorizo to keep you fueled for whatever the day brings.
- Jessica's Fried Green Tomatoes (page 173) The cornmeal and flour crust sets this recipe apart from others. In only a matter of minutes, your tomatoes will be battered and crispy fried.

August

- Cherries-and-Cream Icebox Cake (page 191) This stunning make-ahead chilled dessert will wow your guests. No oven required.
- Herb-Crusted Salmon with Potatoes and Tomatoes (page 192) We like the simplicity of this recipe—flaky salmon, tender potatoes, and garden-fresh tomatoes in a single pan. What could be easier?!
- Sheet Pan Jambalaya (page 196) Jambalaya is a Southern classic and takes hours of simmering to develop rich flavor. This weeknight-friendly version packs in all the Creole flavors and is on the table in 35 minutes.
- Cornmeal Waffles (page 197) These are a delicious change from ordinary, thanks to a light crunch of cornmeal. Top with berries and maple syrup, eggs and cheese, or bacon and spicy honey.

September

- Dark Chocolate-Pear Cake (page 217) Apples often star in fall baking. Here, we give pears the leading role in several desserts. Count on this deliciously dense cake to be a favorite.
- Sticky-Sweet Korean Barbecue Ribs (page 224) These ribs will fall off the bone, thanks to the Korean bulgogi marinade.
- Tortellini Mac and Cheese (page 229) This medley of shell pasta, tortellini, and three cheeses is super creamy and rich. Enjoy with a mixed greens salad.

CINNAMON-RAISIN ALMOND BUTTER DIP

- Cinnamon-Raisin Almond Butter Dip (page 233) We created this recipe to serve with sliced fruit, veggies, or crackers. But it works well as a sandwich spread, too.

BIG-BATCH MULLED CIDER

October

- Chicken Fricot (page 243) This chicken and vegetable soup, dotted with sausage-filled dumplings, is comfort food at its finest. This version of the classic Acadian dish received rave reviews in our Test Kitchen.
- Pumpkin Spice Candied Pecans (page 249) Sweet and buttery pecans are a must-have for holiday entertaining. Keep this Southern staple on hand for topping a frosted cake, gift-giving, or snacking.
- Skillet Pork Chops with Dijon-Buttermilk Sauce (page 253) Boneless chops and a creamy buttermilk-Dijon mustard sauce elevate this dish to weeknight-friendly.
- Autumn Salad with Maple-Cider Vinaigrette (page 259) A little bit sweet, a little bit savory, this vibrant fall salad of tender kale, roasted sweet potatoes, fragrant apples, and savory Manchego cheese is sure to be a hit. Butternut squash, diced pears, and Parmesan cheese are ideal complements and change-ups.
- Big-Batch Mulled Cider (page 259) A must-have recipe for fall entertaining, this slightly sweet mulled cider is infused with fruit and spices.

November

- Penne with Squash and Italian Chicken Sausage (page 268) This lovely fall recipe is easily customized to use what you have on hand. We chose kuri squash, but butternut squash works well also. Mostaccioli or ziti pasta can be swapped for penne pasta.
- Roasted Acorn Squash Salad with Sorghum-Tahini Vinaigrette (page 270) A beautiful salad for Thanksgiving, this dish boasts roasted squash, thinly sliced tart apple, tender kale, sweet dried cranberries, and a not-too-sweet vinaigrette.
- Apple Pie with Rye Crust and Cider Caramel (page 276) We've put a new twist on apple pie with an earthy rye flour crust and tart-sweet cider reduction. The wide lattice-top crust is a beautiful finish.
- John's Sweet Tea-Brined Smoked Turkey (page 280) The wet brine—made with black tea, citrus, herbs, and sorghum—paired with black tea rub and savory-sweet mopping sauce will get rave reviews.
- Lisa's Mashed Potatoes with Herbed Brown Butter (page 284) The essentials for these ultra-rich mashed potatoes are butter, half-and-half, cream cheese, and a drizzle of herbed brown butter.

JOHN'S SWEET TEA-BRINED SMOKED TURKEY

December

- Clementine-Vanilla Bean Marmalade (page 294) 'Tis the season for gift-giving and for juicy, easy-to-peel clementines. Though available year-round, these gems reach peak flavor October through January. Recipients will appreciate a festive tag with serving suggestions for crepes, scones, and croissants.
- Spicy Cheese Twists (page 301) Store-bought puff pastry is the MVP of party nibbles, and it has no higher calling than these slightly spicy, crispy, buttery cheese straws. They're at home as part of an appetizer buffet or serve-along with soups or pasta.
- Ambrosia Cheesecake (page 309) Ambrosia—a sweet mélange of citrus and coconut—is a beloved tradition of the South. This rich New York-style cheesecake can be prepared up to four days in advance, then add the ambrosia topping just before serving.
- Red Velvet Cake Crinkle Cookies (page 317) These little gems, coated in a sprinkling of powdered sugar, are velvety rich and will be the star of your holiday cookie exchange. Make an extra dozen (or two!) for yourself. Your family will thank you!
- Rosemary and Ginger Mule (page 330) Bar owner Chris Marshall created this seasonal sipper as an attractive nonalcoholic option for holiday gatherings. This delicious mocktail is filled with spirit!
- Slow-Cooker Short Ribs with Pork Rind Gremolata (page 332) For a fresh take on a comforting classic, look no further than this savory dish that looks impressive without being fussy. And best of all, it's made in a slow cooker, which gives you time to entertain without standing over a stove.

January–February

Rainbow Chard

Enjoy the leaves and stems, too

Quick Skillet Chard

ACTIVE 15 MIN. - TOTAL 15 MIN.
SERVES 6

Remove stems from 1 lb. **rainbow Swiss chard**; chop into 1-inch pieces. Tear chard leaves into bite-size pieces. Heat 2 Tbsp. **extra-virgin olive oil** in a skillet over medium-high. Add 1 **large garlic clove**, sliced. Cook, stirring often, until starting to brown, about 2 minutes. Stir in chard stems. Cook, covered, until just tender, about 4 minutes. Stir in chard leaves, 1 tsp. chopped **fresh oregano**, ½ tsp. **salt**, and ¼ tsp. **black pepper**. Cook, uncovered, stirring often, until leaves just wilt but are still bright green, about 2 minutes. Remove from heat. Sprinkle with 2 Tbsp. **toasted sliced almonds**.

It's hard not to smile when you spot a bunch of rainbow chard with its emerald leaves and candy-color stems. That's why it's odd that this vibrant, vitamin-packed vegetable isn't as popular as collards or kale. The tender leaves cook as quickly as spinach but retain more texture, so they don't wilt as much in the pan. The crunchy stems are tasty, too.

Tabitha Brown's Recipe for Happiness

The food journey for this North Carolina native made her a social media sensation

IT ALL STARTED WITH A SANDWICH. In 2018, actress Tabitha Brown purchased a TTLA (tempeh bacon, tomato, lettuce, avocado) on ciabatta bread. After eating the first half of her vegan "BLT," she picked up her cell phone to record a review. "Y'all. Lord have mercy," she said in a North Carolina drawl. "You know I can't sing, but this done made me sing."

For over a year prior to that she had experienced depression and debilitating headaches. She decided to go vegan for 30 days; by the tenth day, she had energy and her headaches were gone, and she had transitioned to a plant-based lifestyle. She finds creative ways to enjoy the staples she was raised on. "A Southern favorite would be my vegan mac and cheese," she explains. "This is good comfort food. My granny made it, my mom made it, and when I went vegan, I still had to have it in my life."

Tabitha Brown's Vegan Mac and Cheese

Nutritional yeast is inactive yeast that is used as a seasoning for its cheesy, slightly nutty flavor. It's available at well-stocked grocery stores, but you can omit it from the recipe with good results.

ACTIVE 25 MIN. · TOTAL 1 HOUR
SERVES 8

- 4 cups peeled, seeded, and chopped butternut squash (from 1 small [1½-lb.] squash)
- 3 cups peeled and chopped russet potato (from 1 large [about 12-oz.] potato)
- 1 Tbsp. garlic-herb seasoning blend
- 2 tsp. kosher salt, divided
- 1 cup vegetable broth, divided
- 8 oz. uncooked elbow macaroni
- ¼ cup unsalted dairy-free butter alternative
- ½ cup plain unsweetened dairy-free yogurt alternative
- 1 Tbsp. nutritional yeast
- ½ tsp. garlic powder
- 1 cup shredded vegan mozzarella cheese
- 2 cups shredded vegan cheddar cheese, divided
- ½ tsp. black pepper
- ½ tsp. paprika (optional)

1. Preheat oven to 375°F with rack 6 inches from heat source. Place squash and potato in a large stockpot, and add water to cover by 1 inch. Add garlic-herb seasoning blend and 1 teaspoon of the salt. Bring to a boil over medium-high. Cook, undisturbed, until squash and potato are tender when pierced with a knife, 15 to 20 minutes. Drain; transfer to a blender. Add ½ cup of the broth. Secure lid on blender, and remove center piece to allow steam to escape. Place a clean towel over opening. Process until completely smooth, 1 to 2 minutes.

2. While squash and potato cook, bring a separate large stockpot of salted water to a boil over high. Add pasta; cook according to package directions. Drain.

3. Melt dairy-free butter in a large broiler-safe, ovenproof skillet over medium-low. Add blended squash mixture, dairy-free yogurt, nutritional yeast, and garlic powder. Stir until smooth and combined. Add vegan mozzarella and 1 cup of the vegan cheddar. Cook, stirring constantly, until cheeses melt and mixture is smooth and creamy, about 2 minutes. Stir in pepper and remaining 1 teaspoon salt and ½ cup broth. Add drained pasta; stir together until evenly coated. Sprinkle pasta mixture with remaining 1 cup vegan cheddar; sprinkle with paprika, if using.

4. Cover skillet with aluminum foil, and bake in preheated oven 20 minutes. Remove foil. Increase oven temperature to broil; cook until cheese is melted and bubbling around edges, about 3 minutes.

A New Leaf

A staple on tables across the South, collard greens are surprisingly—and deliciously—versatile

I LEARNED ABOUT COLLARD GREENS from two important women in my life, their lessons delivered decades apart. First was my paternal grandmother, who (with my grandfather) tended a 10-acre farm near Grenada, Mississippi. I realized by the time I was 5 that collards were my favorite. Unlike the pungent mustard greens and bitter turnip greens that unfurled in their garden this time of year, collards were milder and sweeter. I loved the chewiness of the cooked leaves and the heady-green fragrance that filled the kitchen as they simmered.

Grandmama cooked hers for hours with a little bit of salt pork, water, salt, and pepper. She didn't add sugar to the pot, nor vinegar, so the flavor I grew up on was pure goodness. If you wanted extra oomph, you could shake on some pepper vinegar—but I never did. Spooned over split and toasted cornbread (also made without sugar, thank you very much), the simple greens made a soul-warming meal.

Later, when I was in my twenties, my boyfriend's (now husband's) mother, Jeanie, treated me to her collards, and I loved them so much that I overcame my shyness to ask her how she made

them. She happily shared her method: Cook some bacon in the pot, and remove the crispy bits for later. Then add your greens (torn into large pieces, with the stems still attached), and toss them around in the drippings with tongs until they're fully coated and slightly wilted. Add water, salt, and pepper; then cook for about an hour. Sprinkle the crisp bacon on top when serving.

Collards cooked this way have a wonderful texture, thanks to the stems (which offer more bite) and that initial toss in the smoky bacon fat (which makes the leaves silkier). One other thing Jeanie did that blew my mind: She simmered chunks of turnip root with her greens. I had never considered mixing "genres" like this, but the pairing was heaven.

I'm now in my early fifties and have discovered many more ways to enjoy those large sultry leaves. I like them raw in salads, where they bestow a gentle peppery bite. And because their flavor is relatively mild, I use wilted collards instead of spinach or kale in casseroles, soups, pilafs, and more.

My love for this vegetable is rooted in the simplicity of my grandmother's approach combined with the savory innovations of my mother-in-law. Although neither woman is with us now, their lessons remain with me to this day.
—Ann Taylor Pittman

Collard Green-and-Rice Fritters with Green Pesto

Serve these fritters with a crisp white wine for a memorable appetizer.
ACTIVE 30 MIN. · TOTAL 40 MIN.
MAKES 8 FRITTERS AND 1 CUP PESTO

- 6 cups coarsely chopped stemmed collard greens (from 1 [1-lb.] bunch)
- 1 (8.8-oz.) pkg. precooked microwavable long-grain white rice
- 2 large eggs, lightly beaten
- ¼ cup finely chopped shallot (from 1 large shallot)
- 3 Tbsp. cornstarch
- ¼ tsp. black pepper
- 3 oz. Parmesan cheese, grated (about ¾ cup), divided
- 1 tsp. kosher salt, divided
  Canola oil, for frying
- ⅓ cup loosely packed fresh flat-leaf parsley leaves
- ¼ cup chopped toasted pecans
- 1 medium garlic clove
- ½ cup extra-virgin olive oil
- 1 tsp. honey

1. Bring a large pot of water to a boil over high. Add chopped stemmed collards. Cook, stirring often, until bright green and wilted, about 3 minutes. Drain in a colander, then rinse under cold water. Squeeze collards firmly over sink to remove as much liquid as possible. Reserve half of collards (about 1 cup) for making pesto.

2. Place rice and remaining half of collards in a large bowl. Mix well using your hands, breaking up grains of rice. Stir in eggs, shallot, cornstarch, pepper, ½ cup of the cheese, and ½ teaspoon of the salt until thoroughly blended.

3. Pour canola oil to a depth of ¼ inch in a large, deep cast-iron skillet over medium-high. Working in 2 batches, carefully scoop 4 packed ¼ cupfuls of rice mixture into hot oil (oil will splatter). Press fritters with a spatula to flatten slightly. Cook until browned and crisp, 3 to 4 minutes per side. Transfer to a plate lined with paper towels, and cover fritters to keep warm. Repeat process with remaining rice mixture (you do not need to wipe skillet clean or add more oil).

4. Pulse together parsley, pecans, garlic, and reserved 1 cup collards in a food processor until finely chopped, about 10 pulses. Add olive oil, honey, and remaining ¼ cup cheese and ½ teaspoon salt, and process until well blended, about 1 minute. Spoon pesto into a small serving bowl and serve alongside fritters.

CREAMY COLLARD
SOUP WITH BACONY
CROUTONS (PAGE 21)

COLLARD GREEN SALAD
WITH ORANGES AND
PORT-SOAKED CHERRIES
(PAGE 22)

COLLARD-
ARTICHOKE-AND-
MUSHROOM STRATA

Collard-Artichoke-and-Mushroom Strata

A baguette that's firm and chewy, rather than soft and fluffy, will work best in this bread pudding.

ACTIVE 35 MIN. - TOTAL 2 HOURS, PLUS 7 HOURS CHILLING

SERVES 8

- 1 (12-oz.) rustic baguette, cut into 1-inch cubes (about 8 cups)
- 3 Tbsp. unsalted butter, plus more for greasing baking dish
- 1 cup chopped sweet onion (from 1 small onion)
- 1 (8-oz.) pkg. sliced fresh button mushrooms
- 6 cups chopped stemmed collard greens (from 1 [11-oz.] bunch)
- 1 tsp. kosher salt, divided
- 1 tsp. black pepper, divided
- 2 cups coarsely chopped thawed frozen artichoke hearts (about 8 oz.)
- 8 large eggs
- 2 cups half-and-half
- 1 (5.2-oz.) container garlic-and-herb spreadable cheese (such as Boursin)
- 8 oz. Swiss cheese, shredded (about 2 cups), divided

1. Preheat oven to 375°F. Arrange bread pieces in a single layer on a large rimmed baking sheet. Bake 10 minutes. Turn off oven; let bread stand in oven until crisp and dry on the outside and chewy on the inside, 5 minutes.
2. Meanwhile, melt butter in a large skillet over medium. Add onion and mushrooms. Cook, stirring occasionally, until onion is slightly softened, about 4 minutes. Add collards and ½ teaspoon each of the salt and pepper. Cover and cook, stirring occasionally, until collards are wilted, about 5 minutes. Stir in artichoke hearts; cover and cook 3 minutes. Uncover; let cool slightly, about 5 minutes.
3. Whisk eggs in a large bowl until lightly beaten. Add half-and-half, spreadable cheese, 1 cup of the Swiss cheese, and remaining ½ teaspoon each salt and pepper. Whisk until well blended. Add toasted bread and collard mixture; toss well to combine. Spoon into a 13- x 9-inch baking dish greased with butter. Sprinkle evenly with remaining 1 cup Swiss cheese. Cover with aluminum foil; chill at least 7 hours or up to 12 hours.
4. Preheat oven to 350°F. Let the casserole stand at room temperature 30 minutes. Uncover; bake until cheese is browned in spots and filling is set, about 45 minutes. Let stand 5 minutes before serving.

Creamy Collard Soup with Bacony Croutons

(Photo, page 18)

The croutons are baked with bacon drippings for a smoky topping.

ACTIVE 25 MIN. - TOTAL 35 MIN.

SERVES 6

- 8 thick-cut bacon slices, cut crosswise into 1-inch pieces (2 cups)
- 1½ cups chopped yellow onion (from 1 large onion)
- 3 medium garlic cloves, chopped (1 Tbsp.)
- 4 cups unsalted chicken stock
- 1¼ lb. Yukon Gold potatoes, peeled and cut into 1-inch pieces (about 4¼ cups)
- ¼ tsp. black pepper
- 1¾ tsp. kosher salt, divided
- 8 oz. chopped stemmed collard greens (about 8 cups)
- 5 cups torn (1-inch pieces) rustic sourdough bread (from 1 [1-lb.] loaf)
- 1½ cups heavy cream, plus more for drizzling
- 1 Tbsp. hot sauce

1. Preheat oven to 400°F. Cook bacon in a medium Dutch oven over medium-high, stirring occasionally, until crisp, 10 to 12 minutes. Using a slotted spoon, transfer bacon to paper towels to drain. Pour drippings (you should have about ½ cup) from pot into a heatproof bowl; reserve. Do not wipe Dutch oven clean.
2. Return 2 tablespoons of the reserved drippings to Dutch oven over medium-high. Add onion. Cook, stirring occasionally, until slightly softened, about 3 minutes. Add garlic. Cook, stirring often, until onion is softened, about 2 minutes. Add stock, scraping bottom of pot to loosen browned bits. Add potatoes, pepper, and 1¼ teaspoons of the salt. Let mixture come to a boil. Reduce heat to medium-low; simmer, uncovered, 5 minutes. Stir in collards. Cook, partially covered, until potatoes are tender, about 15 minutes.
3. Meanwhile, arrange bread pieces in an even layer on a baking sheet lined with aluminum foil. Drizzle with 4 tablespoons of the reserved drippings; toss to coat. (Reserve any remaining drippings for another use.) Bake in preheated oven until crisp and golden brown, 10 to 12 minutes, stirring once after 7 minutes. Let stand at room temperature 15 minutes.
4. Spoon half of the collard mixture into a blender; process until smooth, about 1 minute. Pour into a large bowl. Repeat process with remaining collard mixture. Stir 1½ cups cream, the hot sauce, and remaining ½ teaspoon salt into pureed collard mixture. Ladle soup into bowls. Drizzle with additional cream, and top with croutons and bacon.

In Praise of Potlikker

Some folks will argue that the best part of a pot of greens is the brothy, green liquid called potlikker (or "pot liquor" if you're fancy). It wasn't always beloved by all, though. Back in pre-Civil War days, plantation owners valued the greens drained of their liquid, but the enslaved cooks knew better and prized the potlikker, nurturing their families with the broth. It's nutrient-dense, as some of the vitamins leach out into the liquid (most notably, 60% of the vitamin C), and it's deliciously savory. Whenever you cook a pot of greens, don't toss it out. Spoon the greens and a pool of the liquid over a split piece of cornbread in a bowl; stir the potlikker into soup or rice; or simply sip it, with appreciation, from a cup.

Collard Green Salad with Oranges and Port-Soaked Cherries

(Photo, page 19)

Port-infused dried cherries make this simple salad extra special. If you'd rather skip the port, plain dried cherries will work well, too.

ACTIVE 25 MIN. - TOTAL 35 MIN.

SERVES 8

- ⅔ cup dried cherries
- ½ cup (4 oz.) port
- ¼ cup plus 1 Tbsp. extra-virgin olive oil
- 2 Tbsp. apple cider vinegar
- 1 Tbsp. whole-grain mustard
- 1 tsp. Dijon mustard
- 1 tsp. honey
- ½ tsp. kosher salt
- ½ tsp. black pepper
- 8 cups thinly sliced, stemmed collard greens (from 2 [1-lb.] bunches)
- ½ cup thinly sliced red onion (from 1 small onion), rinsed and drained
- 2 (6-oz.) navel oranges, peeled and sliced into ¼-inch-thick rounds (about 10 rounds)
- ½ cup toasted walnut halves
- 2 oz. goat cheese, crumbled (about ½ cup)

1. Microwave cherries and port in a small microwavable bowl on HIGH until port comes to a boil, about 90 seconds. Let stand 10 minutes. Drain, reserving cherries and 2 tablespoons port (discard remaining port).
2. Place oil, vinegar, whole-grain and Dijon mustards, honey, salt, pepper, and reserved 2 tablespoons port in a lidded jar. Seal lid; shake well until blended and creamy.
3. Place collards in a large bowl. Drizzle with half (about ⅓ cup) of the vinaigrette. Gently massage together using your hands until collards wilt, about 2 minutes. Add onion and oranges; toss gently to combine. Arrange salad on a platter or in a large bowl. Sprinkle with walnuts, goat cheese, and port-soaked cherries. Drizzle with remaining vinaigrette.

Mashed Potatoes and Rutabaga with Collards

Combine three vegetables into one creamy side dish. The cooked potatoes and rutabaga are a little wet right out of the pot, so let them drain and dry a bit so they can soak up more of the milk and butter.

ACTIVE 30 MIN. - TOTAL 50 MIN.

SERVES 12

- 2 lb. Yukon Gold potatoes, peeled and cut into 1-inch pieces (about 5 cups)
- 3 cups chopped (½-inch pieces) peeled rutabaga (from 1 [1½-lb.] rutabaga)
- 1 Tbsp., plus 1¼ tsp. kosher salt, divided
- ½ cup unsalted butter, cut into 1-Tbsp. pats, softened, divided
- 1 cup chopped scallions (white and light green parts only, from 1 [6-oz.] bunch)
- 6 cups coarsely chopped stemmed collard greens (from 1 [1-lb.] bunch)
- 1 cup whole milk, warmed
- 4 oz. white cheddar cheese, shredded (about 1 cup)

1. Place potatoes and rutabaga in a large Dutch oven or a large heavy-bottom saucepan, and cover with 9 cups cool water. Stir in 1 tablespoon of the salt. Bring mixture to a boil over high. Reduce heat to medium-high, and simmer until vegetables are very tender, about 20 minutes. Remove from heat. Drain; return cooked vegetables to Dutch oven. Let stand 5 minutes, or until they are dry and have a slightly chalky appearance.
2. Meanwhile, heat 3 tablespoons of the butter in a large skillet over medium until foamy. Add chopped scallions. Cook, stirring often, until scallion greens are slightly wilted, about 1 minute. Add collards and ½ teaspoon of the salt. Cover; cook, stirring occasionally, until collards are just tender-crisp, 7 to 8 minutes. Remove skillet from heat.
3. Add warm milk, 2 tablespoons of the butter, and remaining ¾ teaspoon salt to drained potato-rutabaga mixture. Mash to desired consistency using a potato masher. Stir in cheese and collard mixture until cheese is melted. Spoon into a serving bowl; top with remaining 3 tablespoons butter.

Layers of Love

Despite the name, German chocolate cake was born in Dallas in the 1950s.
Thanks to its ridiculously rich coconut–pecan frosting, it remains a classic

German Chocolate Cake

ACTIVE 25 MIN. · TOTAL 2 HOURS, 10 MIN.
SERVES 12

- 2 (4-oz.) German's sweet chocolate baking bars, chopped
- ½ cup strong brewed hot coffee
- 2¼ cups all-purpose flour, divided, plus more for pan
- 1 tsp. baking soda
- ½ tsp. salt
- 1 cup butter, softened
- 1 cup granulated sugar
- 1 cup packed light brown sugar
- 4 large eggs, separated
- 2 tsp. vanilla extract
- 1 cup whole buttermilk
  Vegetable shortening
  Coconut-Pecan Frosting (recipe follows)

1. Preheat oven to 350°F. Stir together chopped chocolate and hot coffee in a medium microwavable bowl. Microwave on HIGH until melted and smooth, 30 seconds to 1 minute, stirring mixture after 30 seconds. Set aside.
2. Whisk together flour, baking soda, and salt in a medium bowl. Beat butter and sugars with a heavy-duty stand mixer on medium speed until light and fluffy, about 3 minutes. Add egg yolks, 1 at a time, beating just until blended after each addition. Add melted chocolate mixture and vanilla, and beat on low speed until blended. Add flour mixture alternately with buttermilk, beginning and ending with flour mixture. Beat on low speed just until blended after each addition.
3. In a clean bowl beat egg whites with an electric mixer on high speed until stiff peaks form, about 3 minutes. Fold into batter. Grease (with shortening) three (9-inch) round cake pans. Line

HERE'S THE TRICKY PART
Don't spread the frosting the usual way—it's too thick. Press it gently into the sides and tops of the layers using a small spatula.

bottom of pans with parchment paper rounds; grease paper and dust pans with flour. Divide batter among pans.
4. Bake in preheated oven until a wooden pick inserted in center comes out clean, 24 to 28 minutes. Remove pans from oven; gently run a knife around outer edge of cake layers to loosen from sides of pans. Cool in pans on wire racks 15 minutes. Remove from pans; transfer to wire racks. Discard parchment paper. Cool completely, about 1 hour. Press slightly warm Coconut-Pecan Frosting between layers and on top and

sides of cake. Let stand until frosting is completely cool and set, about 15 minutes.

Coconut-Pecan Frosting

ACTIVE 25 MIN. · TOTAL 25 MIN., PLUS 40 MIN. STANDING
MAKES ABOUT 5 CUPS

- 1 (12-oz.) can evaporated milk
- ¾ cup butter
- ¾ cup granulated sugar
- ¾ cup packed light brown sugar
- 6 egg yolks, lightly beaten
- 2 cups sweetened flaked coconut
- 2 cups chopped toasted pecans
- 1½ tsp. vanilla extract

Stir together evaporated milk, butter, sugars, and egg yolks in a heavy 3-quart saucepan. Cook over medium heat, stirring constantly, until butter melts and sugars dissolve, 3 to 4 minutes. Cook, stirring constantly, until bubbling and a puddinglike thickness, 12 to 14 minutes. Remove from heat; stir in coconut, pecans, and vanilla. Transfer to a bowl. Let stand, stirring occasionally, until slightly warm and spreading consistency, about 40 minutes.

Pretty Healthy

Spring shouldn't get all the attention. Let fresh winter ingredients shine at dinner

Collard Salad with Chicken, Bell Pepper, and Roasted Squash

ACTIVE 20 MIN. - TOTAL 35 MIN.

SERVES 4

- 1 medium (2½-lb.) butternut squash, peeled, seeded, and cubed (7 cups)
- 1 medium-size red bell pepper, thinly sliced (1¼ cups)
- 2 medium shallots, sliced (½ cup)
- ¼ cup olive oil, divided
- 1½ tsp. kosher salt, divided
- 1 Tbsp. Champagne vinegar
- ¼ tsp. pure maple syrup
- 1 lb. fresh collard greens, stemmed and thinly sliced (about 9 cups)
- 2 cups coarsely shredded rotisserie chicken breast (from 1 rotisserie chicken)
- 2 oz. feta cheese, crumbled (about ½ cup)
- ⅓ cup roasted salted pumpkin seed kernels (pepitas)

1. Place 2 large rimmed baking sheets in oven; preheat oven to 425°F. (Do not remove baking sheets while oven preheats.) Toss butternut squash, bell pepper, and shallots with 2 tablespoons of the oil and 1 teaspoon of the salt in a large bowl. Spread evenly on preheated baking sheets. Roast until browned and tender, 20 to 25 minutes, tossing halfway through roasting time. Remove from oven; set aside to cool.

2. Whisk together vinegar, maple syrup, and remaining 2 tablespoons oil and ½ teaspoon salt in a small bowl.

3. Combine collards and 1 tablespoon of the dressing in a large bowl. Massage dressing into greens with hands until tender, about 30 seconds. Add chicken, squash-and-pepper mixture, feta, and pumpkin seed kernels to greens; toss gently to combine. Arrange on a serving platter; drizzle with remaining dressing.

Orange-Rosemary Roast Chicken

ACTIVE 20 MIN. · TOTAL 45 MIN.
SERVES 6

- 2 medium navel oranges, divided
- 1½ lb. baby Yukon Gold potatoes, cut into ¾-inch-thick wedges
- ⅓ cup loosely packed fresh rosemary leaves, divided
- ¼ cup olive oil, divided
- 2¼ tsp. kosher salt, divided
- ½ tsp. black pepper, divided
- 6 (6- to 7-oz.) bone-in, skin-on chicken thighs
- 1 Tbsp. white balsamic vinegar
- ¼ tsp. honey
- ½ cup mixed Kalamata and Castelvetrano olives, pitted and cut into pieces
- ⅓ cup thinly sliced scallions
- 1 oz. Parmigiano-Reggiano cheese, shaved (about ½ cup)

1. Place a large rimmed baking sheet in oven; preheat oven to 425°F. (Do not remove baking sheet while oven preheats.) Thinly slice 1½ of the oranges; place in a large bowl. Squeeze juice from remaining orange half into a small bowl to equal 2 tablespoons; set aside. Add potato wedges and ¼ cup of the rosemary leaves to orange slices; stir to combine. Add 1 tablespoon of the oil, ¾ teaspoon of the salt, and ¼ teaspoon of the pepper; toss to coat. Scatter potato mixture evenly on preheated pan; roast until starting to brown, about 15 minutes.

2. Meanwhile, season chicken evenly with 1 teaspoon of the salt and remaining ¼ teaspoon pepper. Heat 2 tablespoons of the oil in a large cast-iron skillet over medium-high. Add chicken, skin-side down; cook until deep golden brown, 5 to 7 minutes. Turn chicken; continue cooking until golden brown on both sides, about 4 minutes more. Transfer to baking sheet with potato mixture; return to oven. Roast until potatoes are browned and tender and a meat thermometer inserted into thickest part of chicken thighs registers 165°F, 12 to 15 minutes more.

3. While chicken and potatoes finish roasting, whisk together vinegar, honey, the reserved 2 tablespoons orange juice, and remaining ½ teaspoon salt and 1 tablespoon oil in a small bowl;. Remove baking sheet from oven; scatter olives, scallions, and shaved cheese over chicken and potatoes. Drizzle with juice mixture; sprinkle with remaining rosemary.

START WITH A SEAR

Yes, it requires two pans, but for crisp skin and meat that's never dry, brown the chicken in a skillet first then transfer it to the sheet pan to finish cooking in the oven.

Salmon with Pineapple-Pepper Salsa and Coconut Cauliflower Rice

ACTIVE 15 MIN. - TOTAL 35 MIN.

SERVES 4

- ½ cup finely chopped fresh pineapple
- ⅓ cup finely chopped red bell pepper (from 1 small pepper)
- ⅓ cup finely chopped red onion (from 1 onion)
- ⅓ cup finely chopped ripe avocado (from 1 avocado)
- ¼ cup finely chopped fresh cilantro, divided
- 2 Tbsp. fresh lime juice (from 2 small limes), divided
- 1¾ tsp. kosher salt, divided
- 4 (6-oz.) skin-on salmon fillets
- ½ tsp. black pepper
- ¼ cup canola oil, divided
- 3 garlic cloves, finely chopped (1 Tbsp.)
- 6 cups (24 oz.) riced cauliflower
- 1 cup unsweetened canned light coconut milk (from 1 [13.66-oz.] can)
- ½ cup toasted coconut chips (such as Dang, optional)

1. Combine pineapple, bell pepper, onion, avocado, 1 tablespoon of the cilantro, 2 teaspoons of the lime juice, and ¼ teaspoon of the salt in a bowl; set aside.

2. Season salmon with black pepper and ½ teaspoon of the salt. Heat 2 tablespoons of the oil in a large cast-iron skillet over medium-high. Add fish, flesh-side down; cook until golden brown and crispy, about 4 minutes. Turn fish over; reduce heat to medium-low. Cook until skin has crisped and a thermometer inserted in fish registers 125°F, about 5 minutes more. Remove from skillet to a large plate; cover with aluminum foil to keep warm.

3. Heat remaining 2 tablespoons oil in the same skillet over medium. Add garlic. Cook, stirring constantly, until fragrant, 1 minute. Add riced cauliflower. Cook, stirring occasionally, until starting to soften, 2 minutes. Add coconut milk. Cook, stirring occasionally, until milk is fully absorbed and cauliflower rice is just tender, about 5 minutes. Remove from heat; stir in coconut chips (if using) and remaining 3 tablespoons cilantro, 4 teaspoons lime juice, and 1 teaspoon salt. Divide cauliflower rice among 4 plates; top each with 1 salmon fillet and salsa.

Spicy Spaghetti Squash with Shrimp

ACTIVE 25 MIN. · TOTAL 35 MIN.

SERVES 4

- 1 large (3¼-lb.) spaghetti squash, cut in half lengthwise, seeded, and cut into half-moons
- ¼ cup olive oil, divided
- 1½ lb. medium-size peeled, deveined raw shrimp
- 1½ tsp. kosher salt, divided
- ½ tsp. black pepper, divided
- 1 cup chopped yellow onion (from 1 medium onion)
- 4 garlic cloves, finely chopped (4 tsp.)
- 3 anchovy fillets, finely chopped
- ½ tsp. crushed red pepper
- ⅓ cup dry white wine
- 1 (28-oz.) can crushed San Marzano plum tomatoes
- ¼ cup heavy whipping cream
- 2 oz. Pecorino Romano cheese, grated (about ½ cup), divided
- ¼ cup small fresh basil leaves

1. Preheat oven to 450°F. Place squash on a large baking sheet, and toss with 2 tablespoons of the oil. Roast until squash starts to brown and strands separate from peel when pulled with a fork, 15 to 20 minutes. Remove squash strands from peel, and set aside in a large bowl. Discard peel.

2. While squash roasts, season shrimp with ½ teaspoon of the salt and ¼ teaspoon of the black pepper. Heat remaining 2 tablespoons oil in a large high-sided skillet over medium-high. Add shrimp. Cook, turning once, until opaque and starting to crisp on both sides, 1 to 2 minutes per side. Remove to a plate; set aside. Add onion to skillet. Cook, stirring occasionally, until onion starts to soften, about 5 minutes. Add garlic, anchovies, and crushed red pepper. Cook, stirring constantly, until fragrant, about 1 minute. Add wine, stirring and scraping bottom of pan to release browned bits. Cook, stirring occasionally, until wine has almost fully reduced, 1 to 2 minutes. Add crushed tomatoes and remaining 1 teaspoon salt and ¼ teaspoon black pepper. Cook, stirring occasionally, until sauce starts to thicken, about 5 minutes. Remove from heat; stir in cream, shrimp, and ¼ cup of the grated cheese.

3. Divide spaghetti squash evenly among 4 bowls, and top with shrimp mixture. Sprinkle each bowl with 1 tablespoon each of basil leaves and remaining grated cheese. Serve immediately.

Instant Pot Creamy Root Vegetable Soup

ACTIVE 15 MIN. - TOTAL 45 MIN.
SERVES 4

 2 Tbsp. olive oil
 1 medium-size sweet onion, chopped
 1½ tsp. red curry powder
 1 tsp. finely chopped fresh ginger (from 1 [1-inch] piece)
 3 medium carrots, peeled and cut into ¾-inch pieces (about 1 cup)
 3 medium parsnips, peeled and cut into ¾-inch pieces (about 1½ cups)
 2 medium-size sweet potatoes, peeled and cut into ¾-inch pieces (about 5 cups)
 1 (32-oz.) container vegetable stock
 ½ cup half-and-half, divided
 2 tsp. apple cider vinegar, divided
 ¼ cup plain whole-milk Greek yogurt
 ½ tsp. pure maple syrup
 ½ cup chopped salted pistachios

A SPICE MIX THAT SINGS
Red curry powder (a Thai seasoning blend with chiles, garlic, and ginger) adds bold flavor. Look for it in the spice aisle, or use the same amount of jarred red curry paste—such as Thai Kitchen.

1. Select SAUTÉ setting on a programmable pressure multicooker, such as Instant Pot. (Times, instructions, and settings may vary according to cooker brand or model.) Select HIGH temperature setting; add oil to cooker. Heat oil 1 to 2 minutes; add onion. Cook, stirring occasionally, until onion starts to soften, about 5 minutes. Add curry powder and ginger. Cook, stirring constantly, until toasted and fragrant, 1 minute. Press CANCEL. Add carrots, parsnips, sweet potatoes, and stock. Cover cooker with lid; lock in place. Turn steam release handle to SEALING position. Select PRESSURE COOK setting. Select HIGH pressure for 10 minutes. (It will take 9 to 10 minutes for cooker to come up to pressure before cooking begins.) When cooking has finished, carefully turn steam release handle to VENTING position; let steam fully escape (float valve will drop). This will take about 1 minute. Remove lid.
2. Transfer soup to a blender in batches. Secure lid; remove center piece to allow steam to escape. Place a clean towel over opening. Process until smooth, 1 to 2 minutes. (Or process in cooker using an immersion blender until smooth, 2 minutes.) Stir in ¼ cup of the half-and-half and 1 teaspoon of the vinegar.
3. Combine yogurt, maple syrup, and remaining ¼ cup half-and-half and 1 teaspoon vinegar in a small bowl. Divide soup among 4 bowls; top with yogurt mixture and pistachios.

Get Cracking

Skip the scrambled. Forget the fried. Wake up with baked eggs garnished any way you like them

ITALIAN BAKED EGGS WITH HERBS AND PARMESAN

Tasty Toppings
Three ways to add flavor

American
Chopped bacon, grated sharp cheddar cheese, and chopped fresh chives

Mediterranean
Marinara sauce, crumbled feta cheese, and chopped fresh flat-leaf parsley

Italian
Chopped fresh thyme, chopped fresh rosemary, and finely grated Parmesan cheese

Classic Baked Eggs
ACTIVE 10 MIN. · TOTAL 30 MIN.
SERVES 4

  Unsalted butter, for ramekins
4 tsp. heavy whipping cream
8 large eggs
½ tsp. kosher salt
  Black pepper, to taste

Preheat oven to 375°F. Butter 4 (6-ounce) ramekins; place on a baking sheet. Pour 1 teaspoon cream into each ramekin, and crack 2 eggs over cream in each. Sprinkle each ramekin with ⅛ teaspoon salt and a pinch of pepper. Bake until set around edges and still a bit jiggly in centers, about 15 minutes. (For firm yolks, bake an additional 3 minutes.) Remove from oven; let stand 2 to 3 minutes to set. Garnish with desired toppings, and serve.

The Roots of Red Rice

This classic Low-country dish takes many forms, and it started in West Africa

I CAME ACROSS red rice—a lynchpin dish that connects Africa to the American South—on my first trip to Charleston, South Carolina, in 1983. I was sitting at a local eatery with a group of friends who had each spent time in Senegal. When a starch was proposed to accompany the meal, all of the newcomers to Charleston's cuisine were intrigued by red rice and ordered it. We each took one bite, savored the rich tomatoey flavor with a hint of smoked bacon, and exclaimed in virtual unison: "thieboudienne!" It was a true culinary epiphany, one that's defined my relationship with it ever since.

Senegal is a region of West Africa that has its own form of rice—which is the country's preferred starch. Thieboudienne (pronounced che-boo-JEN), Senegal's national dish, can be prepared in different ways but usually has fish and vegetables served with rice made red with tomato paste. (As tomatoes are not native to Africa, it is thought that it might have originally been prepared using palm oil.) When thieboudienne eventually migrated to other parts of West Africa—notably English-speaking Ghana and Nigeria—it took on the name of the Senegalese empire that originally spawned it: the Jolof Empire (also known as Wolof or Jollof), which ruled the land from the mid-1300s to the mid-1500s. Jollof rice has been adopted and adapted; it swaps fish for chicken and adds and subtracts vegetables at the whim of the cook.

Whether from Senegal, Nigeria, or Ghana, the taste for the dish crossed the ocean with enslaved Africans. On the other side, South Carolina's vast wealth was based on the grain. Slave traders valued the technological and agricultural know-how of Africans from rice-growing regions and sold them for work in the fields. As a result, traditional African dishes were transformed into red rice and other bedrock staples of Gullah Geechee cooking. Farther south, in Louisiana—another area where enslaved Africans labored in rice fields—jambalaya, a close cousin of the West African dish, was created. Both are prime examples of how history can often be found hidden in plain sight at the dinner table. –Jessica B. Harris

Red Rice

ACTIVE 30 MIN. · TOTAL 1 HOUR, 15 MIN.
SERVES 6

- 2 large tomatoes (about 16 oz. total)
- 6 center-cut bacon slices
- ½ cup chopped yellow onion (from 1 small onion)
- 3 scallions, minced
- ¼ cup finely chopped green bell pepper (from 1 pepper)
- 1 Tbsp. hot sauce
- 1 tsp. kosher salt
- ½ tsp. black pepper
- 2 cups chicken broth
- 1 cup uncooked long-grain rice
- ¾ cup minced cooked ham (from 1 [8-oz.] pkg.)

1. Peel and seed tomatoes, capturing juices in a bowl. Coarsely chop to equal 2 cups, and add to bowl with additional juices. Set aside.

2. Preheat oven to 350°F. Heat a 12-inch cast-iron skillet over medium. Add bacon. Cook, turning occasionally, until crisp, about 10 minutes. Remove; drain on paper towels, reserving 1 tablespoon drippings in pan. Add onion, scallions, and bell pepper to pan. Cook, stirring occasionally, until onion is translucent, 5 minutes. Crumble bacon.

3. Add tomatoes and their juices, bacon, hot sauce, salt, and black pepper to pan; stir to combine. Stir in broth and rice; bring to a simmer over medium. Reduce heat to low. Cook, stirring occasionally, until liquid has reduced slightly, 10 minutes. Stir in ham.

4. Transfer to a greased (with cooking spray) 2-quart baking dish. Cover; bake in preheated oven until rice is tender, 40 to 45 minutes, stirring every 15 minutes. Serve hot.

A Little Red Rice Advice

Jessica shares three tips for her traditional recipe

GO VEGETARIAN Red rice is a forgiving dish and can be made without meat if you like. In Step 2, omit the bacon and substitute 1 tablespoon olive oil for the drippings. Use vegetable broth instead of chicken broth in Step 3, and omit the ham.

PEEL LIKE A PRO Don't forget to peel the tomatoes. Cut a small X on the bottom of each with a knife. Blanch them in boiling water about 30 seconds, then transfer to an ice bath. The skins will slip off easily. If fresh ripe tomatoes are unavailable, you use canned peeled ones.

SIMMER BEFORE BAKING My recipe has separate yet tender and fluffy grains because the rice, vegetables, and cooking liquids are all simmered in a skillet on the stove top (to reduce the liquid) then transferred to a baking dish to finish cooking in the oven.

Dressed to Kale

Our lightened-up Caesar salad is made with hearty greens, grated eggs,
and toasted breadcrumbs so crunchy that you won't miss the croutons

Chopped Kale Salad with Toasted Breadcrumbs

Cut prep time by chopping the kale in batches in a food processor.

ACTIVE 15 MIN. - TOTAL 15 MIN.

SERVES 4

Heat 1½ Tbsp. **olive oil** in a small skillet over medium-high. Add ⅓ cup **panko breadcrumbs** and ½ tsp. **black pepper.** Cook, stirring occasionally, until golden brown, 5 minutes. Remove from heat; set aside. Whisk together ¼ cup **mayonnaise,** ¼ cup **plain Greek yogurt,** 1 tsp. grated **lemon zest** plus 3 Tbsp. **fresh juice** (from 1 lemon), 1 tsp. **Dijon mustard,** 1 tsp. **Worcestershire sauce,** 1 tsp. **kosher salt,** 1 tsp. grated **garlic** (from 2 garlic cloves), and 1 Tbsp. finely grated **Parmesan cheese** in a large bowl. Add 8 cups finely chopped **curly kale** (from 1 [8-oz.] bunch); toss with tongs until kale is thoroughly coated. Gently fold in 2 large hard-cooked **eggs** (grated on large holes of a box grater) and panko mixture. Sprinkle with additional Parmesan.

CALORIES: **277** – CARBS: **13G** – FAT: **21G**

Bring On the Brisket

Make-ahead sliders that are a little spicy, a little sweet, and just right for game day

Slow-Cooker Chipotle Brisket Sliders

ACTIVE 10 MIN. · TOTAL 4 HOURS, 10 MIN.

MAKES 12

- 1½ Tbsp. packed light brown sugar
- 2 tsp. kosher salt
- 1 tsp. ground cumin
- ¾ tsp. black pepper
- 1 (2-lb.) trimmed beef brisket
- 2 chipotle chiles in adobo sauce, minced (about 2 Tbsp.)
- 3 garlic cloves, smashed
- 1 cup barbecue sauce
- 12 slider buns, toasted
- ½ cup spicy pickle chips

1. Stir together brown sugar, salt, cumin, and black pepper in a small bowl. Season brisket with sugar mixture. Place brisket, chipotle chiles, and garlic in a 6-quart slow cooker. Cover and cook until tender, 4 to 5 hours on HIGH or about 8 hours on LOW.

2. Transfer brisket to a cutting board, reserving ½ cup cooking liquid. Using 2 forks, shred brisket; place in a large bowl. Add barbecue sauce and reserved cooking liquid; stir until meat is fully coated. Divide meat evenly among bottom halves of buns. Add pickle chips, and cover with bun tops.

Here's Your Game Plan: Prepare the brisket up to two days ahead; chill in an airtight container. Reheat the meat and assemble the sliders when you're ready to eat.

Mardi Gras Memories

Test Kitchen professional and *Hey Y'all* host Ivy Odom
combines king cake and beignets to make one unforgettable treat

WHEN I WAS GROWING UP in Georgia, we didn't pay much attention to Fat Tuesday. I'd heard of the parades, but the celebratory day seemed reserved for those fun-loving crowds in New Orleans or South Alabama. That all changed when I was a teenager visiting family in the small town of Lizana, Mississippi, near the coast. It was my first Carnival, and we were greeted by massive tables mounded with crawfish. That night, I tasted the lip-puckering heat of a crawfish boil and then found the baby in my first slice of king cake.

Every year since, I've celebrated Fat Tuesday like it's my first one all over again. I don't always get around to the boil, but I do make sure some form of king cake is on the menu. This year, I combined two of my favorite Mardi Gras desserts to create King Cake Beignets. These pillowy-soft treats are drizzled in a cream cheese glaze and sprinkled with crunchy sanding sugars in purple, green, and gold. The best part? You can make the dough ahead so you'll have more time to let the good times roll.

King Cake Beignets

ACTIVE 50 MIN. · TOTAL 50 MIN.,
PLUS 4 HOURS CHILLING
MAKES ABOUT 3 DOZEN

- 1 tsp. active dry yeast (from 1 [¼-oz.] envelope)
- ¾ cup warm water (105°F to 115°F), divided
- 4 Tbsp. granulated sugar, divided
- 1 large egg, lightly beaten
- ½ cup evaporated milk
- ¾ tsp. kosher salt, divided
- 2 Tbsp. vegetable shortening
- ¾ tsp. ground cinnamon
- 3½ cups bread flour, divided, plus more for work surface
- 1½ oz. cream cheese (about 3 Tbsp.), at room temperature
- ½ Tbsp. unsalted butter, melted
- ½ Tbsp. whole milk
- ½ tsp. vanilla extract
- ¼ cup plus 2 Tbsp. powdered sugar, sifted
- Vegetable oil, for frying
- Green, purple, and yellow sanding sugars

1. Stir together yeast, ¼ cup of the warm water, and ½ teaspoon of the granulated sugar in a bowl of a stand mixer fitted with a dough hook attachment. Let stand until foamy, about 5 minutes. Stir in egg, evaporated milk, ½ teaspoon of the salt, and remaining 3 tablespoons plus 2½ teaspoons granulated sugar.
2. Stir together shortening and remaining ½ cup warm water in a bowl until melted. Add this to yeast mixture. Beat on low speed until just combined, 30 seconds.

3. Stir together cinnamon and 2 cups of the flour in a medium bowl. Gradually add to yeast mixture; beat on low speed until combined, about 1 minute. Gradually add remaining 1½ cups flour, beating on low speed until a sticky dough forms, 1 minute. Transfer to a large bowl lightly greased with cooking spray; turn dough to grease top. Cover bowl; refrigerate until dough is thoroughly chilled and firm, at least 4 hours or up to 24 hours.
4. Place cream cheese, butter, whole milk, vanilla, and remaining ¼ teaspoon salt in a medium bowl. Beat with an electric mixer fitted with a paddle attachment on medium speed until smooth, 1 minute. Gradually add powdered sugar, beating until smooth, 1 minute. Spoon glaze into a piping bag or a zip-top plastic bag. Set aside.
5. Turn dough out onto a lightly floured work surface, and roll into a 12-inch square (about ¼ inch thick). Using a knife or pizza cutter, cut dough into 2-inch squares (about 36 pieces).
6. Pour oil to a depth of 2 inches in a 5- to 6-quart Dutch oven; heat over medium-high to 360°F, adjusting heat as needed to maintain temperature. Working in about 6 batches, carefully add dough pieces to hot oil. Fry until puffy and golden, about 1½ minutes per side. Remove beignets from oil using a slotted spoon; transfer to a wire rack set over a baking sheet. Let stand until just cool enough to handle, 1 to 2 minutes.
7. Snip a ¹⁄₁₆- to ⅛-inch tip off one corner of the filled piping bag. Drizzle glaze over slightly cooled beignets; sprinkle with sanding sugars. Serve immediately.

COOKING SCHOOL

HOW TO POACH AN EGG

1.

Crack 1 large egg into a fine-mesh strainer set over a bowl. Let stand until the thin, loose parts of egg whites drain into bowl, about 10 seconds. Discard drained egg white parts in bowl.

2.

Combine 4 cups water and 1 tsp. white vinegar in a large nonstick skillet. Bring to a low boil over medium-high; reduce to a simmer over low. Transfer egg to a bowl; gently slip egg into simmering water.

3.

Cover pan; cook on low until white is cooked and set, 2 to 3 minutes. Gently remove egg from skillet using a slotted spoon or spatula. Pat egg dry with a paper towel while still on spoon.

Scrambled Stir-Ins
Bored of the same breakfast? Try these flavor ideas

SOUR CREAM
For extra richness and velvety texture, beat in 1 tablespoon sour cream (or crème fraîche or plain full-fat Greek yogurt) per egg.

SMOKED SALMON
When the eggs start to set in the pan, stir in desired amount of chopped smoked salmon. Top with fresh chives or dill to fancy it even more.

BACON FAT
Replace the usual butter or oil with an equal amount of bacon drippings for extra-savory eggs. (Bonus points if you add shredded cheddar, too.)

CORN TORTILLAS
Turn eggs into a filling meal. Tear up 1 tortilla per egg. Add a few tablespoons of canola oil to a skillet over medium, and cook tortilla pieces until golden and crisp. Pour in beaten eggs, and cook until done.

"I'm a countertop cracker. When breaking eggs on the side of a bowl, I somehow manage to get little bits of shell in there, too."

Karen Schroeder-Rankin
Test Kitchen Professional

THE BEST WAY TO CRACK AN EGG

Melissa Gray
Test Kitchen Professional

"I make one hard crack on the side of a thin-rimmed bowl. Aim for the center of the egg (aka the 'egg-quator') to create a clean break."

March

One-Bowl Wonders

Have your cake (on a Wednesday) and eat it, too. Whenever you're in the mood for a little something sweet, these single-layer desserts are as easy to whip up as any boxed mix

YOU'LL FIND A HOMEMADE LAYER CAKE in my house maybe two or three times a year, a special treat for a birthday or another celebration. But from-scratch snack cakes have a semi permanent spot on the kitchen counter. That's because they're easier to make–a quick pick-me-up you can whisk together (literally) on a whim. These casual desserts have a slightly heartier texture than the delicate crumb of a layer or pound cake, but they still satisfy the same craving for moist, tender forkfuls complete with delightful frostings.

You'll need only one bowl to make each of these five recipes. Stir together the batter, and while it's baking or cooling, quickly wash the bowl to use it to mix up the frosting. You can serve the cake right out of the pan to keep things simple; that's the beauty of it.

Lest you think that because they're easier to make they're less delicious, consider our strawberry cake flavored with rosé wine, the supremely moist coconut poke cake, or the fresh raspberry cake with salted milk chocolate frosting. They might just become mainstays in your home, too. –Ann Taylor Pittman

Strawberry-Rosé Snack Cake

Instead of flavored gelatin, this pink dessert is made with freeze-dried strawberries, which have vibrant color and more concentrated flavor.

ACTIVE 15 MIN. - TOTAL 40 MIN., PLUS 1 HOUR COOLING
MAKES 1 (8-INCH) CAKE

CAKE
- 1½ cups freeze-dried strawberries, divided
- 1½ cups all-purpose flour
- 1 cup granulated sugar
- 2 tsp. baking powder
- ½ tsp. kosher salt
- ⅔ cup rosé wine
- ¼ cup canola oil
- 1 tsp. vanilla extract
- 1 large egg

FROSTING
- ¼ cup unsalted butter, softened
- 4 oz. cream cheese, softened
- ¼ tsp. kosher salt
- 2¼ cups powdered sugar

1. Prepare the Cake: Preheat oven to 350°F. Line an 8-inch square baking pan with parchment paper, leaving a 2-inch overhang on all sides. Process freeze-dried strawberries in a mini food processor until powdered, 30 seconds to 1 minute. Measure 3 tablespoons powdered strawberries into a medium bowl (reserve remaining powdered strawberries in the food processor for Frosting). Add flour, granulated sugar, baking powder, and salt to bowl. Using a spoon, make a well in center of flour mixture, and pour rosé wine, oil, and vanilla into well. Crack egg into rosé mixture. Pierce egg using tip of a whisk, and lightly beat together. Fold egg mixture into flour mixture to form a smooth batter.

2. Spread batter evenly in prepared baking pan. Bake in preheated oven until a wooden pick inserted in center comes out clean, 25 to 28 minutes. Cool in pan 5 minutes. Using parchment paper overhang, lift Cake from pan and transfer to a wire rack. Cool completely, about 1 hour.

3. Prepare the Frosting: Wash and dry the bowl. Place butter, cream cheese, and salt in bowl; beat with an electric mixer fitted with a paddle attachment on medium-high speed until smooth, about 1 minute. Add reserved powdered strawberries, and beat on medium-high speed until thoroughly combined, about 1 minute. Add powdered sugar and beat on low speed until smooth and creamy, about 1 minute. Spread Frosting over cooled Cake.

JUICED UP
This classic gets an extra boost of flavor and color from bottled carrot juice. Look for the bright orange drink in the refrigerated juice section at the supermarket. Check that it's made only with carrots and no other ingredients.

CARROT-WALNUT SNACK
CAKE WITH CREAM CHEESE
FROSTING (PAGE 45)

HUMMINGBIRD SNACK
CAKE WITH BROWN
BUTTER FROSTING
(PAGE 46)

RASPBERRY SNACK
CAKE WITH SALTED MILK
CHOCOLATE FROSTING

Raspberry Snack Cake with Salted Milk Chocolate Frosting

A hint of cardamom gives this dessert unexpected depth. If you don't have that spice, substitute the same amount of ground ginger or cinnamon.

ACTIVE 15 MIN. - TOTAL 50 MIN., PLUS 1 HOUR, 15 MIN. COOLING

MAKES 1 (8-INCH) CAKE

CAKE
- 1½ cups all-purpose flour
- 1 cup granulated sugar
- ¾ tsp. baking soda
- ½ tsp. kosher salt
- ¼ tsp. ground cardamom
- ¾ cup whole buttermilk
- ¼ cup canola oil
- 1½ tsp. vanilla extract
- 1 large egg
- 1 cup fresh raspberries, patted dry, plus more for serving (optional)

FROSTING
- 8 oz. milk chocolate, chopped
- ½ cup unsalted butter, softened
- ½ tsp. vanilla extract
- ¼ tsp. kosher salt
- 1½ cups powdered sugar

1. Prepare the Cake: Preheat oven to 350°F. Line an 8-inch square baking pan with parchment paper, leaving a 2-inch overhang on all sides. Whisk together flour, sugar, baking soda, salt, and cardamom in a large microwavable bowl. Using a spoon, make a well in center of mixture; pour buttermilk, oil, and vanilla into well. Crack egg into buttermilk mixture. Pierce egg using tip of a whisk; lightly beat together. Fold egg mixture into flour mixture in bowl to form a smooth batter.

2. Spread half of the batter evenly in prepared baking pan; sprinkle evenly with ½ cup raspberries. Spread remaining batter evenly over berries; sprinkle with remaining ½ cup berries.

Bake in preheated oven until a wooden pick inserted in center comes out clean, 35 to 38 minutes. Remove from oven; cool in pan 5 minutes. Using parchment paper overhang, lift Cake from pan and transfer to a wire rack. Cool completely, 1 hour.

3. Prepare the Frosting: Wash and dry the microwavable bowl. Place chocolate in bowl; microwave on HIGH until melted, about 90 seconds, stirring every 30 seconds. Cool at room temperature 15 minutes.

4. Add butter to chocolate in bowl; beat with an electric mixer fitted with a paddle attachment on medium speed until smooth and creamy, 1 minute. Beat in vanilla and salt. Add powdered sugar; beat on low speed until smooth and creamy, 1 minute. Spread Frosting over cooled Cake. Serve with additional raspberries, if desired.

Carrot-Walnut Snack Cake with Cream Cheese Frosting

(Photo, page 42)

Let the cream cheese and butter come to room temperature while the cake is cooling so they'll be ready for the frosting.

ACTIVE 15 MIN. - TOTAL 1 HOUR, PLUS 30 MIN. COOLING

MAKES 1 (8-INCH) CAKE

CAKE
- 2 cups shredded carrots (about 4 large carrots)
- ⅔ cup packed light brown sugar
- ¼ cup honey
- ½ tsp. kosher salt
- ½ cup refrigerated bottled carrot juice
- ¼ cup canola oil
- 1½ tsp. vanilla extract
- 1 large egg
- 2 tsp. ground cinnamon
- ¾ tsp. baking soda
- 1½ cups all-purpose flour
- 1 cup coarsely chopped walnuts, toasted, divided

FROSTING
- 8 oz. cream cheese, softened
- 3 Tbsp. unsalted butter, softened
- 1 tsp. vanilla extract
- ⅛ tsp. kosher salt
- 1½ cups powdered sugar

1. Prepare the Cake: Preheat oven to 350°F. Line an 8-inch square baking pan with parchment paper, leaving a 2-inch overhang on all sides. Toss together carrots, brown sugar, honey, and salt in a large bowl; let stand 10 minutes. Add carrot juice, oil, and vanilla. Crack egg into bowl. Pierce egg using tip of a whisk, and lightly beat into carrot juice mixture. Whisk in cinnamon and baking soda. Fold in flour and ½ cup walnuts.

2. Spread batter evenly in prepared baking pan. Bake in preheated oven until a wooden pick inserted in center comes out clean, 35 to 38 minutes. Remove from oven; cool in pan 5 minutes. Using parchment paper overhang, lift Cake from pan and transfer to a wire rack. Cool completely, 30 minutes.

3. Prepare the Frosting: Wash and dry the bowl. Add cream cheese and butter; beat with an electric mixer fitted with a paddle attachment on medium speed until smooth and creamy, about 1 minute. Beat in vanilla and salt. Add powdered sugar; beat on low speed until smooth and creamy, about 1 minute. Spread Frosting over cooled Cake. Sprinkle with remaining ½ cup walnuts.

Hummingbird Snack Cake with Brown Butter Frosting

(Photo, page 43)

Browning the butter in the microwave saves you a pan to clean up. The butter will pop and spatter, so weigh down the parchment that covers the bowl with a plate. Bonus: The parchment also keeps the plate clean.

ACTIVE 20 MIN. - TOTAL 1 HOUR, 15 MIN.,
PLUS 1 HOUR, 25 MIN. COOLING

MAKES 1 (8-INCH) CAKE

CAKE
- 2 medium bananas
- ½ cup canned crushed pineapple in juice (undrained, from 1 [8-oz.] can)
- ¼ cup canola oil
- 1½ tsp. vanilla extract
- 1 large egg
- ¾ cup granulated sugar
- ¾ tsp. baking soda
- ½ tsp. kosher salt
- 1½ cups all-purpose flour
- 1 tsp. ground cinnamon
- ¼ tsp. ground allspice
- ⅔ cup chopped pecans, toasted

FROSTING
- ¾ cup unsalted butter
- 2 Tbsp. heavy whipping cream
- 1 tsp. vanilla extract
- ¼ tsp. kosher salt
- 1½ cups powdered sugar

1. Prepare the Cake: Preheat oven to 350°F. Line an 8-inch square baking pan with parchment paper, leaving a 2-inch overhang on all sides. Mash bananas in a large microwavable bowl until nearly smooth. Stir in pineapple, oil, and vanilla. Crack egg into bowl. Pierce egg using tip of a whisk, and lightly beat into pineapple mixture. Whisk in granulated sugar, baking soda, and salt. Fold in flour, cinnamon, and allspice. Fold in pecans.

2. Spread batter evenly in prepared baking pan. Bake in preheated oven until a wooden pick inserted in center comes out clean, 33 to 35 minutes. Remove from oven, and cool in pan 5 minutes. Using parchment paper overhang, lift Cake from pan and transfer to a wire rack. Cool completely, 1 hour.

3. Prepare the Frosting: Wash and dry the microwavable bowl. Place butter in bowl. Cover bowl with a sheet of parchment paper; place a microwavable plate on top of parchment to cover bowl. Microwave on HIGH until butter is amber color, 6 to 9 minutes (butter will pop as it browns). Remove from microwave, and cool 20 minutes. Transfer bowl to refrigerator, and chill until butter starts to solidify, about 1 hour.

4. Remove butter from refrigerator; add whipping cream to bowl. Beat mixture using an electric mixer fitted with a whisk attachment on medium speed until smooth and fluffy, about 1 minute. Beat in vanilla and salt. Add powdered sugar; beat on low speed until smooth and creamy, about 1 minute. Spread Frosting over cooled Cake.

Triple-Coconut Poke Snack Cake

You can substitute regular sweetened condensed milk and ½ teaspoon coconut extract for the coconut milk.

ACTIVE 25 MIN. - TOTAL 45 MIN.,
PLUS 1 HOUR COOLING

MAKES 1 (8-INCH) CAKE

CAKE
- 1½ cups all-purpose flour
- 1 cup granulated sugar
- 2 tsp. baking powder
- ½ tsp. kosher salt
- ¾ cup well-shaken and stirred coconut milk (from 1 [15-oz.] can)
- ¼ cup canola oil
- 1½ tsp. vanilla extract
- 1 large egg
- ½ cup sweetened condensed coconut milk (from 1 [14-oz.] can)

FROSTING
- 1 cup heavy whipping cream
- ⅛ tsp. kosher salt
- ¼ cup sweetened condensed coconut milk (from 1 [14-oz.] can)

ADDITIONAL INGREDIENT
- ⅓ cup lightly salted toasted coconut chips (such as Bare or Dang)

1. Prepare the Cake: Preheat oven to 350°F. Coat an 8-inch square baking pan with cooking spray, then line with parchment paper, leaving a 2-inch overhang on all sides.

2. Whisk together flour, sugar, baking powder, and salt in a large bowl. Using a spoon, make a well in center of mixture; pour coconut milk, oil, and vanilla into well. Crack egg into coconut milk mixture. Pierce egg using tip of a whisk, and lightly beat together. Whisk egg mixture into flour mixture in bowl to form a smooth batter.

3. Spread batter evenly in prepared baking pan. Bake in preheated oven until a wooden pick inserted in center comes out clean, 25 to 30 minutes. Remove from oven. Immediately poke holes all over Cake using blunt end of a skewer; spread sweetened condensed coconut milk evenly over Cake. Cool in pan 5 minutes. Using parchment paper overhang, lift from pan and transfer to a wire rack. Cool completely, about 1 hour.

4. Prepare the Frosting: Wash and dry the bowl. Add whipping cream and salt; beat with an electric mixer fitted with a whisk attachment on medium-high speed until soft peaks form, about 3 minutes. Increase mixer speed to high; beat until stiff peaks form, about 2 minutes. Add sweetened condensed coconut milk; beat on medium speed until well combined, about 1 minute. Spread Frosting over cooled Cake, and sprinkle with coconut chips.

SUNKEN TREASURE
True to its name, this cake
is poked all over to make
holes that hold a rich filling
of sweetened condensed
coconut milk. Make sure
the cake is still hot when
you reach this step so it
absorbs the liquid.

Go Bananas

Ultra-rich chocolate custard makes this classic cream pie over-the-top delicious

Chocolate-Banana Custard Pie

Choose bright yellow bananas with no brown spots (or very few). Overripe ones will be too mushy. If you want to make the dessert a day in advance, brush any exposed banana slices with fresh lemon juice to keep them from browning. Cover and chill until ready to serve.

ACTIVE 40 MIN. · TOTAL 1 HOUR, PLUS 8 HOURS CHILLING

SERVES 8

- ½ (14.1-oz.) pkg. refrigerated piecrusts (such as Pillsbury)
- ¼ cup all-purpose flour
- ¼ cup unsweetened cocoa
- ¼ tsp. kosher salt
- ¾ cup, plus 3 Tbsp. granulated sugar, divided
- 6 large egg yolks
- 2 cups half-and-half
- 1 cup semisweet chocolate chips
- 3 tsp. vanilla extract, divided
- 5 to 6 medium bananas (about 2 lb.), divided
- 2 cups heavy whipping cream
  Chocolate shavings or chocolate curls

1. Preheat oven to 350°F. Fit piecrust into a 9-inch pie plate; fold edges under, and crimp. Prick bottom and sides of crust with a fork. Line piecrust with aluminum foil or parchment paper, and fill to rim with pie weights or dried beans. Place prepared piecrust on a large rimmed baking sheet. Bake 10 minutes. Remove weights and foil; bake until crust is golden brown, 12 to 14 minutes more. Remove from baking sheet. Cool on a wire rack while preparing filling.

2. Whisk together flour, cocoa, salt, and ¾ cup of the granulated sugar in a medium-size heavy saucepan; set aside. Whisk together egg yolks and half-and-half in a medium bowl. Gradually whisk egg mixture into sugar mixture until well combined. Cook over medium-low, whisking constantly, until it just begins to bubble and is thick enough to hold soft peaks when whisk is lifted, 10 to 12 minutes. Remove saucepan from heat; whisk in chocolate chips and 2 teaspoons of the vanilla. Whisk constantly until chocolate melts and mixture is smooth.

3. Peel and cut half of the bananas into ½-inch slices on a sharp diagonal. Place bananas in prepared crust, covering bottom of crust. Pour chocolate mixture over bananas, and smooth with a spoon or offset spatula. Place plastic wrap directly on warm filling, and chill until set, at least 8 hours or up to overnight.

4. Beat heavy whipping cream and remaining 1 teaspoon vanilla with an electric mixer on medium-high speed until foamy, 30 seconds to 1 minute. Gradually add remaining 3 tablespoons sugar; continue beating until soft peaks form, 2 to 3 minutes more. Just before serving, peel and cut remaining bananas into ½-inch-thick slices on a sharp diagonal. Arrange banana slices on chilled pie; top with whipped cream. Garnish with chocolate shavings or curls.

Spring Into Slow-Cooking

As the seasons change, so should your meals. These five dinners are full of fresh flavors and practically cook themselves

Slow-Cooker Green Minestrone

ACTIVE 10 MIN. · TOTAL 4 HOURS, 40 MIN.
SERVES 8

- 8 cups lower-sodium vegetable broth
- ½ cup thinly sliced scallions (about 5 scallions)
- 4 garlic cloves, thinly sliced (about 1½ Tbsp.)
- 1 large leek, thinly sliced (about 1½ cups)
- 3 celery stalks, cut diagonally into thin slices (about 1 cup)
- 2½ tsp. kosher salt
- ½ tsp. black pepper
- ¼ tsp. crushed red pepper
- 1 (15.5-oz.) can cannellini beans, drained and rinsed
- 8 oz. fresh sugar snap peas, trimmed and diagonally cut in half crosswise (about 1½ cups)
- 2 cups packed fresh baby spinach
- 1 cup frozen sweet peas, thawed
- 1 oz. Parmesan cheese, grated (about ¼ cup)
  Extra-virgin olive oil
  Chopped fresh dill

Stir together broth, scallions, garlic, leek, celery, salt, black pepper, and red pepper in a 4- to 6-quart slow cooker. Cover and cook on LOW until vegetables are tender, about 4 hours. Stir in beans, snap peas, spinach, and sweet peas. Cover and continue cooking on LOW until peas are tender, about 30 minutes more. Top with Parmesan cheese, and garnish with olive oil and dill. Serve immediately.

IT'S EASY BEING GREEN
Preserve the bright hues and delicate flavors of the peas and spinach by adding them toward the end of the cooking process.

Lemony Slow-Cooked Salmon with Potatoes and Fennel

ACTIVE 10 MIN. - TOTAL 4 HOURS, 10 MIN.

SERVES 4

- 1½ lb. small new potatoes, halved lengthwise (about 6 cups)
- 1 small fennel bulb, cored and thinly sliced, fronds reserved for garnish (about 3 cups)
- 1 medium leek, thinly sliced crosswise (about 2 cups)
- 2 tsp. kosher salt, divided
- ½ tsp. black pepper, divided
- 1 large lemon, thinly sliced, plus more lemon slices for garnish
- ½ cup dry white wine (such as Sauvignon Blanc)
- 2 Tbsp. unsalted butter, cubed
- 4 (8-oz.) skin-on boneless center-cut salmon fillets
- Crème fraîche or sour cream (optional)

1. Stir together potatoes, fennel, leek, 1 teaspoon of the salt, and ¼ teaspoon of the pepper in a 6-quart slow cooker. Layer lemon slices evenly over vegetable mixture. Pour wine and ½ cup water over top, and dot with butter. Cover and cook on LOW until vegetables are almost tender, 3 hours and 30 minutes.

2. Season flesh side of salmon with remaining 1 teaspoon salt and ¼ teaspoon pepper. Layer fish, flesh side up, evenly over vegetable mixture. Cover and cook on LOW until salmon is firm and opaque and vegetables are tender, 30 to 45 minutes more. Remove salmon and vegetables; place on a platter. Discard cooking liquid. Garnish with additional lemon slices and the reserved fennel fronds. If desired, dollop each piece of salmon with crème fraîche or sour cream.

Slow-Cooker French Onion Soup

ACTIVE 15 MIN. - TOTAL 6 HOURS, 50 MIN.

SERVES 6

- 2 lb. Vidalia onions, thinly sliced (about 8 cups)
- ¼ cup unsalted butter, melted
- 1½ tsp. granulated sugar
- 1½ tsp. kosher salt
- ½ tsp. black pepper, plus more for garnish
- 6 fresh thyme sprigs, tied with kitchen twine
- 1 dried bay leaf
- 5 cups lower-sodium beef broth
- 1 Tbsp. sherry vinegar
- 12 (½-inch-thick) baguette slices
- 6 oz. Gruyère cheese, shredded (about 1½ cups)
- Fresh thyme leaves

1. Stir together onions, melted butter, sugar, salt, and pepper in a 6-quart slow cooker until onions are fully coated. Place thyme sprigs and bay leaf on onion mixture. Cover and cook on HIGH, stirring once halfway through, until onions are deep golden brown and caramelized, 6 to 7 hours.

2. Remove and discard thyme sprigs and bay leaf. Stir in broth and vinegar. Cover and cook on HIGH until thoroughly heated, about 30 minutes.

3. Preheat oven to broil with oven rack about 6 inches from heat. Spoon soup into 6 ovenproof ramekins; place on a large rimmed baking sheet. Top each ramekin with 2 baguette slices; divide cheese evenly among ramekins (about ¼ cup each). Broil until cheese is melted and golden brown, about 3 minutes. Sprinkle with fresh thyme leaves and black pepper. Serve immediately.

THE CLEVER WAY TO CARAMELIZE

Cut least 30 minutes at the stove by using a slow cooker to cook sweet, tender onions that require (almost) no stirring.

Creamy Slow-Cooker Tarragon Chicken

ACTIVE 15 MIN. - TOTAL 3 HOURS, 45 MIN.

SERVES 6

- 6 (6-oz.) bone-in, skinless chicken thighs
- ½ tsp. black pepper
- 1¼ tsp. kosher salt, divided
- 1 tsp. olive oil
- 8 oz. small carrots with tops, cut in half lengthwise
- 1 medium-size yellow onion, chopped (2 cups)
- 4 large garlic cloves, minced (about 1½ Tbsp.)
- 2 cups lower-sodium chicken broth
- 1 Tbsp. fresh lemon juice (from 1 lemon)
- ¼ tsp. cayenne pepper
- ¼ cup heavy whipping cream, warmed (about 80°F)
- ¼ cup cornstarch
- 1 cup frozen sweet peas, thawed
- 1½ Tbsp. chopped fresh tarragon, plus more for garnish

  Egg noodles or hot cooked rice

1. Season chicken evenly with black pepper and ¾ teaspoon of the salt. Heat oil in a large nonstick skillet over medium-high, and add chicken. Cook, turning once, until golden brown, about 3 minutes per side; remove from heat.
2. Stir together carrots, onion, garlic, chicken broth, lemon juice, cayenne pepper, and remaining ½ teaspoon salt in a 6-quart slow cooker. Layer chicken on vegetable mixture. Cover and cook on LOW for 3 hours. Remove chicken and carrots; set aside.
3. Whisk together warmed cream and the cornstarch in a small bowl until smooth. Add cream mixture to slow cooker, stirring until combined. Layer chicken and carrots evenly on vegetable mixture. Cover and cook on HIGH until chicken is very tender and sauce is thickened, 30 to 45 minutes more, stirring in peas and tarragon during last 15 minutes of cooking. Serve over egg noodles or rice. Garnish with additional tarragon.

Slow-Cooker Lemon-Asparagus Risotto

ACTIVE 10 MIN. - TOTAL 2 HOURS, 10 MIN.
SERVES 4

- ¼ cup unsalted butter
- 2 cups uncooked Arborio rice
- 4 cups lower-sodium vegetable broth, warmed
- ½ cup dry white wine (such as Sauvignon Blanc)
- 1 Tbsp. grated lemon zest, plus 2 Tbsp. fresh juice, plus more zest for garnish (from 2 lemons)
- 1 tsp. kosher salt
- ¼ tsp. white pepper
- 1 lb. fresh thin asparagus, trimmed and cut diagonally into 1-inch pieces (about 3 cups)
- 2 oz. Parmesan cheese, grated (about ½ cup)
- ¼ cup heavy whipping cream
- Chopped fresh flat-leaf parsley

1. Melt butter in a medium saucepan over medium. Add rice. Cook, stirring often, until lightly toasted, about 4 minutes. Place in a 6-quart slow cooker; stir in warmed broth, the wine, lemon zest and juice, salt, and white pepper. Cover and cook on LOW until about half the liquid has been absorbed, about 1 hour.

2. Remove lid, and stir in asparagus. Cover and continue cooking on LOW until rice is al dente and creamy and asparagus is tender, about 1 hour more. Remove lid, and stir in Parmesan and cream until combined. Garnish with chopped parsley and additional lemon zest. Serve immediately.

TAKE TIME TO TOAST
For toasty flavor, cook the rice in butter a few minutes before adding it to the slow cooker.

Wake Up to Cake

A ribbon of tangy strawberry-rhubarb filling runs through this buttery, crumb-topped breakfast treat

Strawberry-Rhubarb Skillet Coffee Cake

ACTIVE 15 MIN. - TOTAL 1 HOUR, 5 MIN.,
PLUS 30 MIN. COOLING

SERVES 12

- 1 tsp. ground cinnamon
- 2½ cups all-purpose flour, divided
- 1¾ cups granulated sugar, divided
- ⅓ cup cold unsalted butter, cubed
  Baking spray with flour
- 1 cup sliced fresh strawberries
- 1 cup finely chopped fresh or thawed frozen rhubarb
- ½ cup unsalted butter, softened
- 1 large egg
- 2 tsp. baking powder
- 1 tsp. kosher salt
- ½ cup whole milk

1. Preheat oven to 350°F. Stir together cinnamon, ½ cup of the flour, and ¾ cup of the sugar in a medium bowl. Using your fingers or a fork, cut cold butter into sugar mixture until coarse crumbs form, leaving some larger pieces. Chill until ready to use.

2. Spray a 10-inch cast-iron skillet with baking spray. Stir together strawberries, rhubarb, and ¼ cup of the sugar in a medium bowl. Let stand, stirring occasionally, until macerated, about 10 minutes.

3. Meanwhile, beat softened butter and remaining ¾ cup sugar with a stand mixer fitted with a paddle attachment on medium-high speed until fluffy, about 4 minutes. Beat in egg until blended. Stir together baking powder, kosher salt, and remaining 2 cups flour in a medium bowl until combined. Alternately add flour mixture and milk to butter mixture, beginning and ending with flour mixture.

4. Drain liquid from macerated fruit, reserving liquid for another use. Gently fold fruit into batter. Spoon into prepared skillet, smoothing top with a spatula. Sprinkle evenly with sugar mixture.

5. Bake in preheated oven until a wooden pick inserted in center comes out clean, 50 to 55 minutes. Cool 30 minutes before slicing. Serve warm, or cool completely.

QUICK TIP

If you're concerned that the cake might absorb savory flavors from the skillet, line the pan with parchment paper.

TEXAS-STYLE
BARBECUE SAUCE

SOUTH CAROLINA-
STYLE MUSTARD SAUCE
(PAGE 58)

ALABAMA-STYLE
WHITE SAUCE

The Stories Behind the Sauce

Every region has a flavor and history of its own

BARBECUE FANS used to have just one favorite sauce. It was typically whatever style they grew up eating at their local joint, and its color, texture, and flavor might vary from one part of the South to another.

Eastern North Carolina diners insisted that proper sauce was just tart vinegar with a strong dose of black and red pepper, and they'd almost come to blows with Tar Heels from farther west who dared to put a little ketchup in the bottle. In Kansas City, Missouri, the sauce was thick, brown, and sweet.

KREUZ MARKET
Lockhart, Texas

For years, the menu board at Kreuz Market, a classic Central Texas brisket joint, announced in bold letters: "No Barbecue Sauce. No Forks. No Kidding." The restaurant sold shirts and Koozies emblazoned with that pugnacious slogan, too. So I was shocked in the summer of 2018 to sit down in a wooden booth in Kreuz's high-ceilinged dining room and find a transparent squeeze bottle filled with dark, reddish-brown sauce.

After years of fielding complaints from cranky out-of-towners demanding sauce, fifth-generation owner Keith Schmidt eventually relented. And it turns out his family had a long-kept secret. Decades before, unbeknownst to the rest of the condiment-averse clan, Schmidt's maternal grandmother, Betty Jean Yates Werme, had come up with her own barbecue sauce.

Shortly before passing away in 1973, Werme shared the recipe with her daughter, Evelyn Schmidt, who eventually revealed it to her son, Keith. A blend of vinegar, ketchup, and more, it has only a touch of sweetness, so it doesn't overwhelm the splendid flavor of

Kreuz's slow-smoked brisket and pork chops. But it's certainly tasty enough to satisfy those sauce-demanding guests.

WHERE TO BUY: Available only in the restaurant

Texas-Style Barbecue Sauce
ACTIVE 5 MIN. - TOTAL 35 MIN.
MAKES 2 CUPS

- 1½ cups ketchup
- ½ cup apple cider vinegar
- ¼ cup packed light brown sugar
- 2 Tbsp. Worcestershire sauce
- 1 Tbsp. chili powder
- 1 Tbsp. ground cumin
- 2 tsp. kosher salt
- 1 tsp. black pepper

Whisk together all ingredients in a medium saucepan. Cook over medium, whisking occasionally, until ingredients are combined and sauce is just starting to simmer, 2 to 3 minutes. Cool to room temperature, about 30 minutes. Store in an airtight container in refrigerator up to 3 weeks.
Note: If you want to really make it Texas-style, stir in up to 1 cup of drippings from brisket or other meat (or beef stock) just before serving.

BIG BOB GIBSON BAR-B-Q
Decatur, Alabama

Alabama barbecue fans might be surprised to learn that their state's signature white sauce has Carolina roots. Back in 1925, Robert "Big Bob" Gibson began cooking pork and chicken in his backyard in Decatur, Alabama, and selling it to friends. "He loved North Carolina-style barbecue sauces, so that's where his inspiration came from," says Chris Lilly, fourth-generation pitmaster at Big Bob Gibson Bar-B-Q, who's married to Big Bob's great-granddaughter.

The family has no clue how Gibson first came across Carolina-style vinegar sauce, but that's what he mopped his pork shoulders with. For split chickens, he came up with his own twist. "He added mayo to the base to keep the chickens from drying out while he hung out in his backyard, waiting for his friends," Lilly says. "I think of white sauce as basically a vinegar-based sauce with mayonnaise."

White sauce was once unknown outside North Alabama, but in recent years, it's become a world traveler. "I've seen it in California in Napa Valley, in Australia, in Ireland—really anywhere there's barbecue," Lilly says. Pitmasters now use it to dress all sorts of barbecued poultry, from smoked turkey to chicken wings. I bet Big Bob would approve.

WHERE TO BUY: Online at *bigbobgibson.com*

Alabama-Style White Sauce
ACTIVE 5 MIN. - TOTAL 5 MIN.
MAKES 2 CUPS

- 1¼ cups mayonnaise (Duke's, of course)
- ¾ cup distilled white vinegar
- 1 Tbsp. black pepper
- 1¼ tsp. kosher salt
- 1 tsp. granulated sugar
- 1 tsp. fresh lemon juice (from 1 small lemon)
- ½ tsp. Worcestershire sauce
- ½ tsp. hot sauce

Whisk together all ingredients in a medium bowl until combined. Use immediately, or store in an airtight container in refrigerator up to 2 weeks.

LILLIE'S OF CHARLESTON
Charleston, South Carolina

The yellow mustard-based sauces from Lillie's of Charleston are deeply rooted in a Low-country South Carolina family. Sisters Tracey Richardson and Kellye Wicker named their company after their Aunt Lillie, who hosted all the relatives for Sunday dinners when they were children. The recipe comes from their father, Hank Tisdale.

Back in the 1980s, Tisdale ran a restaurant called The Rib Shack on King Street. "Customers would always say, 'Hey, Hank, can you bag up some extra sauce?' and someone would dig up a container out of the back to put it in," Richardson remembers. "That was like money walking out the door."

The restaurant lasted just a few years, but the idea of selling the sauce lived on. "It was a family discussion every holiday," Richardson recalls. "Finally, in 2001, we said, 'Okay, let's just bite the bullet,' so we got organized and started doing label designs."

The mild Finger Leek-en and the hot Hab Mussy versions are named in tribute to Gullah culture. The mustard base is their father's recipe, while the pepper blend for the spicy sauce was concocted by Richardson's husband, a former research-and-development chemist with a fondness for heat.

These days, Lillie's products can be found in stores all around Charleston.

And online sales have created fans all the way out in California, which is now the sisters' third-best market.

WHERE TO BUY: Online at *lilliesofcharleston.com*

South Carolina-Style Mustard Sauce

(Photo, page 56)
ACTIVE 10 MIN. - TOTAL 40 MIN.
MAKES 3½ CUPS

- 2 cups yellow mustard
- ½ cup packed light brown sugar
- ½ cup honey
- ½ cup apple cider vinegar
  A few dashes of cayenne pepper
  Black pepper, to taste

Whisk together all ingredients in a medium saucepan. Cook over medium, stirring often, until sugar and honey are dissolved and mixture is just beginning to bubble, 4 to 5 minutes. Remove from heat, and cool to room temperature, about 30 minutes. Store in an airtight container in refrigerator up to 3 months.

SCOTT'S BARBECUE SAUCE
Goldsboro, North Carolina

It all started with a dream. In 1917, a minister named Adam Scott began selling barbecue at his house in Goldsboro, North Carolina, and soon he enclosed his back porch and

converted it into a restaurant. After experimenting for years with sauce recipes, he told his family that the final ratio of ingredients had been revealed to him one night in a dream.

"It's basically an assortment of peppers, vinegar, and some water," says A. Martel Scott Jr., the dreamer's grandson. "I won't go into detail on the peppers." Ruddy orange in color with tongue-tingling heat, it's a classic example of the eastern North Carolina vinegar-and-pepper sauce.

The Scott family helped spread that style far beyond Goldsboro. In 1942, Adam Scott's son, Alvin Martel Scott Sr., packaged it in 6-ounce bottles. "Back then, there were little wholesale houses in each town and city selling to mom-and-pop stores around the county, and that's who he sold his sauce to," A. Martel Scott Jr. recalls.

The Scotts landed their first chain-store account with Winn-Dixie in the 1950s. Things really grew after A. Martel Scott Jr. earned a degree in accounting and took over the sauce operations from his father. Deals with Food Lion and Harris Teeter in the '70s put the yellow-labeled bottles on supermarket shelves across the Carolinas. And in 2002, Walmart began stocking it as far off as New Jersey and California.

Scott is quick to point out that the now-famous sauce is still "fat-free and calorie-free with no sugar." Although the family closed their restaurant a few years ago, their plant is going strong, turning out more than half a million bottles per year right there in Goldsboro.

WHERE TO BUY: Online at *scottsbarbecuesauce.com*

Eastern North Carolina-Style Vinegar Sauce

ACTIVE 5 MIN. - TOTAL 5 MIN., PLUS 4 HOURS STANDING
MAKES 4 CUPS

- 1 qt. distilled white vinegar
- 3 Tbsp. kosher salt
- 1 Tbsp. crushed red pepper, or more to taste
- 1 Tbsp. black pepper

Place all ingredients in a lidded jar or jug. Seal; shake to combine. Let stand at least 4 hours or up to overnight (12 hours). Store in an airtight container at room temperature up to 1 month.

EASTERN NORTH CAROLINA-STYLE VINEGAR SAUCE

ARTHUR BRYANT'S BARBEQUE
Kansas City, Missouri

The roots of Arthur Bryant's sauce go back to the earliest days of barbecue in Kansas City. Bryant's brother Charlie worked for the city's pioneering restaurateur Henry Perry, then branched out to open his own restaurant, which Arthur took over in 1946.

Arthur immediately made a few changes, like replacing wooden tabletops with Formica and putting tiles on the floor instead of sawdust. He adjusted the sauce recipe, too. "Old Man Perry and my brother used to make it too hot," Arthur told *The Kansas City Star* in 1966. "I cut down on the pepper ... I make it so you can put it on bread and eat it. Now it's a pleasure."

It's still a pleasure more than half a century later, especially when slathered across smoky folds of fresh-sliced beef. Rusty orange with strong vinegar tang, the thick sauce has a distinctive grainy texture from plenty of embedded spice. Rich & Spicy and Sweet Heat variants are for those who like more pepper or sugar, but why mess with Arthur Bryant's original?

WHERE TO BUY: Online at *shop.arthurbryantsbbq.com*

Kansas City-Style Barbecue Sauce
ACTIVE 5 MIN. - TOTAL 5 MIN.
MAKES 2⅔ CUPS

- 2 cups ketchup
- ½ cup apple cider vinegar
- 2 tsp. fresh lemon juice (from 1 lemon)
- ¼ cup granulated sugar
- 1 Tbsp. chili powder
- 1½ tsp. kosher salt
- 1 tsp. celery seeds
- 1 tsp. cayenne pepper
- 1 tsp. garlic powder

Whisk together ketchup, vinegar, and lemon juice in a large bowl until combined. Whisk in sugar, chili powder, salt, celery seeds, cayenne, and garlic powder until smooth. Store in an airtight container in refrigerator up to 1 week.

KANSAS CITY-STYLE
BARBECUE SAUCE

Make Way for Mangoes

If you've never tasted a ripe, juicy mango, be sure to try one this spring

Sunshine Smoothie

The fragrant, tropical mango is starting to come into season, and many supermarkets carry several types worth seeking out. Look for varieties like Honey (also called Ataulfo), which has a creamy, smooth texture; the citrusy, green-skin Keitt; or the aromatic Haden.

ACTIVE 5 MIN. · TOTAL 5 MIN.

SERVES 2

Combine 2½ cups chopped **very ripe mango,** ½ cup **fresh orange juice,** 1½ cups **ice cubes,** 2 Tbsp. **honey,** and ⅛ tsp. **kosher salt** in a high-power blender. Process until smooth, about 45 seconds. Pour into 2 glasses, and serve immediately.

How to Cut a Mango

STEP ONE Stem end up, slice from the top of the mango down one side of the pit (about ¼ inch from center). Repeat on opposite side. Discard section with pit.

- -

STEP TWO With the tip of a knife, score a crosshatch pattern into each half, cutting to but not through the skin.

- -

STEP THREE Invert the halves to easily cut the fruit from skin.

- -

Bright mangoes, rich in vitamins A and C and beneficial fiber, can upstage any dessert.

Bright Sides

Perk up proteins with vegetables that
come together in minutes

Sesame-Soy Asparagus

ACTIVE 15 MIN. - TOTAL 15 MIN.
SERVES 6

Heat 2 Tbsp. **toasted sesame oil** in
a large skillet over medium. Add
2 Tbsp. each minced fresh **ginger** and
minced **garlic**. Cook, stirring often,
until fragrant, about 1 minute. Add
6½ cups cut (1½-inch) **fresh asparagus**
pieces (about 2 lb.) and 2 cups cut
(1½-inch) **scallion** pieces; increase
heat to medium-high. Cook, stirring
occasionally, until asparagus is tender-
crisp, 3 to 4 minutes. Stir in 2 Tbsp. each
soy sauce and **mirin** (Japanese sweet
rice wine). Cook, without stirring, until
pan sauce thickens and coats vegetables,
30 seconds to 1 minute. Sprinkle
with 1 Tbsp. **toasted sesame seeds**
before serving.

CALORIES: **138** – CARBS: **14G** – FAT: **8G**

Skillet Radishes with Orange Zest and Tarragon

ACTIVE 15 MIN. - TOTAL 15 MIN.
SERVES 6

Heat 2 Tbsp. **olive oil** in a large skillet
over medium-high. Add 2 lb. **radishes**,
trimmed and halved (or quartered,
if large), and ½ cup sliced **shallots**.
Sprinkle with ½ tsp. **kosher salt** and
¼ tsp. **black pepper**. Cook, stirring
occasionally, until radishes are
browned in spots and tender-crisp, 8 to
10 minutes. Add ½ cup **fresh orange
juice** (from 2 oranges) and 3 Tbsp.
sherry vinegar. Cook, stirring and
scraping bottom of skillet to release
browned bits, until syrupy, about
2 minutes. Remove from heat; stir
in 1 Tbsp. each grated **orange zest**
and chopped **fresh tarragon**. Serve
immediately.

CALORIES: **85** – CARBS: **9G** – FAT: **5G**

Carrot-and-Cabbage Slaw with Sunflower Seeds

ACTIVE 15 MIN. - TOTAL 15 MIN.
SERVES 6

Whisk together 2 Tbsp. each **rice
vinegar, fresh lime juice**, and **canola
oil**; 1 Tbsp. **light brown sugar**; and ½ tsp.
kosher salt in a large bowl until sugar
and salt dissolve, about 1 minute. Add
5 cups thinly sliced **red cabbage** and
2 cups matchstick-cut **carrots**; toss
gently to coat. Add ⅓ cup **dry-roasted,
salted sunflower seed kernels** and
½ cup coarsely chopped **fresh cilantro**;
toss to combine.

CALORIES: **128** – CARBS: **13G** – FAT: **9G**

COOKING SCHOOL

TIPS AND TRICKS FROM THE SOUTH'S MOST TRUSTED KITCHEN

Make Spring Vegetables Last Longer
Tips for savoring three farmers market favorites

ASPARAGUS
Trim and discard the ends of the spears. Place in a glass or jar; fill halfway with water. Cover loosely with a plastic bag. Store in the refrigerator up to one week.

VIDALIA ONIONS
Wrap each onion in a paper towel. Store in the crisper drawer in the refrigerator (with vents closed to keep out moisture) up to two months.

RADISHES
Place bulbs in a plastic bag in the crisper drawer up to one week. Wrap greens in a damp paper towel, place in a plastic bag, store in refrigerator up to three days.

WANT TO MIX THINGS UP?

When stirring a custard or pudding, whisk constantly in a figure eight motion to ensure the mixture cooks evenly without lumps forming. This technique works for gravies and sauces, too.

SECRETS TO SILKY-SMOOTH CUSTARD

1
Choose the right dairy.
Half-and-half isn't just for coffee. The Test Kitchen says it gives custard the right amount of richness and best texture. You can also use equal parts whole milk and heavy cream.

2
Skip the tempering.
Whisking egg yolks into a hot liquid is tricky. Instead, stir together the cold eggs and other ingredients. Then cook over low-to-medium heat to slowly warm and thicken the custard.

3
Look for the jiggle.
If you're baking a custard, check for doneness by carefully jiggling the hot vessel. The center should move slightly, while the edges should be set.

"Before you chill a warm custard or pudding, press a sheet of plastic wrap or waxed paper on its surface to prevent a skin from forming."

—Pam Lolley
Test Kitchen Professional

April

SPICY STRAWBERRY-
GOAT-CHEESE CROSTINI

BUY THE BEST
Before purchasing berries
in a plastic container,
flip the container
over to check for any
bruised fruit.

Strawberry Delights

The sweetest sign of spring in the South

Spicy Strawberry-Goat-Cheese Crostini

ACTIVE 20 MIN. - TOTAL 50 MIN.
SERVES 10

Cut 1 (12-oz.) **French baguette** into ¼-inch-thick diagonal slices; place on a large baking sheet. Bake at 350°F until lightly toasted, about 10 minutes. Cool completely, about 20 minutes. Stir together 2 cups chopped **strawberries**, 1 Tbsp. minced **jalapeño chile**, 2 Tbsp. **honey**, 1 Tbsp. **fresh lime juice**, and ¼ tsp. **kosher salt** in a small bowl. Spread about 1 rounded teaspoon softened **goat cheese** from 2 (4-oz.) logs on each baguette slice. Top goat cheese with 1 slightly rounded teaspoon strawberry mixture. Sprinkle with chopped **fresh mint**.

ROASTED STRAWBERRY COMPOTE

STRAWBERRY FIELDS COCKTAIL

Strawberry Fields Cocktail

ACTIVE 5 MIN. - TOTAL 5 MIN.
SERVES 1

Stir together ¼ cup **Strawberry Syrup** (recipe below), 3 Tbsp. **gin**, and ½ cup plus 2 Tbsp. **tonic water** in a tall glass filled with **ice**. Garnish with a fresh **strawberry**.

Strawberry Syrup

ACTIVE 5 MIN. - TOTAL 5 MIN.
MAKES 1¾ CUPS

Process 1 cup each **granulated sugar** and coarsely chopped **strawberries**, ½ cup fresh **lime juice**, and 2 Tbsp. **water** in a blender until smooth and sugar has dissolved, 1 to 2 minutes. Store in an airtight container in refrigerator up to 2 weeks.

Roasted Strawberry Compote

ACTIVE 10 MIN. - TOTAL 35 MIN., PLUS 30 MIN. STANDING
SERVES 10

Gently stir together 2 lb. **strawberries**, halved (or quartered if large); ¾ cup **powdered sugar**; 1 Tbsp. **fresh lemon juice**; and ⅛ tsp. **kosher salt** in a large bowl. Spoon mixture into a 13- x 9-inch baking dish. Roast at 400°F until strawberries are softened and mixture is bubbly, 25 to 30 minutes, stirring after 15 minutes. Remove from oven; stir in ¼ tsp. **vanilla**. Let stand 30 minutes. Serve warm with vanilla ice cream.

COCONUT
MERINGUE
NESTS

The Magic of Meringue

Sweet treats as light as a spring breeze and as colorful as fresh flowers

Basic Meringue

The following six recipes all begin with a batch of basic meringue. There are several ways to make meringue, but we prefer this Italian-style method, which is very stable and less likely to "weep" in Southern humidity.

ACTIVE 20 MIN. · TOTAL 20 MIN.

MAKES ABOUT 4½ CUPS

- 1   cup granulated sugar
- 4   large egg whites, at room temperature
- ¼   tsp. cream of tartar
- ⅛   tsp. fine sea salt
- ¼   tsp. vanilla extract

1. Place sugar and ⅓ cup water in a small saucepan. Cook over medium-low, swirling pan occasionally, until sugar is dissolved and syrup registers 240°F on an instant-read thermometer, 10 to 14 minutes.

PICK A DRY DAY
Don't make meringues during rainy or very humid weather, if possible. Sugar will absorb water from the air, turning meringues soft and chewy.

2. Meanwhile, after about 7 minutes of cooking sugar syrup, beat egg whites with a stand mixer fitted with a whisk attachment on medium speed until foamy, about 30 seconds. Add cream of tartar and salt. Beat until soft peaks form, 1 to 2 minutes.
3. With mixer running on medium speed, gradually stream hot sugar syrup into whipped egg white mixture. Continue beating until meringue is glossy and forms stiff peaks and the outside of mixer bowl has cooled slightly, 3 to 5 minutes. Reduce speed to low, and beat in vanilla extract. Proceed with desired baked meringue recipe.

Coconut Meringue Nests

ACTIVE 20 MIN. · TOTAL 1 HOUR, 50 MIN., PLUS 2 HOURS COOLING

MAKES 24

  Basic Meringue (recipe precedes), divided
- 2   tsp. instant espresso granules or vanilla bean paste (optional)
- ¾   cup sweetened shredded coconut, lightly toasted
  Small egg-shape malted chocolate candies (such as Mini Robin Eggs)

1. Preheat oven to 200°F with rack in lower third position. Spread about ⅛ teaspoon Basic Meringue into each corner of 2 unrimmed baking sheets. Line each baking sheet with parchment paper; press into meringue to hold parchment in place. Set aside.
2. If desired, for a speckled bird's nest appearance, gently stir espresso granules into remaining Basic Meringue in bowl. Transfer mixture to a large (about 18-inch) piping bag fitted with a ¾-inch open star piping tip (such as Ateco 829). Pipe meringue into 3-inch spiral rounds, starting each in the center and spiraling outward, spaced at least 1 inch apart on prepared baking sheets. (Outer edges of rounds should be slightly raised to resemble nests.) You should have 24 meringues total.

3. Bake in preheated oven until dry and no longer sticky, 1½ to 2½ hours. Turn oven off; let meringues cool completely in oven until crisp, at least 2 hours or up to 12 hours.
4. Spoon coconut into centers of nests (about 1½ teaspoons each). Top with candies. Store in an airtight container at room temperature up to 1 week.

Mini Meringue Kisses

(Photo, page 68)

ACTIVE 20 MIN. · TOTAL 2 HOURS, 20 MIN., PLUS 4 HOURS COOLING

MAKES 160

  Basic Meringue (recipe precedes), divided
  Food coloring gels (such as Wilton Teal, Rose, and Lemon Yellow)
  Nonpareils (optional)

1. Preheat oven to 200°F with rack in lower third position. Spread about ⅛ teaspoon Basic Meringue into each corner of 2 unrimmed baking sheets. Line each baking sheet with parchment paper; press into meringue to hold parchment in place. Set aside.
2. Divide remaining Basic Meringue evenly into separate bowls, and stir different food coloring gels into each bowl. Transfer each dyed meringue mixture to a separate piping bag fitted with desired tip (such as a ½-inch round, closed star, or French star), or swirl 2 dyed mixtures together in a bowl, and place in 1 bag. Pipe small (about 1-inch) kisses evenly spaced at least ½ inch apart onto prepared baking sheets. You should have about 160 meringues total. If desired, decorate with nonpareils.
3. Bake in preheated oven until dry and no longer sticky, about 2 hours. Turn oven off; let meringues cool completely in oven until crisp, at least 4 hours or up to 12 hours. Store in an airtight container at room temperature up to 1 week.

MINI MERINGUE KISSES
(PAGE 67)

LEMON DROP MERINGUES
(PAGE 71)

DARK CHOCOLATE-
PISTACHIO-
ORANGE KISSES

Dark Chocolate-Pistachio-Orange Kisses

ACTIVE 30 MIN. - TOTAL 2 HOURS, 30 MIN.,
PLUS 2 HOURS COOLING
MAKES 48

Basic Meringue (recipe, page 67), divided

1½ tsp. finely grated orange zest (from 1 orange)

Food coloring gel (such as Wilton Golden Yellow)

6 oz. 60% bittersweet chocolate, chopped

1 cup raw pistachios, finely chopped

1. Preheat oven to 200°F with rack in lower third position. Spread about ⅛ teaspoon of the Basic Meringue into each corner of 2 unrimmed baking sheets. Line each baking sheet with parchment paper; press into meringue to hold parchment in place. Set aside.
2. Using a spatula, gently stir orange zest and a very small amount of food coloring into remaining Basic Meringue in bowl until incorporated. Stir in additional coloring until desired color. Transfer mixture to a large (about 18-inch) piping bag fitted with a ¾-inch French star piping tip (such as Ateco 869). Pipe 2-inch-wide (about 1-inch-high) rounds spaced at least ½ inch apart on prepared baking sheets. You should have 48 meringues total.
3. Bake meringues in preheated oven until dry, 1½ to 2½ hours. Turn oven off; let cool completely in oven until crisp, at least 2 hours or up to 12 hours. Store in an airtight container up to 1 week.
4. Microwave chopped chocolate in a medium-size microwavable bowl on HIGH until melted and smooth, about 90 seconds, stopping to stir every 30 seconds. Place chopped pistachios in a small shallow bowl. Working with 1 meringue at a time, carefully dip bottom into melted chocolate about ¼ inch up the sides; let excess drip off. Dip meringue into pistachios to coat chocolate completely, then place on a baking sheet lined with parchment paper. Repeat process with remaining meringues, melted chocolate, and pistachios. Let stand at room temperature until chocolate is set, about 30 minutes. Dipped meringues can be stored in an airtight container at room temperature up to 1 week.

Raspberry-White Chocolate Meringue Sandwiches

(Photo, page 5)
ACTIVE 1 HOUR, 35 MIN. - TOTAL 3 HOURS, 5 MIN.,
PLUS 3 HOURS COOLING
MAKES 16 SANDWICHES

Basic Meringue (recipe, page 67), divided

½ cup freeze-dried raspberries, finely ground

4 oz. white chocolate, finely chopped

2½ Tbsp. heavy whipping cream

1 Tbsp. butter

⅓ cup raspberry preserves

1. Preheat oven to 200°F with rack in lower third position. Spread about ⅛ teaspoon of the Basic Meringue into each corner of 2 unrimmed baking sheets. Line each baking sheet with parchment paper; press into meringue to hold parchment in place. Set aside.
2. Using a spatula, gently stir ground raspberries into remaining Basic Meringue in mixing bowl until incorporated. Transfer mixture to a large (about 18-inch) piping bag fitted with a ½-inch closed star piping tip (such as Ateco 846). Pipe into 3-inch spiral rounds, starting each in the center and spiraling outward, spaced at least ½ inch apart on prepared baking sheets. You should have 32 meringues total.
3. Bake meringues in preheated oven until dry and no longer sticky, 1½ to 2½ hours. Turn oven off, and let meringues cool completely in oven until crisp, at least 2 hours or up to 12 hours. Store in an airtight container up to 1 week.
4. Place white chocolate in a medium-size microwavable bowl. Stir in cream and butter. Microwave on MEDIUM (50% power) until melted and smooth, 1 to 2 minutes, stopping to stir every 30 seconds. Let ganache stand at room temperature, stirring occasionally, until thickened and cooled completely, 1 to 2 hours.
5. Transfer ganache to a piping bag with a ¼-inch hole cut in the corner. Turn half the meringues over, flat-side up, and pipe a thin border of ganache around the edge at top. Spread 1 teaspoon raspberry preserves inside border, then sandwich with remaining meringues, flat sides together. Assembled meringue sandwiches can be stored in an airtight container at room temperature up to 3 days.

Lemon Drop Meringues

(Photo, page 69)
ACTIVE 30 MIN. - TOTAL 2 HOURS,
PLUS 2 HOURS COOLING
MAKES 96

Basic Meringue (recipe, page 67), divided

Food coloring gel (such as Wilton Lemon Yellow)

¼ tsp. lemon extract or 1 tsp. grated lemon zest (from 1 lemon)

1 Tbsp. tiny white nonpareils

1. Preheat oven to 200°F with rack in lower third position. Spread about ⅛ teaspoon of the Basic Meringue into each corner of 2 unrimmed baking sheets. Line each baking sheet with parchment paper; press into meringue to hold parchment in place. Set aside.
2. Using a food-safe paintbrush, paint 4 thin, very light lines of food coloring gel lengthwise along the inside of 2 large (about 18-inch) piping bags; fit 1 of the bags with a ⅓-inch round tip (such as Ateco 804). Gently stir lemon extract into remaining Basic Meringue in bowl. Transfer half the mixture to 1 prepared bag. Pipe meringue into dollops (about 1¼ inches wide at the base) spaced at least ½ inch apart on prepared baking sheets. When bag is empty, transfer round tip to remaining bag. Add remaining meringue mixture to bag; repeat piping process. You should have about 96 meringues total. Sprinkle with nonpareils.
3. Bake in preheated oven until dry, 1½ to 2 hours. Turn oven off; let meringues cool completely in oven until crisp, at least 2 hours or up to 12 hours. Store in an airtight container at room temperature up to 1 week.

AVOID COLD EGGS
Let the whites stand at room temperature for 1 hour. Or place whole eggs in a bowl of warm water for 10 minutes.

CHECK THE BOWL
Make sure the mixing bowl is completely clean. If there are any traces of fat, the egg whites won't whip up.

Almond Meringue Puffs with Hazelnut-Chocolate Filling

ACTIVE 30 MIN. - TOTAL 3 HOURS,
PLUS 2 HOURS COOLING

MAKES 12

¼ cup hazelnut-chocolate spread (such as Nutella), chilled

Basic Meringue (recipe, page 67), divided

¼ tsp. almond extract

Food coloring gels (such as Wilton Violet, Kelly Green, and Royal Blue)

1. Scoop 12 balls (about 1 teaspoon each) of hazelnut-chocolate spread; roll into smooth balls using your hands. Place on a baking sheet lined with parchment paper. Freeze, uncovered, until hard, at least 30 minutes or up to 3 days.

2. Preheat oven to 200°F with rack in lower third position. Spread about ⅛ teaspoon of the Basic Meringue into each corner of 2 unrimmed baking sheets. Line each baking sheet with parchment paper; press into meringue to hold parchment in place. Set aside.
3. Gently stir almond extract into remaining Basic Meringue. Divide mixture evenly among 3 medium bowls (about 1⅓ cups each). Using a wooden pick, add a small amount of violet food coloring gel to 1 bowl; stir gently to combine. Repeat process with remaining 2 bowls of meringue and different food coloring gels.
4. Working with 1 color of meringue at a time, use the back of a spoon to spread about 1 tablespoon meringue into a 1½-inch circle on prepared baking

sheet. Place 1 frozen hazelnut-chocolate ball in center of circle. Using a 2½-inch scoop, drop a spoonful (about ⅓ cup) of the same color meringue onto ball, pressing gently so meringue completely encases the ball and adheres to parchment. Smooth sides using the back of a spoon, if needed. (Dip the scoop in a cup of hot water between puffs.) Repeat process with remaining meringue and balls, spacing them at least 1 inch apart on the 2 baking sheets.
5. Bake in preheated oven until dry, 2 to 3 hours. Turn oven off; let cool completely in oven until crisp, at least 2 hours or up to 12 hours. Store in an airtight container at room temperature up to 1 week.

Gather in the Garden

Nashville entertaining pro Katie Jacobs shares recipes for a mother–daughter DIY centerpiece party

Elderflower-Champagne Cocktail

For Elderflower-Champagne cocktail, Jacobs plucks some flowers from the garden, freezes them in an ice cube tray, and advises to choose blooms wisely. "There are poisonous ones out there, so check a list of edible flowers before you put them in your glass," she says.
ACTIVE 5 MIN. - TOTAL 5 MIN.

SERVES 12

Pour 1 bottle chilled **brut rosé Champagne** or dry sparkling wine, 2 cans chilled **club soda** or **sparkling water** (such as Pure LaCroix), and 1 cup **elderflower liqueur** (such as St Germain) into a large pitcher. Stir until well combined. Pour into wineglasses filled with **ice.**

"The easiest, quickest trick to dazzle your friends is to freeze adornments in ice cubes," says Katie.

Katie's Crudités Platter

A crudités platter can look elegant when you're willing to spend time putting one together. Plus, it's an inexpensive snack for a crowd. "The key is to include pops of color," Jacobs says. "I went to the farmers market and chose carrots that were purple, orange, and yellow, and radishes that were pretty on the inside." Add cauliflower and sprouts for texture, too.

ACTIVE 15 MIN. · TOTAL 15 MIN.

SERVES 12

Combine 1 cup **plain whole-milk Greek yogurt**; 1 (8-oz.) pkg. **cream cheese**, softened; 6 Tbsp. **prepared horseradish**; ¼ cup **whole milk**; ¼ cup chopped **fresh dill**; 1 **lemon**, zested and juiced (about 2 Tbsp. grated zest and 2 Tbsp. juice); and 1 tsp. **kosher salt**. Spoon into a serving bowl; sprinkle with **smoked paprika**. Place on serving platter; surround bowl with alfalfa sprouts, if desired. Arrange **cauliflower, cherry tomatoes, beets, cucumbers, carrots, broccoli,** and **radishes** on platter.

Hummingbird Cake Whoopie Pies

"Hummingbird cake is a long-standing Easter tradition in my family, but I wanted something that was easy to pick up," Jacobs says of her cream cheese frosting-filled whoopie pies. Making individual servings also minimizes how much the host handles guests' food.

ACTIVE 30 MIN. · TOTAL 1 HOUR, 40 MIN.

SERVES 15

COOKIES

- 2 cups all-purpose flour
- 1½ tsp. baking soda
- 1 tsp. baking powder
- ½ tsp. ground cinnamon
- ½ tsp. kosher salt
- 1 cup granulated sugar
- ½ cup vegetable oil
- 1 tsp. vanilla extract
- 2 large eggs
- 2 medium-size ripe bananas, mashed (about ¾ cup)
- ½ cup canned crushed pineapple in juice, undrained (from 1 [8-oz.] can)
- ½ cup finely chopped pecans, toasted

FROSTING

- 1 (8-oz.) pkg. cream cheese, at room temperature
- ½ cup unsalted butter, at room temperature
- ½ tsp. vanilla extract
- 2 cups powdered sugar
  Sweetened shredded coconut, for garnish

1. Prepare the Cookies: Preheat oven to 350°F. Line 2 large rimmed baking sheets with silicone baking mats or parchment paper. Whisk together flour, baking soda, baking powder, cinnamon, and salt in a medium bowl. Set aside.

2. Beat sugar, oil, and vanilla in the bowl of a stand mixer fitted with a paddle attachment on medium speed until combined, about 2 minutes. Add eggs, 1 at a time, beating until just combined after each addition. Continue beating on medium speed until mixture is pale yellow and fluffy, about 3 minutes. With mixer running on low speed, gradually add dry ingredients, beating until just combined. Fold in mashed bananas, pineapple, and pecans until just combined. (Batter will be more like a thick cake batter versus firm like a cookie dough.)

3. Using a 2-teaspoon cookie scoop, scoop batter and level; drop onto 1 of the prepared baking sheets, spacing cookies about 1 inch apart (you should have about 30). Bake in preheated oven until golden brown, 8 to 9 minutes. Transfer baking sheet to a wire rack, and cool 5 minutes. Remove cookies from baking sheet to wire racks, and cool completely, about 30 minutes. Repeat with remaining batter.

4. While Cookies are cooling, prepare the Frosting: Beat cream cheese, butter, and vanilla in the bowl of a stand mixer fitted with a whisk attachment on medium speed until smooth and creamy, about 2 minutes. Add powdered sugar, beating on medium speed until creamy, about 3 minutes, stopping occasionally to scrape down sides of bowl. Transfer Frosting to large piping bag, and cut about 1 inch off tip.

5. Match Cookies into pairs based on diameter. Pipe Frosting (about 1½ tablespoons per whoopie pie) on the flat side of 1 Cookie of each pair; place other Cookie, flat side down, on top of Frosting. Place shredded coconut in a shallow dish. Roll edges of each whoopie pie in shredded coconut, gently pressing to adhere to Frosting. Serve immediately, or cover and chill. If chilled, let come to room temperature before serving.

HUMMINGBIRD CAKE
WHOOPIE PIES

Flourless and Fabulous

This rich and fudgy cake can be made ahead for Passover—
or any time you need a dessert to impress

CHILL FACTOR
For the smoothest top, pour the warm glaze over the chilled cake and gently spread it with a spatula.

Flourless Pecan-Fudge Cake

ACTIVE 25 MIN. - TOTAL 3 HOURS, PLUS 8 HOURS, 20 MIN. CHILLING

SERVES 12

- 1 cup unsalted butter, sliced, divided, plus more for pan (or kosher-for-Passover margarine)
- ¼ cup unsweetened cocoa, plus more for dusting pan
- 8 oz. bittersweet baking chocolate, chopped (2 [4-oz.] bars)
- 10 oz. semisweet baking chocolate, chopped and divided (2½ [4-oz.] bars)
- 5 large eggs
- 1 cup granulated sugar
- 2 Tbsp. strong brewed coffee
- ¼ tsp. kosher salt
- 2½ tsp. vanilla extract, divided
- 4 tsp. light corn syrup or honey
- 1 cup chopped toasted pecans

1. Preheat oven to 300°F. Grease bottom and sides of a 9-inch springform pan with butter. Line bottom with parchment paper; grease with butter. Dust paper with cocoa. Microwave bittersweet chocolate, 4 ounces of the semisweet chocolate, and ¾ cup of the butter in a microwavable bowl on MEDIUM (50% power) until melted and smooth, 2 to 3 minutes, stirring after 1 minute then every 30 seconds. Cool 15 minutes.

2. Beat eggs, sugar, coffee, salt, and 2 teaspoons of the vanilla with a stand mixer fitted with whisk attachment on medium-high speed, until mixture is very foamy, pale in color, and doubled in volume, 3 to 4 minutes. Reduce mixer speed to low; gradually add melted chocolate mixture. Increase speed to medium-high, and beat until well blended, about 30 seconds. Sift the ¼ cup cocoa over mixture; beat on medium-low speed just until blended, 20 to 30 seconds.

3. Pour batter into prepared pan; bake in preheated oven until a thermometer inserted in center of cake registers 140°F, 40 to 45 minutes. Cool in pan on a wire rack 30 minutes.

4. Gently push down edges of cake with your fingertips until top is even. Run a knife around edges of cake; invert onto a wire rack. Remove pan and parchment paper. Cool 1 hour. Cover with plastic wrap. Chill 8 hours or up to overnight.

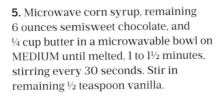

5. Microwave corn syrup, remaining 6 ounces semisweet chocolate, and ¼ cup butter in a microwavable bowl on MEDIUM until melted, 1 to 1½ minutes, stirring every 30 seconds. Stir in remaining ½ teaspoon vanilla.

6. Place wire rack with cake over a rimmed baking sheet. Pour glaze over cake, and spread over top and sides. Press chopped toasted pecans along sides. Chill cake 20 minutes before serving.

The Freshest Catch

Give chicken the night off, and discover new takes on fish, shrimp, and scallops

Simple Seared Fish with Pea Salad

ACTIVE 35 MIN. - TOTAL 35 MIN.

SERVES 4

- ¼   cup rice vinegar
- 2   Tbsp. finely chopped shallot (from 1 large shallot)
- 2   tsp. honey
- 2   tsp. Dijon mustard
- ¼   cup, plus 3 Tbsp. olive oil, divided
- 1¾   tsp. kosher salt, divided
- 1   cup frozen, thawed English peas or fresh, cooked, chilled English peas
- 8   oz. sugar snap peas, cut diagonally into ½-inch slices (about 2 cups)
- ½   cup thinly sliced radishes (from 3 small radishes)
- ¼   cup thinly sliced red onion (from 1 small onion)
- 1   tsp. grated lemon zest (from 1 lemon)
- 4   (6-oz.) skinless grouper fillets
- ½   tsp. black pepper
    Lemon wedges, for serving

1. Whisk together vinegar, shallot, honey, mustard, ¼ cup plus 2 tablespoons of the olive oil, and 1 teaspoon of the salt in a medium bowl. Set aside ⅓ cup dressing. Add English and sugar snap peas, radishes, onion, and lemon zest to shallot mixture in bowl; toss to coat. Let stand at room temperature until ready to serve.
2. Pat fish fillets dry with a paper towel; season with pepper and remaining ¾ teaspoon salt. Heat remaining 1 tablespoon oil in a large nonstick skillet over medium-high until shimmering. Add fillets to skillet. Cook, undisturbed, until a light golden crust appears on outside, about 4 minutes. Turn fillets over; cook until fish is opaque throughout, about 2 minutes. Remove from skillet; place on a plate lined with paper towels.
3. Using a slotted spoon, divide pea mixture among 4 plates. Top each plate with 1 fillet; spoon reserved dressing evenly over salad. Serve with lemon wedges.

FRESH VS. FROZEN
Make this recipe with any thick fillets from white-flesh fish. Buy fish fresh at a seafood counter; frozen fish tends to be watery.

SAVE YOUR SKIN
Keep the skin on the salmon to help the fillet stay intact as it cooks. It will peel right off when the fish is done.

Creamy Fettuccine with Salmon and Spring Vegetables

ACTIVE 35 MIN. - TOTAL 35 MIN.
SERVES 4

- 12 oz. uncooked fettuccine
- 1 (5.2-oz.) pkg. soft Gournay cheese product with garlic and fine herbs (such as Boursin)
- 2 Tbsp. olive oil
- 1 (1-lb.) skin-on salmon fillet
- ¼ tsp. black pepper
- 1¼ tsp. kosher salt, divided
- 2 Tbsp. unsalted butter
- 2 cups thinly sliced leek (from 1 leek)
- 1 lb. fresh thin asparagus, trimmed and sliced diagonally into 2-inch pieces (about 3 cups)
- 1 tsp. grated lemon zest (from 1 lemon)
- 1 cup frozen petite green peas, thawed
- 2 Tbsp. chopped fresh dill, plus more for garnish

1. Cook fettuccine in a large pot of boiling salted water according to package directions for al dente. Drain, reserving 1 cup cooking liquid. Whisk together cheese and ½ cup of the liquid until smooth; set aside.

2. Heat oil in a 12- to 14-inch nonstick skillet over medium-high. Pat salmon dry; season flesh side with pepper and ½ teaspoon of the salt. Add fish, flesh side down, to skillet. Cook, undisturbed, until a deep golden brown crust forms, 5 to 6 minutes. Turn fish over; cook to desired degree of doneness, 1 to 2 minutes for medium. Transfer to a plate lined with paper towels; cover with aluminum foil to keep warm. Wipe skillet clean.

3. Melt butter in skillet over medium. Add leek. Cook, stirring often, until wilted, 2 minutes. Add asparagus and remaining ¾ teaspoon salt. Cook, stirring occasionally, until tender-crisp, 2 minutes. (Reduce heat to medium-low, if needed, to prevent browning.) Stir in cheese mixture, zest, peas, and cooked pasta. Cook, stirring constantly, until heated through, 2 minutes, stirring in cooking liquid, 1 tablespoon at a time, if needed, for creaminess. Remove from heat; stir in dill.

4. Remove skin from salmon; flake into large pieces. Top pasta servings with salmon, and sprinkle with additional dill.

Seared Scallops with Lemon-Herb Rice

ACTIVE 45 MIN. - TOTAL 45 MIN.
SERVES 4

- 5 scallions
- 6 Tbsp. butter, divided
- 1½ cups uncooked long-grain white rice
- ¼ cup dry white wine
- 2¾ cups lower-sodium chicken broth
- 1½ tsp. kosher salt, divided
- 2 tsp. grated lemon zest, plus 2 seeded lemon slices (from 1 lemon), divided
- 16 dry-packed sea scallops (about 1½ lb.)
- ½ tsp. black pepper
- 2 Tbsp. olive oil
- 2 Tbsp. chopped fresh flat-leaf parsley, plus more for garnish

1. Thinly slice white and light green parts of scallions. Thinly slice dark green parts to equal ¼ cup. Melt 2 tablespoons of the butter in a saucepan over medium-high. Add white and light green scallions, and cook, stirring often, 1 minute. Add rice. Cook, stirring constantly, until fragrant and toasted, 2 minutes. Add wine. Cook, stirring constantly, until absorbed, about 30 seconds. Stir in broth and 1 teaspoon of the salt; bring to a boil. Reduce heat to low; cover and simmer until liquid is absorbed, 15 to 17 minutes. Remove from heat; cover until ready to use.
2. While rice cooks, cut remaining 4 tablespoons butter into pieces. Place butter and lemon slices in a microwavable bowl. Microwave on HIGH until butter is almost melted, 30 to 40 seconds. Stir until melted; remove and discard lemons. Cover lemon butter to keep warm.

3. Rinse scallops; pat dry. Remove muscle from side of scallops; discard. Season with pepper and remaining ½ teaspoon salt.
4. Heat 1 tablespoon oil in a large cast-iron skillet over medium-high. Add 8 scallops; press gently with a spatula. Cook until bottom side is deep golden brown, about 4 minutes. Turn scallops over; cook until slightly opaque in center, 3 to 4 minutes more. (Don't overcook.) Transfer to a plate lined with paper towels. Wipe skillet; repeat with remaining oil and scallops.
5. Fluff rice with a fork; stir in parsley and zest. Serve scallops with rice; sprinkle with dark green scallion slices and additional parsley. Spoon lemon butter evenly over scallops before serving.

PREP FOR SUCCESS
On the side of a raw scallop, you might find a small rectangular muscle (called the "foot"). It is chewy and tough compared to the rest of the scallop, so pinch it off and discard it.

Shrimp Cake Sandwiches

ACTIVE 25 MIN. - TOTAL 35 MIN.
SERVES 4

- 1 cup coarsely chopped scallions (from 1 bunch)
- 1 cup loosely packed fresh flat-leaf parsley leaves and tender stems
- 5 Tbsp. chopped fresh basil, divided
- 1 lb. medium-size peeled, deveined raw shrimp
- ½ cup all-purpose flour
- 1 tsp. kosher salt
- ½ cup mayonnaise, divided
- 2 Tbsp. sriracha chile sauce, divided
- ¼ cup canola oil
- 4 brioche hamburger buns, split
- 4 tomato slices
- ¼ cup thinly sliced red onion (from 1 small onion)
- 8 Bibb lettuce leaves (from 1 head)

1. Pulse scallions, parsley, and 2½ tablespoons of the basil in a food processor until finely chopped, about 5 pulses. Scrape down sides of processor bowl. Add shrimp, flour, salt, 2 tablespoons of the mayonnaise, and 1 tablespoon of the Sriracha. Pulse in 1-second bursts just until mixture starts to clump together and you can still see pieces of shrimp, 10 to 12 pulses. Transfer to a medium bowl; let stand 15 minutes.

2. Meanwhile, stir together remaining 6 tablespoons mayonnaise, 2½ tablespoons basil, and 1 tablespoon Sriracha in a small bowl. Set aside.

3. Heat oil in a large skillet over medium-high. Using a ⅔-cup-capacity scoop or measuring cup, scoop 4 mounds of shrimp mixture into hot oil. Flatten with a spatula to form 3½-inch-diameter patties that are about ¾ inch thick. (If mixture sticks to spatula, dip spatula in hot oil.) Cook shrimp cakes until golden brown and opaque throughout, 3 to 4 minutes per side. Transfer to a plate lined with paper towels. Drain oil from skillet. Reduce heat to medium. Add buns in batches, cut sides down, and cook until toasted, 1 to 2 minutes.

4. Evenly spread mayonnaise mixture on cut sides of buns. Top each bun bottom with 1 shrimp cake, 1 tomato slice, red onion slices, and 2 lettuce leaves. Cover with bun top, and serve immediately.

Vietnamese-Style Shrimp Noodle Bowls

ACTIVE 25 MIN. - TOTAL 25 MIN.
SERVES 4

- ⅓ cup sweet chili sauce (such as Mae Ploy)
- ¼ cup fresh lime juice (from 2 limes)
- 1 Tbsp. rice vinegar
- 2 tsp. fish sauce
- 1 (8-oz.) pkg. uncooked rice vermicelli noodles
- 1 lb. large peeled, deveined raw shrimp
- ¼ cup cornstarch
- 1 Tbsp. light brown sugar
- 1 tsp. black pepper
- ¾ tsp. kosher salt
- 3 Tbsp. canola oil

Matchstick-cut carrots, thinly sliced English cucumber, thinly sliced romaine lettuce hearts, chopped fresh cilantro, chopped fresh mint, and chopped roasted peanuts, for topping

1. Stir together ½ cup water, the chili sauce, lime juice, vinegar, and fish sauce in a medium bowl. Set aside.

2. Cook rice noodles according to package directions. Drain, rinse with cold water, and set aside.

3. Pat shrimp very dry with paper towels. Place cornstarch, brown sugar, pepper, and salt in a large zip-top plastic bag. Seal and shake to combine. Add shrimp; seal and gently shake to coat.

4. Heat a wok or large cast-iron skillet over high until very hot. Add 1½ tablespoons oil; swirl to coat wok. Add half of shrimp to hot oil. Cook, separating shrimp with tongs to ensure even browning and turning once, until shrimp are crisp, lightly browned, and cooked through, 3 to 4 minutes. Remove shrimp to a plate lined with paper towels. Repeat procedure with remaining oil and shrimp.

5. Divide noodles and shrimp among bowls. Add desired toppings; drizzle evenly with chili sauce mixture.

Loafing Around

All the flavors of carrot cake served up for breakfast in a delicious quick bread

Carrot Cake Quick Bread with Buttermilk Glaze

ACTIVE 10 MIN. - TOTAL 1 HOUR, 10 MIN., PLUS 1 HOUR, 10 MIN. COOLING

MAKES 2 LOAVES

- 3 cups all-purpose flour, plus more for dusting
- 1½ cups packed light brown sugar
- 1 tsp. baking soda
- 1 tsp. ground cinnamon
- ¾ tsp. kosher salt
- 3 large eggs
- 1 cup unsalted butter, melted, plus softened butter for greasing
- 2 cups grated carrots (from 2 large carrots)
- 1 (8-oz.) can crushed pineapple in juice, drained
- 1 cup unsweetened shredded coconut
- 2 tsp. vanilla extract
- ½ cup, plus 2 Tbsp. whole buttermilk, divided
- 1 cup chopped toasted pecans
- 1 cup powdered sugar

1. Preheat oven to 350°F. Whisk together flour, brown sugar, baking soda, cinnamon, and salt in a medium bowl. **2.** Whisk eggs in a large bowl. Add melted butter, grated carrots, pineapple, coconut, vanilla, and ½ cup of the buttermilk; continue whisking until combined. Gently stir flour mixture into egg mixture just until incorporated. Gently fold in toasted pecans. Spoon mixture evenly into 2 greased (with softened butter) and floured 8- x 4-inch loaf pans. Bake in preheated oven until a wooden pick inserted in center comes out clean, about 1 hour. Tent with aluminum foil, if needed, after 50 minutes to prevent overbrowning. **3.** Cool loaves in pans on a wire rack 10 minutes; remove loaves from pans. Cool completely on rack, about 1 hour. **4.** Whisk together powdered sugar and remaining 2 tablespoons buttermilk in a small bowl; pour or drizzle over cooled loaves.

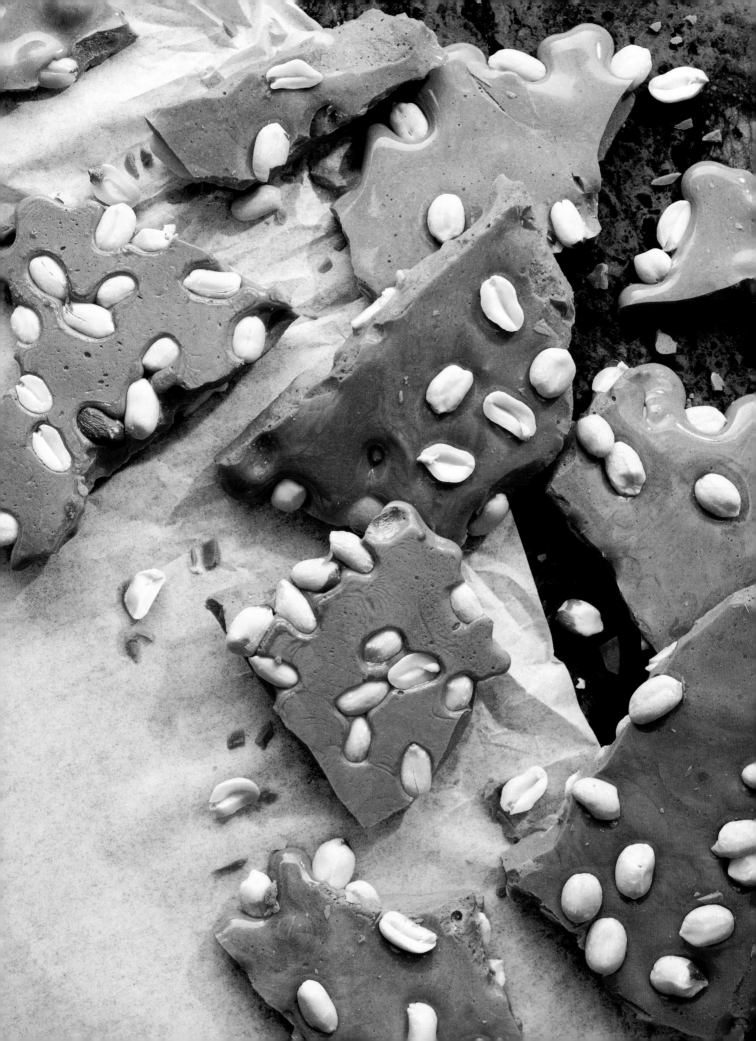

A Nutty Classic

It's always a good time to make a batch of peanut brittle

AFTER MORE THAN 35 YEARS of writing cookbooks, I have to make a culinary confession: I do not bake. No punching down dough or rolling out cookies or delicately fluting the edges of piecrusts for me. I'm not really a dessert eater, so my sweet tooth runs to candy. Cooks make what they like to eat, and while other people may have fond memories of Christmas gingerbread men and Easter rolls, my remembrances are of blocks of fudge and walnut-topped fondant creams.

One recipe, though, has always been my standby: a superquick peanut brittle. I'm not really sure where I got it, probably from my mother, but for decades it has been my go-to. Crumble a bit of it over some store-bought ice cream, and voilà—something special to end a meal. Package some up in a ribbon-tied box, and it's the perfect hostess gift. And if the gummy bears have run out, this candy made of Southern staples is as close as the pantry. I have made the brittle with different types of nuts, but the classic peanut just tastes best to me.

This seems to be a Southern creation, as peanuts have long been common here. They were even the subject of the popular Confederate Civil War song "Eating Goober Peas." Little did those singing know that it had an African connection. Goober (a Southern term for this legume) comes from the Lingala or Kongo word *nguba,* meaning "peanut." When the song was published in 1866, the authors were listed as P. Nutt and A. Pindar, obviously an inside joke. (Pindar is from the word *mpinda,* which is another Kongo term for peanut.)

When the Civil War acquainted the North with this food, its popularity soon spread around the country along with that of peanut brittle. Recipes for the candy made with corn syrup and these nuts began appearing in American cookbooks in the late 19th century.

My version is a very simple one, and it doesn't require cream of tartar, corn syrup, or even a candy thermometer—just butter, peanuts, sugar, a pinch of baking soda, and a cast-iron skillet. –Jessica B. Harris

Jessica's Peanut Brittle

ACTIVE 20 MIN. - TOTAL 20 MIN., PLUS 30 MIN. COOLING

MAKES ABOUT 2 DOZEN 2-INCH PIECES

- ½ Tbsp. unsalted butter
- ½ cup raw shelled peanuts with skins removed
- 2 cups granulated sugar
- ¼ tsp. baking soda

1. Completely coat bottom and sides of a 13- x 9½-inch rimmed baking sheet with butter. Spread nuts in an even layer on prepared pan; set aside.
2. Cook granulated sugar in a heavy cast-iron skillet over medium-low, stirring occasionally with a wooden spoon until the sugar just begins to melt. Stop stirring. Cook, undisturbed, until sugar melts completely and is syrupy and deep golden brown, about 15 minutes total. (If the sugar begins to brown too quickly or clump in some spots, carefully remove skillet from heat, stir gently, and return to heat.) Add baking soda, stirring well to make sure it is mixed thoroughly.
3. Quickly pour the sugar syrup over nuts on baking sheet. (You may not totally cover the bottom of the pan.) Allow it to cool completely, about 30 minutes. Lift peanut brittle from baking sheet. Break into bite-size pieces, and store in an airtight glass jar. The brittle will keep for several weeks—if it doesn't get eaten first.

Peanut Brittle Pointers

Jessica's tips for making this crunchy, buttery candy

PAY ATTENTION Hot sugar is like lava, so care must be taken at all times. This is a recipe that demands your full attention while it cooks, so be sure to have all the necessary tools and ingredients in place before you begin to heat the sugar.

TOAST THE NUTS I prefer to make my brittle with dark-roasted peanuts. I toast them by stirring them around for a few minutes in a hot skillet.

TRY A MARBLE SLAB I prepare candies often enough that I purchased a confectioner's marble slab. Although it isn't necessary, it stays cold, so the candy cools quicker. The slabs are often pricey, but a couple of 12- x 12-inch marble floor tiles will also work well.

Take a Dip

Brighten snack time with three dunk-worthy recipes

BEET-GOAT CHEESE DIP

CARROT-TAHINI DIP

SWEET PEA-PARMESAN DIP

Beet-Goat Cheese Dip

ACTIVE 15 MIN. - TOTAL 1 HOUR, 15 MIN.,
PLUS 1 HOUR CHILLING

SERVES 6

Wrap 3 trimmed (7-oz.) **beets** individually in Reynolds Wrap® aluminum foil; bake at 400°F until tender, about 1 hour. Cool in foil 15 minutes. Peel and quarter beets. Process beets, 4 **dried dates**, ½ tsp. **kosher salt**, and ¼ cup **plain Greek yogurt** in a food processor until smooth, 90 seconds. Transfer to a bowl; chill 1 hour. Stir together 2 oz. crumbled **goat cheese**, 1½ Tbsp. **water**, and ¼ cup **Greek yogurt** in a bowl until smooth. Top beet mixture with cheese mixture. Top with sliced **fresh chives**.

CALORIES: **108** – CARBS: **16G** – FAT: **3G**

Sweet Pea-Parmesan Dip

ACTIVE 15 MIN. - TOTAL 15 MIN.

SERVES 4

Process 3 cups thawed **frozen sweet peas**, ⅓ cup shredded **Parmigiano-Reggiano cheese**, 1½ tsp. grated **lemon zest**, 3 Tbsp. **fresh lemon juice**, 2 Tbsp. **extra-virgin olive oil**, 2 Tbsp. chopped **fresh mint**, 1 **garlic clove**, ½ tsp. **kosher salt**, and ¼ tsp. **black pepper** in a food processor until smooth, about 1 minute, adding **water**, 1 Tbsp. at a time, and processing until smooth. Transfer to a bowl. Sprinkle with chopped **mint** and **lemon zest**.

CALORIES: **172** – CARBS: **15G** – FAT: **9G**

Carrot-Tahini Dip

ACTIVE 20 MIN. - TOTAL 20 MIN.,
PLUS 1 HOUR CHILLING

SERVES 4

Heat 2 Tbsp. **olive oil** in a medium saucepan over medium. Add 3½ cups sliced **carrots** and ½ tsp. **kosher salt**. Cook, covered and stirring occasionally, until carrots start to soften, 6 to 8 minutes. Add 1 smashed **garlic clove**. Cook, stirring occasionally, until carrots are tender, about 5 minutes. Process cooked carrot mixture, 3 Tbsp. **tahini**, 2 Tbsp. **fresh lemon juice**, ½ cup **water**, and 1 Tbsp. **olive oil** in a food processor until smooth, 1 minute. Transfer to a bowl; chill 1 hour. Sprinkle with **za'atar seasoning**.

CALORIES: **217** – CARBS: **17G** – FAT: **16G**

Gussied-Up Grits

This humble pantry staple gets fancy for Easter weekend

Goat-Cheese-and-Spring Onion Grits Soufflés

ACTIVE 30 MIN. - TOTAL 1 HOUR
SERVES 6

- 2 Tbsp. unsalted butter, plus more for greasing ramekins
- 1 cup chopped spring onion bulbs (from 1 medium bunch)
- 2 cups half-and-half
- 1 Tbsp. kosher salt
- 1 cup stone-ground yellow or white grits
- 4 oz. goat cheese, crumbled (about 1 cup), plus more for topping
- 4 large eggs, separated
- 1 tsp. Dijon mustard
- 1 Tbsp. sliced fresh chives

1. Preheat oven to 400°F. Grease 6 (8-oz.) ramekins with butter. Set aside.
2. Heat butter in a large saucepan over medium. Add onions. Cook, stirring occasionally, until softened, about 5 minutes. Add 2 cups water, the half-and-half, and salt to saucepan; bring to a boil over medium-high. Reduce heat to medium-low; whisk in grits. Cook, whisking occasionally, until thickened, about 20 minutes. Remove from heat; whisk in cheese until completely melted.
3. While grits cook, whisk together egg yolks and mustard in a medium bowl; set aside. Beat egg whites with whisk attachment in the bowl of a stand mixer or with an electric hand mixer on medium-high speed until soft peaks form, 2 to 3 minutes.
4. Whisk ¼ cup of the hot grits into yolk mixture to temper; whisk tempered yolk mixture into remaining grits until combined. Gently fold one-third of the egg whites into grits, and repeat until all whites are folded into grits. Divide mixture among prepared ramekins. Bake in preheated oven until puffed and set but still slightly jiggly in centers, about 15 minutes. Sprinkle with chives and additional goat cheese; serve immediately.

SOUFFLÉS AREN'T SCARY
For airy texture, fold the egg whites gently into the grits. Serve right out of the oven, and don't panic when they deflate a bit—that's to be expected.

Spoon Bread with Mushrooms and Herbs

(Photo, page 4)

Don't stir the pot: Let the mushrooms cook undisturbed at first so they can get a good sear, which prevents sogginess.

ACTIVE 1 HOUR · TOTAL 1 HOUR, 40 MIN.

SERVES 8

- ¼ cup unsalted butter, divided, plus more for greasing dish
- 3 cups half-and-half
- 1 Tbsp., plus ½ tsp. kosher salt, divided
- 1½ cups stone-ground yellow or white grits
- 5 large eggs, separated
- 6 oz. Gruyère cheese, shredded (about 1½ cups)
- 3 Tbsp. crème fraîche
- 2 Tbsp. olive oil
- 1 lb. mixed wild mushrooms, halved or sliced
- 2 tsp. finely chopped garlic (from 2 medium garlic cloves)
- ½ cup dry white wine
- 3 Tbsp. heavy cream
- 2 Tbsp. chopped fresh flat-leaf parsley
- 2 tsp. chopped fresh tarragon

1. Preheat oven to 375°F. Grease a 3-quart oval or 13- x 9-inch baking dish with butter; set aside. Bring 3 cups water, the half-and-half, and 1 tablespoon of the salt to a boil in a large pot over medium-high. Once simmering, gradually whisk in grits; reduce heat to medium-low. Cook, whisking occasionally, until grits have absorbed all liquid, pull away from sides of pot, and are completely tender, 20 to 25 minutes. Remove from heat.
2. Whisk egg yolks until smooth. Whisk ½ cup of the hot grits into yolks to temper; stir tempered yolk mixture, Gruyère, crème fraîche, and 2 tablespoons of the butter into remaining grits.
3. Beat egg whites with whisk attachment in the bowl of a stand mixer or with an electric hand mixer on medium-high speed until soft peaks form, 2 to 3 minutes. Gently fold one-third of the egg whites into grits; repeat until all whites are folded into grits. Transfer mixture to prepared baking dish; bake in preheated oven until puffed, golden brown, and just set but still slightly jiggly in center, about 40 minutes.
4. While spoon bread is baking, heat oil in a large high-sided skillet over medium-high. Add mushrooms in an even layer. Cook, undisturbed, until starting to crisp and brown on one side, about 4 minutes. Stir vigorously, and continue to cook, undisturbed, until they start to decrease in volume and brown more evenly, about 4 minutes. Continue cooking, stirring occasionally, until mushrooms are browned and tender, 4 to 6 minutes more. Add garlic. Cook, stirring constantly, until fragrant, 1 minute. Add wine; remove from heat. Stir in cream, parsley, tarragon, and remaining 2 tablespoons butter and ½ teaspoon salt. Cover; keep warm until ready to serve.
5. Once spoon bread is cooked through, remove from oven, and serve immediately topped with mushroom mixture.

Grit Cakes and Pork Grillades

ACTIVE 1 HOUR · TOTAL 3 HOURS, PLUS 1 HOUR CHILLING

SERVES 8

- 2 cups whole milk
- 1 Tbsp. kosher salt, divided
- 1 cup stone-ground yellow or white grits (such as McEwen & Sons)
- 4 oz. sharp white cheddar cheese, shredded (about 1 cup)
- ¾ cup unsalted butter, divided
- 2 Tbsp. canola oil
- 2 lb. boneless pork shoulder, cut into 1½-inch pieces
- 1 medium-size yellow onion, chopped (about 1½ cups)
- 3 medium celery stalks, chopped (about 1 cup)
- 1 medium-size green bell pepper, seeded and chopped (about 1 cup)
- ⅓ cup all-purpose flour
- 2 cups beef broth
- 1 (15-oz.) can fire-roasted diced tomatoes
- ½ cup dry red wine
- 2 Tbsp. Worcestershire sauce
- 2 tsp. Louisiana-style hot sauce (such as Crystal)
- ½ cup thinly sliced scallions (about 4 medium)

1. Line a 15- x 10-inch rimmed baking sheet with parchment paper. Bring milk, 2 cups water, and 1 teaspoon of the kosher salt to a boil in a large saucepan over medium-high. Reduce heat to medium-low; whisk in grits. Cook, stirring occasionally, until grits are tender and thick, 25 to 30 minutes. Remove from heat; stir in cheese and 2 tablespoons of the butter. Pour grits onto parchment-lined pan; spread into an even layer. Cool completely, about 30 minutes. Cover with plastic wrap, and refrigerate until grits are firm, at least 1 hour or up to 3 days.
2. Heat oil in a large Dutch oven over medium-high. Pound each piece of pork to ¼-inch thickness; sprinkle evenly with 1 teaspoon of the salt. Cook pork in batches until browned, flipping once, 3 to 4 minutes per side. Transfer to a plate; set aside. Add onion, celery, and bell pepper to pork drippings. Cook, stirring occasionally, until softened, 6 minutes. Remove; set aside while you prepare the roux.
3. Add 6 tablespoons of the butter to Dutch oven over medium. Add flour to butter, whisking constantly to scrape up browned bits from bottom of pot until flour and butter start to foam. Cook, whisking often, until deep brown, about 10 minutes. Stir in beef broth, tomatoes, wine, Worcestershire, and hot sauce. Add pork, vegetable mixture, and remaining 1 teaspoon salt; bring to a boil. Reduce heat to simmer over medium-low. Cook, uncovered, stirring occasionally, until pork is very tender and sauce has started to reduce, about 2 hours. Remove from heat; cover to keep warm.
4. Remove grits from refrigerator, and cut into 16 rectangles. Working in batches, heat 1 tablespoon of the butter in a large skillet over medium-high. Add 4 grit cakes at a time, and cook until golden brown on both sides, about 2 minutes per side. Repeat with remaining butter and grit cakes. (Keep grit cakes warm in a 200°F oven while cooking remaining batches.)
5. Place 2 grit cakes onto each of 8 plates; top with grillade mixture. Sprinkle with sliced scallions; serve immediately.

JUMP-START BRUNCH
Prepare the grits through Step 1 up to three days ahead. The pork can be made up to two days ahead. Chill in airtight containers; reheat before serving.

GRIT CAKES AND
PORK GRILLADES

RAINBOW-CARROT TART
WITH PEA SHOOTS

Nothing Else Goes Together Like Peas & Carrots

Five reasons these vibrant spring vegetables make the perfect pair

Rainbow-Carrot Tart with Pea Shoots

ACTIVE 25 MIN. · TOTAL 1 HOUR, 25 MIN.

SERVES 12

- 1 (1-lb.) bunch baby multicolor carrots, tops removed, halved lengthwise
- 3 Tbsp. olive oil
- 3 oz. Pecorino Romano cheese, grated (about 1⅓ cups), divided
- 1½ cups whole-milk ricotta cheese (from 1 [16-oz.] container)
- 1 Tbsp. chopped fresh mint, plus small mint leaves for garnish
- 1 garlic clove, grated (¾ tsp.)
- ½ tsp. black pepper
- ¼ tsp. kosher salt
- 2 tsp. grated lemon zest (from 1 lemon), divided
- 20 thawed phyllo pastry sheets (from 1 [16-oz.] pkg.)
- ½ cup unsalted butter, melted
  Fresh pea shoots, for garnish

1. Preheat oven to 425°F with a rimmed baking sheet on center rack. Toss together carrots and oil in a large bowl to coat; spread in an even layer on hot baking sheet. Roast until tender and golden brown, 25 to 30 minutes, tossing once halfway through cook time.
2. Meanwhile, measure 2 tablespoons of the Pecorino Romano into a small bowl; set aside for serving. Place remaining Pecorino Romano in a medium bowl. Add ricotta, mint, garlic, pepper, salt, and 1 teaspoon of the lemon zest; stir to combine. Set aside until ready to use.
3. Once carrots have finished roasting, remove from oven. Reduce oven temperature to 400°F. Place 1 phyllo sheet on a baking sheet lined with parchment paper (cover remaining phyllo sheets with a damp towel to

prevent drying out). Generously brush with some of the melted butter. Repeat layers using remaining phyllo sheets and butter.
4. Spread ricotta mixture in a thin layer over top phyllo layer, leaving a ½-inch border. Arrange roasted carrots over ricotta mixture. Bake at 400°F until phyllo is golden brown and crispy around edges, about 20 minutes. Remove from oven, and let cool slightly, about 10 minutes.
5. Sprinkle tart evenly with reserved 2 tablespoons Pecorino Romano and remaining 1 teaspoon lemon zest. Garnish tart with mint leaves and pea shoots. Serve warm or at room temperature.

Carrot Soup with Pea Pesto

(Photo, page 92)

ACTIVE 35 MIN. · TOTAL 55 MIN.

SERVES 6

- 2½ lb. large carrots, cut into 1-inch pieces
- 1 medium-size sweet onion, cut into wedges
- ½ cup, plus 2 Tbsp. extra-virgin olive oil, divided
- 3½ tsp. kosher salt, divided
- 7 garlic cloves, divided
- 3 oz. Parmigiano-Reggiano cheese, coarsely chopped into 1-inch pieces
- 1 cup fresh or thawed frozen English peas
- 1 cup loosely packed fresh basil leaves
- 3 Tbsp. fresh lemon juice (from 1 lemon)
- 5 cups vegetable stock, divided
- ½ tsp. ground cumin
- ¼ tsp. cayenne pepper
- ¼ cup unsalted butter, cut into cubes
- 1 Tbsp. sherry vinegar
- 2 tsp. pure maple syrup
- 1 cup heavy whipping cream, divided

1. Preheat oven to 400°F. Toss together carrots, onion, 2 tablespoons of the oil, 1 teaspoon of the salt, and 5 of the garlic cloves on a large rimmed baking sheet; spread evenly. Roast until vegetables are very tender and starting to brown, 30 to 40 minutes. Remove from oven; cool 5 minutes.
2. While vegetables roast, place cheese, peas, basil, ¼ cup water, the lemon juice, 1 teaspoon of the salt, and remaining ½ cup oil and 2 garlic cloves in a blender. Process until smooth, stopping to scrape down sides as needed, about 2 minutes. Transfer pesto to a small bowl; set aside. Rinse blender, and wipe dry.
3. Add cooled vegetable mixture and 3 cups of the stock to blender. Process until smooth, stopping to scrape down sides as needed, about 2 minutes. (If needed, process in batches.) Transfer to a large saucepan.
4. Stir cumin, cayenne, and remaining 2 cups stock and 1½ teaspoons salt into carrot mixture in saucepan. Cover; bring mixture to a simmer over medium, stirring occasionally to prevent bottom from scorching (this will take about 10 minutes). Remove from heat. Add butter, vinegar, maple syrup, and ¾ cup of the cream; stir until butter is melted. Ladle soup into 6 bowls. Top each with 1 tablespoon pesto and 2 teaspoons cream. (Reserve remaining pesto for another use.)

CARROT SOUP WITH PEA
PESTO (PAGE 91)

CREAMY SPRING
VEGETABLE POT PIE
(PAGE 94)

Creamy Spring Vegetable Pot Pie

(Photo, page 93)
ACTIVE 35 MIN. - TOTAL 1 HOUR, 20 MIN.
SERVES 6

- 2 Tbsp. unsalted butter
- 2 Tbsp. extra-virgin olive oil
- 1 (8-oz.) pkg. sliced cremini mushrooms
- 4 medium carrots, halved lengthwise and cut into 1½-inch pieces
- 2 medium leeks, white and light green parts only, sliced and rinsed (about 2½ cups)
- 1½ tsp. kosher salt, divided
- ¼ cup all-purpose flour, plus more for work surface
- 3 cups vegetable stock
- 3 Tbsp. heavy whipping cream
- 2 Tbsp. crème fraîche
- 2 Tbsp. whole-grain mustard
- 1 Tbsp. fresh thyme leaves, divided
- 1 frozen puff pastry sheet (from 1 [17.3-oz.] pkg.), thawed
- 1 large egg, lightly beaten
- 6 oz. fresh English peas
- 1 tsp. flaky sea salt

1. Preheat oven to 425°F with rack in lower third position. Heat butter and oil in a 10-inch cast-iron skillet over medium-high until butter is melted and foamy. Add mushrooms in a single layer. Cook, undisturbed, until golden brown and crispy on bottoms, about 5 minutes. Toss mushrooms; cook, stirring occasionally, until liquid releases and evaporates, about 4 minutes. Add carrots, leeks, and ½ teaspoon of the kosher salt. Cook, stirring occasionally, until carrots are just beginning to soften and leeks are tender, 6 to 8 minutes. Sprinkle evenly with flour. Cook, stirring constantly, until vegetables are fully coated and flour smells nutty and turns golden brown, about 1 minute. Add stock; bring to a boil over high. Reduce heat to medium-high. Cook, stirring occasionally, until liquid starts to thicken, about 3 minutes. Remove from heat; stir in whipping cream, crème fraîche, mustard, 2 teaspoons of the thyme, and remaining 1 teaspoon kosher salt. Set aside to cool slightly, about 5 minutes.
2. Meanwhile, roll pastry sheet out onto a lightly floured work surface into a 12-inch square. Cut evenly into 3 (4-inch-wide) strips. Cut each strip evenly into 6 triangles. Stir together egg and 1 tablespoon water in a small bowl.
3. Stir peas into warm vegetable mixture in skillet. Arrange pastry triangles in a concentric-circle pattern over mixture, leaving a slight (about ½-inch) overhang around skillet edges and slightly overlapping triangles (some vegetable mixture will still be exposed around edges). Brush pastry with egg mixture; sprinkle with flaky sea salt.
4. Place a baking sheet lined with aluminum foil on oven rack; place skillet on sheet. Bake in preheated oven until pastry is golden brown and filling is bubbly around edges, about 30 minutes. Remove from oven; let stand 10 minutes. Sprinkle with remaining 1 teaspoon thyme.

Quinoa Salad with Carrots and Sugar Snap Peas

ACTIVE 20 MIN. - TOTAL 20 MIN.
SERVES 4

- 1½ Tbsp. Dijon mustard
- 1 Tbsp. apple cider vinegar
- 1 Tbsp. honey
- ¼ tsp. black pepper
- 1½ tsp. kosher salt, divided
- 8 Tbsp. olive oil, divided
- 8 oz. multicolor carrots (about 4), cut diagonally into ¼-inch-thick slices (about 1¼ cups)
- ½ tsp. ground coriander
- 6 oz. fresh sugar snap peas, cut in half
- 4 cups cooked tricolor quinoa
- 2 cups baby arugula
- 4 oz. goat cheese, crumbled (about 1 cup)

1. Whisk together mustard, vinegar, honey, pepper, and ¾ teaspoon of the salt in a small bowl. Slowly whisk in 6 tablespoons of the oil; set aside.
2. Toss together carrots, coriander, and remaining ¾ teaspoon salt and 2 tablespoons oil in a large bowl. Heat a large skillet over medium-high. Add carrot mixture. Cook, turning occasionally, until golden brown and tender, about 8 minutes, adding snap peas to mixture after 4 minutes cooking time. Remove from heat.
3. Transfer carrot mixture to a large bowl. Add quinoa, baby arugula, crumbled goat cheese, and ¼ cup mustard dressing; gently toss until combined. Divide among 4 bowls, and top with remaining dressing.

Too Good To Leave

Carrot tops and pea shoots are not only edible; they're delicious

CARROT TOPS
If you buy a bunch of carrots with the leafy greens attached, use them in place of parsley. They have a similar bright, grassy flavor. Make sure to wash them well to remove any grit or dirt.

PEA SHOOTS
Delicate leaves and tendrils from pea plants are often sold at farmers' markets in the spring. If you can find them, their mildly sweet flavor and crunchy texture are a lovely garnish or addition to a salad.

QUINOA SALAD
WITH CARROTS AND
SUGAR SNAP PEAS

Braised Chicken with Spring Vegetables and Herbs

ACTIVE 35 MIN. · TOTAL 1 HOUR, 5 MIN.

SERVES 6

- 4 Tbsp. olive oil, divided
- 6 (4-oz.) bone-in, skin-on chicken thighs
- 2 tsp. kosher salt, divided
- 1 tsp. black pepper, divided
- 1½ cups chopped yellow onion (from 1 medium onion)
- 1 Tbsp. finely chopped garlic (from 2 large garlic cloves)
- 1¼ cups dry white wine
- 1 lb. large carrots, cut in half lengthwise and halves cut diagonally into 2-inch pieces
- 12 oz. multicolor baby potatoes, halved
- 3 cups chicken stock
- 8 oz. fresh snow peas, cut in half diagonally

- 6 oz. fresh or thawed frozen English peas
- 3 Tbsp. chopped fresh flat-leaf parsley
- 3 Tbsp. chopped fresh tarragon
- 3 Tbsp. thinly sliced fresh chives
- 1 lemon, cut into wedges

1. Preheat oven to 375°F. Heat 2 tablespoons of the oil in a large Dutch oven over medium-high. Sprinkle chicken evenly with 1 teaspoon of the salt and ½ teaspoon of the pepper. Working in 2 batches, place chicken, skin-side down, in Dutch oven. Cook, undisturbed, until deep golden brown and crispy, 7 to 8 minutes. Flip chicken; cook 1 minute. Remove from Dutch oven, and set aside (chicken will not be cooked through).

2. Add onion to Dutch oven. Cook over medium-high, stirring occasionally, until translucent, about 4 minutes. Add garlic. Cook, stirring constantly, until fragrant,

about 1 minute. Add wine. Cook, scraping up browned bits on bottom of Dutch oven, until reduced by half, about 2 minutes. Add carrots, potatoes, and stock; stir to combine. Bring to a boil over high. Reduce heat to medium-high; simmer, undisturbed, 5 minutes.

3. Nestle chicken, skin-side up, in mixture in Dutch oven. Transfer Dutch oven to preheated oven. Cook, uncovered, until a thermometer inserted in thickest portion of chicken registers 165°F, about 20 minutes. Remove from oven. Transfer chicken to a plate using tongs.

4. Return Dutch oven to stove, and heat over medium. Stir in snow peas, English peas, and remaining 1 teaspoon salt and ½ teaspoon pepper. Cook, stirring occasionally, until snow peas are just cooked through, about 3 minutes. Nestle chicken into mixture, and sprinkle with parsley, tarragon, and chives. Drizzle with remaining 2 tablespoons oil. Serve immediately with lemon wedges.

Very Augusta

No one knows better than Augusta, Georgia, caterer Vera Stewart how to get set for Masters week

Vera spills the secrets to egg salad,
a Masters-week favorite

LEARNING TO ENTERTAIN as a newlywed in Madison, Georgia, was something of a baptism by fire, says Vera Stewart. "In that small town, if I had a dinner party, I invited the people across the street, who were old enough to be my grandparents; the local House of Representatives official, who was my parents' age; and then my peer group," says Vera. "I found out early on that I had to bring my A game if I was hosting in Madison." More than four decades and a move to Augusta later—with a catering company, a cookbook, and nine seasons of a syndicated TV program ("The VeryVera Show") to her name—it's hard to imagine her ever being a novice hostess. She's especially busy during Masters Tournament week in April, when (in a normal year) hordes of golf fans descend upon the city. She and her team have hosted up to 40 events in just one night. "I love the mania, believe it or not," says Vera. "I'm geared up. When it's over, I'm on such a high that I don't even need to take a day off!"

Mama's Egg Salad

ACTIVE 20 MIN. - TOTAL 45 MIN.
SERVES 4

Place 8 **large eggs** in a medium saucepan; cover completely with **water.** Cover saucepan with lid, and cook over high until the water comes to a complete boil. Turn off the heat, and let eggs sit 20 minutes. Remove the lid, and run cold water over eggs until they are cool to the touch, about 3 minutes. Peel immediately. Coarsely chop eggs. Stir together ⅓ cup **sweet pickle relish** (drained of juice), ¼ cup **mayonnaise,** 1 heaping Tbsp. **Durkee Famous Sauce,** ¼ tsp. **kosher salt,** and ¼ tsp. **black pepper** in a large bowl. (If you can't find Durkee locally, substitute yellow mustard and extra mayonnaise.) Add the chopped eggs, and gently mix until incorporated. Store in an airtight container in the refrigerator up to 6 days. Serve the egg salad on toasted **white bread** with **bacon** and **tomato, if desired.**

Ann Ittoop's Easter Memories

A first-generation Indian American who grew up in North Carolina, she keeps cherished traditions alive through food

WHEN ANN ITTOOP thinks back to her childhood Easter celebrations, two distinct images come to mind: appams and floral dresses.

The appams, lacy domes made from a coconut-and-rice batter, are because of her background—her parents came from the robust community of Christians in the Kerala state of India. The dresses, on the other hand, are a product of her upbringing in Charlotte, where her community celebrated a much more Southern, Anglo-Saxon version of the holiday.

In Charlotte, there were few other South Asian families in the area, much less Christian Keralites. As a result, Ittoop, who now runs the South India-meets-American South food blog *The Familiar Kitchen* (thefamiliarkitchen.com), adopted many traditions of her local church. But things weren't always seamless. "My mother didn't know how to wear those dresses," Ittoop says, laughing. "In one picture, she's wearing it backward."

Where Ittoop and her family—which includes her mother, Latha; dad, David; and elder brother, Joseph—could lean into their heritage on Easter was in the food they prepared. For Christian Keralites, Easter starts with Lent, a 40-day period of fasting. During the last week of Lent, Pesaha (or Passover) occurs on Holy Thursday, and families have Pesaha appam, an unleavened bread that's made of rice and coconut, in memory of the Last Supper. The week concludes with a large feast enjoyed on Easter Sunday.

Ittoop's mother would start preparing the Easter meal on Saturday. She'd marinate the chicken in cardamom, cumin, fennel seeds, and black pepper for the biryani and make the appam batter. On Sunday morning, the family attended the earliest church service so that, by 9:30, their plates would be full of appams, the spongy interiors of which were soaked in an aromatic chicken curry flavored with coconut milk, curry leaves, and cardamom. Her mom would eat last, insisting on making the appams to order, ladling batter into a bowl-shape pan and letting it steam into thin domes.

> "When you cook for people you love, it shows."

The meal didn't stop there. After a few hours of television and digging through Easter baskets, it was time for the biryani. Even if no one was hungry, Ittoop's mom would lovingly fluff the rice, make raita, and pull out the fig and date pickle and popadam to eat alongside. For dessert, they kept it simple: a mango fruit salad perfumed with rose water.

What Ittoop remembers most fondly about those meals was her mother's attention to detail. She mixed and fermented the appam batter herself, and instead of buying canned coconut milk, she cracked open fresh coconuts to press the milk before grating the meat. "When you cook for people you love, it shows," she says. "All her heart was being poured into these dishes."

Three years ago, Ittoop moved to East Hanover, New Jersey, with her husband, George. The area has a large community of Christian Keralites. Still, every year, she flies home to celebrate Easter with her family. And Ittoop always helps her mother cook, absorbing kitchen wisdom she hopes will allow her to re-create those food traditions back in New Jersey.

Her blog, started in 2014, was driven in part by this desire to uphold her heritage through food. She recalls her mom telling her about coming to the U.S., trading chiffon saris and long, braided hair for jeans and a short bob, yet feeling grounded by the food she cooked. "I have to document this. I have to pass it down," Ittoop says. "I don't want to lose myself."

Two years ago, for Ittoop's 30th birthday, her mother gave her a book containing all those family recipes, including the chicken curry and the appams. It's one of her favorite keepsakes, and she's been working her way through all the dishes, adding her own spins—using shallots instead of white onions or a little less chili powder.

That book was particularly helpful last year, when (due to the pandemic) Ittoop was unable to travel to Charlotte. She FaceTimed her mom as she made appams and chicken curry in her New Jersey kitchen. It was a sober reminder that, even in nonpandemic times, she won't be able to celebrate Easter with her parents forever.

Ultimately, it's these dishes that will keep the memories of family alive and remind her future children where they came from. "That is what you get to hold on to," Ittoop says. Without those traditions, "Who are you?"
—Priya Krishna

APPAMS (PAGE 100)

KERALA
CHICKEN CURRY
(PAGE 100)

Kerala Chicken Curry

(Photo, page 99)

Ittoop toasts whole spices before grinding them to make a sweet-and-smoky rub for the chicken.

ACTIVE 40 MIN. · TOTAL 1 HOUR, 30 MIN., PLUS 30 MIN. CHILLING

SERVES 6

CHICKEN

- 3 to 4 lb. bone-in, skin-on chicken thighs, skin and most of the fat removed
- 10 yellow baby new potatoes, halved
- 1 cup well-shaken and stirred coconut milk
- ¼ cup white vinegar

MEAT MASALA BLEND

- 2 Tbsp. fennel seeds
- 10 green cardamom pods
- 6 whole cloves
- 1 cinnamon stick, broken in half

MARINADE

- 1 medium-size white onion, thinly sliced (about 2 cups)
- 2 small serrano chiles, stems removed and chiles halved lengthwise
- 8 garlic cloves, minced (about 2½ Tbsp.)
- 1 (2-inch) piece fresh ginger, peeled and minced (2 Tbsp.)
- 2 Tbsp. ground coriander
- 2 Tbsp. Kashmiri red chili powder, plus more for garnish
- 2 tsp. ground turmeric, plus more for garnish
- 12 fresh curry leaves

TEMPERING INGREDIENTS

- 2 Tbsp. virgin coconut oil
- 2 shallots, thinly sliced (about ½ cup)
- 2 tsp. brown mustard seeds
- 12 fresh curry leaves, plus more for garnish
- 2 dried red chiles, broken in half crosswise
  Kosher salt

1. Prepare the Chicken: Separate meatiest side of each chicken thigh from bone, then cut each meaty piece of chicken in half. Leave whatever meat is left on bone as is. Transfer all chicken pieces to a large Dutch oven.

2. Prepare the Meat Masala Blend: Place fennel seeds, cardamom pods, whole cloves, and broken cinnamon stick in a small skillet. Cook over medium, stirring often, just until fragrant, about 1 minute. Remove from heat. Cool completely, about 15 minutes. Transfer to a spice grinder. Process until a slightly coarse powder forms, about 40 seconds.

3. Prepare the Marinade: Add onion, serrano chiles, garlic, ginger, coriander, Kashmiri red chili powder, turmeric, curry leaves, and 2 tablespoons of the Meat Masala Blend to chicken pieces in Dutch oven; toss together until evenly coated. Cover and chill at least 30 minutes or up to 12 hours.

4. Remove Dutch oven from refrigerator. If the chicken marinated more than 4 hours, let stand at room temperature 1 hour. Scatter potatoes around chicken mixture in Dutch oven; pour ½ cup water on top. Place Dutch oven over low heat. Cook, covered, until potatoes and chicken are tender, about 40 minutes, stirring every 10 minutes. During this time, moisture should naturally release from chicken mixture and cooking juices should rise up sides of Dutch oven, partially covering chicken mixture. Stir in coconut milk and vinegar. Bring to a gentle simmer over low. Cook, stirring occasionally, until chicken easily pulls away from the bone and flavors meld, about 10 minutes. Remove from heat.

5. During final 5 minutes of cook time for chicken mixture, prepare the Tempering Ingredients: Heat coconut oil in a medium skillet over medium until hot and fragrant. Add shallots; cook, stirring often, until light golden brown, 4 to 5 minutes. Stir in mustard seeds, curry leaves, and dried red chiles. Cook, stirring constantly, until mustard seeds pop, 10 to 30 seconds. Remove from heat, and stir in remaining Meat Masala Blend.

6. Stir about ¼ cup chicken curry liquid from Dutch oven into Tempering Ingredients in skillet to gather all the spices. Stir mixture back into chicken curry in Dutch oven. Season with salt to taste. Sprinkle a pinch of turmeric and Kashmiri red chili powder on top for color. Garnish with curry leaves.

Appams

(Photo, page 99)

Thin, lacy-edge appams are made from a fermented rice-and-coconut batter and served with the curry.

ACTIVE 50 MIN. · TOTAL 50 MIN., PLUS 6 HOURS CHILLING AND 10 HOURS FERMENTING

SERVES 4

- 1 cup uncooked white basmati rice
- 1½ cups canned coconut water (such as Goya) or tap water
- ½ tsp. active dry yeast (from 1 [¼-oz.] envelope)
- 2 Tbsp., plus ½ tsp. granulated sugar, divided
- 2 Tbsp. warm water (110°F to 115°F)
- 1 cup well-shaken and stirred coconut milk
- ½ cup grated fresh coconut (from 1 coconut)
- ½ cup cooked white basmati rice
- ½ tsp. kosher salt

1. Place uncooked rice in a small bowl, and pour in canned coconut water; rice should be submerged. Cover and refrigerate at least 6 hours or up to 12 hours. Drain. (Soaking the rice in coconut water gives it a sweet tang and supports the fermentation process.)

2. Stir together yeast and ½ teaspoon of the sugar in a small bowl. Add the warm water; stir until yeast mixture dissolves. Let stand until yeast is foamy, about 10 minutes.

3. Meanwhile, place drained rice, coconut milk, grated coconut, cooked rice, ¼ cup tap water, and remaining 2 tablespoons sugar in a blender. Process on low speed, gradually increasing speed to high, until a smooth batter forms, about 1 minute. Batter will feel slightly gritty if you rub it between your fingers.

4. Pour batter into a large bowl, and add yeast mixture. Stir with your hands until combined. The warmth of your hands supports the fermentation process. Cover with a clean kitchen towel; let ferment at warm room temperature or in a turned-off oven for at least 10 hours or up to 12 hours. The batter will have puffed up and will have fermentation holes on top. This is a good sign of fermentation. Stir in salt and, if needed, 1 to 2 tablespoons tap water until mixture is blended and smooth and resembles consistency of thin pancake batter.

5. Heat a nonstick appam pan, a 10-inch nonstick skillet, or a small nonstick wok over medium about 1 minute. Remove pan from heat. Pour in about ⅓ cup of the batter, and swirl once in a circular motion. Return pan to heat over medium. Cover and cook, undisturbed, until center of appam looks set and slightly puffed, edges are speckled with bubbles, and bottom is browned and slightly crisp, 3 to 4 minutes. Remove appam. Repeat process with remaining batter. Serve immediately.

Mango-Rose Fruit Salad

ACTIVE 30 MIN. · TOTAL 30 MIN., PLUS 30 MIN. CHILLING

SERVES 6

- ½ cup heavy whipping cream, warmed
- 2 pinches of dried saffron threads
- 1 large mango, cut into bite-size pieces (about 2 cups)
- 1 large banana, cut into bite-size pieces (about 1 cup)
- 1 medium-size red apple (such as McIntosh), peeled, cored, and cut into bite-size pieces (about 1 cup)
- 1 cup chopped (bite-size pieces) fresh strawberries (from 6 oz. strawberries)
- 1 cup chopped (bite-size pieces) fresh pineapple
- 12 seedless green grapes, halved
- 1½ Tbsp. fresh lemon juice (from 1 lemon)
- 2 tsp. culinary rose essence (such as Preema)
- 1 cup canned mango pulp (such as Deep Kesar Mango Pulp)
- ⅓ cup canned sweetened condensed coconut milk (such as Nature's Charm)
- 6 green cardamom pods, smashed, pods discarded and seeds reserved
- ⅛ tsp. kosher salt

1. Place cream in a large bowl; sprinkle saffron over cream. Let saffron "bloom" for 10 minutes. Place in refrigerator until thoroughly chilled, about 30 minutes. **2.** Meanwhile, gently toss together mango, banana, apple, strawberries, pineapple, grapes, lemon juice, and rose essence in a large bowl. Cover and refrigerate until ready to use. Stir together mango pulp and condensed coconut milk in a small bowl; set aside. **3.** Using a mortar and pestle, grind cardamom seeds to a fine powder. Add to cream mixture in bowl, along with salt. Beat cream mixture with a hand mixer on high speed until stiff peaks form, about 2 minutes, 30 seconds. **4.** Gently stir mango pulp mixture into chopped fruit mixture; fold in whipped cream mixture until combined. Serve immediately, or store, covered, in refrigerator up to 8 hours.

FINISH WITH FRUIT
This memorable dessert gets its golden color from mango pulp and cream infused with dried saffron threads. Rose essence adds a delicate floral aroma.

MANGO-ROSE FRUIT SALAD

COOKING SCHOOL

TIPS AND TRICKS FROM THE SOUTH'S MOST TRUSTED KITCHEN

The Devil's in the Details
Even if you already have a divine deviled egg recipe, consider these tips

1

COOK EXTRA
When hard-cooking the eggs, add a few more to the pot. The additional yolks will give you more filling for overstuffed eggs, and the extra whites might come in handy if any of the others tear.

2

BREAK OUT THE BEATERS
For the smoothest filling, beat the cooked yolks with an electric mixer. This step will remove any tiny lumps, making the filling much easier to pipe.

3

TOP 'EM OFF
Garnishes are half the fun of deviled eggs. Whatever you choose—capers, smoked paprika, pickled onions, or shrimp (to name a few)—the toppings should allow plenty of egg to show.

MAKE EASY-TO-PEEL EGGS

1.
Bring a large saucepan with enough water to cover eggs to a rolling boil.

2.
Use a large spoon to gently lower cold eggs into boiling water. Reduce heat to medium. Cover and boil 13 minutes.

3.
Remove from boiling water and transfer to an ice bath. Let stand 10 minutes.

4.
Crack eggs, and peel under cold running water.

JUST RIGHT
The shrimp has curled into a C shape, and the flesh is pink and opaque white.

STOP OVERCOOKING SHRIMP

Look for these signs of doneness

OVERDONE
An O shape means it has cooked too long and may be firm and chewy.

Seafood Prep Pointer

Whether you cook shrimp on the grill or salmon in the oven, always pat seafood dry with paper towels before seasoning it. This simple step will prevent seafood from steaming and result in a better sear. (It's good advice for meat and poultry, too.)

May

Cool as a Cucumber

We're lucky that cucumbers come into season right as temperatures start to rise. This versatile ingredient deserves much more than a supporting role in salads. Like melons, which are also members of the gourd family, cucumbers have a satisfying crunch and a mild, fruity yet herbal aroma and flavor that make salads, cocktails, soups, and even water more refreshing.

CHILLED CUCUMBER
SOUP

Chilled Cucumber Soup

ACTIVE 10 MIN. - TOTAL 15 MIN.,
PLUS 30 MIN. CHILLING
SERVES 4

Process 3 chopped **English cucumbers**, 1 **avocado**, 3 cups packed **fresh basil leaves**, 1 cup packed **fresh parsley leaves**, ½ cup **plain whole-milk Greek yogurt**, ½ cup **ice-cold water**, 3 sliced **green scallion** tops, 3 Tbsp. **lime juice**, and 1½ tsp. each **Champagne vinegar** and **kosher salt** in a blender until smooth, about 1 minute. Chill until cold, about 30 minutes. Garnish with a drizzle of **extra-virgin olive oil**, thinly sliced **cucumber**, **basil leaves**, and **black pepper.**

CUCUMBER-CHICKPEA
SALAD WITH FETA-MINT
VINAIGRETTE

CUCUMBER-MINT
MOJITOS

Cucumber-Mint Mojitos

ACTIVE 10 MIN. - TOTAL 10 MIN.
SERVES 2

Peel 2 long, thin strips from 1 small **English cucumber.** Peel remaining cucumber; chop into ½-inch pieces to yield ½ cup (discard peels). Process chopped cucumber, 3 oz. **white rum**, 2 Tbsp. **fresh lime juice**, 1 Tbsp. **cane syrup** or **simple syrup**, and 12 large **fresh mint leaves** in a blender until smooth, about 1 minute. Strain; discard solids. Arrange cucumber strips in a spiral inside 2 Collins glasses. Fill half-way with **crushed ice**; pour cucumber-rum mixture over ice. Top each with ¼ cup **lime-flavored sparkling water.** Garnish each glass with 1 **mint sprig.**

Cucumber-Chickpea Salad with Feta-Mint Vinaigrette

ACTIVE 15 MIN. - TOTAL 20 MIN.
SERVES 4

Toss together 2 sliced medium **English cucumbers** and ¼ tsp. **kosher salt** in a bowl. Let stand 5 minutes. Process ½ cup **fresh mint leaves**, ½ cup crumbled **feta cheese**, ⅓ cup **olive oil**, 1½ Tbsp. **lemon juice**, 2 tsp. **lemon zest**, 1 tsp. **Greek seasoning**, ½ tsp. **kosher salt**, ¼ tsp. **black pepper**, and 2 **garlic** cloves in a blender until smooth, about 1 minute. Discard moisture released from cucumbers. Add ½ cup thinly sliced **red onion**; ½ cup **packaged crunchy chickpeas**; ¼ cup crumbled **feta cheese**; and ¼ cup each **fresh parsley**, **dill**, and **mint leaves** to cucumbers. Add ⅓ cup vinaigrette to salad; toss to coat.

True Blue

For Test Kitchen professional Pam Lolley, blueberries are full of sweet memories

BLUEBERRIES HOLD A SPECIAL PLACE
in Pam Lolley's heart. In the late 1990s, her father, Bill Carter, planted multiple varieties of blueberry bushes along a fence, running from his North Mississippi home all the way down to the road. "They would ripen at different times, so he would have fruit starting in May all the way to July," she says. As each bush came into season, Bill would carefully pick the berries, and her mother, Shirley, would freeze them flat on sheet pans then divide them into zip-top bags to share with Pam and her three siblings. The berries were much juicier and more flavorful than any at the grocery store, and Pam would ration them to make family favorites like muffins and her famous buttermilk pancakes. "I would time it just right so they lasted a year, until I got the next batch," she says. Her stash in the freezer became all the more precious after her father passed away in 2017. "He would always give me more than the other kids because he knew how much I loved those berries and that I would actually bake with them and use them up," she says. These gorgeous treats, created by Pam, celebrate the indigo gems of summer and pay tribute to a very special man.

Blueberry-Lemon Layer Cake

The fruit's sweet, floral flavor pairs well with tart and tangy lemons and buttermilk—both of which star in these tender cake layers. Pureed berries give the frosting its naturally beautiful hue. You'll have about ¼ cup of puree left over; stir it into smoothies or yogurt.
ACTIVE 40 MIN. - TOTAL 1 HOUR, 10 MIN.,
PLUS 1 HOUR COOLING
SERVES 12

CAKE LAYERS

- Vegetable shortening, for greasing pans
- 1 cup butter, softened
- 2 cups granulated sugar
- 4 large eggs
- 2 tsp. baking powder
- ½ tsp. kosher salt
- ½ tsp. baking soda
- 3 cups plus 1 Tbsp. all-purpose flour, divided, plus more for pans
- 1¼ cups whole buttermilk
- 1 Tbsp. grated lemon zest, plus ¼ cup fresh juice (from 2 medium lemons)
- 2 tsp. vanilla extract
- 1½ cups fresh blueberries (from 2 [6-oz.] containers)

FROSTING

- 1 cup fresh blueberries (from 1 [6-oz.] container), plus more for garnish
- 1 Tbsp. grated lemon zest, plus 3 Tbsp. fresh juice, divided (from 2 lemons)
- 1 cup butter, softened
- 1 (32-oz.) pkg. powdered sugar

1. Prepare the Cake Layers: Preheat oven to 350°F. Grease (with shortening) and flour 3 (8-inch) round cake pans, and set aside. Beat butter with a stand mixer fitted with a paddle attachment on medium speed until creamy, about 1 minute. Gradually add sugar, beating until light and fluffy, about 4 minutes. Add eggs, 1 at a time, beating just until blended after each addition.

2. Whisk together baking powder, salt, baking soda, and 3 cups of the flour in a medium bowl until well blended. With mixer running on low speed, gradually add flour mixture to butter mixture, alternately with buttermilk, beginning and ending with flour mixture, beating until blended after each addition. Stir in lemon zest, lemon juice, and vanilla. Toss together blueberries and remaining 1 tablespoon flour in a small bowl; gently fold blueberry mixture into batter. Spoon batter into prepared pans.

3. Bake in preheated oven until a wooden pick inserted in center comes out clean, 23 to 25 minutes. Cool in pans on wire racks 10 minutes; remove from pans to wire racks. Cool completely, about 1 hour.

4. Meanwhile, prepare the Frosting: Process blueberries and lemon juice in a blender or food processor until completely smooth, 1 to 2 minutes. Beat butter and lemon zest with a stand mixer fitted with a paddle attachment on medium speed until creamy, 1 to 2 minutes. With mixer running on low speed, gradually add powdered sugar, alternately with blueberry mixture, beating until blended after each addition. Increase speed to medium; beat until light and fluffy, about 1 minute. If desired, reserve 1 cup Frosting; place in a piping bag fitted with a star tip.

5. Place 1 Cake Layer on a platter or cake stand. Spread 1 cup Frosting over top. Add a second Cake Layer; spread top with 1 cup Frosting. Top with third layer; frost top and sides of cake with remaining Frosting. If desired, pipe reserved Frosting around outer edge of cake. Garnish with blueberries.

BLUEBERRY-CITRUS
ROLLS WITH ORANGE
GLAZE (PAGE 110)

BLUEBERRY-HONEY
UPSIDE-DOWN CAKE
(PAGE 110)

Blueberry-Citrus Rolls with Orange Glaze

(Photo, page 108)

Pam's bright and sunny take on cinnamon rolls replaces the usual brown-sugar-and-cinnamon filling with jammy berries and orange zest and adds a sweet citrus glaze. To wake up to these beauties, chill the assembled, unbaked rolls the day before. Then let the dough rise the next morning, and bake as directed.

ACTIVE 30 MIN. - TOTAL 1 HOUR,
PLUS 2 HOURS, 30 MIN. RISING

MAKES 16

DOUGH
- 1 (¼-oz.) envelope active dry yeast
- ¼ cup warm water (100°F to 115°F)
- ½ cup, plus 1 tsp. granulated sugar, divided
- ½ cup butter, softened
- 2 large eggs, lightly beaten
- 1 cup whole milk
- 1 Tbsp. fresh orange juice (from 1 orange)
- 1 tsp. kosher salt
- 5 cups bread flour, divided, plus more for work surface
- ½ cup very soft butter

CITRUS FILLING
- 1 cup granulated sugar
- 2 Tbsp. grated orange zest (from 1 orange)
- 1 cup fresh blueberries (from 1 [6-oz.] container)

CITRUS GLAZE
- 2 cups powdered sugar
- 2 Tbsp. butter, softened
- 2 tsp. grated orange zest plus 3 Tbsp. fresh juice (from 1 orange)

1. Prepare the Dough: Stir together yeast, warm water, and 1 teaspoon of the granulated sugar in a glass measuring cup; let stand 5 minutes.

2. Meanwhile, beat ½ cup softened butter with a stand mixer fitted with a paddle attachment on medium speed until creamy, about 1 minute. Gradually add remaining ½ cup sugar, beating until light and fluffy, about 1 minute. Add eggs, milk, and orange juice; beat just until blended, about 30 seconds. Beat in yeast mixture until combined.

3. Stir together salt and 4½ cups of the bread flour. Gradually add flour mixture to butter mixture, beating on low speed until well blended, about 1½ minutes.

4. Heavily flour a work surface. Turn Dough out; knead until smooth and elastic, about 5 minutes, adding up to ½ cup of the remaining bread flour as needed to prevent sticking. Place in a lightly greased (with cooking spray) large bowl, turning to grease top. Cover with plastic wrap. Let rise in a warm place, free from drafts, until doubled in bulk, 1½ to 2 hours.

5. Punch Dough down; turn out onto a lightly floured surface. Roll into a 22- x 12-inch rectangle. Spread with ½ cup very soft butter, leaving a 1-inch border around edges unbuttered.

6. Prepare the Citrus Filling: Stir together sugar and orange zest. Sprinkle sugar mixture evenly over buttered rectangle; sprinkle blueberries evenly over sugar mixture.

7. Roll up rectangle, jelly-roll style, starting at one long side. Cut into 16 (about 1¼-inch-thick) slices. Place rolls, cut side down, in 2 lightly greased (with cooking spray) 9-inch round cake pans. Cover with plastic wrap. Let rise in a warm place, free from drafts, until doubled in bulk, about 1 hour.

8. Preheat oven to 350°F. Uncover rolls, and bake until golden brown, 25 to 30 minutes. Cool rolls in pans 5 minutes on wire racks.

9. Meanwhile, prepare the Citrus Glaze: Stir together powdered sugar, butter, orange zest, and orange juice in a medium bowl until well combined and smooth. Brush glaze over warm rolls; serve.

Blueberry-Honey Upside-Down Cake

(Photo, page 109)

This not-too-sweet cake gets its lovely texture and subtle toasty flavor from cornmeal, which contrasts with the layer of baked fruit. Any type of honey will work well in the recipe, but we prefer locally sourced varieties. For the finishing touch, serve the cake with a dollop of whipped cream or a scoop of vanilla ice cream.

ACTIVE 20 MIN. - TOTAL 1 HOUR, 20 MIN.,
PLUS 40 MIN. COOLING

SERVES 12

- ¾ cup, plus 2 Tbsp. butter, softened, divided
- ½ cup honey
- 2 cups fresh blueberries (from 2 [6-oz.] containers)
- ⅔ cup granulated sugar
- ⅔ cup packed light brown sugar
- ¼ tsp. almond extract
- 1½ tsp. vanilla extract, divided
- 1¾ cups all-purpose flour
- ¼ cup fine plain yellow cornmeal
- 1 tsp. baking powder
- 1 tsp. kosher salt
- ½ tsp. baking soda
- ¾ cup whole buttermilk
- 3 large eggs
- 1 cup heavy whipping cream

1. Preheat oven to 350°F. Butter a 9-inch square baking pan (at least 2 inches deep) with 2 tablespoons of the butter. Pour honey into pan, tilting pan to spread evenly. Top evenly with blueberries.

2. Beat granulated sugar, brown sugar, and remaining ¾ cup butter with a stand mixer fitted with a paddle attachment on medium speed until light and fluffy, 3 to 4 minutes. Beat in almond extract and 1 teaspoon of the vanilla.

3. Whisk together flour, cornmeal, baking powder, kosher salt, and baking soda in a medium bowl. Whisk together buttermilk and eggs in a small bowl.

4. Add flour mixture to sugar-butter mixture alternately with buttermilk mixture, beginning and ending with flour mixture, beating on medium-low speed just until blended after each addition. Spoon batter on blueberries; spread evenly with a small offset spatula.

5. Bake in preheated oven until a wooden pick inserted in center comes out clean, 45 to 50 minutes, shielding with Reynolds Kitchens® aluminum foil after 40 minutes to prevent excessive browning, if necessary. Cool in pan on a wire rack 10 minutes. Gently run a sharp knife around edges of pan, and invert cake onto a serving platter. Cool at least 30 minutes before serving.

6. Beat heavy cream and remaining ½ teaspoon vanilla with a stand mixer fitted with whisk attachment on medium-high speed until stiff peaks form, 1 to 2 minutes. Serve cake with whipped cream.

Blueberry-Ginger Crumb Cake

(Photo, page 112)

Chopped crystallized ginger gives this cake a slightly spicy note that pairs wonderfully with a cup of coffee. To keep the berries from sinking to the bottom of the pan, Pam tosses them in a little flour before folding them into the batter.

ACTIVE 15 MIN. - TOTAL 1 HOUR, 45 MIN., PLUS 30 MIN. COOLING

SERVES 8

CRUMB TOPPING
- 1 cup all-purpose flour
- ²⁄₃ cup granulated sugar
- ¼ tsp. kosher salt
- ½ cup cold butter, cubed

CAKE
- ½ cup chopped crystallized ginger
- 1½ tsp. baking powder
- ½ tsp. kosher salt
- ½ tsp. ground cinnamon
- ¼ tsp. baking soda
- 2 cups, plus ½ Tbsp. all-purpose flour, divided, plus more for skillet
- ¾ cup butter, softened
- ½ cup granulated sugar
- ½ cup packed light brown sugar
- 2 large eggs
- 1½ tsp. vanilla extract
- ½ cup sour cream
- 1 cup fresh blueberries (from 1 [6-oz.] container)
- Vegetable shortening, for greasing pan

1. Prepare the Crumb Topping: Stir together flour, sugar, and salt in a medium bowl; cut cold butter into flour mixture with a pastry blender or fork until crumbly. Cover; chill until ready to use.

2. Prepare the Cake: Preheat oven to 350°F. Combine crystallized ginger, baking powder, salt, cinnamon, baking soda, and 2 cups of the flour in a food processor; process until ginger is very finely chopped and mixture is well combined, about 2 minutes. Set aside.

3. Beat butter with a stand mixer fitted with a paddle attachment on medium speed until creamy, 1 minute. Gradually add granulated and brown sugars; beat until light and fluffy, 4 to 5 minutes. Add eggs, 1 at a time, beating until just combined after each addition. Beat in vanilla, 10 seconds. With mixer running on low speed, gradually add flour mixture to butter mixture, alternately with sour cream, beginning and ending with flour mixture, beating until just combined after each addition.

4. Toss together blueberries and remaining ½ tablespoon flour in a bowl. Gently fold blueberry mixture into batter. Spoon into a greased (with shortening) and floured 10-inch cast-iron skillet or oven-proof skillet (at least 2 inches deep). Smooth batter into an even layer using an offset spatula. Sprinkle evenly with Crumb Topping.

5. Bake in preheated oven until a wooden pick inserted in center comes out clean, 50 to 55 minutes. Transfer to a wire rack. Cool 30 minutes to serve warm, or cool completely, about 1 hour.

Blueberry-Lavender Hand Pies

(Photo, page 113)

ACTIVE 30 MIN. - TOTAL 1 HOUR, 15 MIN., PLUS 4 HOURS CHILLING, PLUS 1 HOUR COOKING

MAKES 12

DOUGH
- 2½ cups all-purpose flour, plus more for work surface
- 2 Tbsp. granulated sugar
- 1 tsp. kosher salt
- ¾ cup cold butter, cubed
- 4 Tbsp. cold vegetable shortening, cubed
- ½ cup ice-cold water

FILLING
- ¼ tsp. dried culinary lavender
- 4 Tbsp. granulated sugar, divided
- 1 Tbsp. cornstarch
- ⅛ tsp. kosher salt
- 1 cup fresh blueberries (from 1 [6-oz.] container)
- 1 tsp. vanilla extract

GLAZE
- 1 cup powdered sugar
- 4 tsp. whole milk
- ¼ tsp. vanilla extract

1. Prepare the Dough: Place flour, sugar, and salt in bowl of a food processor; pulse until combined, about 3 pulses. Scatter butter and shortening over top of flour mixture; pulse until mixture resembles coarse crumbs, 7 to 8 pulses. Add ice water; pulse until mixture starts to clump together, about 8 pulses. Scrape mixture out onto a lightly floured surface; knead just until it comes together, 2 or 3 times. Divide Dough in half; shape each half into a flat disk. Cover each disk in plastic wrap, and chill 4 hours.

2. Prepare the Filling: Process lavender and 2 tablespoons of the sugar in a spice grinder or food processor until finely ground. Whisk together lavender mixture, cornstarch, salt, and remaining 2 tablespoons sugar in a small saucepan. Whisk in ¼ cup water, and bring to a boil over medium-high, whisking often. Cook, whisking constantly, until thickened, about 30 seconds. Remove from heat, and stir in blueberries and vanilla, lightly crushing half of the berries. Let stand until completely cool, about 30 minutes.

3. Preheat oven to 400°F with oven rack in upper third of oven. Roll 1 chilled Dough disk to ⅛-inch thickness on a lightly floured surface; using a 5-inch round cutter, cut out 4 or 5 circles. Repeat procedure with remaining disk. Reroll scraps; cut out 2 or 3 more circles until you have 12 circles total. Spoon 1 tablespoon Filling in center of each circle. Moisten edges halfway around each circle with water. Fold circles in half over Filling; crimp edges with a fork to seal. Cut 2 or 3 (½-inch) slits on top of each pie. Place pies on a parchment-paper-lined large rimmed baking sheet.

4. Bake in preheated oven until golden brown, 20 to 25 minutes. Transfer baking sheet to a wire rack, and cool 30 minutes.

5. While pies cool, prepare the Glaze: Whisk together powdered sugar, milk, and vanilla until smooth. Drizzle Glaze over slightly warm pies. Serve warm, or let cool completely, about 30 minutes.

BLUEBERRY-GINGER
CRUMB CAKE (PAGE 111)

BLUEBERRY-LAVENDER
HAND PIES (PAGE 111)

Blueberry Chiffon Mini Pies

The mascarpone-cheese-and-whipped-cream combo makes this filling smooth and rich. Although it takes a bit of work to create these adorable treats, Pam says each step is very easy—you even use store-bought pie dough!

ACTIVE 20 MIN. - TOTAL 1 HOUR, 10 MIN., PLUS 4 HOURS, 15 MIN. CHILLING, PLUS 45 MIN. COOLING

MAKES 6

1   (14.1-oz.) pkg. refrigerated piecrusts
    All-purpose flour, for work surface

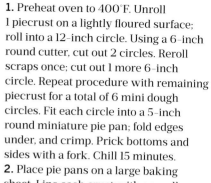

2   cups fresh blueberries (from 2 [6-oz.] containers)
1   Tbsp. fresh lemon juice (from 1 lemon)
1   (¼-oz.) envelope unflavored gelatin
1   (8-oz.) container mascarpone cheese
½   cup, plus 1 Tbsp. granulated sugar, divided
2   cups heavy whipping cream, divided
1½ tsp. vanilla extract, divided
    Fresh blueberries, for garnish

1. Preheat oven to 400°F. Unroll 1 piecrust on a lightly floured surface; roll into a 12-inch circle. Using a 6-inch round cutter, cut out 2 circles. Reroll scraps once; cut out 1 more 6-inch circle. Repeat procedure with remaining piecrust for a total of 6 mini dough circles. Fit each circle into a 5-inch round miniature pie pan; fold edges under, and crimp. Prick bottoms and sides with a fork. Chill 15 minutes.

2. Place pie pans on a large baking sheet. Line each crust with a small square of parchment paper, and fill with pie weights or dried beans. Bake in preheated oven until crust is set and edges are lightly browned, 12 to 15 minutes. Carefully remove weights and parchment, and continue baking until crusts are golden brown, 4 to 5 minutes. Transfer pie pans to wire racks, and let cool completely, about 15 minutes.

3. Meanwhile, process blueberries and lemon juice in a blender or food processor until completely smooth, 1 to 2 minutes. Combine blueberry mixture and gelatin in a small saucepan over medium-low. Cook, stirring constantly, until gelatin has completely dissolved, about 4 minutes. Transfer mixture to a large bowl, and let stand until room temperature, about 30 minutes. Gently stir mascarpone cheese and ¼ cup of the sugar into blueberry mixture until well combined.

4. Beat 1½ cups of the heavy cream and 1 teaspoon of the vanilla with a stand mixer fitted with a whisk attachment on medium speed until foamy, about 30 seconds. Increase speed to medium-high, and gradually add ¼ cup of the sugar, beating until stiff peaks form, about 1 minute. Gradually fold whipped cream into blueberry mixture. Spoon mixture evenly into prepared piecrusts (about ¾ cup per pie). Cover and chill at least 4 hours or overnight (about 8 hours).

5. Beat remaining ½ cup heavy cream and ½ teaspoon vanilla with a stand mixer fitted with a whisk attachment on medium speed until foamy, about 30 seconds. Increase speed to medium-high, and gradually add remaining 1 tablespoon sugar, beating until stiff peaks form, about 1 minute. Dollop or pipe whipped cream on top of pies. Garnish with additional blueberries, if desired.

Going Blond

Brown butter gives these classic bar cookies a tasty new twist

Brown Butter Blondies

ACTIVE 20 MIN. - TOTAL 1 HOUR, 10 MIN.,
PLUS 1 HOUR, 20 MIN. COOLING

MAKES 20

- 1½ cups unsalted butter
- 1 cup granulated sugar
- ½ cup packed light brown sugar
- 3 large eggs
- 2 tsp. vanilla extract
- 2¼ cups all-purpose flour
- 1½ tsp. kosher salt
- 2 (4-oz.) 60% bittersweet chocolate bars, chopped

1. Cook butter in a medium saucepan over medium-high, stirring occasionally, until butter melts, smells toasted, and turns brown, 8 to 10 minutes. Remove from heat; immediately pour butter into a large metal bowl. Let cool about 20 minutes (butter should still be melted, but bowl should be cool enough to handle).
2. Preheat oven to 350°F. Coat a 9-inch square baking pan with cooking spray, and line with parchment paper, leaving a 2-inch overhang on 2 sides. Add granulated sugar and brown sugar to melted butter in bowl; whisk together until smooth. Add eggs and vanilla; whisk together until incorporated. Add flour and salt; fold together using a rubber spatula just until fully incorporated. Fold in chopped chocolate.
3. Pour batter into prepared baking pan. Bake in preheated oven until a wooden pick comes out clean (top will still look moist), about 45 minutes. Cool on a wire rack until pan is cool to the touch, about 1 hour. Remove blondies from pan using parchment paper overhang; transfer to a cutting board. Cut into squares. Store in an airtight container at room temperature up to 3 days.

Put Some Southern in Your Salad

Five simple recipes starring cornbread, buttermilk, pepper jelly, and more

Chicken-and-Quinoa Salad with Pepper Jelly Dressing

ACTIVE 15 MIN. - TOTAL 15 MIN.

SERVES 4

- 1 medium bunch scallions
- ¼ cup fresh orange juice (from 1 medium orange)
- 3 Tbsp. red pepper jelly
- ½ tsp. black pepper
- 1 tsp. kosher salt, divided
- ¼ cup extra-virgin olive oil
- 3 cups cooked, cooled quinoa
- 4 oz. fresh sugar snap peas, thinly sliced (1½ cups)
- 4 small radishes, sliced (1 cup)
- 4 oz. feta cheese, crumbled (about 1 cup)
- 2 Tbsp. chopped fresh mint, divided
- 2 cups shredded rotisserie chicken

1. Slice white parts of scallions to measure about 1 cup, and set aside. Chop green parts of scallions to measure about 3 tablespoons, and set aside. (Reserve remaining scallions for another use.) Whisk together juice, jelly, pepper, and ¼ teaspoon of the salt in a bowl. Gradually whisk in oil until emulsified, 30 seconds; set aside.

2. Stir together quinoa, snap peas, radishes, white parts of scallions, feta, 1½ tablespoons of the mint, and remaining ¾ teaspoon salt in a bowl. Pour ½ cup dressing over quinoa mixture; toss to combine. Transfer to a platter; top with chicken. Drizzle with remaining ¼ cup dressing. Top with remaining ½ tablespoon mint and green parts of scallions.

WANT TO SAVE TIME?
Cook field peas up to 2 days ahead; cover and chill. Or substitute drained, rinsed canned peas.

Seared Steak-and-Field Pea Salad

ACTIVE 35 MIN. - TOTAL 1 HOUR, PLUS 2 HOURS MARINATING

SERVES 4

- 2   Tbsp. light brown sugar
- ½   cup, plus 1 Tbsp. white balsamic or white wine vinegar, divided
- ½   cup olive oil, divided
- 1½ lb. flank steak, halved crosswise
- 2   cups fresh or frozen (not thawed) field peas
- 2   tsp. kosher salt, divided
- 3   ears (1½ lb. total) fresh yellow corn, husks removed
- 1   large orange bell pepper, stemmed, seeded, and cut into large planks (1 cup)
- 1   large red bell pepper, stemmed, seeded, and cut into large planks (1 cup)
- 1   tsp. black pepper
- 2   tsp. thinly sliced fresh chives
- 1   tsp. flaky sea salt

1. Whisk together sugar, ½ cup of the vinegar, and ¼ cup of the oil in a small bowl. Transfer to a large zip-top plastic bag; add steak. Seal bag; massage steak and marinade to coat completely. Chill at least 2 hours or up to 12 hours.

2. Place peas in a large pot; add water to cover by 2 inches. Bring to a boil over high. Reduce heat to medium-low. Simmer, undisturbed, until peas are tender and just cooked through, 25 to 30 minutes. Drain; set aside until ready to use.

3. Meanwhile, remove steak from refrigerator; let come to room temperature, about 30 minutes.

4. While peas cook and steak rests, whisk together 1 tablespoon of the oil, ½ teaspoon of the kosher salt, and remaining 1 tablespoon vinegar in a small bowl. Set aside vinaigrette.

5. Heat 1 tablespoon of the oil in a large cast-iron skillet over medium-high. Add corn ears. Cook, turning corn often, until charred, about 5 minutes. Remove from skillet. Add 1 tablespoon of the oil to skillet, and add bell pepper planks.

Cook over medium-high until starting to soften and charred on both sides, 2 to 3 minutes per side. Remove skillet from heat. Remove peppers from skillet; cool about 5 minutes.

6. Cut corn kernels from cobs; discard cobs. Chop pepper planks into ½-inch pieces. Place corn, peppers, and peas in a large bowl. Add reserved vinaigrette; toss to combine. Set aside until ready to serve.

7. Remove steak from marinade; discard marinade. Pat dry with paper towels; sprinkle evenly with black pepper and remaining 1½ teaspoons kosher salt. Add remaining 1 tablespoon oil to skillet, and return to heat over high. Add steak; cook until charred on both sides and desired degree of doneness (2 to 3 minutes per side for medium-rare, 125°F). Remove from skillet; let rest 15 minutes.

8. Slice steak against the grain into ½-inch-thick strips. Spoon field pea mixture onto a platter, and top with sliced steak. Sprinkle with chives and flaky sea salt.

VEGGING OUT
Bump up the color and health factor by adding extra vegetables to this flexible recipe. We like tomatoes, cucumbers, carrots, and corn kernels.

FRIED CHICKEN SALAD
WITH BASIL-BUTTERMILK
DRESSING

Fried Chicken Salad with Basil-Buttermilk Dressing

ACTIVE 10 MIN. - TOTAL 10 MIN.

SERVES 4

- 1   cup chopped fresh basil
- ½   cup mayonnaise
- ⅓   cup whole buttermilk
- 1   medium garlic clove, coarsely chopped (1 tsp.)
- ½   tsp. granulated sugar
- ½   tsp. onion powder
- 1   tsp. kosher salt, divided
- 6   cups packed mixed greens (8 oz.)
- 8   oz. fried chicken tenders, cooled and cut into 1½-inch pieces (about 2½ cups)
- 2   oz. extra-sharp cheddar cheese, shredded (about ½ cup)

1. Place basil, mayonnaise, buttermilk, garlic, sugar, onion powder, and ¾ teaspoon of the salt in a food processor. Process until completely combined and smooth, 15 to 30 seconds. Transfer to a small bowl; set aside.
2. Place greens, fried chicken, cheese, and remaining ¼ teaspoon salt in a large bowl. Drizzle ½ cup dressing over mixture; gently toss to coat. Divide evenly among 4 plates; drizzle with remaining ½ cup dressing.

Three-Bean Salad with Tomatoes and Tangy Creole Dressing

ACTIVE 10 MIN. - TOTAL 15 MIN.

SERVES 4

- 10   oz. fresh green beans, trimmed and cut into 1½-inch pieces (2 cups)
- 1½   Tbsp. apple cider vinegar
- 2   tsp. spicy brown mustard
- 1½   tsp. Creole seasoning (such as Tony Chachere's)
- 1   tsp. pure maple syrup
- 1   tsp. Louisiana-style hot sauce (such as Crystal)
- ½   tsp. black pepper
- ½   tsp. kosher salt, divided
- ⅓   cup extra-virgin olive oil
- 1   (16-oz.) can dark red kidney beans, drained and rinsed
- 1   (16-oz.) can chickpeas, drained and rinsed
- 3   cups packed baby arugula (4 oz.)
- 1   pt. cherry tomatoes, halved (about 2 cups)
- 1   small shallot, thinly sliced (about ¼ cup)

1. Fill a large pot with water to a depth of 4 inches; bring to a boil over medium-high. Fill a large bowl with ice water, and set aside. Add green beans to boiling water, and cook until tender, 1 to 2 minutes. Remove using a slotted spoon; transfer to ice water. Let stand until cooled, about 1 minute. Remove from ice water. Drain; set aside.
2. Whisk together vinegar, mustard, Creole seasoning, maple syrup, hot sauce, black pepper, and ¼ teaspoon of the salt in a small bowl. Gradually whisk in oil until completely combined, about 30 seconds; set aside vinaigrette.
3. Toss together cooled green beans, kidney beans, chickpeas, arugula, tomatoes, shallot, and remaining ¼ teaspoon salt in a large bowl. Add vinaigrette; toss to coat. Serve immediately, or store in refrigerator up to 1 hour.

THREE-BEAN SALAD WITH
TOMATOES AND TANGY
CREOLE DRESSING

Southern Cobb Salad with Cornbread Croutons

ACTIVE 15 MIN. - TOTAL 35 MIN.
SERVES 4

- 2 cups cubed (about 1-inch pieces) day-old cornbread
- ½ tsp. black pepper
- ½ cup olive oil, divided
- 1 tsp. kosher salt, divided
- 3 Tbsp. red wine vinegar
- 1 tsp. Dijon mustard
- 1 medium garlic clove, grated (½ tsp.)
- ½ tsp. honey
- 6 cups packed chopped romaine lettuce (from 2 [8-oz.] lettuce hearts)
- 3 hard-cooked eggs, quartered lengthwise
- 4 oz. blue cheese, crumbled (about 1 cup)
- 1 medium avocado, chopped (¾ cup)
- 4 thick-cut bacon slices, cooked and chopped (about ½ cup)
- ½ cup drained and rinsed canned black-eyed peas

1. Preheat oven to 375°F. Place cornbread cubes, pepper, 2 tablespoons of the oil, and ½ teaspoon of the salt in a medium bowl. Gently toss to coat, being careful to keep cubes intact. Arrange 1 inch apart on a small baking sheet. Bake until golden brown and crispy, about 15 minutes, turning cubes once halfway through cook time. Cool slightly, about 10 minutes.
2. Meanwhile, whisk together vinegar, mustard, garlic, honey, and remaining ½ teaspoon salt in a small bowl. Gradually whisk in remaining 6 tablespoons oil until completely combined, about 30 seconds; set aside.
3. Toss together lettuce and ⅓ cup vinaigrette in a large bowl. Transfer mixture to a platter; top with cornbread croutons, eggs, cheese, avocado, bacon, and peas. Drizzle salad with remaining ⅓ cup dressing.

CLEAN THOSE GREENS
To wash heads of lettuce, separate the leaves and swish them in cold water. Soak 10 minutes to release any grit. Drain and pat dry.

Hash It Out

Bored with breakfast? Eggs and potatoes will always rise and shine

Hash Brown Frittata

ACTIVE 25 MIN. - TOTAL 35 MIN.
SERVES 6

- 5 large eggs
- ½ cup half-and-half
- ½ tsp. black pepper
- ¾ tsp. kosher salt, divided
- 3 Tbsp. canola oil, divided
- ½ cup chopped yellow onion (from 1 small onion)
- 1 (20-oz.) pkg. refrigerated shredded hash browns (such as Simply Potatoes)
- 2 Tbsp. chopped fresh chives
- 1 Tbsp. chopped fresh dill

1. Preheat oven to 375°F. Whisk together eggs, half-and-half, pepper, and ½ teaspoon of the salt in a medium bowl. Set aside.

2. Heat 1 tablespoon of the oil in a 10-inch nonstick oven-safe skillet over medium-high. Add onion; cook, stirring occasionally, until softened, about 5 minutes. Add hash browns and 1 tablespoon of the oil; spread mixture in an even layer. Cook, undisturbed, until hash browns begin to brown on bottoms, about 4 minutes. Flip mixture in sections using a wide spatula, trying to flip as much of the top as possible onto the bottom of the skillet. (Don't worry if it doesn't flip evenly.) Pour remaining 1 tablespoon oil over hash brown mixture; sprinkle evenly with remaining ¼ teaspoon salt. Cook until hash browns are evenly browned on bottoms, about 3 minutes.

3. Pour prepared egg mixture over hash brown mixture in skillet; reduce heat to medium. Cook, undisturbed, until outer edges are set, about 2 minutes. Transfer skillet to preheated oven. Bake until center is set, 6 to 8 minutes. Remove from oven. Immediately run an offset spatula around edges of frittata to loosen, and turn out onto a cutting board. Let stand 5 minutes. Slice frittata; sprinkle with fresh chives and dill before serving.

TOP TATERS
For easy separating and spreading, use refrigerated rather than frozen hash browns.

SPRING SALAD WITH
BERRIES AND BACON

Be Sweet to Mom

Honor the special women in your life with ideas for a strawberry-inspired lunch

Spring Salad with Berries and Bacon

Make this bold salad more filling by adding shredded rotisserie chicken or cooked whole grains.

ACTIVE 20 MIN. - TOTAL 20 MIN.

SERVES 6

- 2   Tbsp. red wine vinegar
- 1   Tbsp. finely chopped shallot (from 1 shallot)
- 1½ tsp. honey
- ½   tsp. Dijon mustard
- 3   cups sliced strawberries (from 1 lb. fresh strawberries), divided
- ¾   tsp. kosher salt, divided
- ¼   cup extra-virgin olive oil
- 5   cups baby spring mix (from 2 [5 oz.] pkg.)
- 1   (4-oz.) feta cheese block, crumbled
- 1   medium shallot, thinly sliced lengthwise
- 1   cup yellow cherry tomatoes, halved
- 8   bacon slices, cooked and coarsely chopped

1. Place red wine vinegar, finely chopped shallot, honey, Dijon mustard, 1 cup of the strawberries, and ¼ teaspoon of the salt in a blender. Process until smooth, about 30 seconds. With blender running, gradually drizzle in oil, processing until vinaigrette is smooth and combined, about 30 seconds.
2. Arrange spring mix on a large platter. Top with feta, sliced shallot, tomatoes, bacon, remaining 2 cups strawberries, and ½ teaspoon salt. Drizzle vinaigrette over salad, and serve immediately.

STRAWBERRY-BASIL SWEET TEA

Strawberry-Basil Sweet Tea

ACTIVE 25 MIN. - TOTAL 40 MIN., PLUS 1 HOUR CHILLING

SERVES 6

- 1   lb. fresh strawberries, plus more for garnish
- 1   cup granulated sugar
- ½   cup fresh basil leaves, plus basil sprigs for garnish
- 3   family-size black tea bags
- 1½ Tbsp. fresh lime juice (from 1 lime)
    Ice cubes

1. Place strawberries, sugar, and 2 cups water in a medium saucepan; bring to a boil over medium-high. Boil, undisturbed, 1 minute. Reduce heat to medium. Simmer, stirring often, until strawberries are very broken down and mixture is thickened and slightly reduced, about 15 minutes. Carefully skim any foam that rises to top of saucepan, and discard.
2. Pour strawberry mixture into a blender. Secure lid on blender; remove center piece to allow steam to escape. Place a clean towel over opening. Process until smooth, about 30 seconds. Pour mixture into a heatproof bowl; stir in basil, and let stand 10 minutes. Pour mixture through a fine-mesh strainer into a separate bowl; discard solids. Cover; chill until ready to use (or up to 2 weeks).
3. Bring 4 cups water to a boil in a medium saucepan over medium-high. Remove from heat. Add tea bags to water, and let steep 5 minutes. Remove and discard tea bags (do not squeeze bags). Stir lime juice and 2 cups strawberry-basil syrup into tea. (Reserve remaining syrup for another use.) Pour mixture into a pitcher. Cover and chill at least 1 hour or up to 24 hours. To serve, pour chilled tea into ice-filled glasses, and garnish with strawberries and basil sprigs.

Strawberry Short-Sheet Cake

ACTIVE 30 MIN. - TOTAL 1 HOUR, 5 MIN.,
PLUS 1 HOUR, 10 MIN. COOLING

SERVES 12

- 2 lb. fresh strawberries
- 2¼ cups soft wheat self-rising flour (such as White Lily Enriched Bleached Self-Rising Flour)
- 1 cup all-purpose flour, plus more for dusting
- ½ tsp. kosher salt
- ¾ cup granulated sugar, divided
- ¼ cup cold unsalted butter, cut into ¼-inch cubes
- 1 cup whole buttermilk
- 2 tsp. grated lemon zest (from 1 lemon)
- 1⅔ cups heavy whipping cream, divided
- 1 Tbsp. vanilla extract, divided
- 1½ Tbsp. unsalted butter, melted
- 2 Tbsp. sanding sugar
- 1 (8-oz.) container mascarpone cheese
- ¼ cup powdered sugar

1. Hull 1 pound of the fresh strawberries, and cut in half lengthwise; set aside. Hull and chop strawberries from remaining 1 pound berries to measure 1 cup; set aside. (Reserve remaining whole berries for another use.)

2. Preheat oven to 400°F. Coat a 13- x 9-inch rimmed baking sheet with cooking spray. Whisk together self-rising flour, all-purpose flour, salt, and ½ cup of the granulated sugar in a large bowl. Cut cold butter cubes into flour mixture until butter pieces are evenly coated and pea size. Gently fold in buttermilk, lemon zest, ⅔ cup of the whipping cream, and 1 teaspoon of the vanilla until mixture just comes together but is still lumpy. Gently fold in reserved chopped strawberries.

3. Using a ¼-cup measuring cup dusted with all-purpose flour to prevent sticking, scoop slightly rounded dough mounds onto prepared baking sheet in 3 rows of 6 side-by-side mounds, continuing to flour scoop after each mound to prevent sticking. Brush dough mounds evenly with melted butter, and sprinkle with sanding sugar. Bake

in preheated oven until golden brown, 28 to 32 minutes. Transfer baking sheet with shortcake to a wire rack, and cool 10 minutes. Transfer shortcake to wire rack; cool completely, about 1 hour.

4. Meanwhile, stir together halved strawberries and remaining ¼ cup granulated sugar in a medium bowl, and let stand until berries start to release their juices, 10 to 15 minutes.

5. Gently stir together mascarpone cheese, powdered sugar, and remaining 2 teaspoons vanilla in a separate medium bowl just until combined. Pour remaining 1 cup whipping cream into a separate large bowl, and beat with an electric mixer fitted with a whisk attachment on high speed until stiff peaks form, 2 to 3 minutes. Gently fold whipped cream into mascarpone mixture just until combined.

6. Spread whipped-cream-mascarpone mixture on cooled shortcake, leaving edges exposed. Top with strawberry mixture and any accumulated juices. Slice evenly into 12 pieces, and serve immediately.

Chicken with a Kick

Barbecue sauce with no refined sugar? Sweet!

Grilled Chicken Sandwich with Tangy Honey Barbecue Sauce

ACTIVE 25 MIN. - TOTAL 25 MIN.
SERVES 4

- ⅓ cup honey
- ¼ cup tomato paste
- 1 Tbsp. Dijon mustard
- 2 tsp. Worcestershire sauce
- 1 tsp. chili powder
- ½ tsp. onion powder
- ½ tsp. garlic powder
- 1 tsp. kosher salt, divided
- 1 tsp. black pepper, divided
- 1 Tbsp. apple cider vinegar
- 2 (10- to 12-oz.) boneless, skinless chicken breasts, cut in half crosswise
- 4 whole wheat hamburger buns, toasted
- Sliced tomatoes, pickles, lettuce, for topping

1. Cook honey, tomato paste, ¼ cup water, the mustard, Worcestershire, chili powder, onion powder, garlic powder, and ¾ teaspoon each of the salt and pepper in a small saucepan over medium, stirring often, until mixture comes to a boil. Boil, stirring constantly, 1 minute. Remove from heat, and stir in vinegar. Divide sauce into 2 small bowls; set aside.

2. Sprinkle chicken with remaining ¼ teaspoon each salt and pepper. Open bottom vent of a charcoal grill completely. Light charcoal chimney starter filled halfway with briquettes.

When briquettes are covered with gray ash, pour them onto bottom grate of grill. Adjust vents as needed to maintain an internal temperature of about 400°F. Coat top grate with oil, and place on grill. (If using a gas grill, preheat to medium [400°F].) Place chicken on oiled grate. Grill, covered, until grill marks appear, about 3 minutes per side. Using 1 of the bowls of sauce, brush on chicken evenly, a couple tablespoons at a time. Continue to cook, flipping and brushing every minute, until chicken is cooked through, about 5 minutes more. Discard any remaining sauce used for basting.

3. Place tomato slices, pickles, and 1 chicken piece on bottom half of each bun. Brush with sauce from second bowl, and add lettuce. Cover with bun tops.

CALORIES: **451** – CARBS: **51G** – FAT: **6G**

QUICK TIP
Leftover sauce can be chilled in an airtight container for 2 weeks. Reheat gently before using.

Off to the Races

Move over, mint juleps! Test Kitchen pro and *Hey Y'all* host Ivy Odom celebrates Derby Day at home in her own way

WHEN I THINK of the Kentucky Derby, big hats come to mind way before the horses. Fancy headwear instantly says, "I'm going to Churchill Downs." There's no other statement piece quite like it. When I'm at home watching the race, I re-create the fanfare of the event as closely as I can by pulling out my silver julep cups, putting on a bright-color dress and coordinating hat, and making an extravagant menu to match.

Hot Brown Party Rolls fill the bill with gooey cheese, turkey, and bacon sandwiched between sweet rolls topped with brown-sugar-garlic butter. Instead of the usual mint juleps, I make fruity Black-Eyed Susan Slushies. The mix of pineapple and citrus juices and ginger ale is more synonymous with the Preakness Stakes than the Derby. It's a drink that tastes great with or without bourbon—my mocktail version is served frozen and gussied up with garnishes as flashy as sensational hats.

Hot Brown Party Rolls
ACTIVE 15 MIN. · TOTAL 45 MIN.
SERVES 6

- 1 (12-ct.) pkg. small sweet Hawaiian rolls (such as King's Hawaiian)
- 5 oz. Gruyère cheese slices (about 6 slices), divided
- ½ lb. thinly sliced deli turkey
- 1 small tomato, cut into ¼-inch slices
- 6 slices thick-cut bacon (such as Wright Brand), cooked and cut into 2-inch pieces
- 1 oz. Parmesan cheese, shredded (about ¼ cup)
- ¾ cup butter, melted
- 1 Tbsp. Dijon mustard
- 2 tsp. dried minced onion
- 1½ tsp. Worcestershire sauce
- 1 tsp. light brown sugar
- ½ tsp. grated garlic (from 1 medium garlic clove)
- ½ tsp. Mexican-style hot sauce (such as Cholula Hot Sauce)

1. Preheat oven to 375°F. Lightly spray an 11- x 7-inch baking dish with cooking spray. Split rolls horizontally (without separating into individual rolls); place bottoms of rolls in prepared baking dish.
2. Layer bottoms of rolls with 3 slices Gruyère cheese, cutting slices to fit evenly. Add turkey slices, folding to fit evenly on Gruyère. Place tomato slices in an even layer on turkey. Top evenly with bacon pieces. Add remaining slices of Gruyère, cutting to fit, in an even layer on bacon. Sprinkle evenly with Parmesan. Top with roll tops.
3. Stir together melted butter, Dijon mustard, minced onion, Worcestershire, brown sugar, garlic, and hot sauce in a 2-cup liquid measuring cup. Slowly pour mixture over rolls in baking dish to soak into rolls. Cover dish with aluminum foil. Bake sandwiches in preheated oven until cheese is melted, about 15 minutes. Uncover, and continue baking until tops are golden brown and crisp, 8 to 10 minutes. Remove from oven; let stand 5 minutes before serving.

Black-Eyed Susan Slushies
ACTIVE 10 MIN. · TOTAL 10 MIN.
SERVES 6

Process ⅓ cup **fresh lime juice** (from 3 limes); ⅓ cup **fresh lemon juice** (from 2 lemons); ⅓ cup **simple syrup**; ¾ cup **frozen orange juice concentrate**, thawed (from 1 [12-oz.] container); ¾ cup **frozen pineapple juice concentrate**, thawed (from 1 [12-oz.] container); and 4 cups **ice cubes** in a blender on high until mixture is smooth and slushy, 30 to 45 seconds. Divide slushy evenly among 6 glasses. Top each glass with 1 to 2 ounces of **ginger ale** (around 1½ cups total). Garnish with **pineapple leaves, orange** slices, and **maraschino cherries**, if desired.

BLACK-EYED SUSAN
SLUSHIES

SPIKE IT
If desired, add
1½ ounces bourbon
to each glass along
with the ginger ale.

HOT BROWN
PARTY ROLLS

Plate It Pretty
Three easy ways to make your favorite salad shine

COMBINE A FEW LETTUCES
For different colors and textures, use a variety of greens (such as arugula, spinach, chopped romaine, kale, and spring mix).

PLACE PROTEIN ON TOP
Tossing chicken and other meats with dressing can make them look less appetizing. Plate only the dressed salad, add the protein, then drizzle on more dressing, if needed.

ADD A CRUNCHY TOPPING
The finishing touch makes every bite fun. Garnish with toasted nuts and seeds, crushed tortilla or kettle chips, croutons, or a sprinkle of everything bagel seasoning.

FRESH CUTS

BELL PEPPER CONFETTI
Sweet peppers add color and texture to salads. Dice them into small "confetti" to sprinkle on top.

CARROT CURLS
If carrots are large, use a hand peeler to shave them into lengthy curls. Small carrots can be sliced diagonally into bite-size pieces.

CUCUMBER FLOWERS
Place each cucumber on a flat surface; then gently run the tines of a fork lengthwise along one side to score the skin. Turn the cucumber and repeat on all sides, then slice.

DO I REALLY NEED TO...

Boil Water for Tea?

No. In fact, boiling water will scald the tea leaves and make the liquid taste bitter. Instead, just bring the water to a simmer. When you see tiny bubbles and steam, it's time to take it off the heat and add the bags or loose tea. Or skip this step completely, and try our easy cold-brewed method (at right), which makes a clear, clean-tasting batch with no bitterness. Serve it over ice, or heat it up—and don't forget the sugar.

THE SOUTHERN WAY TO MAKE COLD-BREWED ICED TEA
Place 4 cups room-temperature **water** and 3 regular-size **tea bags** (any type) in a quart-size container or pitcher. Cover; refrigerate 8 hours. Remove and discard the tea bags before serving. Store tea, covered, in refrigerator up to 1 week.

June

Pep Rally

Crunchy, versatile, and vibrant, a variety of sweet and hot peppers are popping up in backyard gardens and farmers markets across the South. Here are two ways to make the most of them

Southern Hot-Pepper Vinegar

ACTIVE 5 MIN. · TOTAL 5 MIN., PLUS 3 HOURS COOLING AND 8 HOURS CHILLING
MAKES 2½ CUPS

Split 5 **small jalapeño chiles,** 5 **medium-size red Fresno chiles,** and 1 **medium-size banana wax pepper** lengthwise, and place in a 1-qt. canning jar, glass bottle, or medium-size airtight container. Bring 2¼ cups **white vinegar,** ½ cup **water,** and 2 smashed **garlic cloves** to a boil in a saucepan over high. Discard garlic cloves; pour vinegar mixture over peppers. Cool completely, about 3 hours. Cover; chill at least 8 hours or up to 12 hours before using. Store at room temperature.

Marinated Sweet Pepper Salad with Ricotta and Summer Herbs

ACTIVE 25 MIN. · TOTAL 50 MIN.
SERVES 6

Preheat grill to high (450°F to 500°F). Toss 8 **medium-size multicolor bell peppers** with 1 Tbsp. **olive oil.** Grill peppers on oiled grates, covered, turning occasionally, until charred in spots and softened, 15 to 20 minutes. Transfer to a large bowl; cover with plastic wrap. Let steam 10 minutes. Meanwhile, stir together 1 cup torn **fresh herbs** (such as basil, mint, and oregano), 2½ Tbsp. each **red wine vinegar** and **lemon juice,** ¾ tsp. grated **garlic,** 2 tsp. **kosher salt,** ¾ tsp. **black pepper,** and ¼ cup **olive oil.** Remove and discard skins and seeds from bell peppers; cut flesh into thick strips. Add to herb mixture; toss to coat. Marinate 15 minutes; toss again. Dollop with ¾ cup **whole-milk ricotta cheese;** sprinkle with ¼ cup toasted **pine nuts.** Drizzle with 1 Tbsp. **olive oil;** sprinkle with **flaky sea salt,** additional **herbs,** and **black pepper.**

Herb Appeal

Add vibrant color and aroma to everything from drinks to desserts

HERBED CRAB CAKES WITH GREEN GODDESS DRESSING (PAGE 132)

Herbed Crab Cakes with Green Goddess Dressing

(Photo, page 131)

A trio of herbs (chives, cilantro, and tarragon) pairs well with fresh crabmeat without overpowering its delicate sweetness. The Green Goddess Dressing, which can be made a day in advance and chilled in an airtight container, is a delicious topper for the crab cakes and salad greens.

ACTIVE 30 MIN. - TOTAL 40 MIN.,
PLUS 1 HOUR CHILLING

SERVES 4

CRAB CAKES

- 1 sleeve saltine crackers (about 40 crackers)
- 2 large egg yolks
- ¼ cup mayonnaise
- 2 Tbsp. Dijon mustard
- 2 tsp. grated lemon zest, plus 2 Tbsp. fresh juice (from 1 lemon)
- 2 Tbsp. finely chopped fresh chives
- 2 Tbsp. finely chopped fresh cilantro
- 1 Tbsp. finely chopped fresh tarragon
- ¼ tsp. black pepper
- 1 lb. fresh lump crabmeat, drained and picked over

GREEN GODDESS DRESSING

- ¾ cup mayonnaise
- ½ cup packed fresh cilantro (tender stems and leaves)
- ¼ cup loosely packed fresh tarragon leaves
- ½ tsp. grated lemon zest, plus 3 Tbsp. fresh juice (from 1 lemon)
- 1 small garlic clove, grated
- 1 tsp. kosher salt
- ⅛ tsp. black pepper

ADDITIONAL INGREDIENTS

- ¼ cup canola oil
- 1 (5-oz.) pkg. spring mix salad greens
  Lemon wedges

1. Prepare the Crab Cakes: Process saltines in a food processor until consistency of fine crumbs, about 1 minute. Stir together egg yolks, mayonnaise, mustard, lemon zest and juice, chives, cilantro, tarragon, and pepper in a large bowl until combined. Gently stir in crabmeat and 1 cup saltine crumbs. (Reserve remaining crumbs for another use.) Let stand 10 minutes.

2. Shape crab mixture evenly into 8 (3-inch) patties (about ½ cup each). Arrange on a baking sheet lined with parchment paper. Cover; chill at least 1 hour or up to 12 hours.

3. Meanwhile, prepare the Green Goddess Dressing: Process mayonnaise, cilantro, tarragon, lemon zest and juice, garlic, salt, and pepper in a blender until smooth, about 30 seconds. Cover and refrigerate until ready to serve or up to 24 hours.

4. Heat oil in a large skillet over medium-high. Working in batches, add Crab Cakes to skillet. Cook until browned on both sides, about 5 minutes per batch, flipping once halfway through cook time.

5. Top salad greens with Crab Cakes. Drizzle with Green Goddess Dressing, and serve with lemon wedges.

Focaccia with Ricotta and Crispy Herbs

Crunchy, light-as-air fried herbs are a gorgeous garnish for this simple focaccia made with store-bought pizza dough. Pat the herbs completely dry with paper towels to prevent spattering before adding them to the hot oil.

ACTIVE 15 MIN. - TOTAL 2 HOURS

SERVES 8

- ¾ cup extra-virgin olive oil, divided
- 1 lb. fresh pizza dough
- 1 (15-oz.) container whole-milk ricotta cheese
- 2 tsp. grated garlic (from 3 small garlic cloves)
- 1 tsp. kosher salt
- ½ tsp. black pepper
- ⅓ cup loosely packed fresh flat-leaf parsley leaves
- ⅓ cup loosely packed fresh basil leaves
- ⅓ cup loosely packed fresh mint leaves
- ¼ tsp. crushed red pepper

1. Pour 2 tablespoons of the oil in a 13- x 9-inch rimmed baking sheet, and spread across entire bottom and sides to evenly coat. Place dough on pan, turning and flipping to completely coat in oil. Cover with a clean towel; let stand at room temperature until dough relaxes and is easy to shape, 1 to 1½ hours.

2. Meanwhile, stir together ricotta, garlic, salt, and black pepper in a bowl. Set aside at room temperature up to 1 hour.

3. Preheat oven to 425°F. Using your hands, gently spread dough to cover bottom of baking sheet. (If dough pulls back, cover again, and let rest another 15 minutes.) Using a fork and flipping dough, prick each side of dough 10 to 12 times. Drizzle one side of dough with another 2 tablespoons of the oil.

4. Bake in preheated oven until golden and slightly puffed, 12 to 13 minutes. Remove from oven, and cool 15 minutes.

5. Heat remaining ½ cup oil to 325°F in a small skillet over medium. Working in small batches of 4 to 6 herb leaves, add leaves to oil; fry until crisp and fragrant, 5 to 10 seconds per batch. (Make sure the herbs are dry to prevent them from spattering in the oil.) Using a slotted spoon, transfer leaves to a plate lined with paper towels to drain.

6. Spread ricotta mixture over cooled bread. Arrange crispy herbs over ricotta, and sprinkle with crushed red pepper.

Goat Cheese-Herb Spread

While the recipe calls for parsley, chives, and mint, you could replace some or all of the herbs with tarragon, dill, or thyme.

ACTIVE 5 MIN. - TOTAL 5 MIN.

SERVES 4

- 8 oz. goat cheese, at room temperature
- 1 Tbsp. finely chopped fresh flat-leaf parsley
- 1 Tbsp. finely chopped fresh chives
- 2 tsp. finely chopped fresh mint
  Serving options: black pepper, sliced baguette, or radishes

Stir together goat cheese, parsley, chives, and mint in a small bowl until combined. If desired, sprinkle with pepper and serve with sliced baguette and radishes.

GOAT CHEESE-HERB
SPREAD

FOCACCIA WITH
RICOTTA AND
CRISPY HERBS

CHICKEN WITH
40 LEAVES OF BASIL

Chicken with 40 Leaves of Basil

Inspired by the famous recipe Chicken with 40 Cloves of Garlic, this basil-filled bird is just as aromatic. Serve alongside crusty bread or roasted potatoes to enjoy every last bit of the herb oil.

ACTIVE 15 MIN. - TOTAL 2 HOURS
SERVES 4

1	(4-lb.) whole chicken
3½	tsp. kosher salt
40	fresh basil leaves (about 2 cups loosely packed)
¼	cup extra-virgin olive oil
1	tsp. black pepper
1	medium-size red onion, cut into wedges
8	oz. mini sweet peppers, halved and seeded
12	garlic cloves, smashed

1. Remove giblets and neck from chicken; discard. Let chicken come to room temperature, about 30 minutes. Preheat oven to 375°F.
2. Pat chicken dry. Rub salt evenly inside chicken cavity and on skin. Carefully run your fingers under skin of chicken breast and thighs, lifting skin slightly to loosen (to help the chicken brown). Place 2 to 3 basil leaves inside chicken cavity.
3. Finely chop remaining basil, and transfer to a small bowl. Stir in oil and black pepper. (Alternatively, you can use a mortar and pestle to crush chopped basil, oil, and black pepper together.) Reserve 2 tablespoons basil-oil mixture for serving. Rub remaining basil-oil mixture evenly inside chicken cavity and on chicken skin. Arrange onion wedges and peppers in a large cast-iron skillet; top with chicken. Scatter garlic around chicken in skillet.
4. Roast in preheated oven until chicken is golden brown and a thermometer inserted in thickest portion of thighs registers 165°F, 1 hour to 1 hour, 15 minutes. Remove from oven; spoon or brush reserved basil-oil mixture over chicken. Cool in skillet 10 minutes, and carve. Serve with onion and peppers in skillet.

LINGUINE WITH PARSLEY PESTO

Linguine with Parsley Pesto

With its bright and grassy flavor, fresh parsley makes a tasty stand-in for basil when preparing pesto. This unconventional recipe replaces the usual pine nuts with pistachios, which boost the green color of the sauce and make it taste rich and buttery.

ACTIVE 10 MIN. - TOTAL 15 MIN.
SERVES 4

2	cups packed fresh flat-leaf parsley leaves (from 1 bunch), plus chopped parsley for garnish
⅓	cup roasted salted pistachios
1½	oz. Parmesan cheese, finely grated (about ⅓ cup), plus shaved Parmesan for serving
¼	cup extra-virgin olive oil
2	Tbsp. fresh lemon juice (from 1 lemon)
½	tsp. kosher salt
¼	tsp. black pepper
1	small garlic clove
12	oz. uncooked linguine
2	Tbsp. unsalted butter, cubed
	Crushed red pepper, for topping

1. Bring a large pot of salted water to a boil over high. Meanwhile, place parsley, pistachios, grated Parmesan, oil, lemon juice, salt, pepper, and garlic in a food processor or blender. Process until almost smooth, about 1 minute.
2. Add pasta to boiling water; cook according to package directions until al dente. Drain, reserving 1 cup cooking water. Return pasta to pot over low heat. Add butter and parsley pesto, gradually stirring in reserved cooking water as needed until desired consistency. Garnish with red pepper, shaved cheese, and chopped parsley.

TOMATO-HERB PANZANELLA

Tomato-Herb Panzanella

Think of this rustic bread-and-tomato salad as a blank canvas for fresh herbs. We like the combination of basil and tarragon leaves mixed with baby arugula, but mint and parsley would also be delicious.

ACTIVE 20 MIN. - TOTAL 1 HOUR

SERVES 6

- 8 oz. rustic boule bread (from 1 [16-oz.] loaf), cut into 1-inch cubes (about 6 cups)
- ¼ cup, plus ⅓ cup extra-virgin olive oil, divided
- 2 tsp. kosher salt, divided
- ½ tsp. black pepper, divided
- 2½ lb. assorted tomatoes (such as heirloom or beefsteak), cut into 1-inch pieces
- 1 (14-oz.) English cucumber, halved lengthwise and sliced
- 2 cups loosely packed baby arugula
- 2 cups loosely packed fresh basil leaves
- ½ cup loosely packed fresh tarragon leaves, roughly chopped
- ¼ cup nonpareil capers
- 3 Tbsp. rice wine vinegar
- 1 tsp. Dijon mustard
- 1 small garlic clove, grated

1. Preheat oven to 375°F. Toss together bread, ¼ cup of the oil, ½ teaspoon of the salt, and ¼ teaspoon of the pepper on a large rimmed baking sheet; spread mixture in an even layer. Bake until golden brown and crispy, about 15 minutes, tossing once halfway through cook time.

2. Toss together tomatoes, cucumber, arugula, basil, tarragon, capers, and toasted bread in a large bowl; set aside.

3. Stir together vinegar, mustard, garlic, and remaining ⅓ cup oil, 1½ teaspoons salt, and ¼ teaspoon pepper in a small bowl until combined. Drizzle over tomato mixture in bowl; gently toss to combine. Let stand at room temperature 30 minutes. Serve.

BASIL-LEMON BARS
(PAGE 138)

Basil-Lemon Bars

(Photo, page 137)

This herb-and-citrus combo is hard to beat in savory or sweet dishes, like these lively lemon bars. While this recipe works wonderfully with regular basil, it's even better with lemon basil, which is easy to grow and available at many nurseries and greenhouses.

ACTIVE 20 MIN. - TOTAL 1 HOUR, 30 MIN., PLUS 1 HOUR COOLING

MAKES 16

- 25 large fresh basil leaves (1 cup loosely packed)
- ½ tsp. kosher salt
- 2 Tbsp. grated lemon zest, plus ½ cup fresh juice (from 3 lemons), divided
- 2¼ cups all-purpose flour, divided
- 2½ cups granulated sugar, divided
- 1 cup cold unsalted butter, cubed
- 4 large eggs
- ½ tsp. baking powder
- Powdered sugar
- Thin lemon slices and small basil leaves, for topping (optional)

1. Preheat oven to 350°F. Place basil, salt, lemon zest, 2 cups of the flour, and ½ cup of the granulated sugar in a food processor; process until basil is very finely chopped, about 1 minute.

2. Add butter cubes to flour mixture in food processor; pulse until mixture resembles coarse meal, about 15 pulses. Line a 13- x 9-inch baking pan with parchment paper, leaving a 2-inch overhang on all sides; lightly coat with cooking spray. Firmly press flour mixture into bottom of pan.

3. Bake in preheated oven until light golden brown, 30 to 35 minutes. Remove from oven (do not turn oven off); let cool completely on a wire rack, about 20 minutes.

4. Whisk together eggs, baking powder, lemon juice, and remaining ¼ cup flour and 2 cups granulated sugar in a large bowl until smooth. Pour over cooled crust in baking pan; gently tap pan on counter 2 to 3 times to release any air bubbles in lemon curd.

5. Bake at 350°F until lemon curd is set, 30 to 35 minutes. Remove from oven; let cool completely on a wire rack, about 1 hour.

6. Sift powdered sugar over top of bars. Cut into 2-inch squares. Top with lemon slices and basil leaves, if desired. Cover and refrigerate up to 3 days.

Fresh Mint-Chocolate Pie

If you grow mint, you'll have a bumper crop before you know it. The pie's decadent dark chocolate custard filling is infused with lots of this herb for an intense flavor that you just can't get from an extract.

ACTIVE 25 MIN. - TOTAL 1 HOUR, 25 MIN., PLUS 4 HOURS CHILLING

SERVES 8

CRUST
- 1 (9-oz.) pkg. chocolate wafer cookies (such as Nabisco Famous), finely crushed
- 5 Tbsp. unsalted butter, melted
- 3 Tbsp. granulated sugar

FILLING
- 2½ cups whole milk
- 1 cup packed mint sprigs
- 5 large egg yolks
- ½ cup granulated sugar
- 3 Tbsp. cornstarch
- ⅛ tsp. kosher salt
- 4 Tbsp. unsalted butter, cut into 1-Tbsp. pieces
- 1 (4-oz.) semisweet chocolate candy bar (such as Ghirardelli), chopped
- 1 (1-oz.) unsweetened chocolate baking square, chopped
- 2 tsp. vanilla extract

ADDITIONAL INGREDIENTS
- 2 cups heavy whipping cream
- ⅓ cup powdered sugar
- Chocolate shavings
- Small fresh mint leaves

1. Prepare the Crust: Preheat oven to 350°F. Stir together crushed cookies, melted butter, and granulated sugar in a medium bowl. Firmly press mixture into bottom and up sides of a 9-inch pie plate. (You will have about 2 tablespoons left over. Discard or reserve for another use.) Bake until just set, about 10 minutes. Remove from oven; cool completely on a wire rack, about 20 minutes.

2. Prepare the Filling: Heat milk in a medium saucepan over medium-high until it just comes to a simmer. Stir in mint sprigs, and remove from heat. Cover and let steep 15 minutes. Remove and discard mint.

3. Stir together egg yolks, granulated sugar, cornstarch, and salt in a medium bowl until combined. Very slowly and gradually whisk half of the steeped milk into egg mixture. Whisk egg mixture into remaining steeped milk in saucepan. Bring to a simmer over medium, stirring constantly. Continue simmering, stirring constantly, until thickened and bubbly, about 2 minutes. Reduce heat to low; stir in butter 1 tablespoon at a time until incorporated. Add chocolate bar, chocolate square, and vanilla, stirring until mixture is melted. Remove from heat.

4. Spoon Filling into cooled Crust; cool on wire rack 10 minutes. Place a piece of plastic wrap directly over surface of Filling. Refrigerate until firm, about 4 hours.

5. Beat whipping cream and powdered sugar with an electric mixer fitted with a whisk attachment on high speed until stiff peaks form, 1 to 2 minutes. Remove plastic wrap from pie. Spread top with whipped cream. Garnish with chocolate shavings and small mint leaves.

FRESH MINT-
CHOCOLATE PIE

Mint Margaritas

Perk up a batch of your usual margaritas with the taste of mint. Or if you prefer, substitute an equal amount of fresh basil.
ACTIVE 5 MIN. - TOTAL 5 MIN.
SERVES 4

Lime wedges, as needed
Coarse sea salt
Crushed ice
¾ cup (6 oz.) tequila
¾ cup fresh lime juice (from 6 limes)
½ cup (4 oz.) orange liqueur (such as Cointreau)
¼ cup agave syrup
8 fresh mint sprigs, plus more for garnish

1. Run a lime wedge around rims of 4 glasses. Place salt in a small saucer; dip rims in salt to coat. Fill glasses with crushed ice.
2. Place tequila, lime juice, orange liqueur, agave syrup, and mint sprigs in a pitcher or large measuring cup. Gently muddle using handle of a wooden spoon. Pour mixture through a fine-mesh strainer evenly into prepared glasses, and discard solids. Garnish with additional mint sprigs.

Best Ways to Store Herbs

Keep Them Fresh

Treat bunches of herbs like bouquets of flowers. Trim the stems, and place in a glass with enough water to cover the ends (remove any leaves under the water). Place in a room-temperature spot; change the water daily. Herbs will stay fresh longer with a plastic shopping bag over the glass to loosely cover the leaves.

Freeze Them

Preserve individual leaves and sprigs by flash-freezing them. Clean the herbs, and pat dry. Spread them out on a sheet pan, and place in the freezer. Chill 30 minutes or until frozen. Then transfer herbs to zip-top plastic freezer bags, and press out excess air. Use within a month in cooked dishes (no need to thaw).

Tarragon-Hibiscus Gin Spritzer

This herb has a slight anise flavor, which shines in a sparkling cocktail made with citrusy hibiscus tea, tonic water, and gin. The tea mixture is also refreshing on its own without alcohol.
ACTIVE 10 MIN. - TOTAL 30 MIN.
SERVES 4

½ cup granulated sugar
½ oz. fresh tarragon sprigs, plus more for garnish
2 regular-size hibiscus tea bags (such as Celestial Seasonings Red Zinger)
1½ cups tonic water
¾ cup (6 oz.) gin
¼ cup fresh lemon juice (from 2 lemons)
Ice cubes
Lemon slices, for garnish

1. Place ½ cup water and the sugar in a medium saucepan, and bring to a boil over high, stirring occasionally. Continue boiling, stirring occasionally, until sugar is dissolved, about 1 minute. Remove from heat, and add tarragon and tea bags. Let steep 10 minutes. Pour mixture through a fine-mesh strainer into a heatproof bowl, and discard solids. Let cool completely, about 10 minutes.
2. Stir together tonic water, gin, lemon juice, and ¼ cup strained hibiscus mixture in a pitcher. Taste spritzer, and if desired, add more hibiscus mixture until desired sweetness. (Remaining hibiscus mixture can be stored in an airtight container in refrigerator up to 1 week.)
3. Fill 4 glasses with ice. Pour gin mixture evenly into glasses. Garnish with additional tarragon sprigs and lemon slices.

MINT MARGARITAS

TARRAGON-HIBISCUS GIN SPRITZER

Just Peachy

This beautifully rustic dessert is even easier than pie

Gingered Peach Galette

ACTIVE 15 MIN. · TOTAL 1 HOUR, 35 MIN.

SERVES 8

- 1 (14.1-oz.) pkg. refrigerated piecrusts (such as Pillsbury), at room temperature
  All-purpose flour, for dusting
- ¼ cup packed light brown sugar
- 1 Tbsp. cornstarch
- 2 tsp. grated lemon zest, plus 1 Tbsp. fresh juice (from 1 lemon), divided
- ½ tsp. kosher salt
- ½ tsp. ground ginger
- 1½ lb. firm-ripe peaches (about 5 peaches), cut into ¾-inch-thick wedges (about 6 cups wedges)
- 1 tsp. vanilla extract
- 1 Tbsp. heavy whipping cream
- 1 Tbsp. sparkling or turbinado sugar
  Vanilla ice cream or whipped cream

1. Preheat oven to 375°F. Position oven rack in bottom third of oven. Unroll 1 piecrust on a lightly floured surface, and lightly brush top of piecrust with 2 tablespoons water. Unroll remaining piecrust, and place on top of crust on lightly floured surface. Roll out stacked piecrusts into a 13-inch circle. Transfer to a large rimmed baking sheet lined with parchment paper. Refrigerate, uncovered, until ready to use, up to 15 minutes.

2. Whisk together brown sugar, cornstarch, lemon zest, salt, and ground ginger in a large bowl until combined. Gently stir in peaches, vanilla, and lemon juice until peaches are fully coated. Arrange peach slices in an even layer in concentric circles on piecrust, starting from outside and leaving a 2-inch border around edges. Drizzle peaches with any remaining juices from bowl. Fold edges of piecrust over fruit, pleating as needed. Brush crust with cream; sprinkle crust and fruit with sparkling sugar.

QUICK TIP
Choose firm-ripe peaches, which won't fall apart when baked.

3. Bake in bottom third of preheated oven until filling is bubbling and crust is golden brown, about 50 minutes. Transfer baking sheet to a wire rack; let galette cool to room temperature, about 30 minutes. Serve with ice cream or whipped cream.

The Art of the Burger

From beef to black bean, five recipes for cooking all week long

EASY CLEAN
Before you get grilling, make sure the grates are free of debris. Use tongs and a ball of aluminum foil to scrape off any residue.

Lamb Burgers with Feta and Dijonnaise

ACTIVE 30 MIN. · TOTAL 30 MIN.,
PLUS 30 MIN. CHILLING
SERVES 4

- 1 lb. ground lamb
- 2 Tbsp. finely chopped shallot (from 1 shallot)
- 2 Tbsp. Worcestershire sauce
- 2 tsp. chopped fresh thyme
- 2 Tbsp. Dijon mustard, divided
- 1 tsp. kosher salt, divided
- ¾ tsp. black pepper, divided
- ½ cup mayonnaise
- ¼ cup sour cream
- 1 tsp. grated garlic (from 1 garlic clove)
- 4 brioche hamburger buns, toasted

Toppings: crumbled feta cheese, thinly sliced red onion rings, arugula

1. Stir together ground lamb, shallot, Worcestershire, thyme, 1 tablespoon of the mustard, and ¼ teaspoon each of the salt and pepper in a large bowl until well combined. Divide evenly into 4 (about 4½-ounce) balls. Shape each ball into a 4-inch-wide, ¾-inch-thick patty. Arrange patties on a baking sheet lined with parchment paper; cover with plastic wrap. Chill patties at least 30 minutes or up to 8 hours.

2. Stir together mayonnaise, sour cream, garlic, ¼ teaspoon each of the salt and pepper, and remaining 1 tablespoon mustard in a small bowl until well combined. Cover; place in refrigerator until ready to use or up to 3 days.

3. Preheat a grill to medium-high (400˚F to 450˚F). Sprinkle patties evenly with remaining ½ teaspoon salt and ¼ teaspoon pepper. Place patties on oiled grates. Grill, covered, until a thermometer inserted into thickest portion of patties registers 140˚F to 145˚F for medium doneness, about 5 minutes per side. Serve on toasted buns topped with Dijonnaise mixture, feta, onion, and arugula.

Turkey Cheeseburgers with Grilled Vidalia Onion Rings

ACTIVE 35 MIN. - TOTAL 40 MIN.,
PLUS 30 MIN. CHILLING

SERVES 4

- ½ cup cold unsalted butter
- 1 lb. lean ground turkey breast
- 2 tsp. poultry seasoning
- 1 large Vidalia onion, cut crosswise into ½-inch-thick rounds (individual rings not separated)
- 2 tsp. kosher salt, divided
- 1 tsp. black pepper, divided
- 2 Tbsp. olive oil
- 4 provolone cheese slices
- 4 potato hamburger buns, toasted
  Toppings: ketchup, pickles, green leaf lettuce, or mayonnaise

1. Grate butter using largest holes on a box grater; transfer to a medium bowl. Add ground turkey and poultry seasoning; gently mix using your hands until well combined. Divide mixture into 4 (about 5-ounce) balls; shape each ball into a 4-inch-wide, ¾-inch-thick patty. Arrange patties on a baking sheet lined with parchment paper. Cover; chill at least 30 minutes or up to 8 hours.
2. Preheat a grill to medium-high (400°F to 450°F). Sprinkle onion rounds evenly with 1 teaspoon of the salt and ½ teaspoon of the pepper, and drizzle evenly with oil. Place onion rounds on unoiled grates. Grill, uncovered, rotating rounds on grates often, until completely charred, about 7 minutes per side. Transfer grilled onions to a medium bowl, discarding outer blackened rings, and cover tightly with plastic wrap. Let onion rounds stand until completely tender, about 5 minutes.
3. Place a cast-iron griddle plate or a large cast-iron skillet on grill grates, and preheat about 3 minutes. Remove patties from refrigerator; sprinkle evenly with remaining 1 teaspoon salt and ½ teaspoon pepper. Place patties on preheated unoiled griddle plate on grill. Cook, covered, until well seared and golden in color, about 5 minutes. Flip patties; cook, covered, 3 minutes. Top each patty with 1 cheese slice. Cook, covered, until cheese is melted and a thermometer inserted into thickest portion of patties registers 165°F, about 2 minutes. Serve patties on toasted buns with ketchup, pickles, grilled onions, lettuce, and mayonnaise.

JUST ADD BUTTER
Lean turkey meat can be dry, so we mixed in grated cold butter to make these burgers juicy. Use a cast-iron griddle or skillet to cook the patties; the melting butter can cause flare-ups on the grill.

Black Bean Burgers with Avocado Slaw

ACTIVE 40 MIN. - TOTAL 55 MIN.,
PLUS 30 MIN. CHILLING

SERVES 4

- 2 (15½-oz.) cans black beans, drained and rinsed
- ¼ cup olive oil, divided
- ⅔ cup finely chopped yellow onion (from 1 medium onion)
- ⅔ cup finely chopped orange bell pepper (from 1 large bell pepper)
- 1 Tbsp. finely chopped garlic (from 2 garlic cloves)
- 1 Tbsp. chili powder
- 2 large egg yolks
- ¼ cup panko breadcrumbs
- 1 tsp. kosher salt
- 1 tsp. black pepper
- 1 cup packed shredded coleslaw mix
- 3 Tbsp. bottled cilantro-avocado yogurt dressing (such as Bolthouse Farms)
- 2 Tbsp. chopped fresh cilantro
- 4 hamburger buns, toasted
- 1 medium avocado, sliced

1. Preheat oven to 350°F. Spread beans in an even layer on a baking sheet lined with Reynolds Wrap® aluminum foil. Bake until beans are dry and cracked, about 15 minutes. Remove from oven, and cool about 10 minutes.

2. Meanwhile, heat 2 tablespoons of the oil in a large skillet over medium. Add onion, bell pepper, garlic, and chili powder. Cook, stirring occasionally, until tender and fragrant, about 5 minutes. Transfer mixture to a medium bowl, and set aside. Wipe skillet clean.

3. Place egg yolks, panko, salt, black pepper, 2 cups of the beans, and 2 tablespoons of the onion mixture in a food processor. Process until mostly smooth, about 15 seconds. Transfer pureed mixture to bowl with remaining onion mixture. Add remaining 1 cup beans; stir until well combined. Divide evenly into 4 (about 6-ounce) balls; shape each ball into a 4-inch-wide, ¾-inch-thick patty. Arrange patties on a baking sheet lined with parchment paper, and cover with plastic wrap; chill 30 minutes.

4. Meanwhile, toss together coleslaw mix, dressing, and cilantro in a large bowl, and cover with plastic wrap. Chill until ready to use or up to 1 hour.

5. Add remaining 2 tablespoons oil to cleaned skillet; heat over medium. Add patties; cook until crisp, about 5 minutes per side. Serve patties on toasted buns with avocado slices and slaw.

Beef Sliders with Bacon Jam

ACTIVE 30 MIN. - TOTAL 50 MIN.

SERVES 6

- 1 lb. bacon, roughly chopped
- 1¼ lb. 80/20 ground beef
- 1 Tbsp. Dijon mustard
- 1 tsp. kosher salt
- ¼ cup, plus 1 Tbsp. balsamic vinegar, divided
- 1 tsp. black pepper, divided
- 1 cup finely chopped red onion (from 1 medium onion)
- ¼ cup granulated sugar
- 1 Tbsp. chopped fresh thyme
- 1 (12-oz.) pkg. savory butter rolls (such as King's Hawaiian)
- 6 extra-sharp cheddar cheese slices
- 3 small round tomatoes, cut into 12 slices total

  Hamburger dill pickle chips

1. Preheat oven to 350°F. Cook bacon in a large saucepan over medium, stirring often, until mostly crisp, 8 to 10 minutes. Remove bacon from pan using a slotted spoon, and transfer to a plate lined with paper towels; set aside. Reserve 1 tablespoon drippings in pan.

2. While bacon cooks, place beef, mustard, salt, 1 tablespoon of the vinegar, and ¾ teaspoon of the pepper in an 11- x 7-inch baking dish. Mix using your hands until well combined. Press mixture into an even layer. Bake in preheated oven until browned (meat will not be fully cooked), 10 to 12 minutes. Remove from oven; let stand 5 minutes. (Keep oven on.)

3. Meanwhile, add onion to reserved drippings in pan; cook over medium, stirring occasionally, until tender, about 5 minutes. Remove pan from heat. Transfer bacon to a cutting board; finely chop.

4. Using a long spatula, transfer beef patty from baking dish to a baking sheet lined with paper towels to drain. Wipe dish clean; coat with cooking spray.

5. Add bacon, sugar, and remaining ¼ cup vinegar to onion in pan. Bring to a boil over high, stirring constantly. Reduce heat to low. Simmer, stirring often, until almost completely reduced, about 5 minutes. Stir in thyme and remaining ¼ teaspoon pepper. Remove from heat; set aside.

6. Without separating individual rolls, cut roll loaf in half horizontally, creating 1 top and 1 bottom. Place roll bottom in prepared baking dish. Cover with cooked beef patty; spread patty with bacon jam. Add cheese and tomato slices; cover with roll top. Bake at 350°F until cheese is melted and rolls are golden, about 8 minutes. Slice into sliders before serving with pickles.

FRESH CATCH
These burgers are made with salmon, herbs, capers, and lemon. The fish mixture has a chunky texture to help the patties keep their shape and stay moist.

Salmon Burgers with Creamy Tartar Sauce

ACTIVE 40 MIN. - TOTAL 40 MIN., PLUS 30 MIN. CHILLING

SERVES 4

- 2 Tbsp. finely chopped shallot (from 1 medium shallot)
- 2 tsp. Dijon mustard
- 1 lb. skinless salmon fillets, cut into ½-inch pieces, divided
- ¼ cup chopped capers, divided, plus 1 tsp. reserved brine (from 1 [2-oz.] jar)
- 2 Tbsp. finely chopped fresh dill, divided
- 2 Tbsp. finely chopped fresh tarragon, divided
- 2 tsp. grated lemon zest, plus 1 Tbsp. fresh juice (from 1 lemon), divided
- ¼ cup plain dry breadcrumbs
- 1 tsp. kosher salt, divided
- ½ tsp. black pepper, divided
- ½ cup mayonnaise
- 2 Tbsp. olive oil
- 4 brioche hamburger buns, toasted
- Toppings: shredded iceberg lettuce, beefsteak tomato slices

1. Place shallot, mustard, one-fourth (4 ounces) of the salmon, 1 tablespoon of the capers, 1 tablespoon of the dill, 1 tablespoon of the tarragon, and 1 teaspoon of the lemon zest in a food processor. Pulse until mixture is mostly smooth, 5 or 6 pulses, stopping to scrape down sides as needed using a spatula. Add remaining 12 ounces salmon to food processor; pulse until salmon is chopped into about ¼-inch pieces and well combined with pureed salmon mixture, 5 or 6 pulses.

2. Transfer mixture to a medium bowl. Add breadcrumbs, ¾ teaspoon of the salt, and ¼ teaspoon of the pepper; gently mix together using your hands. Divide mixture evenly into 4 (about 4-ounce) balls; shape each ball into a 4-inch-wide, ½-inch-thick patty. Arrange on a baking sheet lined with parchment paper. Cover with plastic wrap; chill 30 minutes.

3. Meanwhile, stir together mayonnaise, lemon juice, caper brine, and remaining 3 tablespoons capers, 1 tablespoon dill, 1 tablespoon tarragon, 1 teaspoon lemon zest, ¼ teaspoon salt, and ¼ teaspoon pepper in a small bowl. Cover and chill tartar sauce until ready to use.

4. Heat oil in a large skillet over medium-high. Add salmon patties. Cook until golden, crisp on top and bottom, and a thermometer inserted into thickest portion of patties registers 145°F, about 3 minutes per side. Serve patties on toasted buns with tartar sauce, lettuce, and tomato slices.

Good Morning, Honey

Start the day on a sweet note with fruit–and–nut muffins served with a flavored butter

Raspberry-Almond Muffins with Honey Butter

ACTIVE 15 MIN. - TOTAL 50 MIN.

MAKES 12

- 6 Tbsp. unsalted butter, melted
- 2 large eggs
- ½ cup whole buttermilk
- 1 tsp. vanilla extract
- ¾ cup honey, divided
- 1¾ cups all-purpose flour
- 1 cup almond flour
- ½ cup granulated sugar
- 1½ tsp. baking powder
- 1¼ tsp. kosher salt, divided
- 2 cups fresh raspberries, divided
- ¼ cup sliced almonds, finely chopped
- ½ cup unsalted butter, softened

1. Preheat oven to 350°F. Lightly grease a 12–cup muffin pan with cooking spray.

2. Whisk together melted butter, eggs, buttermilk, vanilla, and ½ cup of the honey in a large bowl until combined. Whisk together all–purpose flour, almond flour, sugar, baking powder, and 1 teaspoon of the salt in a medium bowl until combined. Gradually add flour mixture to butter mixture, stirring just until combined. Coarsely crush 1 cup of the raspberries in a small bowl. Fold crushed raspberries into batter. Spoon batter into prepared muffin cups. Top with almonds and remaining 1 cup raspberries.

3. Bake in preheated oven until a wooden pick inserted in center comes out clean, about 20 minutes. Cool muffins in pan 5 minutes. Transfer to a wire rack to cool slightly before serving, about 10 minutes.

4. Meanwhile, stir together softened butter and remaining ¼ cup honey and ¼ teaspoon salt until well combined. Serve warm muffins with honey butter.

Marvelous Mix–Ins

Use our basic honey butter recipe (Step 4) as a jumping–off point for creative spreads.

Berry Honey Butter

Omit salt; stir ½ cup chopped fresh berries into honey butter until combined.

Chai Honey Butter

Omit salt, and stir ¼ tsp. each ground cinnamon, cardamom, and ginger and a pinch of black pepper into honey butter until combined.

Orange-Vanilla Honey Butter

Stir ½ tsp. freshly grated orange zest and ½ tsp. vanilla bean paste into honey butter until combined.

A Spoonful of Summer

The taste of this fresh corn soup is as rich as its golden hue

Sweet-and-Spicy Corn Soup

ACTIVE 30 MIN. - TOTAL 30 MIN.
SERVES 4

- 8 ears fresh yellow corn, husked
- 2 bacon slices, chopped
- 1 Tbsp. olive oil
- 1½ cups chopped sweet onion (from 1 medium onion)
- 1 tsp. kosher salt, divided
- 2 garlic cloves, minced
- 1 (8-oz.) russet potato, peeled and cut into ½-inch cubes (about 1½ cups)
- 4 cups lower-sodium vegetable broth
- ½ cup whole milk
- 1 Tbsp. apple cider vinegar
- 1 tsp. Louisiana-style hot sauce (such as Crystal), plus more for serving
- ¼ cup plain whole-milk Greek yogurt
- 2 Tbsp. chopped fresh basil
- 1 Tbsp. chopped fresh chives
- ½ tsp. black pepper

MAKE IT MEATLESS
Skip the bacon, and use olive oil in place of the drippings.

1. Cut corn kernels off cobs onto a rimmed baking sheet. Using the back of a knife, scrape the corn milk and remaining pulp from cobs onto baking sheet. (You should have about 5 cups.) Reserve 3 cobs; discard remaining 5.

2. Cook bacon in a large Dutch oven over medium, stirring occasionally, until crisp, about 5 minutes. Transfer bacon to a plate lined with paper towels. Reserve 1 tablespoon drippings in Dutch oven; discard remaining drippings.

3. Add oil to drippings; heat over medium. Add onion and ½ teaspoon of the salt. Cook, stirring occasionally, until softened, about 5 minutes. Add garlic and potato. Cook, stirring occasionally, until potato is just starting to soften, about 2 minutes. Add vegetable broth, 4 cups corn kernels, and the reserved corn cobs to Dutch oven. Increase heat to medium–high; bring to a boil. Reduce heat to medium, and simmer until potato is tender, about 12 minutes. Remove from heat; discard cobs.

4. Pour soup into a blender. Secure lid on blender, and remove center piece to allow steam to escape. Place a clean towel over opening. Process until smooth, 30 to 45 seconds. Return mixture to Dutch oven, and stir in milk, vinegar, hot sauce, and remaining ½ teaspoon salt.

5. Divide soup among 4 bowls; top each with Greek yogurt, basil, chives, bacon, remaining 1 cup corn kernels, and pepper. Serve with additional hot sauce, if desired.

CALORIES: **385** – CARBS: **60G** – FAT: **14G**

How to Milk a Cob

Corn milk, the starchy, sweet liquid inside the cob, enhances the taste of the soup and adds creaminess without extra fat

STEP 1
Hold a shucked ear of corn upright on a rimmed baking sheet. Using a chef's knife, shave the kernels from the cob.

STEP 2
Using the back of the knife or a metal spoon, scrape all sides of the cob from top to bottom to remove the remaining bits of kernels and extract the milk. The cob will resemble an empty honeycomb.

Let It Marinate

Spice up happy hour with this make–ahead appetizer

Marinated Feta with Cherry Tomatoes

ACTIVE 10 MIN. · TOTAL 40 MIN.,
PLUS 6 HOURS CHILLING

SERVES 12

Cut 2 (3-inch) strips of orange peel from 1 **navel orange** using a vegetable peeler, and place in a large bowl. Squeeze juice from orange to equal 2 tablespoons, and add to bowl with orange peel strips. Add 2 thinly sliced **red Fresno chiles** (about ⅓ cup), 1 thinly sliced medium **shallot** (about ¼ cup), 2 minced **garlic cloves** (about 2 tsp.), 1 cup roughly chopped fresh **basil** leaves, ⅓ cup roughly chopped **fresh flat-leaf parsley**, 1 Tbsp. **red wine vinegar**, 2 tsp. **fresh thyme leaves**, ¼ tsp. **kosher salt**, and ¼ tsp. **black pepper**. Stir to combine. Add 1 lb. **feta cheese**, cut into ½-inch cubes (about 3 cups); gently toss to fully coat in herb mixture. Pour 2 cups **extra-virgin olive oil** over feta-and-herb mixture; stir gently to distribute and submerge mixture in oil. Cover with plastic wrap; chill 6 hours or up to overnight. Remove feta mixture from refrigerator, and let come to room temperature, about 30 minutes. Add 1 pt. halved **cherry tomatoes** (about 2 cups) to feta mixture; transfer to a serving bowl. Serve with toasted **baguette slices**.

CHANGE UP THE CHEESE

Goat cheese rounds

Sharp cheddar cubes

Fresh mozzarella balls

COOKING SCHOOL

Honey Dos (and Don'ts)

Helpful tips for cooking with this natural sweetener

NOTICE THE COLOR
Raw honey varies in appearance and flavor more than processed honey. Generally, darker kinds are richer and more robust. An exception: tupelo honey, which is pale gold and prized for its complex buttery, herbal, and floral taste.

AVOID WASTE
When measuring honey, coat spoons or cups with cooking spray so every bit of golden goodness will slide right off. (This makes cleaning up easier, too.)

TRY THE COMB
Yes, the honeycomb is edible—and delicious. Chop it to stir into oatmeal or yogurt. Serve on a cheese board with baguette slices. Sprinkle small chunks onto salads. Spread it over hot buttered toast or an English muffin.

WATCH THE TEMPERATURE
High heat, like that of a microwave, can lower the quality of honey. If honey has crystallized, place the closed jar in a saucepan of warm (not hot) water for a few minutes; then stir until it liquefies.

Southern Staple
Pure Southern Honey

Harvested in Georgia, this raw, unfiltered honey has a smooth consistency and lovely flavor from a mix of gallberry, tupelo, black gum, and palmetto flowers. The family-run company sells honey by the jar and the pound—even in 5-gallon buckets.
puresouthernhoney.com

A FEW FAVORITE WAYS TO ENJOY IT

LEMONADE
Make honey syrup by mixing together equal parts honey and warm water. Stir it into lemonade or any beverage you want to sweeten (including cocktails).

ROASTED VEGETABLES
Add flavor and caramelization by drizzling root vegetables with honey during the last 10 minutes of cooking.

BAKED GOODS
Use an equal amount of honey as a substitute for maple syrup or molasses in certain recipes, such as bar cookies, cakes, and quick breads.

July

Pretty as a Plum

Whether you go for purple-, black-, or red-skinned varieties, these stone fruits have
the ideal balance of sweet and tart, and they taste great cooked or raw

TANGY PLUM
POPS

Tangy Plum Pops

ACTIVE 20 MIN. - TOTAL 40 MIN.,
PLUS 4 HOURS FREEZING
MAKES 10

Bring 2½ cups **water**, 2 cups chopped
ripe, firm black or red plums, ⅔ cup
granulated sugar, and ½ cup **fresh
blueberries** to a boil in a medium
saucepan over medium-high. Reduce
heat to medium. Simmer, stirring
occasionally, until fruit is softened,
12 to 15 minutes. Transfer to a medium
bowl, and chill until cooled slightly,
about 20 minutes. Place plum mixture,
1 tsp. grated **lime zest**, and 2 Tbsp. **fresh
lime juice** in a blender. Process until
completely smooth, about 1 minute. Pour
mixture evenly into 10 (3-oz.) ice-pop
molds, and insert ice-pop sticks. Freeze
until solid, about 4 hours. To serve,
run the molds under warm water for
a few seconds, and gently pull pops
from molds.

Sparkling Plum Punch

ACTIVE 25 MIN. - TOTAL 25 MIN.,
PLUS 1 HOUR, 30 MIN. CHILLING
SERVES 6

Cut 4 **ripe, firm black or red plums**
into ½-inch slices, and chill until ready
to serve. Cut 4 **ripe, firm black or red
plums** into small cubes, and place in
a medium saucepan. Add 1 cup each
granulated sugar and **water.** Bring to a
simmer over medium. Simmer, stirring
occasionally, until plums are tender,
about 10 minutes. Pour plum mixture
through a fine-mesh strainer into a
medium bowl; discard solids. Cover;
chill syrup 30 minutes. Stir together
plum syrup, reserved plum slices, ¼ cup
fresh lemon juice, and 5 cups **water**
in a large **ice**-filled container. Chill at
least 1 hour or up to overnight. Ladle
or pour chilled punch and fruit into
glasses; top each with ¼ cup **sparkling
cranberry juice.**

PUNCH IT UP
This big-batch nonalcoholic drink is refreshing as is, or you can stir in 1 cup vodka.

SPARKLING
PLUM PUNCH

Spiced Plum Compote

ACTIVE 30 MIN. - TOTAL 30 MIN.

SERVES 8

Bring 1½ cups **water**, ⅔ cup packed **brown sugar**, 1 tsp. grated **fresh ginger**, 3 **whole cloves**, and 1 **cinnamon stick** to a boil in a medium saucepan over medium-high. Cook until sugar has dissolved and mixture thickens, about 5 minutes. Remove and discard cinnamon stick and cloves. Cut 6 **ripe, firm red or black plums** into ½-inch slices; add to pan. Return to a boil over medium-high; reduce heat to medium. Simmer, stirring occasionally, until plums are tender but hold their shape, 10 to 12 minutes. Using a slotted spoon, transfer plums to a bowl. Continue to simmer sauce until syrupy, 8 minutes more. Remove from heat; stir in ⅛ tsp. **kosher salt.** Add sauce to plums. Serve chilled with yogurt and granola.

LEMON-LIME POKE CAKE

Lemon Lime Love

These refreshingly tart and tangy desserts are made for summer

Lemon-Lime Poke Cake

ACTIVE 15 MIN. - TOTAL 40 MIN., PLUS 1 HOUR
COOLING AND 1 HOUR CHILLING

SERVES 15

Baking spray with flour
- 1 (15.25-oz.) pkg. white cake mix (such as Duncan Hines)
- 4 large eggs
- 4 Tbsp. canola oil
- 1 tsp. grated lemon zest (from 1 lemon)
- 1 tsp. grated lime zest (from 1 lime)
- 1⅓ cups whole buttermilk, divided
- 1 (14-oz.) can sweetened condensed milk
- ¼ cup fresh lemon juice (from 2 lemons)
- ¼ cup fresh lime juice (from 2 large limes)
- 1½ (8-oz.) containers frozen whipped topping, thawed
- Lemon and lime slices, for garnish

1. Preheat oven to 350°F. Grease a 13- x 9-inch baking pan with baking spray.
2. Beat cake mix, eggs, oil, lemon and lime zests, and 1 cup of the buttermilk in a large bowl with an electric mixer on medium speed 2 minutes. Pour into prepared pan.
3. Bake in preheated oven until a wooden pick inserted in center comes out clean, 25 to 28 minutes.
4. Meanwhile, whisk together sweetened condensed milk, lemon and lime juices, and remaining ⅓ cup buttermilk until smooth. While the cake is still warm and using the round handle of a wooden spoon, poke holes all over top of cake, about 1½ inches apart. Pour condensed milk mixture over cake, spreading evenly over top with a spatula. Cool until room temperature, about 1 hour.
5. Spread whipped topping over top. Refrigerate until chilled, about 1 hour. Garnish with lemon and lime slices, if desired. Cake can be stored, covered, without whipped topping, in the refrigerator up to 3 days. Spread with whipped topping just before serving.

Coconut-Lime Cupcakes

(Photo, page 157)

ACTIVE 25 MIN. - TOTAL 40 MIN.
PLUS 25 MIN. COOLING

SERVES 24

CUPCAKES
- 2¾ cups bleached cake flour
- 1 tsp. baking powder
- 1 tsp. kosher salt
- 1½ cups granulated sugar
- ¾ cup unsalted butter, softened
- 3 large eggs
- 1 cup well-shaken and stirred unsweetened coconut milk
- 1 Tbsp. grated lime zest, plus 2 Tbsp. fresh juice (from 2 limes)

FROSTING
- 6 Tbsp. unsalted butter, softened
- 6 oz. cream cheese, at room temperature
- 3 Tbsp. well-shaken and stirred unsweetened coconut milk
- 1½ Tbsp. fresh lime juice (from 1 lime)
- 3¾ cups powdered sugar
- Toasted sweetened shredded coconut and lime slices, for garnish

1. Prepare the Cupcakes: Preheat oven to 350°F. Place paper baking cups in 2 (12-cup) muffin pans, and coat with cooking spray. Stir together flour, baking powder, and salt in a medium bowl; set aside.
2. Beat sugar and butter in bowl of a stand mixer fitted with a paddle attachment on medium speed until light and fluffy, about 4 minutes. Add eggs, 1 at a time, beating well after each addition. Add flour mixture alternately with coconut milk, lime zest, and lime juice, beginning and ending with flour mixture, beating on low speed just until blended after each addition. Beat on low speed 1 minute. Spoon batter into baking cups, filling two-thirds full.
3. Bake in preheated oven until a wooden pick inserted in center comes out clean, 18 to 20 minutes. Cool in pans on wire racks 5 minutes. Remove Cupcakes from pans to wire racks, and cool completely, about 20 minutes.
4. Meanwhile, prepare the Frosting: Beat butter and cream cheese in a large bowl with an electric mixer on medium-high speed until smooth, about 2 minutes, scraping down sides of bowl, if needed. Add coconut milk and lime juice, and beat on low speed just until combined, about 1 minute. With mixer running on low speed, gradually add powdered sugar until combined. Increase speed to high, and beat until fluffy, about 2 minutes.
5. Spoon Frosting into a zip-top plastic bag. Snip one corner of bag to make a small hole, and swirl on cooled Cupcakes. Or spread Frosting evenly over cooled Cupcakes. Garnish with toasted sweetened shredded coconut and lime slices, if desired.

NO-CHURN KEY LIME PIE
ICE CREAM (PAGE 159)

COCONUT-LIME
CUPCAKES (PAGE 155)

Meyer Lemon Cheesecake Bars

ACTIVE 20 MIN. - TOTAL 1 HOUR, PLUS 5 HOURS
CHILLING AND 1 HOUR, 5 MIN. COOLING

SERVES 16

CURD

- ⅓ cup fresh Meyer lemon juice (from 2 large Meyer lemons)
- ⅓ cup granulated sugar
- 2 large eggs
- 4 Tbsp. unsalted butter, cubed
- 2 tsp. grated Meyer lemon zest (from 1 Meyer lemon)

CRUST

- 2½ cups graham cracker crumbs
- ½ cup unsalted butter, melted
- 3 Tbsp. granulated sugar

FILLING

- 3 (8-oz.) pkg. cream cheese, at room temperature
- 1½ cups granulated sugar
- ⅓ cup sour cream
- 4 large eggs
- 2 tsp. vanilla extract

1. Prepare the Curd: Whisk together lemon juice, sugar, and eggs in a saucepan. Cook over medium-low, whisking constantly, until slightly thickened, about 3 minutes. Add butter a few cubes at a time, and cook, whisking constantly, until melted before adding more butter. Continue cooking, whisking constantly, until Curd is smooth and coats the back of a spoon, about 2 minutes. Pour through a fine-mesh strainer into a heatproof bowl; discard solids. Stir in zest, and chill 1 hour.
2. Meanwhile, prepare the Crust: Preheat oven to 350°F. Line a 13- x 9-inch baking pan with parchment paper, leaving a 2-inch overhang on all sides. Stir together crumbs, melted butter, and sugar in a medium bowl until combined. Press on bottom and ½ inch up sides of prepared pan. Bake until Crust begins to brown, about 10 minutes. Transfer to a wire rack to cool slightly, about 15 minutes. Reduce oven temperature to 325°F.
3. Meanwhile, prepare the Filling: Beat cream cheese and sugar in the bowl of a stand mixer fitted with a paddle attachment on medium speed until smooth, about 2 minutes, scraping down sides as needed. Add sour cream, eggs, and vanilla, beating on medium speed until smooth, about 2 minutes. Pour cream cheese mixture over Crust. Using a tablespoon, dollop chilled Curd on top; swirl Curd into mixture using the tip of a knife.
4. Bake at 325°F until Filling is almost set but jiggles slightly in center, 35 to 40 minutes. Transfer to a wire rack, and cool 1 hour. Refrigerate until well chilled, about 4 hours. Using the parchment paper overhang, lift cheesecake out of pan. Cut into 16 (2¼- x 3¼-inch) bars, and serve.

No-Churn Key Lime Pie Ice Cream

(Photo, page 156)

ACTIVE 15 MIN. - TOTAL 15 MIN.,
PLUS 6 HOURS CHILLING

MAKES ABOUT 1 QT. / SERVES 8

- 4 graham cracker sheets, coarsely crumbled
- 2 Tbsp. unsalted butter, melted
- 2 tsp. granulated sugar
- 1 (14-oz.) can sweetened condensed milk
- 1 Tbsp. grated Key lime zest (from 4 Key limes)
- ⅓ cup fresh Key lime juice (from 5 to 6 Key limes, or use bottled juice, such as Nellie & Joe's)
- 1 tsp. vanilla extract
- ¼ tsp. kosher salt
- 2 cups heavy whipping cream

1. Stir together graham cracker crumbs, melted butter, and sugar in a medium bowl; set 1 tablespoon graham cracker mixture aside.
2. Stir together condensed milk, lime zest and juice, vanilla, and salt in a large bowl; set aside. Beat cream in a separate large bowl with an electric mixer fitted with a whisk attachment on high speed until stiff peaks form, 2 minutes. Fold whipped cream and remaining graham cracker mixture in bowl into condensed milk mixture.
3. Spoon into a 9- x 5-inch loaf pan. Sprinkle with reserved 1 tablespoon graham cracker mixture. Cover; freeze until firm, about 6 hours.

The Lowdown on Lemons and Limes

Lemons

Regular lemons (usually Eureka or Lisbon varieties) are more acidic and tart than Meyer lemons. That boldness is good for balancing rich, strongly flavored dishes, such as roast chicken and grilled salmon.

Meyer Lemons

A cross between regular lemons and mandarin oranges, this fruit has orangish skin, a heady floral aroma, and a slightly sweet taste. Use the juice and zest in recipes where it can really shine, like drinks, dairy-based desserts, and lemon curd.

Persian Limes

Bright green and about the size of a golf ball, Persian limes are easy to find at the grocery store. They have a balanced acidity that's ideal to add a pop of brightness to a dish like guacamole. Their juiciness also makes them ideal for cocktails.

Key Limes

These are smaller with yellowish skin and an astringent flavor that works best in very sweet desserts like Key lime pie. The fresh fruit doesn't produce much juice. Nellie & Joe's brand is a good bottled version.

A Word About "That Pie"

North Carolina chef Bill Smith had no idea that a dessert from his childhood would become an overnight sensation.

GROWING UP in eastern North Carolina in the 1950s, we were taught that if you ate dessert after a seafood dinner, you would die (just like swimming after lunch). No explanation—in those days, you believed what your elders told you. For some reason, the one exception to this rule was lemon pie, so all of the restaurants in the beach towns along our coast had that on the menu. Their crusts were often made of cracker crumbs (saltines, Ritz, or Captain's Wafers). They were all good—and you never found this dessert anywhere else. I loved this pie, then forgot about it for 40 years. By then, I was the chef at Crook's Corner in Chapel Hill.

In June of 2012, the Southern Foodways Alliance invited its membership to a field trip in my hometown of New Bern. Wood-cooked whole-hog barbecue is the most famous food to come from those parts, but they wanted to showcase all kinds of local specialties. I worked with Cindy and Sam McGann from the wonderful Blue Point restaurant in Duck, North Carolina, to put on a coastal supper in the gazebo at Union Point Park on the banks of the Neuse River. Corned-ham biscuits, fish muddle, hard-crab stew, and lemon pie were on the menu. I cobbled together a recipe for the pie using mostly old church and community cookbooks. The evening was a success and ended with my sisters, nieces, and their friends dancing around me dressed in crab costumes. These are grown women. A video of this pops up, unbidden, on Facebook every six months or so.

The pie was as good as I had remembered—and, best of all, easy—so I put it on the menu at Crook's. I had to call it something, so sort of offhandedly, I chose the name of one of our closest beach towns, Atlantic Beach. Enter food writer and cookbook author Katie Workman. She came in for dinner right afterward and liked it so much that she arranged for us to record a piece for NPR's *All Things Considered* called "A North Carolina Pie that Elicits an 'Oh My God' Response."

As luck would have it, the night the segment aired, I was back in Duck with Sam and Cindy, photographing a magazine piece about the food of coastal North Carolina. My phone started ringing. At the restaurant, there was a line of people at the door, and we were about to run out of pie. That was a prediction of my future. Soon enough, I was hearing things like: "The event is in a field about 10 miles outside town. There really isn't any refrigeration to speak of. We'll need about 80 slices," and "There are some ovens in that tent over there. We're expecting about 700 people." And that was before the rest of the press even caught on.

Of course, I'm sort of flattered. But it never quite dies down, and there are factions. The summer before the pandemic, I was challenged to a baking contest by cooks out on Harkers Island, North Carolina, to benefit the Core Sound Waterfowl Museum & Heritage Center. You see, they use Ritz crackers and meringue. I use saltines and whipped cream. Being ladies and gentlemen, we agreed that the result was a tie.

I don't remember when I started calling it "that stupid pie," but today it awaits me at every turn. It's really good, and anyone can make it—so they do. Bringing it to the table guarantees plenty of praise and compliments. I just stand back and watch.

Atlantic Beach Pie

Our Test Kitchen's version of Smith's beloved recipe

ACTIVE 15 MIN. · TOTAL 1 HOUR, PLUS 1 HOUR, 10 MIN. COOLING AND 2 HOURS CHILLING

SERVES 8

- 1½ cups finely crushed saltine crackers (from 1 sleeve, about 37 crackers)
- 6 Tbsp. unsalted butter, melted
- 3 Tbsp. granulated sugar
- 1 large egg white, lightly beaten
- 1 (14-oz.) can sweetened condensed milk
- 4 large egg yolks
- ¼ cup fresh lime juice (from 2 large limes)
- ¼ cup fresh lemon juice (from 2 lemons)
- 1½ cups heavy whipping cream
- ¼ cup powdered sugar
- Lemon and lime zests, for garnish

1. Preheat oven to 350°F. Stir together crushed crackers, melted butter, sugar, and egg white in a medium bowl until combined. Transfer mixture to a 9-inch glass pie plate; firmly press to form a crust on bottom and sides. Freeze 10 minutes.

2. Bake in preheated oven until crust is lightly browned, about 20 minutes. Transfer to a wire rack; cool slightly, about 10 minutes.

3. Meanwhile, whisk together condensed milk and egg yolks until smooth. Whisk in lime juice and lemon juice until combined. Pour juice mixture into warm crust.

4. Bake at 350°F until center is just set, about 15 minutes. Transfer to a wire rack; cool 1 hour. Refrigerate until chilled, about 2 hours.

5. Beat cream and powdered sugar in a large bowl with an electric mixer on high speed until stiff peaks form, about 2 minutes. Spread whipped cream topping over chilled pie, leaving about a ½-inch border of custard showing around crust. Garnish with lemon and lime zests, if desired. Pie can be stored, covered, without whipped cream topping, in the refrigerator up to 4 days. Spread with topping just before serving.

The New Southern Veggie Plate

It's the best time of the year to make a meal of fantastic finds from the farmers market

Cucumber-and-Vidalia Onion Salad

Buttered Corn on the Cob with Creole Seasoning

CREAMED NEW POTATOES

FIELD PEA SALAD WITH TOMATOES AND FETA

SUMMERTIME is an opportunity to visit enticing farmers markets and produce stands to pick up fresh, seasonal, and local foods, and to discover new varieties and tastes. Peak-season produce usually has admirers who crave at least one favorite food and are eager to relive that taste. One benefit of most in-season foods is that they are typically easy to prepare–keeping prep simple to highlight taste, texture, color, and shape.

With summer produce, it's easy to assemble a platter of what's abundant, aiming for a combination of at least three veggies. From tender and creamy new potatoes, sweet and juicey corn, crisp cucumbers, zesty onions, petite tomato globes, just-picked peas and beans, and more–you'll find in-season produce that will add healthful complements to summertime dining.

Creamed New Potatoes

Not quite mashed or smashed, but something in between. It's okay to be a little rough when stirring the potatoes into the white sauce to break them down a bit.

ACTIVE 20 MIN. - TOTAL 35 MIN.

SERVES 6

- 2 lb. red new potatoes, quartered (about 6 cups)
- 2 Tbsp. unsalted butter
- 1 Tbsp. all-purpose flour
- 1 cup whole milk
- ¾ tsp. black pepper
- ½ tsp. kosher salt
- 2 Tbsp. chopped fresh chives

1. Place potatoes in a large saucepan; cover with salted cold water by 1 inch. Bring to a boil over high. Reduce heat to medium; simmer until potatoes are tender, about 15 minutes. Drain.
2. Add butter to saucepan, and melt over medium. Whisk in flour; cook, whisking constantly, 1 minute. Gradually whisk in milk. Bring to a boil over medium, whisking occasionally. Boil, whisking occasionally, until slightly thickened, about 2 minutes. Stir in pepper and salt. Add potatoes. Cook, stirring constantly,

until potatoes start to break apart and mixture is thickened, about 2 minutes. Sprinkle with chives.

Field Pea Salad with Tomatoes and Feta

Lady peas are creamy, tender, and less starchy than other varieties of field peas. They also have a mild earthiness that's just delicious. When lady peas aren't available, though, other varieties easily take their place in this recipe.

ACTIVE 45 MIN. - TOTAL 1 HOUR

SERVES 6

- 1 Tbsp. unsalted butter
- 1 small onion, finely chopped (about 1 cup)
- 1 lb. shelled fresh lady peas or purple hull peas (about 4 cups)
- 1 dried bay leaf
- 1 tsp. kosher salt, divided
- ¾ tsp. black pepper, divided
- 3 Tbsp. extra-virgin olive oil
- 2 Tbsp. minced shallot (from 1 [2-oz.] shallot)
- 1 Tbsp. whole-grain Dijon mustard
- 2 tsp. chopped fresh thyme
- 1 tsp. grated lemon zest, plus 2 Tbsp. fresh juice (from 1 lemon)
- 1 pt. cherry tomatoes, halved
- ⅓ cup chopped fresh flat-leaf parsley
- 2 oz. feta cheese, crumbled (about ½ cup)

1. Melt butter in a large saucepan over medium-high. Add onion; cook, stirring occasionally, 5 minutes. Stir in peas, 2 cups water, bay leaf, ¾ teaspoon of the salt, and ½ teaspoon of the pepper. Bring water to a boil over medium-high. Cover and reduce heat to medium. Cook, stirring occasionally, until peas are tender, about 30 minutes. Remove from heat; let stand 10 minutes. Drain; remove and discard bay leaf.
2. Whisk together oil, shallot, mustard, thyme, lemon zest and juice, and remaining ¼ teaspoon each salt and pepper in a large bowl. Add pea mixture, tomatoes, and parsley; toss gently to combine. Sprinkle with cheese. Serve warm or at room temperature.

No-Fuss Veggie Sides

Round out plates with recipes fresh and colorful

Cabbage
Top boiled cabbage wedges with fresh thyme leaves and scallions.

Corn
Spread boiled corn with butter; sprinkle with Creole seasoning blend.

Cucumbers
Toss sliced, seasoned cucumbers and Vidalia onion in rice vinegar.

Okra
Roast halved, seasoned okra pods.

Lima Beans
Mix cooked lima beans with butter and roasted red peppers.

One-Pot Fresh Corn Mac and Cheese

Fresh corn kernels add a sweet crunch to every bite of this mac and cheese. The one-pot method yields tender pasta and a creamy sauce with minimal effort.

ACTIVE 25 MIN. - TOTAL 30 MIN.

SERVES 6

- 4 Tbsp. unsalted butter, divided
- 3 cups fresh corn kernels (about 2 large ears)
- ⅔ cup sliced scallions (from 1 bunch)
- 1¼ tsp. kosher salt, divided
- 1 cup finely chopped Vidalia onion (from 1 small onion)
- 8 oz. uncooked large elbow macaroni
- ½ cup whole milk
- ½ tsp. black pepper
- 8 oz. Colby Jack cheese, shredded (about 2 cups)

1. Melt 2 tablespoons of the butter in a large high-sided skillet over medium-high. Add corn, scallions, and ½ teaspoon of the salt. Cook, stirring occasionally, 2 minutes. Remove mixture from skillet, and set aside. Do not wipe skillet clean.
2. Add remaining 2 tablespoons butter to skillet, and melt over medium-high. Add onion; cook, stirring occasionally, 3 minutes. Add macaroni, 2¼ cups water, and ½ teaspoon of the salt. Bring to a boil over medium-high. Cover and reduce heat to medium. Cook, stirring occasionally, until liquid is almost fully absorbed and pasta is tender, about 7 minutes. Stir in corn mixture and remaining ¼ teaspoon salt; cook, stirring occasionally, 1 minute.
3. Remove skillet from heat. Add milk and pepper; stir until combined. Gradually stir in cheese until smooth.

Smoky Pole Beans and Tomatoes

Flat pole beans (or Romano beans) have a meatier texture than regular green beans. They also take more time to cook, so be sure to blanch them long enough.

ACTIVE 30 MIN. - TOTAL 40 MIN.

SERVES 6

- 3 Tbsp., plus ¾ tsp. kosher salt, divided
- 1½ lb. fresh flat pole beans or Romano beans, trimmed and snapped into 3- to 4-inch pieces (about 6 cups)
- 3 bacon slices, cut into 1-inch pieces (about ½ cup)
- ½ tsp. ground cumin
- ½ tsp. black pepper
- 1 Tbsp. canola oil
- 1 pt. cherry tomatoes
- 2 garlic cloves, thinly sliced (about 1½ tsp.)
- ¼ tsp. smoked paprika

1. Bring 8 cups water and 3 tablespoons of the salt to a boil in a large pot over medium-high. Add beans; cook until almost tender, 5 to 7 minutes. Drain. Rinse with cold water; drain well.
2. Cook bacon pieces in a large skillet over medium, stirring occasionally, until crisp, about 12 minutes. Remove bacon from skillet using a slotted spoon, and drain on a plate lined with paper towels. Reserve drippings in skillet. Add cumin and pepper to drippings. Cook over medium, stirring constantly, 30 seconds. Add drained beans and ½ teaspoon of the salt; toss gently to coat. Increase heat to high. Cook, stirring occasionally, until beans begin to char, about 5 minutes. Spoon beans into a bowl or onto a platter. Do not wipe skillet clean.
3. Reduce heat under skillet to medium-high. Add oil, and swirl skillet to coat. Add tomatoes, garlic, smoked paprika, and remaining ¼ teaspoon salt. Cook, stirring often, until tomatoes begin to burst, 3 to 4 minutes. Spoon mixture over beans. Sprinkle with reserved bacon, and serve.

Roasted Okra

Boiled cabbage with scallions and thyme

ONE-POT FRESH CORN MAC AND CHEESE

SMOKY POLE BEANS AND TOMATOES

Easiest Balsamic Pickled Beets

The beets cook quickly in the pickling liquid, becoming tender and tangy to serve as soon as they cool.

ACTIVE 10 MIN. - TOTAL 30 MIN., PLUS 45 MIN. COOLING

SERVES 6

- ¾ cup white balsamic vinegar
- 3 Tbsp. granulated sugar
- 1½ tsp. kosher salt
- 1 fresh tarragon sprig
- 1 lb. trimmed red beets (about 3 medium-large beets), peeled and cut into ¼-inch wedges (about 4 cups)
- 1 medium shallot, thinly sliced (about ⅓ cup)

1. Stir together vinegar, ⅔ cup water, the sugar, salt, and tarragon in a small saucepan; bring to a boil over medium-high. Stir in beets and shallot. Cover and reduce heat to medium. Cook until beets are tender when pierced with a knife, 15 to 20 minutes.

2. Remove from heat. Uncover and let cool to room temperature, about 45 minutes. Store in an airtight container in refrigerator up to 2 weeks. Serve using a slotted spoon.

Summer Squash Gratin

This light dish features young and tender summer squashes that have fewer seeds. The buttery, cheesy breadcrumb topping makes it company-ready.

ACTIVE 30 MIN. - TOTAL 30 MIN.

SERVES 6

- 3 garlic cloves
- 4 Tbsp. unsalted butter, divided
- 1½ cups thinly sliced Vidalia onion (from 1 small onion)
- 1 lb. yellow squash, sliced ¼ inch thick (about 4 cups)
- 1 lb. zucchini, sliced ¼ inch thick (about 4 cups)
- 2 tsp. chopped fresh thyme
- ½ tsp. black pepper
- 1 tsp. kosher salt, divided
- ½ cup panko breadcrumbs
- 2 oz. Parmesan cheese, grated (about ½ cup)

1. Preheat oven to broil with rack 6 inches from heat source. Mince 2 of the garlic cloves, and set aside. Grate remaining garlic clove; set aside separately.

2. Melt 2 tablespoons of the butter in a 10-inch cast-iron skillet over medium. Add onion. Cook, stirring occasionally, until starting to soften, about 3 minutes. Stir in squash, zucchini, thyme, and reserved minced garlic. Increase heat to medium-high. Cover and cook until mixture starts to soften, about 6 minutes, stirring once halfway through cook time. Uncover and cook, stirring occasionally, until mixture is tender, about 6 minutes. Stir in pepper and ¾ teaspoon of the salt. Remove from heat.

3. Microwave remaining 2 tablespoons butter in a small microwavable bowl on HIGH until melted, about 30 seconds. Add panko, cheese, reserved grated garlic, and remaining ¼ teaspoon salt; stir together until combined. Sprinkle evenly over squash mixture. Broil in preheated oven until topping is browned and crisp, 1 to 2 minutes.

EASIEST BALSAMIC PICKLED BEETS

SUMMER SQUASH GRATIN

Buttered lima beans with roasted red peppers

Sliced tomatoes with salt and pepper

Garden to Grill

Throw some peak-season vegetables on the fire for these tasty weeknight dinners

Southern-Style Grilled Cobb Salad

ACTIVE 30 MIN. - TOTAL 35 MIN.
SERVES 4

- 3 Tbsp. red wine vinegar
- 1 Tbsp. Dijon mustard
- 3½ tsp. kosher salt, divided
- ⅓ cup, plus 2 Tbsp. olive oil, divided
- 2 ears fresh corn, shucked
- 4 oz. fresh okra, sliced in half lengthwise
- 1½ lb. boneless, skinless chicken breasts
- ½ tsp. black pepper, divided
- 4 thick-cut bacon slices
- 2 large (12 to 16 oz. each) heads red leaf or green leaf lettuce
- 1 lb. small heirloom tomatoes, cored and cut into ½-inch-thick slices
- 3 oz. aged cheddar cheese, crumbled into small pieces (about ¾ cup)

1. Preheat grill to medium-high (400°F to 450°F) with an oiled metal grilling basket positioned on 1 side of grill grates. For the dressing, whisk together vinegar, mustard, and 1 teaspoon of the salt in a small bowl until combined. Slowly add ⅓ cup of the oil, whisking constantly to combine. Set aside.

2. Place corn and okra on half of a rimmed baking sheet lined with aluminum foil. Drizzle with 1 tablespoon of the oil, then sprinkle with 1 teaspoon of the salt; transfer okra to a grilling basket and set aside. Add chicken to opposite half of baking sheet; brush with remaining 1 tablespoon oil, and sprinkle with 1 teaspoon of the salt and ¼ teaspoon of the pepper.

3. Place bacon slices on unoiled grates. Place grilling basket on grill. Grill, covered, until bacon is lightly charred, crisp, and cooked through and okra is softened and charred, 2 to 3 minutes per side. Remove bacon and grilling basket from grill. Add corn and chicken to grates. Grill, covered, until corn and chicken are lightly charred and a thermometer inserted into thickest portion of chicken registers 165°F, 12 to 16 minutes, turning corn occasionally and turning chicken once. Remove corn and chicken from grill; cool 5 minutes.

4. Chop chicken into 1-inch pieces. Cut corn kernels from cobs; discard cobs. Cut bacon into ½-inch pieces. Tear lettuce into 2-inch pieces; place in a large bowl or on a serving platter. Add dressing, okra, bacon, chicken, corn, tomatoes, cheese, and remaining ½ teaspoon salt and ¼ teaspoon pepper; toss to combine.

Rigatoni with Grilled Veggies and Mozzarella

ACTIVE 30 MIN. - TOTAL 40 MIN.

SERVES 6

- 1 large (about 1½ lb.) eggplant, cut crosswise into ¾-inch-thick rounds
- 7 Tbsp. olive oil, divided
- 2 Tbsp. kosher salt, divided
- 2¼ lb. vine-ripened tomatoes, halved lengthwise through stems
- 1 lb. uncooked rigatoni pasta
- 3 Tbsp. capers
- 2 Tbsp. red wine vinegar
- 2 Tbsp. chopped fresh flat-leaf parsley
- 2 garlic cloves, minced (about 1 Tbsp.)
- 1 (8-oz.) container small mozzarella cheese balls, drained, cheese roughly torn in half
- ½ cup loosely packed small fresh basil leaves, plus more for garnish

1. Preheat grill to medium–high (400°F to 450°F). Arrange eggplant rounds on a large baking sheet; drizzle evenly on both sides with 3 tablespoons of the oil, and sprinkle with 1 tablespoon of the salt. Move eggplant to opposite side of baking sheet. Place tomato halves on other half of baking sheet; drizzle evenly with 1 tablespoon of the oil, and sprinkle with 1 teaspoon of the salt.

2. Place eggplant on unoiled grates. Grill, covered, until charred and softened, about 3 minutes per side. Remove from grill; set aside. Add tomato halves, cut-side down, to grates. Grill, covered and undisturbed, until charred and softened slightly, 3 to 4 minutes. Remove from grill, and cool 5 minutes. Peel off and discard tomato skins. Cut tomato pieces into quarters; cut eggplant rounds into quarters.

3. Bring a large pot of water to a boil over high. Add pasta, and cook according to package directions.

4. Meanwhile, stir together capers, red wine vinegar, parsley, garlic, 1 teaspoon of the salt, and remaining 3 tablespoons oil in a medium bowl to combine; set aside.

5. Drain cooked pasta, reserving ¼ cup cooking water. Return pasta to pot. Gently stir in eggplant, tomatoes, mozzarella, basil, caper mixture, and remaining 1 teaspoon salt. Stir in reserved cooking water, 1 tablespoon at a time, as needed until desired consistency. Sprinkle pasta with additional basil.

Spiced Chicken and Veggie Kebabs with Grilled Pita Bread

ACTIVE 30 MIN. · TOTAL 30 MIN.

SERVES 4

- 1 Tbsp. tomato paste
- 2 tsp. ground coriander
- 4 Tbsp. olive oil, divided
- 4 tsp. kosher salt, divided
- 2 lb. boneless, skinless chicken thighs, cut crosswise into 1-inch strips
- 1 cup plain whole-milk Greek yogurt
- ¼ cup chopped fresh mint
- 1 pt. (10 oz.) cherry tomatoes
- 1 medium-size red onion, cut into 1-inch wedges
- 4 (6-inch) pita bread rounds

1. Whisk together tomato paste, ground coriander, 3 tablespoons of the oil, and 2 teaspoons of the salt in a medium bowl until combined. Add chicken; toss until evenly coated. Set aside.

2. Preheat grill to medium (350°F to 400°F). Stir together yogurt, mint, and 1 teaspoon of the salt in a medium bowl until combined. Chill until ready to serve.

3. Thread tomatoes and onion wedges alternately onto 4 (8-inch-long) skewers. Thread chicken onto 4 separate skewers. Discard remaining marinade. Arrange chicken kebabs on half a baking sheet lined with aluminum foil; arrange vegetable kebabs on opposite half. Drizzle vegetables with remaining 1 tablespoon oil; sprinkle with remaining 1 teaspoon salt.

4. Place chicken kebabs on well-oiled grill grates. Grill, covered, until lightly charred and a thermometer inserted into thickest portion of meat registers 165°F, 12 to 15 minutes, rotating halfway through cook time. Remove from grill. Add vegetable kebabs to grates. Grill, covered, until charred and some tomatoes have burst, 3 to 4 minutes per side. Remove from grill.

5. Wrap pita tightly in aluminum foil. Place on grates; grill until warmed, 2 minutes.

6. Serve pitas and kebabs with yogurt sauce.

Grilled Pork-and-Peach Salad with Honey-Mustard Dressing

ACTIVE 40 MIN. · TOTAL 45 MIN.

SERVES 4

- 1 (1½-lb.) pork tenderloin, silver skin removed
- 1 Tbsp. barbecue seasoning (such as Bone Suckin' Seasoning & Rub or Stubb's BBQ Rub)
- 3½ tsp. kosher salt, divided
- ¼ cup, plus 5 Tbsp. olive oil, divided
- 3 medium peaches, unpeeled, halved, and pitted
- 1 small Vidalia onion, halved lengthwise through stem end
- 5 oz. baguette (from 1 [10-oz.] baguette), cut into ¼-inch slices
- 2 Tbsp. apple cider vinegar
- 1 Tbsp. Dijon mustard
- 1 Tbsp. stone-ground mustard
- 1 Tbsp. honey
- 2 (5-oz.) containers baby arugula

1. Preheat a grill to medium-high (400°F to 450°F). Pat pork dry with paper towels. Sprinkle all over with barbecue seasoning and 2 teaspoons of the salt; rub with 1 tablespoon of the oil. Set aside.
2. Line a baking sheet with aluminum foil. Toss together peaches, onion, and 2 tablespoons of the oil on prepared baking sheet; push mixture to half of baking sheet. Place baguette slices on opposite half. Brush bread evenly on both sides with 2 tablespoons of the oil; sprinkle with 1 teaspoon of the salt.
3. Arrange peaches and onion, cut-sides down, on one section of oiled grill grates. Arrange baguette slices on separate section of oiled grates; grill bread, uncovered, until toasted and crisp, 1 to 2 minutes per side. Remove from grill. Grill peaches and onion, uncovered and undisturbed, until charred and slightly softened, 3 to 4 minutes. Remove from grill. Let peaches cool 5 minutes; slice into 1-inch wedges. Set aside.
4. Reduce heat on one side of grill to low (250°F to 300°F); keep opposite side at medium-high (400°F to 450°F). Place pork on grates over medium-high heat. Grill, uncovered, until browned on all sides, turning occasionally, 6 to 8 minutes. Move pork to grates over low heat; add onion, cut-sides down, to grates over low heat. Grill, covered and undisturbed, until onion is softened and a thermometer inserted into thickest portion of pork registers 140°F, about 12 minutes. Remove onion and pork from grill; cool 10 minutes.
5. Meanwhile, whisk together vinegar, Dijon, stone-ground mustard, and honey in a large bowl until combined. Slowly whisk in remaining ¼ cup oil.
6. Thinly slice pork. Remove and discard onion cores; cut onion into 1-inch wedges. Add arugula and remaining ½ teaspoon salt to salad dressing bowl; toss to coat. Arrange arugula mixture on plates; top with pork, peaches, and onion. Tear grilled baguette slices and add to salad before serving.

Grilled Shrimp and Squash Kebabs with Herbed Couscous

ACTIVE 25 MIN. - TOTAL 35 MIN.

SERVES 4

- 2 cups uncooked Israeli couscous
- 4 Tbsp. extra-virgin olive oil, divided
- 24 jumbo peeled, deveined raw shrimp, tail on (about 1½ lb.)
- ½ tsp. black pepper
- 3½ tsp. kosher salt, divided, plus more for salting water
- 4 small (1 lb. total) zucchini and/or summer squash, halved lengthwise and cut into 2-inch pieces
- 3 oz. feta cheese, crumbled (about ¾ cup)
- ½ cup chopped pitted Castelvetrano olives
- ¼ cup chopped fresh flat-leaf parsley
- 3 Tbsp. chopped fresh dill
- 2 Tbsp. fresh lemon juice (from 1 lemon)
- 1 lemon, cut into 6 wedges

1. Preheat grill to medium-high (400°F to 450°F). Fill a medium saucepan with salted water; bring to a boil over high. Add couscous. Cook, undisturbed, until al dente, 8 to 10 minutes. Drain; rinse under cold water, and drain again. Return to saucepan. Add 2 tablespoons of the oil, and stir to combine. Set aside.

2. Meanwhile, toss together shrimp, pepper, 1 tablespoon of the oil, and 1 teaspoon of the salt in a medium bowl until combined. Thread evenly onto 4 (8-inch-long) skewers. Toss together squash, 1 teaspoon of the salt, and remaining 1 tablespoon oil in a separate bowl until combined. Thread evenly onto 4 separate skewers. Place squash kebabs on unoiled grates. Grill, uncovered, until charred and tender, about 3 minutes per side. Remove from grill. Place shrimp on unoiled grates. Grill, uncovered, until cooked through, 1 to 2 minutes per side. Remove from grill.

3. Add feta, Castelvetrano olives, parsley, dill, lemon juice, and remaining 1½ teaspoons salt to couscous in saucepan, and gently stir to combine. Spoon onto a platter. Top with shrimp and squash kebabs and lemon wedges.

Texas for Breakfast

These hearty tacos are quick to make and keep you fueled all morning long

Chorizo Breakfast Tacos

ACTIVE 20 MIN. - TOTAL 20 MIN.
SERVES 4

- 1 cup finely chopped white onion (from 1 medium onion)
- ¾ cup chopped fresh cilantro
- 3 Tbsp. fresh lime juice (from 2 limes)
- 1 tsp. kosher salt, divided
- 12 oz. fresh Mexican chorizo
- 6 large eggs
- 1 Tbsp. olive oil
- 1 small avocado, cut into wedges
- 1 oz. queso fresco (fresh Mexican cheese), crumbled (¼ cup)
- 8 (6-inch) corn or flour tortillas, warmed
- Hot sauce

1. Stir together onion, cilantro, lime juice, and ½ teaspoon of the salt in a bowl. Let stand, stirring occasionally, until ready to use.

2. Heat a large nonstick skillet over medium-high. Add chorizo. Cook, stirring often and breaking up meat with a wooden spoon, until most of the fat has rendered and chorizo is cooked through, about 5 minutes. Remove from heat. Transfer to a plate lined with paper towels. Wipe skillet clean.

3. Whisk together eggs and remaining ½ teaspoon salt in a bowl. Add oil to skillet; heat over medium. Add eggs. Cook, stirring constantly, just until set, about 3 minutes. Remove from heat.

4. Divide chorizo, scrambled eggs, avocado, queso fresco, and onion mixture evenly among warm tortillas. Serve with hot sauce.

The Best of Our Tortilla Taste Test

Favorite Flour: Tortilla Land
These uncooked tortillas are sold refrigerated at supermarkets. After a minute in a hot pan, they puff up and deflate for a tender, flaky texture that's hard to beat.

Favorite Corn: La Tortilla Factory
Handmade-style tortillas have stone-ground corn and wheat flour for flavor as well as sturdy texture to hold up well when filled.

A Tale of Two Tomatoes

How a classic Southern dish forged a lifelong friendship

I MET Ronni Lundy in the early 1990s at The Book and The Cook, an early food event in Philadelphia for cookbook authors. She was there as a journalist, and I later learned that she was writing a book on Appalachian foodways.

Shortly thereafter, I traveled to Louisville, Kentucky, for a book signing with Ronni. She became my designated escort, driving me to a store in a shopping mall where we were both scheduled to do cooking demonstrations. We hit it off right away, falling into easy chatter about all manner of things.

As was common practice back then, I carried with me an electric frying pan and the ingredients necessary to prepare the recipe that would be sampled by those in attendance—usually a few folks who were out wandering the mall on a Saturday afternoon. That day, my dish was fried green tomatoes. At some point that morning, I realized she was planning to make the same thing.

We watched each other's dueling demos, reveling in the minute differences between our recipes. Over the years, mine has changed slightly, and I now use buttermilk to hold the dredge. Back then, though, we were enthralled by our tomatoes' twinship—commenting on how interesting it was that Black and White recipes for the same dish varied so slightly. We parted as friends.

As our friendship grew, our discussions about the interconnectedness of African-American and Appalachian traditions and foods deepened. We talked about the similarities that some dishes made by White Appalachians have with their Black neighbors' and that some techniques and ingredients are shared.

Over time, Ronni became the leading advocate for the foods of Appalachia. In 2017, I watched with delight as her book *Victuals: An Appalachian Journey, with Recipes* won the James Beard Foundation Book Award for American Cooking and was named Book of the Year. I was among the first to hop to my feet for her standing ovation, thinking all the while of the fried green tomatoes that had united us more than two and a half decades ago. –Jessica B. Harris

Jessica's Fried Green Tomatoes

ACTIVE 20 MIN. - TOTAL 20 MIN.

SERVES 6

- 4 large unripe green tomatoes, cut into ¼-inch-thick slices
- 1 cup whole buttermilk
- ¼ cup all-purpose flour
- ¼ cup fine yellow cornmeal
- 1 tsp. kosher salt
- ½ tsp. black pepper
- Vegetable oil or bacon drippings, for frying
- Cooked bacon or sausage

1. Place tomato slices and buttermilk in a medium bowl; set aside. Combine flour, cornmeal, salt, and pepper in a small brown paper bag; set aside.

2. Add vegetable oil or drippings to a large cast-iron skillet or other heavy skillet to a depth of ½ inch. Heat over medium-high until the oil shimmers. Meanwhile, remove 3 or 4 tomato slices from buttermilk, letting excess drip off; add to flour mixture in paper bag. Close bag, and shake gently until tomato slices are well coated.

3. Place coated tomato slices in hot oil. Fry until golden brown on both sides, turning often to avoid sticking, about 4 minutes. Drain on paper towels.

4. Repeat coating-and-frying process with remaining tomato slices. Serve hot with bacon or sausage.

The Fried–Green–Tomato BLT

Jessica enjoys this sandwich with a twist

FRIED GREEN TOMATOES are a Southern breakfast staple, often gracing the table alongside sausage, bacon, or country ham. They can show up at other times of the day, too. JoAnn Clevenger, the owner of New Orleans' Upperline Restaurant, created a modern Creole dish by using them as a base for shrimp rémoulade.

My favorite way to eat them is in a BLT sandwich. Pile the fried tomatoes on thinly sliced sourdough bread slathered with mayonnaise, then add a few leaves of butter lettuce and slices of ripe tomato and crispy bacon. Voilà!

"I'll Bring Potato Salad"

Three freshened-up takes on a favorite side dish for cookouts and barbecues

LEMON-TARRAGON
POTATO SALAD

Lemon-Tarragon Potato Salad

ACTIVE 10 MIN. - TOTAL 35 MIN.

SERVES 6

- 1 large shallot, thinly sliced (½ cup)
- 2 Tbsp. white wine vinegar
- 1 (24-oz.) pkg. small (about 1½-inch round) red potatoes, quartered
- 2½ tsp. kosher salt, divided
- 1 Tbsp. fresh lemon juice (from 1 lemon)
- 1 tsp. Dijon mustard
- ¼ tsp. black pepper
- 2 Tbsp. olive oil
- ½ cup thinly sliced celery (from 1 stalk)
- 1 Tbsp. chopped fresh tarragon, plus more leaves for garnish

1. Stir together shallot and vinegar in a small bowl; set aside. Place potatoes and 2 teaspoons of the salt in a large saucepan. Cover with 10 cups water; bring to a boil over medium-high. Reduce heat to medium. Cook, undisturbed, until potatoes are fork-tender, 12 to 15 minutes. Drain; transfer to a large bowl.

2. Using a slotted spoon, remove shallot from vinegar, and transfer to large bowl with potatoes. Reserve vinegar in small bowl. Add lemon juice, mustard, pepper, and remaining ½ teaspoon salt to vinegar; whisk together until combined. Gradually whisk in oil until combined.

3. Add lemon-vinegar mixture, celery, and tarragon to potato mixture. Toss to coat, using back of a spoon to gently smash about one-third of potatoes. Serve immediately, or cover and refrigerate until ready to serve (up to 12 hours). Garnish with additional tarragon leaves before serving.

CALORIES: **132** – CARBS: **21G** – FAT: **5G**

SPICY ROASTED
SWEET POTATO SALAD

WARM POTATO SALAD
WITH MUSTARD
AND BACON

Spicy Roasted Sweet Potato Salad

ACTIVE 15 MIN. · TOTAL 40 MIN.,
PLUS 1 HOUR CHILLING

SERVES 6

- 1½ lb. sweet potatoes, peeled and cut into 1-inch pieces (about 5 cups)
- ½ cup fresh corn kernels (from 1 large ear)
- 3 Tbsp. olive oil, divided
- 1½ tsp. kosher salt, divided
- ¾ tsp. black pepper, divided
- 2 Tbsp. fresh lime juice (from 1 lime)
- 2 tsp. honey
- ½ cup black beans (from 1 [15-oz.] can), drained and rinsed
- ¼ cup drained sliced pickled jalapeños (from 1 [7-oz.] can), chopped
- 2 Tbsp. chopped fresh cilantro
   Sliced scallions

1. Preheat oven to 425°F. Line a large rimmed baking sheet with aluminum foil. Stir together sweet potatoes, corn kernels, 2 tablespoons of the oil, 1 teaspoon of the salt, and ½ teaspoon of the black pepper in a large bowl. Spread in an even layer on prepared baking sheet. Roast until vegetables are tender, about 30 minutes.

2. Meanwhile, whisk together lime juice, honey, and remaining 1 tablespoon oil, ½ teaspoon salt, and ¼ teaspoon black pepper in a large bowl until combined.
3. Add sweet potato mixture, beans, and jalapeños to lime juice mixture; stir until evenly coated. Cover with plastic wrap, and refrigerate until completely chilled, at least 1 hour or up to 12 hours. Add cilantro to salad; toss to combine. Garnish with scallions, and serve.

CALORIES: **196** – CARBS: **32G** – FAT: **7G**

Warm Potato Salad with Mustard and Bacon

ACTIVE 30 MIN. · TOTAL 1 HOUR

SERVES 6

   Ice water
- 1 (24-oz.) pkg. baby Yukon Gold potatoes, halved
- 4 large eggs
- 2½ tsp. kosher salt, divided
- 4 center-cut bacon slices
- 2 Tbsp. dark brown sugar
- 2 Tbsp. whole-grain mustard
- 1 Tbsp. sherry vinegar
- ¼ tsp. cayenne pepper
- 2 Tbsp. chopped fresh flat-leaf parsley, plus more for garnish

1. Fill a bowl with ice water; set aside. Place potatoes, whole eggs, and 2 teaspoons of the salt in a large saucepan. Cover with 12 cups tap water; bring to a boil over medium-high. Boil, undisturbed, 3 minutes. Using a slotted spoon, transfer eggs to ice water. Continue boiling potatoes, undisturbed, until fork-tender, about 15 minutes. Drain potatoes well. Peel eggs; roughly chop. Set both aside.
2. Place bacon in a 10-inch cast-iron skillet. Cook over medium, turning occasionally, until crispy, 10 to 12 minutes. Transfer to a plate lined with paper towels; reserve drippings in skillet. Cool 5 minutes; crumble.
3. Add sugar, mustard, vinegar, cayenne, and remaining ½ teaspoon salt to drippings. Bring to a simmer over medium, stirring constantly, until thickened, about 2 minutes. Remove from heat.
4. Place potatoes, crumbled bacon, and parsley in a large bowl. Add sugar-mustard mixture, and toss to coat evenly. Stir in eggs; garnish with additional parsley. Serve immediately.

CALORIES: **237** – CARBS: **23G** – FAT: **10G**

CRISPY CEREAL-AND-
BERRY BARS

A Berry Special Fourth

Test Kitchen pro and *Hey Y'all* host Ivy Odom calls for freeze-dried fruit to give treats a pop of patriotic color

WHEN I WAS GROWING UP my mama would always take me along for her weekly grocery runs to Winn-Dixie. I'd help with the shopping and even had my own kid-size buggy that I'd push around the store to get the things she wrote down for me.

Of course, while shopping, I'd pick out a few extras that weren't on my list of necessities. One of my go-to treats was Kool-Aid Blue Raspberry Lemonade mix. She rarely let me buy it but did give in on a few occasions, like when we stocked up for our annual Fourth of July beach vacation. The blue punch was festive, and these trips were meant for splurging.

I remember unpacking beach groceries and finding the prized packet of blue powder. I would quickly mix it with water and put it in the fridge to chill so we could enjoy it throughout the week. Although my Firecracker Punch won't give you a blue tongue, the recipe is made with freeze-dried (dehydrated) fruit for an all-natural version of that classic summer drink. It's sweet, tart, slightly effervescent, and sure to please both young and old.

When you make the punch, it would be a shame not to whip up some ridiculously easy crispy cereal treats with freeze-dried fruit, too. They come together in no time and will disappear in even less.

Crispy Cereal-and-Berry Bars

ACTIVE 10 MIN. - TOTAL 15 MIN.,
PLUS 2 HOURS STANDING

MAKES 16 BARS

- ¾ cup freeze-dried raspberries (from 1 [0.8-oz.] pkg.), coarsely chopped
- ¾ cup freeze-dried blueberries (from 1 [1.2-oz.] pkg.), coarsely chopped
- ¼ cup butter
- 1 (10-oz.) pkg. miniature marshmallows
- ¼ tsp. kosher salt
- 4 cups crisp rice cereal (such as Rice Krispies)

1. Line an 8-inch square baking dish with parchment paper, leaving a 1-inch overhang on all sides. Coat with cooking spray. Stir together berries in a bowl; set aside.
2. Melt butter in a large Dutch oven over medium. Stir in marshmallows and salt. Cook, stirring constantly, until melted, 2 to 3 minutes. Remove from heat. Using a rubber spatula greased with cooking spray, fold in cereal and 1¼ cups of the berry mixture until cereal and berries are fully coated in marshmallow mixture.
3. Transfer to prepared dish using greased spatula; press in an even layer. Sprinkle with remaining ¼ cup berry mixture; press into cereal mixture. Let stand, uncovered, at room temperature until set, about 2 hours. Remove from dish using parchment overhang as handles. Cut and serve.

Firecracker Punch

ACTIVE 10 MIN. - TOTAL 10 MIN.

SERVES 8

- 1½ cups freeze-dried raspberries (1 [1.3-oz.] pkg.)
- 1½ cups freeze-dried strawberries (from 2 [0.8-oz.] pkg.)
- 1 (52-oz.) bottle refrigerated lemonade (6¾ cups, such as Simply Lemonade)
- 2 cups chilled nonalcoholic ginger beer
  Frozen fresh blueberries
  Lemon slices
  Ice

1. Process raspberries and strawberries with a food processor until very finely ground and powdery, about 30 seconds. Sift berry powder through a fine-mesh strainer into a bowl, and discard any large clumps.
2. Measure ¼ cup berry powder into a ½-gallon (8-cup) pitcher, and reserve remaining berry powder for another use. Add lemonade and ginger beer to pitcher; whisk until powder is dissolved. Garnish punch with frozen blueberries and lemon slices. Serve immediately over ice. If mixture separates, stir before serving.

FIRECRACKER PUNCH

COOKING SCHOOL

Your Guide to Fresh Grilled Veggies
Consider this a cheat sheet for tender, flame-kissed produce every time

BELL PEPPER
Prep it: Cut into quarters; remove seeds and stem. Drizzle with olive oil. Sprinkle with salt and black pepper.

Cook it: Grill, covered, on oiled grates over high heat until slightly charred, about 3 minutes on each side.

EGGPLANT
Prep it: Cut into ½-inch slices; season with salt. Drain in a colander 30 minutes; pat dry. Drizzle with olive oil. Sprinkle with salt and black pepper.

Cook it: Grill, covered, on oiled grates over medium-high until tender and charred on each side, 4 to 5 minutes per side.

RED ONION
Prep it: Cut through the root end into ½-inch wedges. Drizzle with olive oil. Sprinkle with salt and black pepper.

Cook it: Grill, covered, on oiled grates over medium-high until lightly charred and tender, 3 to 4 minutes per side.

CHERRY TOMATOES
Prep them: Thread tomatoes onto 12-inch skewers, or keep them on the vine. Drizzle with olive oil. Sprinkle with salt and black pepper.

Cook them: Grill, uncovered, on oiled grates over high until lightly charred, about 4 minutes, turning kebabs once halfway through.

GREEN BEANS
Prep them: Align beans in a row; chop off ends. Drizzle with olive oil. Sprinkle with salt and black pepper. Toss to coat.

Cook them: Grill, uncovered, over medium-high in a grill basket or cast-iron skillet, tossing often with tongs, until beans begin to char and soften, about 10 minutes.

SQUASH
Prep it: Cut medium-size squash diagonally into ½-inch-thick slices. Drizzle with olive oil. Sprinkle with salt and black pepper. Toss to coat.

Cook it: Grill, covered, on oiled grates over high until tender and lightly charred, about 3 minutes on each side.

YES, YOU SHOULD FREEZE CITRUS ZEST!

Half the flavor of these fruits is in the peels, so preserve them. Use a Microplane grater to make fine zest for baked goods and sauces; a citrus zester to create delicate curls for pasta dishes; or a vegetable peeler or paring knife to cut off large strips as drink garnishes or sliced in marinades. Store in a plastic bag in the freezer up to three months.

Bright Idea

KOSIN BARBECUE GRILL LIGHT
Attach this magnetic light with an adjustable neck to your grill, and never cook in the dark again.

August

Bring On the Blackberries

Time to enjoy these late-summer beauties

BLACKBERRY FLOATS

Blackberry Floats

ACTIVE 5 MIN. - TOTAL 5 MIN.
SERVES 4

Process 2 cups **blackberries**, ⅓ cup **hot water**, ⅓ cup **granulated sugar**, and 1 Tbsp. **lemon juice** in a blender until pureed, about 2 minutes. Strain; discard solids. Scoop ⅓ cup **vanilla ice cream** into each of 4 glasses. Spoon ⅓ cup blackberry mixture into each glass; top each with 1 cup **club soda**. Garnish with **blackberries** and **mint**.

Blackberry-Lime Drop Biscuits

ACTIVE 15 MIN. - TOTAL 30 MIN.
SERVES 6

Whisk together 2 cups **self-rising flour**, ¼ cup **brown sugar**, and 1 tsp. **lime zest** in a bowl. Cut in ½ cup cold cubed **unsalted butter** until crumbly. Add 1 cup **blackberries**, ¾ cup **sour cream**, and ⅓ cup **buttermilk**; stir until dough comes together. Drop dough in ¼-cup mounds 2 inches apart on 2 parchment-paper-lined baking sheets. Bake at 400°F on upper- and lower-third racks until tops begin to brown, about 14 minutes, rotating baking sheets halfway through. Whisk together 1 cup **powdered sugar** and 2 Tbsp. **lime juice** in a bowl; drizzle over warm biscuits.

Blackberries are very perishable; eat them within a day or two.

BLACKBERRY-LIME
DROP BISCUITS

The Book of Ouida

As with the historic homes she works to preserve, HGTV star Erin Napier keeps her grandmother's memory alive the best way she knows how—by creating something to pass down

MY GRANDMOTHER, Ouida Walters Rasberry, kept the dented aluminum biscuit bowl in one of her two little closet pantries, beside the strainers, jars, and presses she used for canning. A layer of newspaper loosely lined the linoleum floor of the closet for reasons unknown. In the other pantry closet, freezer tape on the back of the door marked the heights for me; my brother, Clark; and my cousin Jim for a decade. These measurements kept watch over the simple ingredients she used time and again: yellow cornmeal, Crisco, cocoa powder, and parboiled rice. There was no fancy truffle oil or balsamic vinegar, but there was a metal canister stamped with the word "grease" that kept what was left behind by the bacon she cooked. She ate collards and eggs fried in it daily and lived to be 97.

When I was in high school, I spent the weekend with Mammaw (as we called her) a couple months after my grandfather, Pappaw, passed away. One night, while doing my homework at her dinner table, I put a mix CD I'd made into the hulking six-disc CD changer my uncle had given her when it was the hottest new technology, and the song "Video" by the musician India.Arie

came on. Mammaw had been cleaning up the kitchen, and then I noticed her shadow shuffling into the room—a little clap and sidestep, and she danced to the music. I'd never seen her move that way before and certainly didn't expect it in the fog of grief we'd been living in, but in that moment, we were two girlfriends, dancing to an acoustic guitar with a hip-hop beat. And I adored her even more fiercely for it.

That was the weekend I asked her to teach me the secrets of biscuit making. She pulled out the dented aluminum bowl and poured a few cups of Martha White self-rising flour into it. Then with her tiny, sun-weathered hands, she made a fist to form the crater to add the other ingredients for the dough. Her instructions weren't quantifiable: "Pour in the buttermilk until it looks about like this," she said. I wrote down my closest estimates so I would have proof, since I was now the official keeper of the Rasberry family biscuit secrets.

Next, she taught me two more of her most beloved dishes: spicy rice and tomato gravy. The rice was always served for Sunday lunch, when we would all descend on her house ravenous after an hour-long Baptist sermon. It was waiting on the Formica kitchen counter in her biggest skillet, as tempting as her homemade mac and cheese. I took for granted that we would have time to cook like this again. She was healthy, her mind was sharp, and the weekends stretched out in front of us.

But in January of 2008, she suffered a stroke that stole the words from her mouth and memories from her mind. By that point, I was a recent Ole Miss graduate and was engaged to the love of my life, Ben. As I was about to become a wife, I realized how badly I wanted to know all of those untold recipes. I felt a new wave of grief in realizing that chance was gone, even if we still had

Ouida's Chocolate Delight

ACTIVE 15 MIN. - TOTAL 1 HOUR, 15 MIN.,
PLUS 2 HOURS CHILLING
SERVES 8

- 1½ cups self-rising flour
- 1½ cups chopped toasted pecans
- ½ cup unsalted butter, melted
- 1 (8-oz.) pkg. cream cheese, softened
- 1 cup unsifted powdered sugar
- 1 (16-oz.) container frozen whipped topping (such as Cool Whip), thawed, divided
- 4 cups whole milk
- 1 (5.9-oz.) pkg. chocolate instant pudding mix
- 1 (3.4-oz.) pkg. vanilla instant pudding mix
- Chocolate syrup (optional)

1. Preheat oven to 350°F. Coat a 13- x 9-inch baking dish with cooking spray. Stir together flour, pecans, and butter in a bowl. Press mixture into prepared baking dish in a thin layer, patting mixture evenly into all corners. Bake until set, about 20 minutes. Remove from oven; cool about 30 minutes.
2. Beat cream cheese with an electric mixer on medium speed until creamy, about 2 minutes. Gradually add powdered sugar, beating until well blended, 45 seconds to 1 minute. Fold in 1 cup of the thawed whipped topping. Spread mixture evenly over cooled crust.
3. Whisk together milk and the chocolate and vanilla pudding mixes in a large bowl until well combined. Let stand until slightly set, about 10 minutes. Pour mixture over cream cheese layer; spread with remaining whipped topping. Drizzle with chocolate syrup, if desired. Cover, and chill at least 2 hours or up to 8 hours.

Story continued on next page

HIDDEN TREASURE
These large fruit-shape ceramic canisters were stuffed full of Mammaw's handwritten recipes.

SWEET MEMORIES
The Book of Ouida is filled with family recipes and other keepsakes.

Story continued from previous page

her with us. She was eventually able to piecemeal sentences together with the small vocabulary she relearned after post-stroke therapy. For a few years, she managed living by herself and preparing her own meals, even if she couldn't remember all the steps. In 2015, we began to lose her again. Ministrokes stole her freedom this time, and she moved to assisted living.

We helped Daddy sort out her home: the crocheted table doilies, the wooden rotary-dial phone on the kitchen wall, a copy of *The Swiss Family Robinson* and several Danielle Steel books, the mint-condition issues of *Southern Living* dating back to the early 1990s stacked neatly in a magazine rack. I took photos of each room, exactly as she had left it, so we would always remember the Christmases and birthdays spent around her out-of-tune piano and the dinner table. I packed her Blue Willow dishes, the glass tea pitcher, the cobalt blue ceramic canisters, and the dented biscuit bowl into the back of my Grand Wagoneer. I felt a bit of her soul attached

to those objects, talismans that would make me feel like I was closer to her, even as she felt so far away now. I found a few cookbooks, none seeming particularly worn or used. But the things I really hoped to discover—her handwritten recipes—were nowhere to be found. Everything else was neatly packed and placed in storage until "later."

The "later" no one wanted to think about finally came one bright morning in May 2020, when she passed away. After a few weeks, Daddy felt ready to give her modest belongings to Goodwill. Ben, Clark, and Jim were helping him load huge pieces of furniture into a truck when the door of the dining room console flung open, nearly spilling the contents onto the pavement. Inside were two ceramic canisters, shaped like a ripe peach and a basket of strawberries, stuffed to the brim with her recipes that were scribbled on any paper she'd had handy. They were all there: the peanut brittle, Jim's favorite Christmas cake, spaghetti and meatballs, and her famous

creamy layered dessert called Chocolate Delight—a simple and frequent character on her dinner table alongside the hand-battered fried chicken and butter beans. It felt like she was alive and well and giving us this one final gift that would carry on in us and our children and their children.

I carefully scanned the recipes, one by one, onto the computer and compiled them into a chapter book of her favorite dishes, along with tips she had clipped from magazines (like how to keep your meringue from sweating and when to trim your crepe myrtles). I included those photos of her house and pictures of her with her head thrown back as she laughed on the front porch, with a straw sun hat resting on the table beside her.

Last year, I gave *The Book of Ouida* to everyone in our family for Christmas. This year, I expect we'll have a buffet of all her recipes at our holiday dinner, and when we hear "Blue Christmas" on the radio and sing it loud enough, we'll hear her and Pappaw joining in, too, with an off-pitch piano accompanying us all.

Fruit Cocktails

Refreshing drinks that show off the sweet side of summer melons

HONEYDEW
SLUSHIES

CANTALOUPE
SLUSHIES

WATERMELON
SANGRÍA
(PAGE 186)

HONEYDEW
MOJITOS
(PAGE 186)

WATERMELON
SLUSHIES

Melon Slushies

ACTIVE 5 MIN. - TOTAL 5 MIN.

SERVES 2

2 cups frozen melon cubes (1-inch pieces, such as cantaloupe, honeydew, and red or yellow watermelon), plus more for garnish

½ cup crushed ice cubes

¼ cup (2 oz.) vodka

¼ cup (2 oz.) white wine aperitif (such as Lillet Blanc)

¼ cup Simple Syrup (recipe, page 186)

2 Tbsp. fresh lemon juice (from 1 lemon)

Process all ingredients in a blender until smooth, about 45 seconds. Pour evenly into 2 glasses. Garnish glasses with additional melon pieces.

Honeydew Mojitos

(Photo, page 185)

ACTIVE 15 MIN. - TOTAL 15 MIN.

SERVES 4

- 1 medium-size thin-skin lime, plus lime slices for garnish
- 4 cups honeydew melon cubes (1-inch pieces)
- ¾ cup (6 oz.) white rum (such as Bacardí)
- ½ cup loosely packed fresh mint leaves, plus mint sprigs for garnish
- ½ cup Simple Syrup (recipe follows) Ice cubes
- 1 cup sparkling water, seltzer water, or club soda

1. Cut lime lengthwise into quarters. Using a knife, remove center white pith from lime wedges; discard. (Do not remove the peels.)
2. Place lime wedges, melon cubes, rum, mint leaves, and Simple Syrup in a blender. Process until mixture is smooth, about 1 minute. Pour through a fine-mesh strainer into a measuring cup or a bowl, stirring and pressing lightly on solids to extract as much juice as possible. Discard solids.
3. Fill 4 glasses with ice cubes. Pour ¾ cup strained mixture into each glass. Top with ¼ cup sparkling water; stir. Garnish glasses with lime slices and mint sprigs.

Watermelon Sangría

(Photo, page 185)

ACTIVE 25 MIN. - TOTAL 25 MIN., PLUS 2 HOURS CHILLING

SERVES 4

- 14 cups watermelon cubes (1½-inch pieces, from ½ [22-to 24-lb.] watermelon)
- 1 (750-milliliter) chilled bottle dry rosé wine
- 4 cups melon balls (1-inch pieces, such as cantaloupe, honeydew, and red or yellow watermelon)
- ½ cup (4 oz.) elderflower liqueur (such as St-Germain)

1. Working in batches, process watermelon cubes in a blender until smooth, about 30 seconds per batch. Pour blended watermelon through a fine mesh strainer into a bowl, and discard solids. (You may need to stir the processed watermelon gently to help strain it, but don't press on the pulp.) Store watermelon juice in an airtight container in refrigerator up to 3 days; shake well before using.
2. Place chilled rosé, melon balls, elderflower liqueur, and 2 cups watermelon juice in a large pitcher; stir to combine. (Reserve remaining watermelon juice for another use.) Chill sangría at least 2 hours or up to 24 hours before serving.

Simple Syrup

ACTIVE 5 MIN. - TOTAL 35 MIN.

MAKES 1½ CUPS

Cook 1 cup **water** and 1 cup **granulated sugar** in a medium saucepan over medium-high, stirring constantly, until sugar dissolves, about 5 minutes. Remove from heat; cool to room temperature, about 30 minutes. Refrigerate, covered, until ready to use or up to 2 weeks.

Melons made for mixing

1 — **SEEDLESS RED WATERMELON**
Firm and crunchy, the fruit has an intense, candylike sweetness (and no seeds), making it ideal for drinks.

2 — **CANTALOUPE**
The juicy, rich, and smooth flesh is denser than most melons. It has a strong sugary flavor and a musky aroma.

3 — **CANARY**
This fruit has a mildly sweet and tangy taste, a crisp and pearlike texture, and a delicate tropical fragrance.

4 — **CRENSHAW**
One of the sweetest melons, the Crenshaw is prized for its complex flavor, which some describe as slightly spicy.

5 — **HONEY KISS**
Similar to a cantaloupe, the flesh of this melon has a creamy texture and a syrupy sweetness.

6 — **ORANGE DEW**
A cross between a honeydew and cantaloupe, this melon is thin-skinned with a tender and sweet interior.

7 — **HONEYDEW**
The meltingly soft texture of this fruit complements its intense sweetness and light floral aroma.

8 — **MINI SEEDLESS WATERMELON**
This version tastes just like its larger counterpart but is smaller and also has a much thinner rind.

9 — **CASABA**
The flesh is tender and slightly creamy, and it has a light sweetness with notes of pear and cucumber.

10 — **YELLOW WATERMELON**
Even though it has the same crisp and juicy texture as a red watermelon, this variety is more mellow.

Roll Models

Janice Nguyen Hudgins owns a popular Vietnamese restaurant outside
Charleston, South Carolina, and it all started with a beloved egg roll recipe

JANICE NGUYEN HUDGINS grew up
making egg rolls with her mother, Thu-
Ha Nguyen, but you won't find those
on the menu at Little Miss Ha, Hudgins'
Vietnamese eatery in Mount Pleasant,
South Carolina. "We do imperial rolls at
the restaurant," she says. "We use rice
paper, the way they do it in Vietnam."

For as long as Hudgins can remember,
her mom, who emigrated from Vietnam
to Charleston in 1979, has made egg rolls
using wheat-flour wrappers. And until
two years ago, Hudgins just assumed
that was the most authentic version
of the dish. "I was selling egg rolls out
of the trunk of my car, and I had this
awesome couple who would order, like,
four dozen at a time," she says. "They
had lived in Vietnam for nine years, and
one day, they said, 'We love your egg
rolls, but do you have the extra-crispy
ones like they make in Vietnam?' "
Bewildered, Hudgins asked her mother
what they meant, and it was then that
she learned the traditional Vietnamese
egg rolls she had grown up making

weren't exactly that. "Mom said, 'Oh
yeah, they make them with rice paper
there. That's the original way.' I said,
'What? We're not making them the
original way?' I was totally duped."

Her mother's preference for the
wheat-based wrappers was born of
practicality, says Hudgins. "Rice paper
is really, really sticky and fickle. When
my mom and aunts moved to the States,
they came across the wheat ones.
Everybody was using those instead. It's
a lot easier, and you can freeze them, so
those are what we grew up on."

While the wheat-flour shells of
Hudgins' childhood may not be part of
the imperial rolls at Little Miss Ha, she
still credits her mom's recipe as the one
that started it all.

When Nguyen immigrated to
Charleston, she didn't speak much
English, but she could count money
and landed herself a job at the since
shuttered Piggly Wiggly on Meeting
Street. "People couldn't really pronounce
Thu-Ha (two-HA), so they were like,
'We'll just call you Miss Ha,' " says
Hudgins. It stuck. After a stint as a
cashier at the cigarette counter, "Miss
Ha" moved to the deli, where she
eventually started selling her egg rolls
and fried rice on the hot bar, right
alongside the fried chicken and okra
stew. Well versed in making the recipe
for a crowd, Nguyen also began selling
them to a local caterer, who would buy
a few hundred every other week. Filling
the orders became a family affair. "Mom
would make the mix; [my younger
brother] Ryan would have to peel all the
egg roll shells—he was only 5 or 6, so
that was his job; and Mom and I would
roll," says Hudgins.

Now, years later, Ryan is the head chef
at Little Miss Ha and Hudgins is teaching
her oldest daughter, Ellie, to help out, too.
"Once you roll a couple thousand, you'll
get it!" Hudgins says.

Thu-Ha Nguyen's Vietnamese Egg Rolls

*These crisp, golden egg rolls are full of
savory flavor and are fun to assemble and
fry with family or friends. If you can't find
unseasoned, freshly ground pork at the
supermarket, ask your butcher to grind a
pork tenderloin.*

ACTIVE 1 HOUR, 15 MIN. - TOTAL 1 HOUR, 15 MIN.
MAKES 60

- 1 **cup thinly sliced yellow onion (from 1 small onion)**
- 1 **cup chopped scallions (from 1 bunch scallions)**
- 1 **cup shredded carrots (from 2 medium carrots)**
- 3 **oz. cellophane noodles (mung bean threads), prepared according to package directions, drained, and coarsely chopped (1 cup)**
- ¾ **tsp. kosher salt**
- 1½ **tsp. granulated sugar, divided**
- ¾ **tsp. black pepper, divided**
- 6 **oz. fresh ground pork (not sausage)**
- 6 **oz. peeled, deveined raw shrimp, finely chopped**
- 2¼ **tsp. fish sauce (such as Red Boat)**
- 60 **spring roll shells (such as Wei-Chuan)**
  Vegetable oil, for frying
  Dipping sauce of choice

1. Place yellow onion, scallions, carrots,
cellophane noodles, salt, ¾ teaspoon of
the sugar, and ½ teaspoon of the pepper
in a large bowl; toss together until
thoroughly combined.
2. Place pork, shrimp, fish sauce,
and remaining ¾ teaspoon sugar and
¼ teaspoon pepper in a medium bowl.
Stir using your hands or a fork until well
combined. Add pork mixture to onion
mixture; stir again until combined.
3. Fill a small bowl with cold water. Lay
1 spring roll shell on a cutting board or
a clean work surface positioned in a
diamond shape (with corners pointing

north, south, east, and west). If wrappers seem dry when you take them out of the package, drape a warm, damp paper towel or kitchen towel over them to keep them from drying out as you work. Fold the corner closest to you (pointing south) in toward center. Place about 1 tablespoon filling in the center of the folded corner, and shape it into a 3-inch log running crosswise on wrapper. Fold left and right corners of the wrapper in toward center (A). Dip fingertips in cold water, and brush water onto the top edges of the wrapper (B). Using too much water will cause the wrapper to break, but using too little will not seal the wrapper. Starting from the bottom of the spring roll shell, roll wrapper over the filling tightly without tearing the wrapper; roll up around the filling 2 times (C). Press damp tip of wrapper down to seal roll (D). Place assembled egg roll on a baking sheet; cover with a damp paper towel. Repeat process with remaining spring roll shells and filling.

4. Fill a 12-inch skillet with oil to a depth of ½ inch. Heat over high until oil reaches 350°F. Working in batches, add about 10 egg rolls to hot oil. Cook, turning occasionally, until rolls are golden brown and a thermometer inserted into centers registers 165°F, 4 to 5 minutes. Transfer egg rolls to a large baking sheet lined with several layers of paper towels to drain. Repeat process with remaining egg rolls, adjusting heat as needed to maintain oil temperature of 350°F. Serve with your favorite dipping sauce.

Cherry Jubilee

This cool, creamy (make-ahead!) dessert is a real treat on a hot day

Cherries-and-Cream Icebox Cake

ACTIVE 25 MIN. - TOTAL 25 MIN., PLUS 8 HOURS CHILLING

SERVES 12

- ½ cup, plus 1 Tbsp. cherry preserves (from 1 [13-oz.] jar, such as Bonne Maman)
- 4 cups heavy whipping cream, divided
- 2 tsp. vanilla extract, divided
- ¾ tsp. almond extract, divided
- 1 (8-oz.) pkg. cream cheese, softened
- ¾ cup, plus 3 Tbsp. powdered sugar, divided
- 21 (2¼- x 5-inch) graham crackers (from 1 [14.4-oz.] pkg.)
- Fresh cherries, for topping

1. Process cherry preserves in a food processor until completely smooth, 1 to 2 minutes; set aside.

2. Beat 3 cups of the cream, 1 teaspoon of the vanilla, and ½ teaspoon of the almond extract with a stand mixer fitted with a whisk attachment on medium speed until foamy, about 30 seconds. Increase speed to medium-high, and beat until stiff peaks form, 1 to 2 minutes; set aside.

3. Beat cream cheese, ¾ cup of the powdered sugar, and 3 tablespoons of pureed cherry preserves in a large bowl with an electric mixer on medium speed until smooth and completely combined, about 2 minutes. Gently fold one-third of whipped cream mixture into cream cheese mixture until thoroughly combined. Repeat in 2 more additions with remaining whipped cream mixture.

4. Lightly coat a 9-inch springform pan with cooking spray. Line bottom of pan with a layer of graham crackers, breaking them in order to cover bottom (don't worry if there are some small gaps). Spread 2 cups whipped cream mixture over graham crackers. Dollop with 1 tablespoon pureed cherry preserves; swirl with a wooden skewer or the tip of a knife. Repeat layers 3 more times with remaining graham crackers and whipped cream mixture and 3 tablespoons of the remaining preserves, ending with whipped cream mixture and preserves (reserve 1 tablespoon preserves for topping). Cover; chill 8 to 24 hours.

5. Before serving, beat remaining 1 cup cream, 1 teaspoon vanilla, and ¼ teaspoon almond extract with a stand mixer fitted with a whisk attachment on medium speed until foamy, about 30 seconds. Increase speed to medium-high, and gradually add remaining 3 tablespoons powdered sugar; beat until medium peaks form, 1 to 2 minutes. Remove cake from springform pan; spread top with whipped cream. Dollop remaining 1 tablespoon preserves onto whipped cream; swirl gently with a wooden skewer or the tip of a knife. Top with fresh cherries.

SECRET TO THE SWIRL

Ribbons of pureed cherry preserves run through the layers of this dessert. Dollop the center of each whipped cream layer with 1 tablespoon preserves. Use a wooden skewer or the tip of a knife to drag and swirl the preserves evenly throughout the whipped cream.

Cheat Sheets

Five garden-fresh weeknight dinners that look fancy and come together in a single pan

Rosemary Chicken Thighs with Summer Vegetables

ACTIVE 20 MIN. - TOTAL 50 MIN.
SERVES 4

- 1 small (1-lb.) eggplant
- 1 small orange bell pepper, sliced into thin strips (about 2 cups)
- 1 Tbsp. olive oil
- 2 tsp. kosher salt, divided
- ½ tsp. black pepper, divided
- 1 Tbsp. grated lemon zest (from 2 lemons)
- 3 tsp. finely chopped fresh rosemary, divided
- 4 (7- to 8-oz.) bone-in, skin-on chicken thighs
- 1 medium zucchini, cut into half-moons (2½ cups)
- 1 pt. yellow cherry tomatoes, halved
- 2 Tbsp. finely chopped fresh flat-leaf parsley, plus more for garnish
- 1 tsp. balsamic glaze

1. Preheat oven to 475°F with racks in upper third and lower third positions. Cut eggplant in half lengthwise. Reserve 1 of the eggplant halves for another use. Cut remaining eggplant half in half lengthwise; then slice crosswise into ½-inch-thick pieces. Place in a medium bowl. Add bell pepper strips, oil, and ¼ teaspoon each of the salt and black pepper to eggplant; toss to coat. Spread mixture in an even layer on an 18- x 13-inch rimmed baking sheet; set aside.
2. Stir together lemon zest, 2 teaspoons of the rosemary, ¼ teaspoon of the salt, and remaining ¼ teaspoon black pepper in a small bowl. Using your hands, rub about ½ teaspoon lemon mixture under

skin of each chicken thigh. Sprinkle chicken skin evenly with ½ teaspoon of the salt. Place chicken thighs, skin-side up, on baking sheet with eggplant mixture. Bake on lower rack in preheated oven 15 minutes.
3. Remove baking sheet from oven. Increase oven temperature to broil. Stir zucchini, tomatoes, and ¼ teaspoon of the salt into eggplant mixture on baking sheet; spread in an even layer. Immediately return to lower oven rack; broil just until zucchini is tender-crisp, about 10 minutes. Transfer baking sheet to upper rack, and broil until chicken skin is crisp and zucchini mixture is charred in spots, about 3 minutes. Sprinkle zucchini mixture with parsley and remaining 1 teaspoon rosemary and ¾ teaspoon salt. Drizzle with balsamic glaze, and stir to combine. Garnish with additional parsley, and serve.

Herb-Crusted Salmon with Potatoes and Tomatoes

ACTIVE 25 MIN. - TOTAL 40 MIN.
SERVES 4

- 1½ lb. yellow baby new potatoes, quartered
- 1 Tbsp. herbes de Provence
- ¼ tsp. black pepper
- 5 Tbsp. olive oil, divided
- 2 tsp. kosher salt, divided
- ⅓ cup finely chopped mixed fresh tender herbs (such as flat-leaf parsley, chives, and tarragon)
- ¼ cup panko breadcrumbs
- 1 Tbsp. Dijon mustard
- 4 (6- to 7-oz.) skin-on salmon fillets
- 1 (14-oz.) pkg. multicolor cherry tomatoes
- 2 tsp. white wine vinegar
- ½ tsp. grated garlic

1. Preheat oven to 450°F. Toss together potatoes, herbes de Provence, pepper, 2 tablespoons of the oil, and 1 teaspoon of the salt on an 18- x 13-inch rimmed baking sheet. Arrange potatoes on baking sheet. Roast 10 minutes. Remove from oven.
2. While potato mixture roasts, stir together mixed herbs, panko, mustard, and 1 tablespoon of the oil in a small bowl. Rub salmon evenly with 1 tablespoon of the oil, and sprinkle with ½ teaspoon of the salt. Spoon herb-panko mixture evenly over salmon, pressing to adhere.
3. Add tomatoes to baking sheet with potatoes, and spread mixture evenly (leaving potatoes cut-side down). Return to oven; roast for 5 minutes. Meanwhile, stir together vinegar, garlic, and remaining 1 tablespoon oil and ½ teaspoon salt in a small bowl; set aside.
4. Remove baking sheet from oven. Push potato-tomato mixture to outer edges of baking sheet; arrange salmon in center of baking sheet. Return to oven; roast until salmon is just firm and opaque, about 12 minutes. Remove from oven. Spoon vinegar mixture over potato-tomato mixture, and stir to combine. Divide salmon and potato-tomato mixture evenly among 4 plates.

HERB-CRUSTED SALMON
WITH POTATOES AND
TOMATOES

ROSEMARY CHICKEN
THIGHS WITH SUMMER
VEGETABLES

Sheet Pan Vegetable Lasagna

ACTIVE 25 MIN. - TOTAL 1 HOUR

SERVES 6

- 1 (10-oz.) pkg. frozen chopped spinach, thawed
- 1 lb. zucchini and/or yellow squash, cut lengthwise into 1/8-inch-thick slices
- 1 1/2 tsp. kosher salt, divided
- 1 (15-oz.) container whole-milk ricotta cheese
- 1/2 cup packed coarsely chopped fresh basil, plus small leaves for garnish
- 1/3 cup drained sun-dried tomatoes in oil (from 1 [8 1/2-oz.] jar), chopped
- 3/4 tsp. crushed red pepper
- 3 oz. Parmesan cheese, grated (about 3/4 cup), divided
- 1 (32-oz.) jar marinara sauce
- 1 (9-oz.) pkg. no-boil lasagna noodles
- 8 oz. low-moisture part-skim mozzarella cheese, shredded (about 2 cups)

  Olive oil, for aluminum foil

1. Preheat oven to 450°F with 1 rack in middle position and 1 rack positioned 6 inches from heat source. Place spinach on a clean kitchen towel, and squeeze firmly over sink to remove as much liquid as possible. Transfer spinach to a medium bowl, and pull apart using 2 forks; set aside.

2. Place zucchini in a colander set in sink, and toss with 1/2 teaspoon of the salt. Let stand until zucchini begins to soften, about 15 minutes. Toss zucchini in colander to drain any remaining water.

3. While zucchini softens, add ricotta, basil, sun-dried tomatoes, crushed red pepper, 1/2 cup of the Parmesan, and remaining 1 teaspoon salt to spinach in bowl; stir until combined.

4. Spread 2 cups of the marinara sauce in bottom of a 15- x 10-inch rimmed baking sheet. Layer with enough noodles to cover sauce (about 6 noodles), overlapping noodles slightly. Spread ricotta mixture evenly over noodles, and top with 1 cup of the mozzarella.

Arrange zucchini slices in a single layer over mozzarella, overlapping slightly. Cover with another layer of noodles (about 6), overlapping slightly, and remaining 2 cups marinara sauce, 1 cup mozzarella, and 1/4 cup Parmesan (your baking sheet should be brimming to the top). Lightly coat 1 side of 2 large pieces of aluminum foil with oil; wrap lasagna tightly with foil, oiled side down. Place on a larger baking sheet (in case of overflow), and bake on middle rack in preheated oven until noodles are tender, about 20 minutes.

5. Remove lasagna from oven; remove and discard foil. Increase oven temperature to broil. Place lasagna on rack 6 inches from heat source in oven; broil until cheese and noodles are browned and crisp in spots, about 7 minutes. Garnish with basil leaves.

Baked Caprese Chicken with Green Beans and Corn

ACTIVE 25 MIN. - TOTAL 35 MIN.

SERVES 4

- 1 cup multicolor grape tomatoes, halved
- 1 Tbsp. rice vinegar
- 2 Tbsp., plus 1 tsp. olive oil, divided
- 2 tsp. kosher salt, divided
- ¾ tsp. black pepper, divided
- 4 small ears fresh corn, shucked and halved crosswise
- 12 oz. fresh green beans, trimmed
- 4 (6- to 7-oz.) boneless, skinless chicken breasts, patted dry
- 1 Tbsp. grated lemon zest (from 2 lemons)
- 4 (1½-oz.) deli-style mozzarella cheese slices
- ¼ cup unsalted butter, softened
- ¼ tsp. grated garlic
- ¼ cup, plus 2 Tbsp. finely chopped mixed fresh tender herbs (such as basil, tarragon, and/or chives), divided

1. Preheat oven to 425°F. Stir together tomatoes, vinegar, 1 tablespoon of the oil, and ¼ teaspoon each of the salt and pepper in a small bowl. Let stand at room temperature until ready to use.
2. Toss together corn pieces, green beans, 1 teaspoon of the oil, and ½ teaspoon of the salt on an 18- x 13-inch rimmed baking sheet, and spread mixture in an even layer. Bake in preheated oven 10 minutes. Remove from oven.
3. While corn mixture bakes, sprinkle chicken evenly with 1 teaspoon of the salt and ¼ teaspoon of the pepper. Heat 1½ teaspoons of the oil in a large skillet over medium-high. Add 2 of the chicken breasts to skillet. Cook, undisturbed, until browned on bottoms, about 4 minutes. Transfer chicken to a plate. Repeat process with remaining 1½ teaspoons oil and chicken.
4. Push corn mixture to 1 narrow end of baking sheet. Arrange chicken, browned-side up, along other narrow end of baking

sheet. Sprinkle chicken evenly with lemon zest; top each breast with 1 cheese slice. Return baking sheet to oven, and bake until a thermometer inserted into thickest portion of chicken registers 160°F, 8 to 10 minutes.
5. Meanwhile, stir together butter, garlic, ¼ cup of the herbs, and remaining ¼ teaspoon each salt and pepper in a bowl.
6. Remove corn from baking sheet, and spread evenly with 2 tablespoons butter mixture. Toss together green beans and remaining 2 tablespoons butter mixture on baking sheet. Stir remaining 2 tablespoons mixed herbs into tomato mixture in bowl; spoon over chicken on baking sheet. Divide chicken, tomatoes, green beans, and corn evenly among 4 plates, or transfer to a large platter.

Sheet Pan Jambalaya

ACTIVE 15 MIN. - TOTAL 35 MIN.
SERVES 4

- 2 small mixed yellow, orange, and/or red bell peppers, cut into thin slices and slices halved crosswise
- 1 (12-oz.) pkg. andouille sausage, sliced
- 1 medium-size yellow onion, thinly sliced (3 cups)
- 1½ Tbsp. chopped fresh thyme
- 1 Tbsp. olive oil
- ½ tsp. garlic powder
- 2 tsp. Creole seasoning (such as Tony Chachere's), divided
- 3 large scallions
- 12 oz. jumbo peeled, deveined raw shrimp
- 1 (10-oz.) can diced tomatoes and green chiles (such as Rotel), drained
- 2 (8.8-oz.) pkg. precooked microwavable white rice

1. Preheat oven to 425°F. Toss together bell peppers, sausage, onion, thyme, oil, garlic powder, and 1 teaspoon of the Creole seasoning on a 13- x 18-inch rimmed baking sheet; spread mixture in an even layer. Bake until mixture is almost tender-crisp, 15 to 17 minutes, stirring mixture once halfway through cook time.

2. Meanwhile, thinly slice dark green parts of scallions; set aside. Thinly slice white and light green parts of scallions; transfer to a large bowl. Add shrimp, drained tomatoes and green chiles, and remaining 1 teaspoon Creole seasoning. Using your hands, crumble rice into shrimp mixture to separate any clumps; stir to combine. Set aside until ready to use.

3. Remove baking sheet from oven. Stir shrimp mixture into bell pepper mixture on baking sheet; return to oven. Bake in preheated oven until shrimp are pink and opaque throughout and rice is warm and tender, about 9 minutes. Sprinkle with dark green parts of scallions.

Waffling Around

Cornmeal adds crunch and a toasty flavor to this breakfast favorite

Outside-the-Box Toppings

Go beyond maple syrup and fresh seasonal fruit

Fully Loaded
Shredded cheddar cheese, sunny-side up egg, crumbled breakfast sausage, and minced chives

Smokin' Hot
Thick-cut bacon, spicy honey, and black pepper

Garden Variety
Ricotta cheese, halved cherry tomatoes, fresh corn kernels, and fresh basil leaves

Cornmeal Waffles

ACTIVE 40 MIN. · TOTAL 40 MIN.
MAKES 16

- 2 large eggs
- 2 cups whole buttermilk
- ½ cup unsalted butter, melted
- 1¼ cups all-purpose flour
- ¾ cup plain yellow cornmeal
- 1 Tbsp. granulated sugar
- 2 tsp. baking powder
- 1 tsp. baking soda
- ½ tsp. kosher salt

1. Preheat oven to 200°F. Set a wire rack inside a large rimmed baking sheet. Preheat waffle iron according to manufacturer's instructions. Process eggs in a blender until frothy, about 15 seconds. Add buttermilk and melted butter. Pulse until combined, about 10 pulses. Add flour, cornmeal, sugar, baking powder, baking soda, and salt. Pulse until fully combined, about 5 pulses, stopping to scrape down sides of blender as needed.

2. Lightly coat hot waffle iron with cooking spray. Pour about ¼ cup batter per waffle in center of waffle iron. Cover with lid, and cook until golden brown, 4 to 5 minutes. Carefully remove waffle from waffle iron, and place on prepared baking sheet. Transfer to preheated oven to keep warm. Repeat process with remaining batter, letting waffle iron reheat and recoating it with cooking spray between batches.

That's a Wrap

Tuck shrimp, cilantro, and quick-pickled veggies into lettuce leaves for a light lunch or appetizer

Grilled Shrimp Lettuce Wraps

ACTIVE 20 MIN. - TOTAL 20 MIN.

SERVES 4

- 1 lb. medium peeled, deveined raw shrimp
- 2 Tbsp. canola oil
- 1 Tbsp. rice vinegar
- 1 garlic clove, grated (about 1 tsp.)
- 1 (1-inch) piece fresh ginger, peeled and grated (about 1 tsp.)
- 1 Tbsp., plus ½ tsp. lower-sodium soy sauce, divided
- ½ cup thinly sliced radishes
- ½ cup thinly sliced matchstick carrots
- ½ tsp. kosher salt
- ½ tsp. granulated sugar
- ⅓ cup mayonnaise
- 1 Tbsp. finely chopped fresh cilantro, plus leaves for garnish
- 2 tsp. grated lime zest, plus 1 tsp. fresh juice (from 1 lime)
- 16 large butter lettuce leaves or Bibb lettuce leaves

1. Preheat grill to medium-high (400°F to 450°F). Stir together shrimp, oil, vinegar, garlic, ginger, and 1 tablespoon of the soy sauce in a medium bowl until combined. Toss together radishes, carrots, salt, and sugar in a small bowl until combined; set aside. Stir together mayonnaise, chopped cilantro, lime zest, lime juice, and remaining ½ teaspoon soy sauce in a separate small bowl until combined; set aside.

2. Place shrimp on oiled grates. Grill, uncovered, until lightly charred and cooked through, about 2 minutes per side; transfer shrimp to a plate to rest.

3. To assemble each wrap, stack 2 lettuce leaves together; spread a generous ½ tablespoon of the mayonnaise mixture on top lettuce leaf. Top with some of the shrimp and some of the vegetable mixture; garnish with cilantro. Serve immediately.

CALORIES: **284** – CARBS: **4G** – FAT: **22G**

MAKE IT AHEAD
Prepare and chill the shrimp, pickled vegetables, and mayonnaise mixture the day before.

Lickety-Split Pops

Beat the heat with healthy spins on a summer staple

RASPBERRY-PEACH
PARFAIT POPS
(PAGE 200)

FIND YOUR FLAVOR
Almost any type of fresh
fruit is delicious in these
frozen treats.

ADD SOME CRUNCH
Sprinkle the pops with
your favorite granola
before freezing them.

Raspberry-Peach Parfait Pops

ACTIVE 15 MIN. - TOTAL 15 MIN.,
PLUS 6 HOURS FREEZING

SERVES 8

- 1¼ cups vanilla whole-milk Greek yogurt
- ¼ cup half-and-half or whole milk
- 2 Tbsp. honey
- ¾ cup fresh raspberries, coarsely chopped
- ½ cup chopped peeled peach (from 1 fresh ripe peach)
- ⅓ cup granola (without raisins)

1. Stir together Greek yogurt, milk, and honey in a medium bowl.

2. Fill each of 8 (3-ounce) ice-pop molds halfway with yogurt mixture. Top each with about 1½ tablespoons chopped raspberries and 1 tablespoon chopped peach, gently pressing some of the fruit into yogurt mixture (you can use a wooden or metal skewer). Top evenly with remaining yogurt mixture. Sprinkle evenly with granola, gently pressing granola to ensure it adheres to yogurt. Insert ice-pop sticks, and freeze at least 6 hours.

3. To serve, run molds under warm water for a few seconds, and gently pull out ice pops.

SKIP THE DAIRY

Swap out the yogurt and milk for 1¼ cups **vanilla coconut milk yogurt** and 2 tablespoons **coconut milk beverage** (such as Silk Coconutmilk), or use 1¼ cups **vanilla almond milk yogurt** and 2 tablespoons **unsweetened almond milk beverage.**

MANGO-LIME
Replace peach and raspberries with chopped fresh mango; stir lime zest into yogurt.

BERRY-ORANGE
Stir juice and zest of 1 small orange into yogurt; replace peach with chopped strawberries.

PIÑA COLADA
Use coconut yogurt; replace peach and raspberries with chopped fresh pineapple.

BLUEBERRY COBBLER
Swap out peach and raspberries for blueberries; stir cinnamon and nutmeg into yogurt.

COOKING SCHOOL

TIPS AND TRICKS FROM THE SOUTH'S MOST TRUSTED KITCHEN

The Right Pan for the Job
Two workhorses every home cook needs

HALF SHEET PAN
With its rolled edges, this option is designed for cakes, but it's the ideal size for sheet pan suppers and roasted vegetables. Its nonstick surface makes cleaning up after meals a snap.
OUR PICK: OXO Good Grips Non-Stick Pro Half Sheet 13 x 18 Inches, $25; *amazon.com*

COOKIE SHEET
The best ones have a layer of air inside the aluminum to keep sheets from overheating and burning cookies.
OUR PICK: AirBake Natural Aluminum 2 Pack Insulated Cookie Sheets, 14 x 12, $19; *amazon.com*

TIPS FOR SLICING ICEBOX CAKES

1.
PICK A SPRINGFORM PAN
Removable sides eliminate the need to lift the cake out of the pan to be sliced.

2.
CHILL COMPLETELY
The cookies need time to soften to set the cake layers and make it easier to serve.

3.
KEEP THE KNIFE CLEAN
Warm a serrated knife under hot water, dry it off, then make a clean cut. Repeat for each serving.

"I like the simple, homemade look of an icebox cake, but you can **make it appear neater by smoothing the sides** with an offset spatula."
—Pam Lolley,
Test Kitchen professional

SECRETS TO SHEET PAN SUCCESS

1
Use a Cooling Rack
Cook breaded foods on an oven-safe cooling rack set on top of the sheet pan. This helps the outer coating get crisp, not soggy.

2
Fire Up the Broiler
Use this direct heat source at the very end of the cooking time to melt or to crisp up ingredients. (Just be sure to keep an eye on it.)

3
Remember the Garnishes
Add fresh herbs, a squeeze of citrus juice, or a handful of chopped toasted nuts to a meal for extra flavor, color, and texture.

September

Carrots of Many Colors

Most people associate these root vegetables with spring, but gardeners know the
sweetest ones are harvested in fall, when the weather turns cooler

Skillet-Roasted Carrots

ACTIVE 10 MIN. - TOTAL 10 MIN.
SERVES 4

Heat 1 Tbsp. **olive oil** in a large
skillet over medium-high. Add 1 lb.
small rainbow carrots, trimmed
and cut on a bias (halved, if large).
Sprinkle with ½ tsp. **kosher salt**
and ¼ tsp. **black pepper.** Cook,
stirring occasionally, until carrots
are browned in spots and tender-
crisp, 6 to 8 minutes. Add 3 Tbsp.
apple cider vinegar and 2 Tbsp.
honey to skillet. Cook, stirring
often, until liquid is syrupy and
carrots are evenly coated, about
1 minute. Remove from heat, and
sprinkle with 1 tsp. **fresh thyme
leaves.** Serve immediately.

Look for multicolor
bunches at the farmers
market. They're an
easy way to brighten
meals. If carrots are
scrubbed clean, you
don't need to peel
them, especially if they
are small.

Feeding Her Soul

Trisha Yearwood gives us a taste of her new cookbook

TRISHA YEARWOOD has become as famous for her cooking as she is for her music, and that's saying something. Over the past three decades, she's racked up around 60 award nominations for songs like "How Do I Live" and "Walkaway Joe," but she's also produced an Emmy-winning television show on the Food Network, *Trisha's Southern Kitchen,* and published a string of best-selling cookbooks. Her latest, *Trisha's Kitchen: Easy Comfort Food for Friends and Family,* is out now. Like her others, it was written with her sister Beth, drawing on recipes and traditions they learned from their mother. We caught up with the Monticello, Georgia, native, who talked about making a mess in the kitchen, what being a Southerner means to her, and how she and her husband, Garth Brooks, came up with a breakfast lasagna.

Pecan Sticky Buns with Bacon Caramel

ACTIVE 25 MIN. - TOTAL 55 MIN.

MAKES 12

- 4 Tbsp. unsalted butter, melted, plus more for greasing pan
- 1 lb. bacon (about 16 slices), chopped
- 1½ cups packed light brown sugar, divided
- ¼ cup pure maple syrup
- ¼ cup heavy whipping cream
- ¼ tsp. kosher salt
- 1 (17.3-oz.) pkg. frozen puff pastry sheets, thawed
- 1 Tbsp. ground cinnamon
- 1¾ cups pecans, chopped, divided

1. Preheat oven to 400°F. Grease a 12-cup muffin pan with butter. Place pan on a baking sheet lined with parchment paper; set aside.

2. Cook bacon in a medium saucepan over medium, stirring occasionally, until almost crispy but not quite cooked through, 8 to 10 minutes. Using a slotted spoon, transfer bacon to a plate lined with paper towels to drain, and reserve drippings in pan.

3. Reduce heat under pan to medium-low, and add 1 cup of the brown sugar to drippings. Cook, whisking often, until sugar has melted and mixture is no longer granular, about 5 minutes. Slowly add maple syrup in a thin drizzle, whisking constantly, until combined and bubbling. Whisk in whipping cream and kosher salt. Remove from heat, and cover to keep warm.

4. Unfold both sheets of puff pastry; arrange them on a work surface with the crease lines parallel to the edge of work surface. Brush sheets evenly with 4 tablespoons melted butter. Stir together cinnamon and remaining ½ cup brown sugar in a small bowl until combined, then sprinkle evenly over buttered pastry sheets. Sprinkle evenly with ½ cup of the bacon and 1 cup of the pecans. Gently press bacon and pecans into sugar mixture with your palms. Tightly roll up each pastry sheet away from you, forming 2 tight logs. Then, using a sharp knife, cut each log crosswise into 6 equal pieces.

5. Pour 1 tablespoon bacon-caramel sauce in pan into each greased muffin well. Sprinkle each muffin well with 1 tablespoon of the bacon and 1 tablespoon of the pecans. Place 1 rolled-up pastry bun, cut-side down, in each muffin well, and gently press down, ensuring that buns maintain their round shape.

6. Place baking sheet with muffin pan in preheated oven. Bake until caramel bubbles and buns are deep golden brown, 25 to 30 minutes. Remove from oven. Working quickly while they are still hot, run a small knife around sides of buns in muffin wells to release. Carefully invert muffin pan onto baking sheet. Spoon any remaining bacon-caramel sauce in muffin pan over buns. Serve immediately.

Cooks of the Year

A celebration of passionate Southern cooks

Each year we set out to celebrate cooks who are using food as a way to make the South a better, more delicious place. And every time, we are overwhelmed by the number of people who are accomplishing that and then some. Our 2021 Cooks of the Year come from different places and backgrounds, and all share an exceptional passion for what they do. The group includes a plant-based pitmaster in Georgia who is redefining barbecue, a bighearted bakery owner in Maryland who feeds her community in more ways than one, and a Kentucky teacher who built a high school culinary program from scratch. Over the past year, as the world changed and businesses shuttered and transformed, these five people faced the uncertainty with optimism, bravery, and grace—and the South is all the better for it.

50,000 Instagram followers. "I get a lot of suggestions from readers," she says. "I'll take requests for things I don't even like."

Yes, she bakes everything herself—usually in one day with one oven. (Sometimes her landlord shares her oven, like the time Kwee made nine apple pies.) "Baking multiple recipes isn't that much more work compared to making one, because you have to get out all those ingredients anyway," she says. "And the payoff is better."

Kwee's favorite part of the process is bringing people together to taste test. (During the pandemic, she doled out samples into muffin pans from a distance.) "It's the best feeling to see your friends enjoy all these different recipes," she says. "That community aspect is really fun for me." –Lisa Cericola

ERIKA KWEE

Helps home cooks have fewer kitchen fails

Finding the Internet's best chocolate chip cookie recipe is like trying to choose the prettiest flower in a meadow. The options seem endless, and each is just a little different. One day, Houston-based food blogger Erika Kwee had a cookie craving and found herself in this situation. So she baked them all—sort of.

Just for fun, Kwee and a friend searched for 20 popular chocolate chip cookie recipes. She then narrowed them down to a dozen, created a chart to compare all the ingredients, baked 200, had 30 people sample and survey them, collected the data, put it in a spreadsheet, ranked them with tasting notes (because, as she discovered, opinions on cookies vary as widely as the recipes), and then posted the results on her blog, *The Pancake Princess*.

The response to this data-driven ranking was so positive that now, four years later, Kwee is a trusted source for cooks around the world. Following the same process, she has tested baked goods ranging from apple crisp to zucchini bread and gained almost

Erika Kwee's Carrot Spice Cake with Candied Pecans and Brown Sugar Caramel Sauce

ACTIVE 55 MIN. · TOTAL 4 HOURS, 15 MIN.
SERVES 16

CAKE LAYERS

2	cups granulated sugar
1½	cups vegetable oil
4	large eggs
1	Tbsp. ground cinnamon
2	tsp. baking soda
1	tsp. kosher salt
½	tsp. ground ginger
¼	tsp. ground nutmeg
¼	tsp. ground cloves
2	cups all-purpose flour
1	lb. large carrots (about 6), peeled and finely grated (about 2¾ cups)

Continued on page 208

ERIKA KWEE'S CARROT SPICE CAKE WITH CANDIED PECANS AND BROWN SUGAR CARAMEL SAUCE

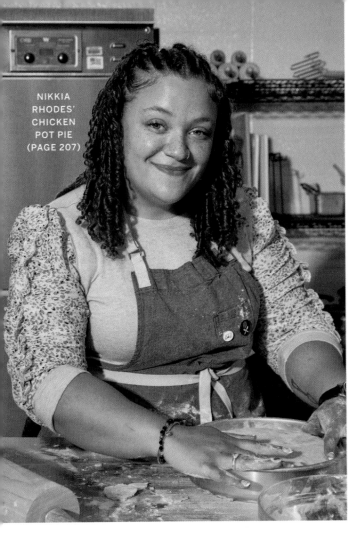

NIKKIA RHODES' CHICKEN POT PIE (PAGE 207)

TERRY SARGENT'S VEGAN "BONELESS RIBS" (PAGE 207)

AMANDA MACK'S APPLE-ALMOND SPICE CAKE WITH BROWN BUTTER FROSTING

TARA JENSEN'S SOURDOUGH CHOCOLATE CHIP COOKIES

Continued from page 206

- ¾ cup chopped toasted pecans
- 1 (8-oz.) can crushed pineapple in juice, drained well
- ¾ cup sweetened shredded coconut

CANDIED PECANS
- 1 large egg white
- 3 cups pecan halves
- ¼ cup granulated sugar
- ¼ cup packed light brown sugar
- 2 tsp. ground cinnamon
- ½ tsp. kosher salt

CARAMEL SAUCE
- 1 cup, plus 2 Tbsp. packed light brown sugar
- ½ cup heavy whipping cream
- 1 large egg yolk
- 1 Tbsp. unsalted butter
- 1 tsp. vanilla extract
- Pinch of kosher salt

FROSTING
- 1 (8-oz.) pkg. cream cheese, softened
- ½ cup unsalted butter, softened
- 1 tsp. vanilla extract
- Pinch of kosher salt
- 4 cups powdered sugar

1. Prepare the Cake Layers: Preheat oven to 350°F. Spray a half sheet pan (13- x 18-inches) with cooking spray, and line with parchment paper. Whisk together sugar, oil, eggs, cinnamon, baking soda, salt, ginger, nutmeg, and cloves in a large bowl. Whisk in flour until just incorporated. Fold in carrots, pecans, pineapple, and coconut (don't overmix batter). Pour into prepared pan; smooth top.

2. Bake in preheated oven until a wooden pick inserted into cake comes out clean, 30 to 35 minutes. Cool in sheet pan on a wire rack completely, about 1 hour. Chill cake in pan, uncovered, until cold, about 2 hours.

3. Meanwhile, prepare the Candied Pecans: Preheat oven to 300°F. Line a rimmed baking sheet with parchment paper. Whisk egg white in a medium bowl until foamy, 1 minute. Add pecans; toss until well coated. Add granulated sugar, light brown sugar, cinnamon, and salt. Stir until pecans are evenly coated. Spread in a single layer on prepared baking sheet. Bake at 300°F until browned and fragrant, about 40 minutes, gently stirring halfway through cook

time. (Pecans will continue to crisp up as they cool.) Set baking pan aside to cool completely at room temperature, about 30 minutes. Reserve 1 cup of Candied Pecan halves; roughly chop remaining (about 2½ cups). Set aside.

4. Prepare the Caramel Sauce: Whisk together brown sugar, whipping cream, and egg yolk in a small saucepan until well combined. Bring mixture to a boil over medium, stirring often. Boil, stirring constantly, 1 minute. Remove saucepan from heat; stir in butter, vanilla extract, and salt. Let stand at room temperature to cool completely, about 1 hour, stirring occasionally.

5. Prepare the Frosting: Beat cream cheese and butter in a stand mixer fitted with a paddle attachment on medium speed until smooth, about 2 minutes. Beat in vanilla and salt. With mixer running on low speed, gradually add powdered sugar, beating until fully incorporated. Increase speed to medium; beat until Frosting is smooth, about 3 minutes, stopping occasionally to scrape sides of bowl. Transfer Frosting to a large piping bag or zip-top plastic bag with a ½-inch hole cut in 1 corner; set aside.

6. Assemble the Cake: Run a knife along sides of cake to loosen it from pan. Carefully cut cake into 4 (about 8½- x 6-inch) rectangles. Place 1 cake rectangle on a large serving platter. Pipe about ⅓ cup of Frosting on top; spread into an even layer with an offset spatula. Drizzle with 2 tablespoons Caramel Sauce, and sprinkle with ½ cup chopped Candied Pecans. Repeat process 2 more times with 2 cake rectangles, ending with chopped pecans. Place remaining cake rectangle on top. Pipe remaining Frosting over top of cake, and spread into an even layer. Drizzle top of cake with about ¼ cup Caramel Sauce; garnish with chopped and halved Candied Pecans. Serve remaining Caramel Sauce and Candied Pecans with cake slices.

NIKKIA RHODES
Trains a new generation of cooks to give back

At 24, this Kentucky native has forged a path in the culinary world that she didn't think would be possible. Raised in Louisville's Smoketown

neighborhood, Nikka Rhodes sometimes had just crackers and peanut butter for supper, but she always understood the value of giving back. Her mother and grandmother managed the Volunteers of America family shelter kitchen, and as Rhodes spent time there, she saw the power of serving others and sharing a meal.

In high school, she met Food Network star Damaris Phillips, who encouraged her to enroll in advanced-level cooking classes at Jefferson Community & Technical College. Soon after that, Rhodes was accepted into the LEE Initiative's Women Culinary & Spirits Program, which was cofounded by chef Edward Lee to offer female chefs training and mentorship.

Rhodes wanted to be a teacher, and in 2018, she started a culinary program at Iroquois High School. "I was given a room with one sink, moldy carpets, and 140 students," she says. "Now we have nice things, quality ovens and stoves, equipment the kids can be proud of."

Last year, just as her classroom kitchen was coming together, COVID-19 hit. Then Louisville erupted in protests over the deaths of Breonna Taylor and, later, David McAtee, a beloved local barbecue chef. When Rhodes saw a photo of McAtee at the Volunteers of America kitchen that she grew up in, she wanted to honor him in the same way. Working again with the LEE Initiative, Rhodes helped establish the McAtee Community Kitchen and took on the responsibility of running it, with help from her culinary students.

"I am an example of how people can have a positive impact on your life," she says. "If I can show my students how to find their talents and then use them to serve others and better their communities, that is the best part of my job." –Patricia S. York

Nikkia Rhodes' Chicken Pot Pie
(Photo, page 207)
ACTIVE 40 MIN. - TOTAL 2 HOURS
SERVES 8

CRUST
- 3¾ cups all-purpose flour, plus more for dusting
- 1½ tsp. kosher salt
- ¾ tsp. garlic powder
- ¾ tsp. onion powder

1½ cups cold unsalted butter, cut into ½-inch cubes

8 to 10 Tbsp. cold water

FILLING

2 Tbsp. olive oil

1 medium-size yellow onion, chopped (about 2 cups)

4 medium carrots, peeled and chopped (about 1 cup)

1½ cups Yukon Gold potatoes, chopped (from 3 medium potatoes)

½ cup roughly chopped shiitake mushrooms

½ cup roughly chopped baby portobello mushrooms

4 tsp. kosher salt, plus more to taste

1½ tsp. black pepper, plus more to taste

½ tsp. dried thyme

½ tsp. dried sage

½ tsp. garlic powder

3 Tbsp. unsalted butter, plus more for greasing

5 Tbsp. all-purpose flour

3 cups chicken stock

2 cups whole milk

3 Tbsp. cream cheese

4 cups shredded rotisserie chicken (skin removed)

2 cups packed fresh spinach, chopped

ADDITIONAL INGREDIENTS

Butter, for greasing

1 large egg, lightly beaten

1 tsp. flaky sea salt

1. Prepare the Crust: Pulse flour, salt, garlic powder, and onion powder in a food processor until well combined, about 5 pulses. Add cold butter; continue pulsing until butter is pea size, about 10 pulses. Add 4 tablespoons cold water; pulse until incorporated, about 5 pulses. Slowly add up to 6 tablespoons cold water, 1 tablespoon at a time, pulsing until dough just comes together. (You may have to take dough out of food processor and bring it together with your hands. Do not knead the dough.) Shape into a 1-inch-thick disk; wrap tightly with plastic wrap. Chill at least 30 minutes or up to 24 hours.

2. Prepare the Filling: Heat oil in a large Dutch oven over medium-high. Add onion, carrots, potatoes, and shiitake and portobello mushrooms. Cook, stirring often, until vegetables are tender and beginning to caramelize,

5 to 8 minutes. Add salt, pepper, dried thyme, dried sage, and garlic powder. Continue cooking, stirring constantly, until vegetables are evenly coated, about 1 minute. Add butter, and cook, stirring often, until completely melted. Stir in flour. Continue cooking, stirring constantly, until flour mixture is golden brown and nutty, about 2 minutes. Add stock, milk, and cream cheese; bring to a boil over medium-high, stirring often. Reduce heat to medium. Simmer, stirring often, until thickened, about 10 minutes. Remove Dutch oven from heat, and stir in shredded chicken and spinach; season to taste with salt and pepper.

3. Preheat oven to 400°F. Grease a 13- x 9-inch baking dish with butter; set aside. Remove and discard plastic wrap from dough. Cut dough disk in half; roll 1 half into a ⅛-inch-thick, 17- x 13-inch rectangle on a work surface lightly dusted with flour. Place dough in prepared baking dish; gently push into bottom and up sides of dish, allowing about 1 inch to extend over sides. (It is okay if it gets a hole in it; just press dough back together.) Add Filling mixture to baking dish. Roll remaining dough half into a ⅛-inch-thick, 10- x 14-inch rectangle. Cut 9 (13- x 1-inch) strips from dough; arrange in a lattice pattern on top of Filling mixture, pressing ends to bottom Crust layer to seal. Trim excess dough from strips; discard. Fold down dough overhang on sides; pinch to seal to lattice strips. Brush dough lattice and border with egg, and sprinkle evenly with flaky sea salt. Bake until Crust is golden and Filling is bubbling, 40 to 45 minutes. Let rest at room temperature 5 minutes before serving.

TERRY SARGENT

Redefines Barbecue in the South

"Barbecue is a way of cooking, not a type of meat," says Terry Sargent. At Grass VBQ Joint, his plant-based restaurant in Stone Mountain, Georgia, he's changing the hearts and minds of carnivores one "veef" brisket sandwich at a time.

Seven years ago, while he was working as a corporate chef in Atlanta, Sargent became a vegan for health reasons and spent his free time

experimenting with meat- and dairy-free recipes. Looking for a challenge, he tried his hand at making barbecue that mimicked the real thing—sausage, "chic'n," brisket, and smoked jackfruit (a close stand-in for pulled pork). "It's a day-and-a-half process," Sargent explains. "Barbecue is a technique, and one thing I had to learn was patience."

In 2019, wanting other people to enjoy these cookout favorites, Sargent held a pop-up on the Fourth of July. When the food sold out in 45 minutes, he knew he was on to something. "We didn't have a website. All this was via social media and word of mouth," he says.

Soon after that, Sargent landed a small stall in a food court, then a full-time spot at Orpheus Brewing. Early last year, Sargent moved into his current storefront, offering an expanded takeout menu around the time that many restaurants closed their doors. His scratch-made 'cue is smoked for hours then served with creative toppings (Roasted Vidalia Onion VBQ Sauce) and sides (Red Curry Coconut Greens and Stout Baked Beans).

"Some people will walk in and have no idea that it's vegan. Then they'll come back another day and say, 'Wait a minute. This is a vegan restaurant?'" Sargent says. "One guy said, 'Dude, I was born and raised in Texas, where we barbecue to death. This is by far the best I've had in my life.'" –Lisa Cericola

Terry Sargent's Vegan "Boneless Ribs"

(Photo, page 207)

ACTIVE 25 MIN. - TOTAL 1 HOUR, 55 MIN., PLUS 4 HOURS CHILLING

SERVES 4

1 cup canned jackfruit, drained and shredded (from 1 [20-oz.] can green jackfruit in brine)

1 cup vital wheat gluten (such as Bob's Red Mill)

5 Tbsp. chickpea flour (such as Bob's Red Mill)

3 Tbsp. pea protein powder (such as Bob's Red Mill)

2 Tbsp. nutritional yeast

1 Tbsp. smoked paprika

2 tsp. onion powder

1 tsp. garlic powder

1 tsp. kosher salt

Continued on page 210

Continued from page 209

1 tsp. black pepper

2 Tbsp. natural creamy peanut butter

1 tsp. liquid smoke

1 Tbsp. soy sauce

3 cups vegetable broth, divided

½ cup bottled barbecue sauce

Neutral oil (such as canola, vegetable, or grapeseed), for grilling

Thinly sliced scallions

1. Preheat oven to 375°F. Lightly grease an 8-inch square baking dish with cooking spray; set aside.

2. the Stir together jackfruit, wheat gluten, chickpea flour, pea protein powder, nutritional yeast, smoked paprika, onion powder, garlic powder, salt, and pepper in bowl of a stand mixer until well combined. Whisk together peanut butter, liquid smoke, soy sauce, and 1 cup of the vegetable broth in a medium bowl until well combined.

3. Add broth mixture to jackfruit mixture, stirring gently until mixture is well combined and has formed a soft dough. Beat dough with a stand mixer fitted with a paddle attachment on medium speed until dough comes together and is slightly elastic, 5 to 7 minutes.

4. Place dough in prepared baking dish, flattening dough so it spreads evenly across entire dish while keeping top as flat and smooth as possible. Cut dough in half lengthwise; then cut 8 (1-inch-thick) strips crosswise to yield 16 (4- x 1-inch) slices. (Don't pull the slices apart; you just want the ability to easily separate them after grilling.) Pour remaining 2 cups broth on top of dough; cover dish with aluminum foil. Bake in preheated oven until ribs have almost doubled in size, about 45 minutes (broth will not be completely absorbed). Remove baking dish from oven, uncover, and carefully pour off and discard excess broth. Cool at room temperature 30 minutes. Cover baking dish with plastic wrap; chill completely, at least 4 hours or up to 24 hours. Remove baking dish from refrigerator. Carefully remove ribs from dish, but do not separate individual pieces. Gently separate ribs along lengthwise cut to yield 2 (4- x 8-inch) slabs; gently pat slabs dry with paper towels.

5. Preheat grill to medium (350°F to 400°F). Brush tops of ribs evenly with ¼ cup barbecue sauce. Place ribs, sauce-side down, on grates well coated with neutral oil. Grill, uncovered, until ribs are deeply browned, 6 to 8 minutes; brush tops with remaining ¼ cup barbecue sauce. Carefully flip ribs. Continue grilling, uncovered, until deeply browned on all sides, 6 to 8 minutes. (Alternatively, preheat a grill pan over medium heat; lightly grease grill pan with neutral oil. Brush tops of ribs evenly with ¼ cup barbecue sauce. Place ribs, sauce-side down, on grill pan; cook until ribs are deeply browned, 6 to 8 minutes. Brush tops with remaining ¼ cup barbecue sauce. Flip ribs; continue cooking until deeply browned on all sides, 6 to 8 minutes.) Transfer ribs to a large serving platter; garnish with scallions.

AMANDA MACK

Feeds her community in more ways than one

When a bakery takes its name from a recipe, it stands to reason that the recipe has a solid reputation. Amanda Mack, owner of Crust by Mack in Baltimore, taught by her grandmother, Yvonne Roy, worked for two years to replicate Roy's recipe. Once Mack felt she'd perfected the crust and shared it with her grandmother, Roy's simple reaction was, "It's good." Mack was ecstatic. "You would have thought I had won the lottery. If it's good to her, then it's great to everybody else."

And it is. In 2018, Mack began to sell pastries at pop-ups, coffee shops, and events. Her signature crust—in tarts, sprinkle-covered pastries, and all varieties of pies—earned a devoted following and helped her raise thousands of dollars for local organizations and charities. Around Baltimore, she became known as much for supporting the community as for her strawberry-basil hand pies. "I'm intentional about raising money for Black-owned businesses and minorities," she says. "My customers are of all races and ethnicities, and they want to support me in supporting others."

Last summer, Mack's first retail shop opened in Whitehall Market, a food hall in Hampden. The welcoming space is mostly run by her family, and she wants customers to feel like they are walking into her home. "You don't know what people are carrying. We want to make sure that this is a bright spot on their journey," she says.

In addition to supporting and raising money to help social- and food-justice organizations, Mack opened Layers, a space where she can host mentoring programs and events for other entrepreneurs. "I know firsthand what it's like to come from a situation where you don't have very much. I wanted to provide a platform for people like me who have a dream and a vision but just need some help getting there."

—Lisa Cericola

Amanda Mack's Apple-Almond Spice Cake with Brown Butter Frosting

(Photo, page 207)

ACTIVE 20 MIN. - TOTAL 2 HOURS, 30 MIN., PLUS 1 HOUR, 30 MIN. COOLING

SERVES 8

CAKE

2 cups granulated sugar

½ cup canola oil

2 large eggs, at room temperature

1 large egg white, at room temperature

2 tsp. vanilla extract

½ tsp. almond extract

2¼ cups all-purpose flour

2 tsp. baking powder

1 tsp. kosher salt

1 tsp. ground cinnamon

½ tsp. ground ginger

¼ tsp. ground nutmeg

¼ tsp. ground allspice

¼ tsp. ground cardamom

½ cup whole buttermilk

1 large Honeycrisp apple, peeled, cored, and shredded on largest holes of a box grater

1 cup sliced almonds

BROWN BUTTER FROSTING

¾ cup butter, softened, divided

3 cups powdered sugar

2 Tbsp. whole milk

GARNISHES
    Apple chips
    Toasted sliced almonds

1. Prepare the Cake: Preheat oven to 350°F. Grease 1 (9½- x 5½-inch) loaf pan with cooking spray. Line bottom of pan with parchment paper, and grease parchment paper. Whisk together sugar, oil, eggs, egg white, vanilla extract, and almond extract in a large bowl until well combined. Whisk together flour, baking powder, salt, cinnamon, ginger, nutmeg, allspice, and cardamom in a separate large bowl until well combined. Gradually whisk flour mixture into sugar mixture, alternately with buttermilk, until combined (be careful not to overmix batter). Stir in apple and almonds. Spoon batter evenly into prepared pan. Bake until a wooden pick inserted in center comes out clean, about 1 hour and 30 minutes to 1 hour and 40 minutes, covering loosely with aluminum foil after 1 hour to prevent excessive browning. Cool in pan 10 minutes before removing and transferring to a wire rack. Remove and discard parchment paper. Cool completely, about 1 hour.
2. Prepare the Brown Butter Frosting: Cook ¼ cup of the butter in a skillet over medium, stirring often, until rich amber in color, about 6 minutes. Transfer butter to bowl of a stand mixer; cool completely at room temperature, about 30 minutes. Add remaining ½ cup butter to brown butter, and beat with a stand mixer fitted with a paddle attachment on medium speed until creamy, about 1 minute. Gradually add powdered sugar, beating on low speed until blended, about 2 minutes. Increase speed to medium; gradually add milk, 1 tablespoon at a time, beating to desired consistency, about 1 minute. Spread frosting over top of cake as desired, and garnish with apple chips and toasted sliced almonds.

TARA JENSEN
Spreads the gospel of artisanal baking

Whether hosting a virtual cooking class on croissant making or a weeklong sourdough camp, Tara Jensen helps people find their inner bakers.

A native of rural Maine, Jensen landed in Asheville, North Carolina, in 2006, working for Farm & Sparrow, the baking-and-milling project founded by David Bauer that focuses on heirloom grains. When Bauer moved on in 2012, Jensen opened her first bakery, Smoke Signals, in the space. It had an outdoor wood-fired oven, which became an impromptu school for bakers of all skill levels and the heart of her business. "The quality of heat in a wood-fired oven is the very best to bake with," she says. Cooking this way also means people hang around and tend the fire. This leads to conversation. "They would come in and ask me questions," she says. "Sharing my craft just came naturally."

And so did her following. Thanks to Instagram, she became known all over the world for rustic loaves made with freshly milled grains and flours and fruit from local orchards. Although her work is beautiful—Jensen uses handmade paper stencils to pattern the tops of loaves with flour and embellishes her pies with pastry shapes—she doesn't aim for perfection. "It should look like it came from your hands," she says.

In 2018, Jensen closed Smoke Signals to focus on teaching at her home and other locations, like the Pine Mountain Settlement School in Kentucky, where she offers in-depth workshops on one of her favorite topics: sourdough. Jensen loves talking about starters, fermentation, and how the natural bacteria give bread a "tangy, interesting, and just plain delicious taste."

With a new cookbook and a studio for virtual and in-person classes, Jensen will have even more opportunity to do what she loves: gathering people together so they can make and break bread. –Patricia S. York

Tara Jensen's Sourdough Chocolate Chip Cookies
(Photo, page 207)
ACTIVE 25 MIN. - TOTAL 1 HOUR, 30 MIN., PLUS 8 HOURS CHILLING
MAKES 12

- 1 cup unsalted butter, at room temperature
- 1 cup granulated sugar
- ⅓ cup packed light brown sugar
- ¾ tsp. kosher salt
- ½ tsp. baking soda
- 2 large eggs
- ¼ cup sourdough starter discard
- 1 Tbsp. vanilla extract
- 2¼ cups all-purpose flour
- 12 oz. (about 2 cups) semisweet chocolate chips
- 8 oz. 60% cacao bittersweet chocolate, roughly chopped (about 1½ cups)
- 1½ tsp. flaky sea salt

1. Beat butter, granulated sugar, brown sugar, salt, and baking soda with a stand mixer fitted with a paddle attachment, starting on low and gradually increasing speed to medium, until batter climbs up the wall of the bowl, about 3 minutes. Stop mixer; scrape sides of bowl with a rubber spatula. Repeat process 2 more times, starting on low and gradually increasing to medium, until mixture is light, fluffy, and pale, 9 to 10 minutes.
2. With mixer running on medium speed, add eggs, 1 at a time, beating well after each addition. Add sourdough starter discard and vanilla extract. Beat on medium-low speed until batter is smooth and shiny, about 3 minutes, stopping to scrape sides and bottom of bowl as needed.
3. Add flour and semisweet chocolate chips. Beat on low speed just until flour is completely incorporated and there are no visible streaks in the batter, 15 to 30 seconds. Transfer dough to an airtight container, or wrap tightly in plastic wrap. Chill at least 8 hours or up to 48 hours.
4. Preheat oven to 350°F. Divide dough into 12 pieces (about ⅓ cup each). Working quickly, shape each piece into a ball. Transfer to a baking sheet lined with parchment paper. Chill, uncovered, 15 minutes.
5. Arrange 4 dough balls at least 2 inches apart on a baking sheet lined with parchment paper. Keep remaining dough balls chilled. Bake in preheated oven 10 minutes. Remove from oven, and top half-baked cookies with about ½ cup of roughly chopped 60% cacao bittersweet chocolate. Sprinkle with ½ teaspoon flaky sea salt among the 4 cookies. Return to oven; bake at 350°F until cookies are golden and firm around edges with soft and slightly risen centers, 12 to 14 minutes. Cool cookies on pan for 5 minutes. Transfer to a wire rack to cool at least 20 minutes. Repeat baking process with remaining dough balls, chopped chocolate, and flaky sea salt. The cooled cookies can be stored in an airtight container up to 5 days.

PEAR-PLUM
TARTLETS

Perfect Pears

Apples get most of the attention, but these fall fruits are just as sweet

Pear-Plum Tartlets

ACTIVE 20 MIN. - TOTAL 1 HOUR, 15 MIN.

SERVES 6

  Pie Dough (recipe follows)
  All-purpose flour, for work surface
3 medium-size firm-ripe Bartlett pears, thinly sliced (about 4 cups)
2 firm-ripe red plums, thinly sliced (about 2 cups)
½ cup granulated sugar
1½ Tbsp. cornstarch
1 Tbsp. fresh lemon juice
2 Tbsp. cold unsalted butter, cubed
1 large egg, beaten
2 Tbsp. sanding sugar or sparkling sugar

1. Preheat oven to 375°F. Line a large rimmed baking sheet with parchment paper.
2. Roll Pie Dough into a 12½- x 18½-inch rectangle (about ⅛ inch thick) on a lightly floured surface. Cut 6 (6-inch) squares; place on prepared baking sheet. (They will overlap slightly.) Chill dough squares.
3. Stir together next 5 ingredients in a bowl. Spoon about ¾ to 1 cup fruit mixture into center of each chilled dough square. Fold up edges to create a ½-inch rim; pinch corners to seal. Place on prepared baking sheet. Top with cubed butter. Brush edges with egg; sprinkle with sanding sugar.
4. Bake in preheated oven until golden and filling is bubbly, about 35 to 40 minutes. Cool slightly on pan, about 20 minutes.

Caramel Apple-Pear Pie

ACTIVE 30 MIN. - TOTAL 1 HOUR, 35 MIN., PLUS 2 HOURS COOLING

SERVES 8

  Pie Dough (recipe follows)
¼ cup all-purpose flour, plus more for work surface
3 cups peeled, cubed Honeycrisp apples (about 2 medium)
3 cups peeled, cubed, firm-ripe Bartlett pears (about 3 medium)
⅓ cup granulated sugar

1 Tbsp. fresh lemon juice
1 tsp. ground cinnamon
¼ tsp. ground ginger
½ cup store-bought salted-caramel topping or sauce, plus more for serving
1 large egg, beaten
2 Tbsp. turbinado sugar

1. Preheat oven to 375°F with oven rack in bottom position. Line a large rimmed baking sheet with parchment paper.
2. Roll 1 Pie Dough disk into a 12-inch circle on a lightly floured surface. Press dough into bottom and up sides of a 9-inch pie plate. Roll remaining Pie Dough disk into a 12-inch circle on a lightly floured surface. Cut dough into 10 (1-inch-wide) strips. Cut 5 of the strips in half again lengthwise. You should have 5 (1-inch-wide) strips and 10 (½-inch-wide) strips. Place all strips on prepared baking sheet. Refrigerate both crust and strips until ready to assemble.
3. Gently stir together apples, pears, granulated sugar, the ¼ flour, the lemon juice, cinnamon, and ginger until combined. Spoon apple mixture into chilled crust. Drizzle evenly with caramel topping. Remove dough strips from baking sheet, and set aside prepared baking sheet. Arrange dough strips in a lattice design over filling,

alternating 1 thick strip with 2 thin strips. Trim excess dough, and crimp edges as desired. Brush crust with beaten egg, and sprinkle with turbinado sugar. Freeze pie 10 minutes.
4. Place pie on prepared baking sheet, and bake in preheated oven on bottom rack until crust is golden brown and filling is bubbly, about 55 minutes, covering loosely with aluminum foil during last 10 minutes to prevent excessive browning, if necessary. Let cool completely on a wire rack, about 2 hours. Drizzle with additional caramel topping just before serving.

Pie Dough

ACTIVE 10 MIN. - TOTAL 1 HOUR, 10 MIN.

MAKES 2 DISKS OR 1 RECTANGLE

Pulse 2½ cups **all-purpose flour;** 1 Tbsp. **granulated sugar;** 2 tsp. **kosher salt;** and 1 cup **cold unsalted butter,** cut into pieces, in a food processor until mixture resembles coarse wet sand, about 15 pulses. With processor running, slowly drizzle in 6 to 8 Tbsp. **cold water,** processing until a dough forms, about 15 seconds. For a double-crust pie, divide dough in half and shape into 2 disks. For tartlets, shape all of dough into a large rectangle. Wrap each disk or rectangle in plastic wrap; refrigerate until firm, about 1 hour.

CARAMEL APPLE-PEAR PIE

POACHED PEARS WITH
VANILLA CUSTARD SAUCE

DARK CHOCOLATE-
PEAR CAKE

Poached Pears with Vanilla Custard Sauce

(Photo, page 214)

ACTIVE 20 MIN. - TOTAL 20 MIN.,
PLUS 8 HOURS CHILLING

SERVES 6

POACHED PEARS

- 6 medium-size firm-ripe Bosc pears, peeled (leaving stems attached)
- ½ cup honey
- ⅓ cup granulated sugar
- 1 (3-inch) lemon peel strip, plus 1 Tbsp. fresh lemon juice (from 1 lemon)
- 1 (3- to 4-inch) cinnamon stick
- 2 hibiscus tea bags (such as Celestial Seasonings Red Zinger)
- 1 vanilla bean pod, split
- 2 cups fresh or frozen cranberries

VANILLA CUSTARD SAUCE

- ⅓ cup granulated sugar
- 2 tsp. cornstarch
- 1½ cups whole milk
- 4 large egg yolks
- ½ tsp. vanilla extract

1. Prepare the Poached Pears: Place pears upright and close together, but not touching, in an even layer in a large saucepan. Add water to barely cover, about 4 to 5 cups. Add honey, sugar, lemon peel strip and juice, cinnamon stick, and tea bags. Scrape seeds from split vanilla bean into saucepan. Bring to a simmer, undisturbed, over medium-high. Reduce heat to medium; simmer until pears are just tender when pierced, about 10 minutes. Add cranberries; return to a simmer. Simmer until cranberries burst, about 3 minutes. Discard tea bags. Cover; chill at least 8 hours or up to 3 days.

2. Meanwhile, prepare the Vanilla Custard Sauce: Whisk together sugar and cornstarch in a saucepan. Gradually whisk in milk until smooth. Bring to a simmer over medium, stirring constantly. Simmer, stirring constantly, until slightly thickened, about 2 minutes. Remove from heat.

3. Whisk egg yolks in a small bowl. While whisking, gradually add about one-third of hot milk mixture to beaten yolks. Whisk egg mixture into remaining milk mixture in pan. Cook over medium-low, stirring constantly, until mixture thickens slightly (do not boil), 1 to 2 minutes. Remove from heat; stir in vanilla. Transfer to a medium bowl. Place a piece of plastic wrap directly on surface; chill about 3 hours.

4. To serve, remove pears and cranberries from poaching liquid; arrange on a serving platter. Lightly blot pears with paper towels. Serve with chilled sauce.

Dark Chocolate-Pear Cake

(Photo, page 215)

ACTIVE 15 MIN. - TOTAL 2 HOURS

SERVES 8

- Baking spray with flour
- 3 (4-oz.) semisweet chocolate bars, chopped and divided (3 cups)
- ½ cup canola oil
- 3 large eggs
- ¾ cup granulated sugar
- 1⅓ cups self-rising flour
- ¼ cup unsweetened cocoa
- 1 medium-size firm-ripe Bosc pear, thinly sliced
- ⅓ cup chopped unsalted almonds

1. Preheat oven to 325°F. Line bottom of a 10-inch cast-iron skillet with parchment paper. Spray with baking spray.

2. Place 2 cups of the chocolate in a microwavable bowl. Microwave on HIGH, stirring every 30 seconds, until melted, about 1½ minutes. Stir in oil until smooth.

3. Beat eggs and sugar in a large bowl with an electric mixer on high speed until pale in color and slightly thickened, about 2 minutes. Stir in melted chocolate mixture. Fold in flour and cocoa until just combined. Fold in remaining 1 cup chopped chocolate until combined. Spoon into skillet; smooth with a spatula. Top with pear and almonds.

4. Bake in preheated oven until edges are crisp but center is still slightly gooey, 45 to 50 minutes. Cool in skillet on a wire rack until room temperature, about 1 hour.

Poached Pears with Simplest Pear Tart

ACTIVE 10 MIN. - TOTAL 45 MIN.

SERVES 9

- ½ (17.3-oz.) pkg. frozen puff pastry sheets, thawed (1 sheet)
- All-purpose flour, for work surface
- 1 medium-size firm-ripe Bosc pear, cut lengthwise into ⅛-inch-thick slices
- 1 large egg
- ⅓ cup cane syrup
- 2 Tbsp. butter, melted
- ½ tsp. freshly ground nutmeg
- Powdered sugar

1. Preheat oven to 350°F. Line a large rimmed baking sheet with parchment paper. Roll puff pastry sheet into a 12-inch square on a lightly floured surface. Transfer to baking sheet. Arrange pear slices in 1 layer over pastry, leaving a 1-inch border.

2. Whisk together egg and 1 tablespoon water in a small bowl until combined. Brush egg mixture over pastry. Bake in preheated oven 15 minutes.

3. Stir together syrup, melted butter, and nutmeg in a small bowl. Reserve 2 tablespoons of the syrup mixture. Remove pastry from oven; brush with remaining syrup mixture. Bake in preheated oven until deep golden brown, 15 to 20 minutes more. Remove from oven; brush with reserved 2 tablespoons syrup mixture. Cool slightly on pan, 5 to 10 minutes. Sift powdered sugar over tart just before serving.

BROWN SUGAR BAKED PEARS

Brown Sugar Baked Pears

ACTIVE 10 MIN. · TOTAL 50 MIN.

SERVES 8

- 4 medium-size firm-ripe Bartlett pears, halved lengthwise and cored
- ¼ cup butter, melted, plus more for greasing baking dish
- ½ cup packed light brown sugar
- 1 tsp. ground cinnamon
- 2 tsp. cornstarch
- ⅔ cup apple cider (such as Martinelli's)
  Vanilla ice cream

1. Preheat oven to 350°F. Put pears, cut-side up, in a buttered 13- x 9-inch baking dish.
2. Stir together butter, brown sugar, and cinnamon. Spoon into centers of pears.
3. Whisk cornstarch with apple cider in a small bowl until smooth. Pour into bottom of baking dish. Cover with aluminum foil.

4. Bake, covered, in preheated oven 20 minutes. Uncover; bake until tender, about 20 minutes more. Top each pear half with ice cream. Stir cooking liquid in baking dish to combine into sauce; drizzle 1 tablespoon sauce over each serving.

Maple-Pecan-Pear Cheesecake

ACTIVE 25 MIN. · TOTAL 2 HOURS, 15 MIN.,
PLUS 2 HOURS COOLING AND 6 HOURS CHILLING

SERVES 12

CRUST
- 1½ cups graham cracker crumbs
- ½ cup finely chopped toasted pecans
- ¼ cup granulated sugar
- 6 Tbsp. butter, melted

FILLING
- 3 (8-oz.) pkg. cream cheese, at room temperature
- 4 large eggs

- 1 cup granulated sugar
- ¾ cup sour cream
- 2 Tbsp. all-purpose flour
- 2 tsp. vanilla extract
- 3½ cups chopped peeled firm-ripe Bartlett pears, divided (from about 4 pears)
- ⅓ cup pure maple syrup
- ¼ tsp. ground ginger
- ½ cup chopped toasted pecans

1. Prepare the Crust: Preheat oven to 325°F. Wrap outside of a 9-inch springform pan with aluminum foil. Stir together graham cracker crumbs, pecans, sugar, and butter in a bowl until combined. Firmly press into bottom and 1½ inches up sides of prepared pan. Bake until set, 12 minutes. Remove from oven; cool 15 minutes. Move oven rack to bottom position. Leave oven on.
2. While Crust bakes, prepare the Filling: Beat cream cheese in a large bowl with an electric mixer on medium speed until smooth, about 1 minute. Add eggs, 1 at a time, beating well after each addition. Add sugar, sour cream, flour, and vanilla; beat on medium speed until smooth and combined, about 2 minutes. Fold in 1½ cups of the chopped pears until evenly distributed. Pour into slightly cooled Crust. Place springform pan in a large roasting pan, and place roasting pan on oven rack in bottom position. Carefully add enough hot water to roasting pan to come halfway up sides of springform pan.
3. Bake at 325°F until center is set, about 1 hour and 15 minutes. Remove cheesecake from water bath. Carefully remove and discard foil from pan. Let cheesecake cool completely in pan on a wire rack, about 2 hours. Wrap in plastic wrap; chill at least 6 hours or up to 3 days.
4. Cook maple syrup, ground ginger, and remaining 2 cups chopped pears in a large skillet over medium-high, stirring often, until pears are just tender and maple syrup has thickened, 10 minutes. Remove from heat. Stir in pecans; cool 10 minutes. To serve, remove from pan; spoon warm pear mixture over chilled cheesecake.

SPICY GRILLED
CHICKEN WINGS

Korean Meets Southern Barbecue

What happens when ribs and wings team up with soy sauce, chile paste, garlic, and ginger? Food so good that it makes a lasting impression

WHENEVER MY FAMILY gets together with my parents for Korean food, a favorite memory always emerges, as though awakened by the spicy, garlicky sting of the kimchi that's always on the table. I'm about 6 years old, in the back seat of our station wagon with my brother, as our mom—who somehow looks just the same today—helps our dad navigate the drive to a place on the outskirts of Memphis. They're taking us for a special dinner, and we bristle with excitement. I'm sure the trip from Grenada, Mississippi, took awhile, and I know we were a little confused (at least I was) that the restaurant looked like a regular redbrick house. But what I really recall, what stands out most in my mind, is the savory smell of charred meat in the smoky air, the almost unbearable wait for our food to arrive as that aroma played on my imagination.

It was my first time eating Korean barbecue, raw meat delivered and cooked on a little grill right in the middle of the table. "Bulgogi is one of the most popular dishes in my home country," my mom explained. The thinly sliced rib eye was salty, sweet, garlicky, and wonderfully charred from the grill's searing heat. It's one of my earliest and most powerful food-and-family memories: My parents hauling us kiddos to a special experience that would stick with us for life.

Korean barbecue, whether enjoyed at a restaurant or at home, consists of meat and sometimes vegetables cooked quickly on a tabletop grill. Popular offerings include bulgogi, like what we had at that restaurant (thinly sliced beef marinated in soy sauce, brown sugar, and garlic), galbi (flanken-cut beef short ribs in a similar marinade), and samgyeopsal (sliced pork belly)—all served with kimchi, rice, red leaf lettuce, sauces, and lots of little relishes and side dishes called banchan. It's such a wonderful meal to share with a group.

Just as my mother did when I was growing up—flavoring her omurice (fried rice rolled up inside an egg crepe) with Jimmy Dean sausage, for example—I have learned to blend Korean dishes or flavors with Southern ones. It comes naturally as a way for me to combine the food traditions I love most, reflecting both my mom's Korean influence and my dad's Mississippi roots.

All of these main dishes are meant to go on an outdoor grill, as I would venture to guess that most Southern kitchens don't contain a tabletop grill. Instead of traditional bulgogi, I use that dish's flavors to give these baby back ribs salty-sweet Korean swagger. Chargrilled chicken wings pick up lots of kick from gochujang, a spicy-sweet Korean fermented chile paste that has become increasingly available in grocery stores. Pork tenderloin-stuffed biscuits get a savory edge from a fish sauce glaze and gochujang mayo. Even my Korean take on coleslaw, which is made with napa cabbage and loaded with kimchi, has the familiar touch point of a lightly sweetened mayonnaise dressing.

These recipes add more fun to a family dinner or a game-day spread, as you can enjoy them as either main dishes or appetizers. While the meats might be the same (ribs, wings, pork tenderloin, chicken), the flavors are bolder, more surprising, absolutely delicious, and (who knows?) perhaps enough to create your own memories that will last a lifetime. –Ann Taylor-Pittman

BARBECUE SAUCE · KIMCHI · CHOWCHOW · SCALLIONS · SOY SAUCE · GOCHUJANG

HONEY-BUTTER
CHICKEN SKEWERS

KIMCHI-
SESAME SLAW

PORK TENDERLOIN
BISCUITS WITH
GOCHUJANG MAYO

Spicy Grilled Chicken Wings

(Photo, page 220)

Gochujang and grated fresh ginger give this dish a tasty kick. The honey in the marinade chars a good bit on the grill for a rich, caramelized flavor that balances out the heat.

ACTIVE 30 MIN. - TOTAL 30 MIN.,
PLUS 1 HOUR MARINATING

SERVES 6

- ½ cup gochujang
- 2 Tbsp. toasted sesame oil
- 2 Tbsp. honey
- 1 Tbsp. grated fresh ginger
- 3 large garlic cloves, grated
- 4 lb. chicken wings, separated into flats and drumettes, wing tips discarded
- ¼ cup chopped scallions
- 1 Tbsp. toasted sesame seeds

1. Whisk together gochujang, oil, honey, ginger, and garlic in a large bowl. Add chicken wings, and toss well to coat. Let marinate in refrigerator 1 hour.
2. Preheat grill to medium (350°F to 400°F). Remove wings from marinade, letting excess drip off; discard marinade. Arrange wings on oiled grates. Grill, covered, until a thermometer inserted into thickest portion of meat registers 165°F, about 20 minutes, turning wings every 4 to 5 minutes. Arrange wings on a platter, and sprinkle with scallions and sesame seeds.

Sticky-Sweet Korean Barbecue Ribs

(Photo, page 3)

These ribs have the flavor of classic Korean bulgogi—soy sauce, brown sugar, garlic, and sesame oil—but with that fall-off-the-bone pork rib texture instead of the usual thinly sliced beef seared over a tabletop grill.

ACTIVE 35 MIN. - TOTAL 35 MIN., PLUS 2 HOURS
MARINATING AND 2 HOURS BAKING

SERVES 6

- 2 (2½- to 2¾-lb.) slabs baby back ribs
- 6 garlic cloves, grated
- ½ cup, plus 3 Tbsp. packed brown sugar, divided
- ¼ cup, plus 3 Tbsp. soy sauce, divided
- 3 Tbsp. honey
- 2 Tbsp. toasted sesame oil
  Chopped scallions (optional)

1. Remove membrane from back side of ribs. Arrange each slab, meaty-side up, on a double layer of heavy-duty aluminum foil. Stir together garlic, ½ cup of the sugar, and 3 tablespoons of the soy sauce in a small bowl. Rub mixture evenly over meaty side of ribs. Wrap foil around ribs, and let marinate in refrigerator at least 2 hours or up to 4 hours.
2. Preheat oven to 300°F. Place ribs, still wrapped in foil, on a large rimmed baking sheet. Bake until tender, about 2 hours.
3. Meanwhile, stir together honey, oil, and remaining 3 tablespoons sugar and ¼ cup soy sauce in a small saucepan; bring to a boil over medium. Reduce heat to medium-low. Boil, stirring occasionally, until syrupy, 2 to 3 minutes. Remove from heat. Reserve about half (⅓ cup) of sauce for serving. Set aside remaining sauce for basting.
4. Preheat grill to medium-high (400°F to 450°F). Unwrap ribs, and discard any liquid in foil. Place ribs on oiled grates. Grill, uncovered, basting with sauce reserved for basting, until lightly charred, about 5 minutes per side. Transfer ribs to a platter, and drizzle with sauce reserved for serving. If desired, garnish with scallions.

Honey-Butter Chicken Skewers

(Photo, page 222)

In Korea, honey-butter potato chips are a popular snack that's pretty irresistible. This recipe captures that flavor in meaty, charred-from-the-grill form. It's rich, salty, and sweet all at once.

ACTIVE 25 MIN. - TOTAL 25 MIN.

SERVES 6

- ½ cup unsalted butter
- 2 large garlic cloves, grated
- ⅓ cup honey
- 1 tsp. kosher salt
- 1 tsp. rice vinegar
- ¼ cup, plus 2 Tbsp. soy sauce, divided
- 3½ lb. boneless, skinless chicken thighs, cut into bite-size (about 1-inch) pieces
- 2 medium-size red onions, cut into wedges

1. Preheat grill to medium-high (400°F to 450°F). Melt butter in a medium saucepan on stove-top over medium. Add garlic, and cook, stirring often, 2 minutes. Stir in honey, salt, vinegar, and 2 tablespoons of the soy sauce. Reduce heat to medium-low, and bring to a boil. Cook, stirring occasionally, until syrupy, about 2 minutes. Remove from heat.
2. Toss together chicken pieces and remaining ¼ cup soy sauce in a large bowl. Thread chicken and onion pieces alternately onto 12 (10- to 12-inch) skewers. Place prepared skewers on oiled grill grates. Grill, uncovered, turning and basting often with butter mixture, until lightly charred and cooked through, 10 to 12 minutes.

Kimchi-Sesame Slaw

(Photo, page 222)

Kimchi, toasted sesame oil, and ginger give this slaw undeniable Korean flavor, and whisking mayo into the dressing adds a familiar creamy consistency and richness. Napa cabbage has a soft crunch, and little bits of chopped kimchi add funk, texture, and touches of heat.

ACTIVE 15 MIN. - TOTAL 15 MIN.

SERVES 8

- ⅓ cup very thinly sliced red onion (from 1 small [5-oz.] onion)
- 3 Tbsp. mayonnaise
- 2 Tbsp. fresh lime juice (from 1 medium lime)
- 2 Tbsp. toasted sesame oil
- 1 Tbsp. packed light brown sugar
- 1 tsp. grated fresh ginger
- ½ tsp. kosher salt
- ½ tsp. black pepper
- 9 cups thinly sliced napa cabbage (about 1 lb., 3 oz.)
- ½ cup chopped kimchi
- ⅓ cup chopped fresh cilantro

Rinse onion slices well with cold water; drain well, and set aside. Whisk together mayonnaise, lime juice, oil, brown sugar, ginger, salt, and pepper in a large bowl. Add onion, cabbage, and kimchi; toss well to coat. Stir in cilantro. Serve immediately, or chill 1 hour.

Pork Tenderloin Biscuits with Gochujang Mayo

(Photo, page 223)

Pork biscuits are a treat in their own right. But the slightly spicy gochujang mayonnaise enriched with toasted sesame oil is the real star of these sandwiches. Brushing the pork with fish sauce enhances its savory quality without giving it a fish flavor. Because this sauce has so much sodium, you don't need to add any salt to the meat. You can serve the pork, mayo, biscuits, and Kimchi-Sesame Slaw on a large platter and just let everyone help themselves.

ACTIVE 45 MIN. - TOTAL 1 HOUR, 10 MIN.

SERVES 5

- 2 (1-lb.) pork tenderloins, trimmed
- 2 Tbsp. fish sauce
- ¼ cup packed brown sugar
- 4 large garlic cloves, grated
- 2¾ cups all-purpose flour, plus more for work surface
- 3½ tsp. baking powder
- 1¼ tsp. kosher salt
- 1 tsp. baking soda
- 11 Tbsp. unsalted butter, cut into small pieces
- 1⅓ cups whole buttermilk
- ½ cup mayonnaise
- 3 Tbsp. gochujang
- 1 tsp. toasted sesame oil

1. Preheat a gas grill to medium-high (400°F to 450°F) on 1 side, or push hot coals to 1 side of a charcoal grill. Preheat oven to 425°F.
2. Brush pork evenly all over with fish sauce, then rub evenly with brown sugar and garlic. Let stand 5 minutes. Arrange pork on oiled grates over lit side of grill. Grill, covered, until meat is well marked, 3 to 4 minutes per side. Move pork to oiled grates over unlit side of grill. Grill, covered, until a thermometer inserted into thickest portion of meat registers 142°F to 145°F, about 15 minutes. Remove from grill, and let stand 5 minutes. Thinly slice the pork, and set aside until ready to use.
3. Whisk together flour, baking powder, kosher salt, and baking soda in a large bowl. Add butter pieces; rub butter into flour mixture using your fingertips until mixture resembles coarse meal. Stir in buttermilk; knead in bowl until dough comes together, about 30 seconds. Turn dough out onto a lightly floured work surface. Roll to ½-inch thickness. Cut dough into rounds using a 2½-inch biscuit cutter, rerolling scraps as needed, to form 20 biscuits. Arrange biscuits on a baking sheet lined with parchment paper. Bake in preheated oven until golden brown, about 15 minutes. Cool 5 minutes.
4. Meanwhile, stir together mayonnaise, gochujang, and sesame oil in a small bowl; set aside until ready to use.
5. Split biscuits. Top each bottom half with 2 to 4 pork slices and mayonnaise mixture, divided evenly among biscuits. Cover with biscuit tops.

The Korean Pantry

Kimchi
This ubiquitous Korean "pickle" is made from fermented cabbage mixed with garlic, dried red chile pepper, and often fish sauce or dried shrimp (though you can find vegan versions). Think of it as a chunky, spicy distant relative of sauerkraut. Nasoya is an easy-to-find brand with legit flavor; it meets with my mom's approval.

Fish Sauce
You'll likely see it in the Asian-food section of any grocery. The thin liquid is made from fermented fish (usually anchovies) and adds lots of savory—not necessarily fishy—taste to food. Red Boat brand is my favorite.

Gochujang
Spicy and slightly sweet, this Korean red chile paste packs a punch. Traditionally, it's sold in Asian markets in tubs and has a texture similar to miso or almond butter. Many grocery stores sell gochujang sauce, which comes in bottles and has a consistency akin to barbecue sauce. Either type will work in these recipes.

Toasted Sesame Oil
You'll also find this in the Asian-food aisle. Most brands deliver plenty of nutty sesame flavor, but if you can, I urge you to seek out a quality Korean sesame oil, such as Beksul or Ottogi. They each have an exquisite taste and aroma.

Give It a Swirl

Ribbons of spices and apples run through a sweet bread that's surprisingly simple to pull off

Spiced Apple-Pecan Swirl Bread

ACTIVE 40 MIN. · TOTAL 3 HOURS,
PLUS 8 HOURS CHILLING

SERVES 12

DOUGH

- 1 (8-oz.) container sour cream
- 6 Tbsp. unsalted butter
- 1¾ tsp. kosher salt
- ¼ cup, plus 1 tsp. granulated sugar, divided
- ⅓ cup warm water (100°F to 110°F)
- 1 (¼-oz.) envelope active dry yeast
- 2 large eggs, beaten
- 3¾ to 4¼ cups bread flour, divided, plus more for work surface

FILLING

- ½ cup granulated sugar
- ½ cup packed light brown sugar
- ½ cup finely chopped peeled Honeycrisp or Gala apple (from 1 small apple), plus 1 cup thinly sliced unpeeled Honeycrisp or Gala apple (from 1 small apple), divided
- ½ cup toasted pecans, chopped
- 4 Tbsp. unsalted butter, softened
- 1½ tsp. ground cinnamon
- 1 tsp. ground cardamom
- ½ tsp. ground ginger
- 1 tsp. fresh lemon juice (from 1 lemon)

GLAZE

- 1 cup sifted powdered sugar
- 1 to 2 Tbsp. apple cider, as needed

1. Prepare the Dough: Cook sour cream, butter, kosher salt, and ¼ cup of the granulated sugar in a small saucepan over medium-low, stirring occasionally, until butter just melts, 4 to 5 minutes. Remove from heat; cool to 110°F to 115°F, about 10 minutes.

2. Stir together warm water, yeast, and remaining 1 teaspoon granulated sugar in a small bowl. Let stand until foamy, about 5 minutes.

3. Beat sour cream and yeast mixtures and eggs with a stand mixer fitted with a dough hook attachment on medium-low speed, gradually adding 3¾ cups of the flour until a soft Dough forms and pulls away from sides but still adheres to bottom of bowl, about 2 minutes.

4. Turn out on a lightly floured work surface. Knead until smooth and elastic, about 10 minutes, adding up to remaining ½ cup flour in very small increments, if needed, to keep the Dough workable. (It should be tacky but not sticky.) Place in a lightly greased (with cooking spray) bowl, turning to coat all sides. Cover and chill at least 8 hours or up to 24 hours.

5. Turn Dough out on a lightly floured work surface. Roll into a 20- x 16-inch rectangle. Coat a 12-inch cast-iron skillet with cooking spray, and place a round sheet of parchment paper in bottom of the skillet. Set aside.

6. Prepare the Filling: Stir together granulated sugar, brown sugar, finely chopped apple, toasted pecans, softened butter, cinnamon, cardamom, and ginger in a bowl until mixture is well combined and the texture of wet sand.

7. Gently spread Filling over Dough, carefully pressing to adhere, leaving a 1-inch border on both long sides. Starting at 1 long side, roll Dough up, jelly-roll style, into a log (A). Using a serrated knife, cut log in half lengthwise (B). Arrange Dough pieces side by side, cut sides up, on work surface. Carefully twist together, keeping cut sides facing up (C). Shape twisted Dough into a 9-inch ring, tucking ends under. Place in prepared skillet. Toss together lemon juice and sliced apple in a small bowl to coat. Gently tuck apple slices in between layers of Dough and Filling. Cover loosely with plastic wrap; let stand in a warm place until almost doubled in size, 1 to 1½ hours.

8. Preheat oven to 350°F with rack in lower third position. Remove and discard plastic wrap from skillet. Bake until golden brown and cooked through, 50 minutes to 1 hour, tenting with aluminum foil after 30 minutes, if needed, to prevent excessive browning. Remove from oven. Let cool 15 minutes.

9. Prepare the Glaze: Whisk together powdered sugar and 1 tablespoon apple cider in a bowl. Add remaining 1 tablespoon cider, if needed, until desired consistency. Drizzle Glaze over bread. Serve warm, or transfer bread to a wire rack. Cool completely, about 1 hour.

Use Your Noodles

Reinvent pasta night with these delicious new twists on old favorites

Creamy Chicken Noodle Soup

ACTIVE 25 MIN. - TOTAL 25 MIN.

SERVES 4

- ¼ cup unsalted butter
- 1 medium-size yellow onion, finely chopped (about 1 cup)
- 3 medium carrots, sliced into ½-inch rounds (about 1½ cups)
- 2 medium celery stalks, chopped (about 1 cup)
- 1½ tsp. kosher salt, divided
- ¼ cup all-purpose flour
- 4 medium garlic cloves, finely chopped (4 tsp.)
- ¼ tsp. smoked paprika
- 6 cups chicken stock
- 8 oz. old-fashioned wide egg noodles (such as Mrs. Miller's)
- 12 oz. cooked chicken, torn into bite-size pieces (4 cups)
- ½ cup heavy whipping cream
- 1 Tbsp. sherry vinegar
- 2 tsp. fresh thyme leaves

1. Melt butter in a large pot over medium-high. Add onion, carrots, celery, and ½ teaspoon of the salt. Cook, stirring occasionally, until softened, about 5 minutes. Add flour, garlic, and paprika. Cook, stirring constantly, until mixture is fragrant and flour turns light brown, about 1 minute.
2. Add stock to flour mixture, and increase heat to high. Bring to a boil, stirring occasionally. Add egg noodles. Cook, stirring occasionally, until tender and just cooked through, about 10 minutes. Reduce heat to medium-low. Add chicken. Cook, stirring constantly, until chicken is heated through, about 1 minute. Remove from heat. Stir in cream, sherry vinegar, and remaining 1 teaspoon salt. Divide soup evenly among 4 bowls; top with thyme leaves.

VEGGING OUT
Make this soup more nutritious by stirring in baby spinach or frozen peas along with the pasta.

Tortellini Mac and Cheese

ACTIVE 25 MIN. - TOTAL 25 MIN.

SERVES 4

8	oz. uncooked medium shell pasta
20	oz. uncooked cheese tortellini
5	Tbsp. unsalted butter, divided
¼	cup all-purpose flour
3	cups whole milk
4	oz. cream cheese
2	tsp. Dijon mustard
1½	tsp. kosher salt
½	tsp. black pepper
4	oz. white cheddar cheese, shredded (about 1 cup)
4	oz. fontina cheese, shredded (about 1 cup)
½	cup panko breadcrumbs
1	Tbsp. finely chopped fresh chives

1. Bring a large pot of salted water to a boil over medium-high. Add shell pasta; return to a boil. Cook, stirring occasionally, 9 minutes. Add tortellini. Cook, stirring occasionally, until shells and tortellini are al dente, about 3 minutes. Drain; set aside.

2. While pasta cooks, melt 4 tablespoons of the butter in a broiler-safe Dutch oven over medium-high. Cook, stirring occasionally, until butter smells nutty, about 2 minutes. Add flour. Cook, whisking constantly, until toasted and light brown, about 2 minutes. Reduce heat to medium; gradually whisk in milk. Cook over medium, stirring occasionally, until mixture can coat the back of a wooden spoon, 5 minutes. Add cream cheese, mustard, salt, and pepper. Cook, whisking constantly, until smooth, 1 minute. Gradually add cheddar and fontina, whisking between additions, until smooth, 1 minute. Remove from heat. Stir drained pastas into sauce in Dutch oven; toss to fully coat. Set aside.

3. Preheat oven to broil with rack about 8 inches from heat source. Microwave remaining 1 tablespoon butter in a small microwavable bowl on MEDIUM (50% power) until melted, about 30 seconds. Add panko to melted butter; toss to coat. Sprinkle evenly over pasta mixture. Broil until golden brown and crispy, about 3 minutes, checking often to prevent burning. Top with chives before serving.

Spaghetti with Meatless Ragù

ACTIVE 30 MIN. - TOTAL 30 MIN.

SERVES 4

- 1 small yellow onion, roughly chopped (about 1 cup)
- 1 medium carrot, roughly chopped (about ½ cup)
- 1 medium celery stalk, roughly chopped (about ¼ cup)
- 2 Tbsp. olive oil
- 2 Tbsp. tomato paste
- 3 medium garlic cloves, finely chopped (about 1 Tbsp.)

- 12 oz. plant-based ground-meat substitute (such as Impossible Burger)
- ¾ cup red wine
- 1½ tsp. kosher salt
- ½ tsp. ground fennel
- ½ tsp. black pepper
- 1 (28-oz.) can crushed San Marzano plum tomatoes
- ⅓ cup whole milk

- 12 oz. uncooked spaghetti
- 3 Tbsp. unsalted butter
- 3 oz. Parmesan cheese, grated (about ¾ cup), divided
- 2 Tbsp. finely chopped fresh parsley

1. Bring a large pot of heavily salted water to a boil over high. Meanwhile, pulse onion, carrot, and celery in a food processor until very finely chopped (but not pureed), about 5 pulses, scraping down sides of bowl as needed. Heat oil in a large Dutch oven over medium-high. Add chopped vegetable mixture. Cook, stirring occasionally, until softened, about 5 minutes. Add tomato paste and garlic. Cook, stirring constantly, until tomato paste starts to darken, about 2 minutes. Add meat substitute in chunks. Cook, undisturbed, until browned on bottom, about 2 minutes. Break up meat substitute using a wooden spoon. Cook, stirring occasionally, until browned, about 4 minutes. Add wine, salt, fennel, and pepper. Cook, stirring occasionally, until wine has reduced, about 1 minute. Add tomatoes and milk. Reduce heat to medium. Cook, stirring occasionally, until ragù is thickened and saucy, about 12 minutes.

2. During final 10 minutes of ragù cook time, add spaghetti to boiling water. Cook until almost al dente, 9 to 11 minutes.

3. Using tongs, transfer spaghetti to ragù in Dutch oven, reserving cooking water in pot. Add about ¾ cup reserved cooking water to spaghetti mixture. Cook over medium, stirring with tongs, until noodles are loosened and coated with sauce. Remove from heat. Add butter and ½ cup of the Parmesan; stir and fold together until butter has melted. Divide among 4 plates; sprinkle with parsley and remaining ¼ cup Parmesan.

One-Pan Garlic-Butter Shrimp with Orzo

ACTIVE 30 MIN · TOTAL 30 MIN.
SERVES 4

- ¼ cup unsalted butter, divided
- ¼ cup olive oil, divided
- 2 medium shallots, finely chopped (½ cup)
- ½ cup white wine
- 3 cups vegetable broth
- 1½ cups uncooked orzo
- 1½ tsp. kosher salt, divided
- 6 medium garlic cloves
- 1 Tbsp. grated lemon zest, plus 2 Tbsp. fresh juice (from 2 lemons), divided, plus lemon wedges for serving
- ¼ tsp. crushed red pepper
- ¼ cup chopped fresh flat-leaf parsley, divided
- 1 lb. large peeled, deveined raw shrimp
- 2 Tbsp. drained capers, roughly chopped

1. Heat 2 tablespoons each of the butter and oil in a large, deep skillet over medium. Add shallots. Cook, stirring occasionally, until softened, about 3 minutes. Add wine. Cook, stirring occasionally, until reduced by about half, about 2 minutes. Remove from heat.

2. Transfer 3 tablespoons shallot mixture to a medium bowl; reserve remaining shallot mixture in skillet. Add remaining 2 tablespoons each butter and oil to shallot mixture in medium bowl, and whisk to combine. Set aside.

3. Add broth to remaining shallot mixture in skillet, and bring to a boil over high. Stir in orzo and 1 teaspoon of the salt. Reduce to a simmer over medium-low. Cover and cook, undisturbed and without uncovering, 10 minutes.

4. Meanwhile, finely chop garlic. Add remaining ½ teaspoon salt to garlic; using the flat side of a chef's knife, press and rub together to form a paste. Add garlic paste, lemon juice, crushed red pepper, and 2 tablespoons of the parsley to shallot mixture in medium bowl, and stir to combine. Add shrimp, and toss to fully coat (mixture will start to solidify because shrimp are cold).

5. Uncover cooked orzo; spoon shrimp in a single layer over orzo. Spoon remaining shallot mixture in bowl over shrimp and orzo. Cover and cook over medium-low until shrimp are just opaque, about 4 minutes. Remove from heat. Uncover; sprinkle with capers, lemon zest, and remaining 2 tablespoons parsley. Serve immediately alongside lemon wedges.

Cheesy Lasagna Soup

ACTIVE 25 MIN. - TOTAL 25 MIN.

SERVES 4

- 8 oz. whole-milk ricotta cheese (about 1 cup)
- 2 oz. Parmesan cheese, finely grated (about 1¼ cups)
- ⅛ tsp. ground nutmeg
- 1¼ tsp. kosher salt, divided
- 1 Tbsp. olive oil
- 1 lb. ground chuck
- 1 medium-size yellow onion, chopped (about 1 cup)
- 3 medium garlic cloves, finely chopped (about 1 Tbsp.)
- 2 (15-oz.) cans diced tomatoes
- 6 cups chicken stock
- 1½ Tbsp. granulated sugar
- 8 oz. uncooked lasagna noodles, broken into 1½- to 2-inch pieces
- 1 Tbsp. red wine vinegar
- 4 oz. low-moisture mozzarella cheese, shredded (about 1 cup)
- ¼ cup small fresh basil leaves

1. Stir together ricotta, Parmesan, nutmeg, and ¼ teaspoon of the salt in a medium bowl. Cover and refrigerate until ready to serve.

2. Heat oil in a large Dutch oven over medium-high. Add ground chuck. Cook, stirring and breaking up into pieces, until browned and just cooked through, about 3 minutes. Using a slotted spoon, transfer beef to a small bowl lined with paper towels; set aside.

3. Do not wipe Dutch oven clean. Add onion to Dutch oven. Cook over medium-high, stirring occasionally, until softened and starting to caramelize, about 4 minutes. Add garlic. Cook, stirring constantly, until fragrant, about 1 minute. Stir in diced tomatoes and stock; bring to a boil over high. Stir in sugar and remaining 1 teaspoon salt. Add lasagna pieces. Cook, stirring occasionally, until noodles are just cooked through and almost al dente, about 8 minutes. Stir in browned beef. Remove from heat, and stir in vinegar. Divide soup evenly among 4 bowls; top with mozzarella and dollops of reserved ricotta mixture. Top bowls with basil leaves before serving.

MAKE WAVES

Skip the no-boil pasta for this soup—it will overcook and turn mushy. Regular lasagna noodles with wavy edges will add more texture to the dish.

Put Down the Peanut Butter

Satisfy after-school cravings with a creamy stir-together dip that's
packed with protein and easy enough for kids to make

Cinnamon-Raisin Almond Butter Dip

ACTIVE 5 MIN. · TOTAL 5 MIN.
SERVES 8

Whisk together ¾ cup **vanilla whole-milk Greek yogurt,** ½ cup **almond butter** (such as Barney Butter), 3 Tbsp. **pure maple syrup,** ½ tsp. **vanilla extract,** and ¼ tsp. **ground cinnamon** in a medium bowl until smooth. Fold in ¼ cup **raisins** until well combined. Sprinkle with **cinnamon** before serving with **apple slices.** Store in an airtight container in refrigerator for up to 3 days.

I Love You, Greens

These leafy vegetables are as much a staple around the world as they are in the South

OVER THE YEARS, I have learned just how Southern my Northern upbringing was. Many custodians of African American foodways live across the North, Midwest, and West because of the Great Migration. My grandmother, a Tennessean transplanted to New York City, made her own lye soap on the stove in her apartment and grew her own collards in a small plot behind her building in the projects. She wasn't a great cook, but she could "put a hurtin' " on a mess of greens. As a special treat, she would put them into Mason jars and send them to me when I was away at college. I guess I really owe my love of them to her.

Greens have always been a part of my life. I am particularly partial to collards but chow down on any kind with gusto—whether collard, kale, mustard, or turnip greens. I'm happiest when they are jazzed up with chopped onion and a dash or two of spicy seasoned vinegar, which I prefer to hot sauce.

It was with both surprise and delight that, on my first trips exploring the African diaspora, I found almost every kind of greens imaginable. When I visited Benin, in West Africa, they were the basis for the deep verdant hue of the sauce feuille that my friend prepared for dinner. One taste, and I realized it was probably the ancestor of chef Leah Chase's New Orleans gumbo z'herbes. In Bahia, Brazil, they turned up as couve, the traditional accompaniment to feijoada (the national dish), and the markets there overflowed with every variety of kale.

In my favorite Ethiopian restaurant, I enjoy them as gomen, which winks at the world from a round of injera (a type of flatbread). In Tunisia, greens are served up proudly as molokhia. I've also been seduced by sautéed pea shoots in Shanghai and bitter greens called horta in Greece. Virtually all over the globe, greens are eaten in some form. I guess it's their ease of cooking, the multiple ways in which they can be prepared,

and that they can even be foraged during times of necessity.

Several years back, I was fortunate enough to be invited to Blackberry Farm in Tennessee to speak about these veggies. I began by paraphrasing a poem by Spanish author Federico García Lorca that I remembered from college: "Greens, I love you, greens." I guess that sums it up.

Jessica's Mixed Greens

ACTIVE 2 HOURS, 45 MIN. - TOTAL 2 HOURS, 55 MIN.
SERVES 6

- 4 lb. mixed fresh collard, mustard, and/or turnip greens
- 8 bacon slices, chopped
- 1½ tsp. kosher salt
- ½ tsp. black pepper

  Hot sauce; chopped onions; additional chopped, cooked bacon; and Spicy Vinegar (recipe follows)

1. Wash mixed fresh greens well, picking them over to remove any brown spots or blemishes. Drain well. Discard any discolored outer leaves, and remove and discard thick ribs. Tear greens into 3- to 4-inch pieces.

2. Place chopped bacon in a large Dutch oven. Cook over medium, stirring often, until translucent and bottom of Dutch oven is coated with rendered bacon fat, about 8 minutes. Add greens and 6 cups water, and bring to a boil over medium. Reduce heat to low. Cook, uncovered, stirring occasionally, until greens are tender, about 2 hours. Stir in salt and pepper. Add desired toppings.

Spicy Vinegar

ACTIVE 15 MIN. - TOTAL 15 MIN., PLUS 1 WEEK STANDING
MAKES 1 PT.

- 1 small carrot
- 1 small (½-inch) piece fresh ginger, peeled
- 4 fresh thyme sprigs
- 3 garlic cloves
- 1 small piece seeded fresh habanero chile or other chile, to taste
- 1 pt. apple cider vinegar

Using a vegetable peeler, peel carrot into thin strips. Place in a sterilized pint-size bottle with a tight lid. Add ginger, thyme, garlic, and chile to bottle. Pour in vinegar; seal bottle. Let stand at room temperature for 1 week.

Which Greens Do You Go For?

There's a world to choose from, and everyone has a favorite

While they fall under the generic heading of greens, there are different types of these vegetables, each with its own partisans. I prefer collards—perhaps the most robust of them all—for their dense flavor and the fact that they are deemed better and sweeter after the first frost hits them. Then there are fans of mustard greens, which are a bit tangier and have an almost mustard-like zing to them. Some opt for a mix, and might even add turnip tops (aka turnip greens) to the pot. Finally, there is kale. After one too many salads made from these leaves, the refreshing taste of the cooked version is most welcome.

Fall Is for Football

Tailgating is a family tradition for *Hey Y'all*
host and Test Kitchen pro Ivy Odom

IN THE SOUTH, the seasons are as follows: winter, spring, summer, and football. The region's favorite sport is as anticipated as the color-changing leaves and crisp mornings that fall eventually brings.

The only thing that can rival the devotion to our college team of choice is our love of tailgating. Because my parents set up a spread at every single University of Georgia home game during my college years, my mama's recipes quickly became touchdowns among all of my friends. She had her go-to dishes that made the roster week after week, but she was also famous for serving more out-of-the-box game-day foods, like fajitas and ravioli with marinara sauce.

Depending on the kickoff time, she went with brunch or snacks or full-on dinner made over a camping grill or heated up with Sterno. Her trusty cast-iron skillet was always at hand, ready to cook anything on the grill. Inspired by one of her melted cheese dips, this Pimiento Queso Fundido is sure to be the perfect addition to your lineup this year.

Whether you make it on your stove-top at home or under a tent in your beloved college town, this gooey riff on pimiento cheese is best served piping hot with warm tortillas or chips for dipping. It will instantly become a fan favorite that will have all of your guests going for two.

Pimiento Queso Fundido

ACTIVE 20 MIN. - TOTAL 20 MIN.
SERVES 6

- 2 tsp. olive oil
- 1 cup thinly sliced sweet onion (from 1 medium onion)
- ¼ tsp. kosher salt
- ¼ tsp. smoked paprika
- 3 (4-oz.) jars sliced pimientos, well drained and patted dry, divided
- 8 oz. sharp cheddar cheese, shredded (about 2 cups)
- 8 oz. Monterey Jack cheese, shredded (about 2 cups)
- 4 oz. Gouda cheese, shredded (about 1 cup)
- 1½ tsp. Worcestershire sauce
- Charred flour tortillas, for serving

1. Heat oil in a 10-inch cast-iron skillet over medium. Add sliced onion. Cook, stirring often, until softened and beginning to caramelize, 8 to 9 minutes. Add kosher salt, paprika, and all but ¼ cup of the sliced pimientos. Cook, stirring constantly, until paprika is fragrant, about 1 minute. Add cheddar, Monterey Jack, Gouda, and Worcestershire, stirring until cheeses begin to melt. Cook, stirring occasionally, until cheeses are melted and bubbly, 5 to 7 minutes.
2. Remove skillet from heat; top mixture with remaining ¼ cup sliced pimientos. Serve with charred tortillas, and garnish with desired toppings (below).

Take your queso to the next level with flavorful ingredient combos.
Extra Spicy Sliced jalapeño chiles or red Fresno chiles, crumbled cooked chorizo, and spicy corn chips (such as Fritos Flamin' Hot)
Farm to Queso Pickled red onions, charred corn kernels, diced fresh tomatoes, diced fresh bell peppers, chopped scallions, and cilantro
Fully Loaded Crumbled cooked bacon, crumbled queso fresco (fresh Mexican cheese), crispy fried onions, sliced pickled jalapeños, and chopped scallions

BEST FOR DIPPING
Heat tortillas in a cast-iron skillet until slightly charred on both sides—or just dig in with tortilla chips.

The Do-It-All Casserole

Yes, comfort food can still taste fresh. The proof is in this one-pan wonder
that can be customized in creative ways

Lightened-Up Chicken-Broccoli Casserole

ACTIVE 20 MIN. - TOTAL 40 MIN.

SERVES 6

- 1/3 cup all-purpose flour
- 4 cups 2% reduced-fat milk, divided
- 2 (8.8-oz.) pkg. precooked microwavable brown rice
- 3 cups fresh broccoli florets
- 3 cups shredded cooked chicken (from 1 large rotisserie chicken)
- 6 oz. reduced-fat extra-sharp cheddar cheese, shredded (1½ cups)
- 3/4 tsp. kosher salt
- 1/2 tsp. black pepper
- 1/2 cup whole-wheat panko breadcrumbs
- 1 Tbsp. canola oil

1. Preheat oven to 400°F with rack 6 inches from heat source. Whisk together flour and 1 cup of the milk in a small bowl until smooth. Bring remaining 3 cups milk to a boil in a large broiler-safe skillet over medium-high, stirring often. Reduce heat to medium, and gradually whisk in flour mixture until smooth. Return to a boil over medium-high. Boil, stirring constantly, until thickened, 2 to 3 minutes.
2. Stir rice and broccoli into milk mixture until combined. Cook over medium-high, stirring occasionally, until broccoli is bright green, about 2 minutes.
3. Add chicken, cheddar, salt, and pepper to rice mixture; stir until cheese is melted. Remove from heat. Stir together panko and oil in a small bowl; sprinkle evenly over chicken mixture.
4. Bake in preheated oven until casserole is bubbly, about 15 minutes. Increase oven temperature to broil (do not remove skillet from oven). Broil until top is golden brown, 1 to 2 minutes. Remove from oven, and let cool 5 minutes before serving.

CALORIES: **467** – CARBS: **44G** – FAT: **16G**

Four Fantastic New Spins

1. Crispy Onions and Parmesan

Prepare recipe as directed, substituting **part-skim mozzarella** for cheddar and substituting ½ cup **crispy fried onions** and ¼ cup finely shredded **Parmesan** for panko-oil mixture in Step 3.

CALORIES: **459** – CARBS: **42G** – FAT: **16G**

2. Pimiento Cheese

Prepare recipe as directed, substituting 8 oz. **whole grain penne** pasta (cooked to al dente) for the rice at the beginning of Step 2. Add 1 (4-oz.) jar **diced pimiento peppers** (drained) and ½ tsp. **onion powder** in with chicken and cheese to pasta-broccoli mixture at the beginning of Step 3. Substitute ½ cup crushed **whole grain crackers** (such as Ritz) for the panko.

CALORIES: **490** – CARBS: **47G** – FAT: **15G**

3. Mushrooms and Thyme

Prepare recipe as directed, substituting **fontina cheese** for cheddar and stirring in 8 oz. quartered and sautéed **cremini mushrooms** with chicken and cheese at the beginning of Step 3. Add 1 Tbsp. chopped **fresh thyme** to panko mixture.

CALORIES: **495** – CARBS: **45G** – FAT: **19G**

4. Buffalo Ranch

Prepare recipe as directed, adding 1 cup finely chopped **carrots** with rice and broccoli at the beginning of Step 2. Add 2 Tbsp. **Buffalo-style hot sauce** (such as Frank's RedHot), 1 Tbsp. chopped **fresh dill**, and ¾ tsp. **garlic powder** with chicken and cheese at the beginning of Step 3. Sprinkle with 1 additional Tbsp. **fresh dill**, and top with additional **hot sauce**.

CALORIES: **477** – CARBS: **46G** – FAT: **16G**

Puff Pastry Pointers

Tips for turning frozen dough into light, flaky layers

DO

Defrost It
Thaw the frozen puff pastry in the refrigerator overnight or for 40 minutes at room temperature.

Keep It Cool
If the pastry starts to soften and turn limp, pop it back in the refrigerator to resolidify the butter. Keep unused sheets frozen or chilled.

DON'T

Skip the Flour
Generously flour the work surface and rolling pin to prevent the puff pastry from sticking and tearing.

Toss the Scraps
Roll extra bits of pastry in cinnamon sugar, and bake it for a cook's treat. Or roll in Parmesan cheese and black pepper for a savory snack.

"Don't unfold puff pastry sheets until they are **fully thawed and pliable.** If the pastry is still a bit frozen, it will crack or tear."

—*Jasmine Smith,* Test Kitchen professional

THE BEST WAY TO SLICE GREENS

1.
Use a chef's knife to cut off center ribs and stems of washed, dried leaves. Place the greens on top of each other to make a stack. Flatten gently with your hands.

2.
Roll trimmed leaves as tightly as possible into a cigar shape. (If they can't be rolled, hold the stack in place on one end, then slice through the layers, starting at the opposite end.)

3.
Holding the roll, use a knife to slice greens, starting from one end. Cut the leaves into wide or narrow ribbons, depending on recipe.

October

CHICKEN FRICOT

Southern Stews and Brews

Bragging rights will be on the line when you team up these comforting recipes with regional beers

Chicken Fricot

When talk turns to Cajun food, gumbo and boudin usually get all the attention, but there's a lesser-known dish that's just as tasty. Chicken fricot (derived from the French word fricoter, *which loosely translates to "cook something up") is a stew with Acadian roots. This version is made with a whole chicken and finished with pillowy sausage-filled dumplings.*

ACTIVE 30 MIN. - TOTAL 1 HOUR
SERVES 4

- 1 (3-lb.) whole chicken
- 1½ Tbsp. Cajun seasoning
- 2 Tbsp. canola oil
- 2 cups diagonally sliced peeled carrots (from 2 large carrots)
- 1 cup coarsely chopped yellow onion (from 1 onion)
- 1 cup diagonally sliced celery (from 3 stalks)
- 3 large garlic cloves, finely chopped
- ¼ cup all-purpose flour, plus more for work surface
- 6 cups chicken stock
- 8 oz. russet potatoes, peeled and cut into ½-inch pieces (about 2 small potatoes)
- 1 tsp. ground savory (optional)
- 1¼ tsp. kosher salt, divided
- 1 cup self-rising flour
- ¾ cup heavy cream
- 1 (2½-oz.) Cajun-style smoked chicken sausage link, very finely chopped (about ¾ cup)
- 2 Tbsp. chopped fresh chives, for garnish

1. Cut chicken into 6 pieces, discarding skin, backbone, giblets, and neck. Sprinkle chicken with Cajun seasoning. Heat oil in a large Dutch oven over medium-high. Add chicken, meaty side down; cook until well browned, about 7 minutes. Turn over; cook 2 minutes. Transfer to a plate.
2. Add carrots, onion, celery, and garlic to Dutch oven. Cook, stirring occasionally, until they begin to soften, about 5 minutes. Add all-purpose flour and cook, stirring often, 1 minute. Stir in chicken stock, stirring and scraping to loosen browned bits from bottom of Dutch oven. Let the mixture come to a boil. Add chicken, potatoes, ground savory (if using), and ¾ teaspoon of the salt. Cover and reduce heat to medium-low. Simmer until chicken is cooked through and vegetables are tender, about 20 minutes. Remove from heat. Transfer chicken to a plate and let stand 10 minutes. Shred chicken, discarding bones.
3. While chicken stands, stir together self-rising flour and remaining ½ teaspoon salt in a medium bowl. Add cream, stirring to combine. Stir in sausage. Place mixture on a lightly floured surface and knead gently once or twice until dough comes together. Pat into ½-inch thickness then cut into 8 pieces. Round edges of dumplings to make a uniform round shape.
4. Return Dutch oven to high heat; bring to a boil. Stir in shredded chicken and reduce heat to medium. Drop dumplings into stew. Cover; cook 7 minutes. Uncover; cook until dumplings are cooked through, about 5 minutes. Sprinkle servings with fresh chives.

Beer Pairing *Abita Andygator Abita Brewing Company; Covington, Louisiana*

Slow-Cooker Burgoo

(Photo, page 244)

Kentuckians have counted on a pot of burgoo showing up at family reunions and church socials ever since chef Gustave Jaubert, employed by Frankfort's Buffalo Trace Distillery, made it popular in the late 1800s. Along with a variety of fresh vegetables, burgoos usually include a mixture of mutton, beef, pork, or poultry. No two recipes are alike, but one thing remains the same—it feeds a crowd.

ACTIVE 20 MIN. - TOTAL 30 MIN.,
PLUS 8 HOURS COOKING
SERVES 6

- 2 Tbsp. unsalted butter
- 2 (4-oz.) spicy pork sausage links, casings removed
- 1 (2½-lb.) boneless pork shoulder, trimmed and cut into 4 pieces
- 1 cup chopped yellow onion (from 1 onion)
- ¾ cup chopped carrot (from 1 large carrot)
- ¾ cup chopped green bell pepper (from 1 small pepper)
- 3 garlic cloves, minced (about 1 Tbsp.)
- 3 cups chicken stock
- 12 oz. russet potatoes, cut into ¾-inch pieces
- 2 cups chopped green cabbage (from 1 small head)
- 2 cups frozen corn kernels
- 1 (15.5-oz.) can cannellini beans, drained and rinsed
- 3 Tbsp. Worcestershire sauce
- 1 Tbsp. kosher salt
- 2 tsp. black pepper

1. Melt butter in a large Dutch oven over medium-high. Add sausage links. Cook, stirring occasionally, until browned, about 6 minutes. Transfer to an 8-quart slow cooker.
2. Add pork to Dutch oven. Cook until well browned, about 12 minutes, turning once. Transfer to slow cooker.
3. Add onion, carrot, bell pepper, and garlic to Dutch oven. Cook, stirring often, until tender, about 6 minutes. Stir in stock. Bring to a boil, scraping to loosen browned bits from bottom of pot. Transfer to slow cooker. Add potatoes, cabbage, corn, beans, Worcestershire, salt, and black pepper. Cover; cook on LOW until pork is tender, 8 hours. Transfer pork to a plate. Shred pork; return to slow cooker before serving.

Beer Pairing *Kentucky Coffee Barrel Stout Lexington Brewing & Distilling Co.; Lexington, Kentucky*

SLOW-COOKER BURGOO
(PAGE 243)

FISH MUDDLE
(PAGE 247)

SLOW-COOKER
CARNE GUISADA

Slow-Cooker Carne Guisada

Guisada means "stewed" in Spanish, and variations of this slow-cooked beef in spicy gravy can be found throughout Texas, Latin America, and the Caribbean. It's best served with warm tortillas on the side.

ACTIVE 30 MIN. - TOTAL 30 MIN., PLUS 6 HOURS COOKING

SERVES 6

- 2 Tbsp. canola oil
- 3½ lb. beef chuck roast, trimmed and cut into 1-inch pieces
- 1 small bunch fresh cilantro
- 2 cups chopped white onion (from 1 large onion)
- 2 cups chopped poblano chiles (from 2 large chiles)
- 4 large garlic cloves, smashed
- 3 Tbsp. all-purpose flour
- 2 tsp. ground cumin
- 2 tsp. ground chili powder
- 2 tsp. dried oregano
- 1 (12-oz.) bottle dark Mexican beer (such as Modelo Negra)
- 3 cups beef stock
- 1 (15-oz.) can fire-roasted diced tomatoes
- 2 Tbsp. light brown sugar
- 1 Tbsp. kosher salt
- 1 tsp. black pepper
  Flour tortillas, warmed, for serving

1. Heat 1 tablespoon of the canola oil in a large skillet over medium-high. Add half the beef to skillet. Cook, turning occasionally, until well browned on all sides, 6 to 7 minutes. Transfer browned beef to a 6-quart slow cooker. Repeat with remaining oil and beef.
2. Coarsely chop cilantro leaves and set aside. Finely chop cilantro stems. Add chopped onion and poblanos, smashed garlic, and cilantro stems to skillet. Cook onion mixture over medium-high, stirring occasionally, until tender, about 5 minutes.
3. Add all-purpose flour, cumin, chili powder, and oregano to skillet; stir until combined. Cook, stirring often, about 1 minute. Add beer to skillet and cook about 2 minutes, stirring and scraping to loosen browned bits from bottom of skillet.

4. Stir in stock, fire-roasted tomatoes, brown sugar, salt, and black pepper. Let the stock mixture come to a boil. Remove skillet from heat. Add stock mixture to browned beef in slow cooker. Stir to combine.
5. Cover slow cooker; cook carne guisada on LOW until beef is tender, about 6 hours (or cook on HIGH 3 hours and 30 minutes). Ladle stew into bowls, and sprinkle each serving with reserved chopped cilantro leaves. Serve with warm tortillas on the side.

Beer Pairing *Shiner Bock Spoetzl Brewery; Shiner, Texas*

Fish Muddle

(Photo, page 245)

In North Carolina, a muddle is a stew that's made with the fresh catch of the day, taking advantage of the abundance of seafood available along the state's coastline. While local opinions may differ on how to prepare this hearty dish, it's usually served over grits or rice. Some cooks garnish it with parsley or add chopped hard-cooked eggs on top.

ACTIVE 30 MIN. - TOTAL 1 HOUR

SERVES 6

- 2½ lb. large unpeeled, head-on, raw shrimp (about 20)
- 2 Tbsp. canola oil
- 4 large garlic cloves, smashed
- 2 celery stalks, chopped (about ¾ cup)
- 2 small carrots, chopped (about ¾ cup)
- 1 small onion, chopped (about ¾ cup)
- 2 large thyme sprigs, plus leaves for garnish
- 1 bay leaf
- 4 cups chicken stock
- 1 tsp. kosher salt
- 5 oz. thick-cut bacon slices, chopped (about 3 slices)
- 8 oz. baby Yukon Gold potatoes, halved (about 1 cup)
- 1 (15-oz.) can fire-roasted diced tomatoes
- 1 lb. skinless snapper fillet, cut into 1-inch pieces
  Cooked grits or rice, for serving

1. Remove heads and shells from shrimp. Devein shrimp; set aside. Heat oil in a Dutch oven over medium. Add shrimp heads and shells. Cook, stirring and pressing on shrimp heads and shells occasionally, until starting to crisp, about 6 minutes. Add garlic, celery, carrots, onion, thyme, and bay leaf. Cook, stirring occasionally, until juices start to brown, about 4 minutes. Add stock and salt; bring to a boil over medium-high. Cover, and reduce heat to medium. Simmer 15 minutes. Remove from heat; pour mixture through a fine-mesh strainer into a bowl. Discard solids.
2. Add bacon to Dutch oven over medium-high. Cook, stirring occasionally, until crispy, 6 minutes. Add strained cooking liquid, potatoes, and tomatoes; bring to a boil. Cover; reduce heat to medium. Simmer 12 minutes. Add fish and reserved shrimp; simmer until cooked through, 7 to 8 minutes. Remove from heat.
3. Serve fish muddle in bowls over grits or rice, and sprinkle with thyme leaves.

Beer Pairing *Saloon Style Pilsner Lonerider; Wake Forest, North Carolina*

One-Hour Brunswick Stew

The origin of this fall classic has been debated for generations. Both Georgians and Virginians claim that their state is the birthplace—and believe their variation is the best. In Brunswick County, Virginia, chicken is favored in the thick tomato-based stew, and it's served as a full meal. In Brunswick, Georgia, it's made with pork and hot spices and usually enjoyed as a side.

ACTIVE 40 MIN. · TOTAL 1 HOUR

SERVES 10

- 2 Tbsp. olive oil, divided
- 2 lb. bone-in, skinless chicken thighs
- 10 oz. smoked chicken sausage, chopped
- 12 oz. Yukon Gold potatoes, cut into 1-inch cubes (about 2 large potatoes)
- 2 cups chopped yellow onion (from 1 large onion)
- 1 cup chopped celery (from 3 celery stalks)
- 1 cup chopped carrots (from 2 medium carrots)
- 6 large garlic cloves, crushed
- 2 Tbsp. tomato paste
- 4 cups chicken stock
- ¼ cup apple cider vinegar
- 2 Tbsp. Dijon mustard
- 2 Tbsp. chopped fresh thyme
- 1 Tbsp. kosher salt
- 1 tsp. black pepper
- 1 (28-oz.) can diced tomatoes
- 3 cups diagonally sliced fresh okra (about 9 oz.)
- 3 cups frozen lima beans (about 14 oz.)

1. Heat 1 tablespoon of the oil in a large Dutch oven over medium-high. Add chicken, meaty-side down, and cook 7 minutes. Turn over, and cook 1 minute. Transfer to a plate.
2. Heat remaining 1 tablespoon oil in Dutch oven. Add smoked sausage. Cook, stirring often, until browned, about 6 minutes. Add potatoes, onion, celery, carrots, and garlic. Cook over medium-high, stirring occasionally, until vegetables soften, 5 minutes. Add tomato paste; cook, stirring often, 1 minute. Stir in stock, vinegar, mustard, thyme, salt, pepper, and tomatoes. Bring to a boil.
3. Return chicken to Dutch oven. Reduce heat to medium, and simmer 10 minutes. Remove chicken; let stand 10 minutes. Stir okra and beans into Dutch oven, and cook until tender, about 20 minutes. Remove from heat. Shred chicken, discarding bones, and stir into stew.

Beer Pairing *Cooter Brown Ale Jekyll Brewing; Alpharetta, Georgia*

Prime Time for Pecans

You can buy pecans all year long, but fall is when they come into season across
the South on stately trees in landscapes, in the wild, and at orchards

SQUIRREL AWAY THESE NUTS

Store them in an air-tight container in the refrigerator or freezer to prevent natural oils from turning rancid.

Pumpkin Spice Candied Pecans

ACTIVE 10 MIN. - TOTAL 55 MIN.,
PLUS 30 MIN. COOLING

MAKES 6 CUPS

Preheat oven to 250°F. Whisk 1 large **egg white** in a large bowl until foamy. Whisk in ½ cup packed **light brown sugar**, 1 tsp. **vanilla extract**, 1 tsp. **kosher salt**, and ¾ tsp. **pumpkin pie spice**. Stir 6 cups (about 21 oz.) **pecan halves** into brown sugar mixture until thoroughly coated. Place pecans in a single layer on a large rimmed baking sheet lined with parchment paper and lightly sprayed with cooking spray. Bake, stirring every 15 minutes, until pecans have browned and coating has set and begun to harden, about 45 minutes. Remove from oven; cool completely on baking sheet, about 30 minutes. Store in an airtight container up to 5 days.

These native nuts are rich in healthy fats, protein, and vitamins. The sweet, buttery flavor is so wonderful that you probably need little convincing to enjoy them by the handful.

One–Bowl Winners

Satisfy cravings between meals with tasty no–bake treats

NO-BAKE CHOCOLATE-
PEANUT BUTTER
OATMEAL COOKIES

No-Bake Chocolate-Peanut Butter Oatmeal Cookies

ACTIVE 10 MIN. - TOTAL 25 MIN.
MAKES 3 DOZEN

- 1½ cups granulated sugar
- ½ cup whole milk
- 6 Tbsp. unsalted butter
- 1 tsp. vanilla extract
- 2½ cups uncooked quick-cooking oats
- ¾ cup dry-roasted, lightly salted peanuts
- ⅔ cup creamy peanut butter
- ¼ cup unsweetened cocoa

1. Stir together sugar, milk, butter, and vanilla in a large saucepan; bring to a boil over medium–high. Boil 1 minute, stirring constantly. Remove from heat; carefully stir in oats, peanuts, peanut butter, and cocoa until well combined.
2. While mixture is warm, use a 1-tablespoon cookie scoop or rounded measuring spoon to drop tablespoons of dough onto a baking sheet lined with parchment paper. Let stand at room temperature until completely cool, about 15 minutes. Store in an airtight container at room temperature up to 1 week.

Trail Mix Bites

ACTIVE 10 MIN. - TOTAL 10 MIN., PLUS 1 HOUR CHILLING
MAKES 12

Place ½ cup **creamy peanut butter,** ½ cup **honey,** and 1 tsp. **vanilla extract** in a large microwavable bowl; microwave on HIGH 20 seconds. Stir to blend until smooth. Add 1¼ cups uncooked **quick–cooking oats,** ¾ cup **crisp rice cereal,** ½ cup **lightly salted whole almonds,** ½ cup **raisins,** and (if desired) ¼ cup **miniature chocolate chips.** Stir until well coated. Using hands, shape

TRAIL MIX BITES

mixture into 12 balls (about 2 generous tablespoons each), and place in a single layer on a baking sheet lined with parchment paper. Chill until firm, about 1 hour. Store in an airtight container in refrigerator up to 5 days.

Salted Caramel Popcorn Bars

ACTIVE 10 MIN. - TOTAL 20 MIN.
MAKES 18

- 2 Tbsp. unsalted butter, plus more for greasing dish
- 10 caramel candies (such as Kraft)
- 1 (10-oz.) pkg. marshmallows
- 12 cups popped popcorn (from 1 [5-oz.] pkg.
- ¾ tsp. kosher salt

1. Melt butter in a large saucepan over medium. Add caramels and 2 tablespoons water. Cook, stirring often with a silicone spatula, until caramels melt completely, about 3 minutes. Add marshmallows. Cook, stirring constantly, until smooth, 1 to 2 minutes. Remove from heat.

NO-STICK TRICK
To prevent the popcorn mixture from adhering to the spatula, coat the spatula with cooking spray before stirring ingredients together and pressing into the baking dish.

SALTED CARAMEL POPCORN BARS

2. Working quickly, fold in popcorn and kosher salt until coated. Press into a lightly greased (with butter) 13- x 9-inch baking dish. Let stand until completely set, about 10 minutes. Cut into 18 bars. Store in an airtight container at room temperature up to 1 week.
Extra Sweet: Stir in 1 cup **candy–coated milk chocolate pieces** (such as M&M's), 1 cup **miniature peanut butter cup candies** (such as Reese's), and 1 cup **gummy bears** with the popcorn and salt in Step 2.
Flavors of Fall: Stir in 2 tsp. **apple pie spice,** 1 cup **dried apple chips,** and 1 cup chopped **candied pecans** with the popcorn and salt in Step 2.
Spiced S'mores: Stir in 2 tsp. **cinnamon;** 1 cup **miniature marshmallows;** 1 (1.55–oz.) **milk chocolate candy bar,** broken into pieces; and 1 cup **Golden Grahams cereal** with the popcorn and salt in Step 2.

Secret's in the Sauce

Jazz up tried-and-true proteins with flavorful recipes that practically make themselves

Chicken Thighs with Tomato-Caper Sauce

ACTIVE 20 MIN. · TOTAL 45 MIN.

SERVES 4

1½	Tbsp. extra-virgin olive oil
4	(6-oz.) bone-in, skin-on chicken thighs
½	tsp. black pepper
1¼	tsp. kosher salt, divided
½	cup thinly sliced yellow onion (from 1 small onion)
2	Tbsp. drained capers
3	large garlic cloves, chopped (1½ Tbsp.)
1	Tbsp. dried Italian seasoning
1	(28-oz.) can whole peeled plum tomatoes
	Hot cooked grits, for serving
	Chopped fresh flat-leaf parsley

1. Preheat oven to 450°F. Coat bottom of a large cast-iron skillet with oil. Pat chicken dry, then sprinkle all over with pepper and 1 teaspoon of the salt. Arrange chicken, skin-side down, in prepared skillet. Cook over medium, undisturbed, until chicken skin is crisp and golden, about 12 minutes (chicken will not be cooked through). Transfer chicken, skin-side up, to a plate; do not wipe skillet clean.

2. Add onion to skillet. Cook over medium, stirring and scraping bottom of skillet using a wooden spoon to loosen browned bits, until softened, about 2 minutes. Add capers, garlic, Italian seasoning, and remaining ¼ teaspoon salt. Cook, stirring constantly, until very fragrant, about 1 minute. Stir in tomatoes; bring to a simmer over medium, breaking tomatoes apart using a wooden spoon.

3. Return chicken, skin-side up, and any juices to mixture in skillet. Transfer skillet to preheated oven. Roast until sauce reduces slightly and a thermometer inserted in thickest portion of chicken registers 165°F, 15 to 20 minutes. Remove from oven. Serve over hot cooked grits; sprinkle with parsley.

Skillet Pork Chops with Dijon-Buttermilk Sauce

ACTIVE 20 MIN. - TOTAL 30 MIN.

SERVES 4

- 1½ Tbsp. olive oil
- 4 (9-oz., 1-inch-thick) bone-in (or boneless) center-cut pork chops
- 1¼ tsp. kosher salt
- ½ tsp. black pepper
- 1 Tbsp. unsalted butter
- 1 medium shallot, finely chopped (about 3 Tbsp.)
- 3 medium garlic cloves, finely chopped (1 Tbsp.)
- 1½ tsp. all-purpose flour
- 1 tsp. finely chopped fresh rosemary, plus more for garnish
- 1 cup unsalted chicken stock
- 2 tsp. coarse-grain Dijon mustard
- ½ cup whole buttermilk
  Hot cooked egg noodles, for serving

1. Preheat oven to 400°F. Heat oil in a large cast-iron skillet over medium-high. Pat pork chops dry. Sprinkle both sides evenly with salt and pepper. Add pork to skillet. Cook, undisturbed, until bottoms are golden brown, 5 to 6 minutes (pork will not be cooked through). Transfer pork to a plate; set aside.

2. Reduce heat under skillet to medium. Add butter to skillet; scrape up browned bits stuck to bottom of skillet using a wooden spoon. Add shallot, garlic, flour, and rosemary. Cook, stirring constantly, until fragrant, about 30 seconds. Stir in stock and mustard. Bring to a simmer over medium. Simmer, undisturbed, until slightly reduced, about 3 minutes.

3. Return pork, browned-side up, and any juices to mixture in skillet. Transfer skillet to preheated oven; roast until a thermometer inserted into thickest portion of chops registers 145°F, 6 to 8 minutes. Remove skillet from oven. Transfer pork to serving plates.

4. Return skillet to stovetop; bring mixture to a simmer over medium. Simmer, undisturbed, 2 minutes. Whisk in buttermilk; return to a simmer over medium. Simmer, whisking often, until buttermilk sauce is slightly thickened, 1 to 2 minutes. Serve pork over hot cooked egg noodles and top with buttermilk sauce; garnish with additional rosemary.

Seared Flank Steak with Zesty Herb Sauce

ACTIVE 30 MIN. - TOTAL 35 MIN.

SERVES 6

- ½ cup, plus 1 Tbsp. extra-virgin olive oil, divided
- 1 (1½- to 2-lb.) flank steak (about ¾ inch thick), trimmed
- 2 tsp. kosher salt, divided
- 1½ tsp. black pepper, divided
- 1 cup packed fresh flat-leaf parsley
- ½ cup packed fresh cilantro leaves
- 1 medium shallot, coarsely chopped (about ¼ cup)
- 2½ Tbsp. red wine vinegar
- 1 large garlic clove
- Hot roasted potatoes, for serving

1. Heat a 12-inch cast-iron skillet over medium-high. Add 1 tablespoon of the oil to skillet, and swirl to coat. Sprinkle both sides of steak evenly with 1½ teaspoons of the salt and 1 teaspoon of the pepper. Cook steak in hot skillet, flipping about every 2 minutes, until a thermometer inserted in thickest portion of meat registers 125°F (for medium-rare), 5 to 7 minutes. Transfer steak to a cutting board; cover loosely with aluminum foil and let rest 10 minutes.

2. While steak rests, pulse parsley, cilantro, shallot, vinegar, garlic, and remaining ½ teaspoon each salt and pepper in a food processor until finely chopped, about 10 pulses, stopping to scrape down sides as needed. With processor running, slowly pour remaining ½ cup oil through food chute until mixture is thoroughly combined but still chunky, about 10 seconds.

3. Cut steak diagonally against the grain into ¼-inch-thick slices, and arrange slices on a platter. Serve with roasted potatoes and herb sauce.

GOING GREEN

This bright and herbaceous sauce is inspired by chimichurri, which is typically served with steak in Argentina. Make an extra batch to drizzle on grilled chicken, seafood, or vegetables.

Skillet Turkey Meatloaves with Mushroom Gravy

ACTIVE 45 MIN. - TOTAL 1 HOUR, 5 MIN.

SERVES 4

- 1 lb. 85/15 lean ground turkey (white and dark meat)
- ½ cup finely chopped yellow onion (from 1 small onion)
- ⅓ cup panko breadcrumbs
- 2 tsp. Worcestershire sauce
- 2½ Tbsp. extra-virgin olive oil, divided
- 3 tsp. finely chopped garlic (from 3 large cloves), divided
- 3 tsp. fresh thyme leaves, divided, plus more for garnish
- 1½ tsp. kosher salt, divided
- ½ tsp. black pepper, divided
- 8 oz. fresh Brussels sprouts, trimmed and halved (2 cups)
- 3 medium carrots (halved lengthwise if wider than ¾ inch), sliced on an angle into 1-inch pieces (1⅓ cups)
- 1 Tbsp. unsalted butter
- 1 (8-oz.) pkg. fresh sliced cremini mushrooms (about 3 cups)
- 1 Tbsp. all-purpose flour
- 1 cup unsalted chicken stock
  Hot cooked mashed potatoes, for serving

1. Preheat oven to 450°F. Place turkey, onion, panko, Worcestershire sauce, 1½ tablespoons of the oil, 2 teaspoons of the garlic, 2 teaspoons of the thyme, 1 teaspoon of the salt, and ¼ teaspoon of the pepper in a large bowl; gently mix together using your hands just until incorporated. Divide turkey mixture evenly into 4 portions. Form each portion into a football-shape loaf about 4 inches long and 1½ inches thick (don't pack mixture too tightly). Set aside.

2. Place Brussels sprouts and carrots in a large cast-iron skillet. Add ¼ teaspoon of the salt and remaining 1 tablespoon oil; toss to coat, then spread in an even layer. Arrange uncooked meatloaves on vegetable mixture. Bake in preheated oven until vegetables are browned and tender and a thermometer inserted into thickest portion of each meatloaf registers 165°F, about 25 minutes.

3. Remove skillet from oven. Transfer meatloaves and vegetable mixture to a platter, or divide evenly among 4 plates. Cover with aluminum foil to keep warm. Do not wipe skillet clean.

4. Add butter to skillet, and melt butter over medium-high until sizzling. Add mushrooms in an even layer. Cook, undisturbed, until bottoms are lightly browned, about 4 minutes. Stir mushrooms. Cook, stirring often, until tender, about 2 minutes. Sprinkle with flour, and stir in remaining 1 teaspoon each garlic and thyme. Cook, stirring constantly, 1 minute. Slowly stir in stock, scraping up any flour stuck to bottom of skillet. Bring to a simmer over medium, stirring occasionally. Simmer, stirring often, until thickened to desired consistency, 4 to 5 minutes. Remove from heat; stir in remaining ¼ teaspoon each salt and pepper.

5. Serve meatloaves and vegetables alongside hot cooked mashed potatoes; top with mushroom gravy. Garnish with additional thyme leaves.

Superfast Shrimp with Honey-Garlic Sauce

ACTIVE 15 MIN. · TOTAL 15 MIN.

SERVES 4

- 3 Tbsp. unsalted butter
- 1 tsp. grated garlic (from 2 medium garlic cloves)
- ¼ cup honey
- 1 Tbsp. soy sauce
- 1 Tbsp. fresh lemon juice (from 1 lemon)
- ¼ tsp. kosher salt
- 1 lb. large peeled, deveined raw shrimp, tail-on

  Chopped fresh flat-leaf parsley

  Lemon wedges

  Hot cooked rice and broccoli, for serving

1. Melt butter in a large nonstick skillet over medium-high. Add garlic. Cook, stirring constantly, until fragrant, about 30 seconds. Add honey and soy sauce. Cook, stirring constantly, until sauce is very foamy and thick enough to coat the back of a spoon, about 1 minute. Stir in lemon juice and salt. Pour half of the honey mixture into a small bowl; reserve for serving. Transfer remaining honey mixture to a separate small bowl for glazing shrimp. Do not wipe skillet clean.

2. Add half of the shrimp to skillet in an even layer. Cook over medium-high just until shrimp are pink on both sides but still translucent in centers, about 1 minute per side. Transfer cooked shrimp to a plate. Repeat process with remaining shrimp.

3. Return shrimp to skillet and add honey mixture reserved for glazing. Cook, stirring constantly, about 1 minute. Transfer mixture to a platter, and garnish with parsley. Serve with lemon wedges, hot cooked rice, broccoli, and reserved sauce.

SPICE IT UP

Add kick to this dish by stirring 1 teaspoon grated fresh ginger or ½ teaspoon diced jalapeño chile into the pan along with the garlic.

Morning, Pumpkin!

Our best-ever buttermilk pancakes get a new flavor for fall

Pumpkin Spice Pancakes

ACTIVE 40 MIN. - TOTAL 45 MIN.

SERVES 6

- 1¾ cups all-purpose flour
- 2 Tbsp. light brown sugar
- 1 Tbsp. baking powder
- 1 tsp. baking soda
- 1 tsp. kosher salt
- ¾ tsp. pumpkin pie spice
- 2 large eggs
- 1½ cups whole buttermilk
- 1 cup canned pumpkin (from 1 [15-oz.] can)
- 1 tsp. vanilla extract
- ¼ cup butter, melted, plus unmelted butter for griddle and serving
  Pure maple syrup

1. Whisk together flour, sugar, baking powder, baking soda, salt, and pumpkin pie spice in a large bowl. Set aside.
2. Whisk together eggs, buttermilk, pumpkin, and vanilla in a medium bowl. Gradually stir buttermilk mixture into flour mixture just until combined. Gently stir in melted butter just until combined (mixture will be lumpy). Let stand 5 minutes.

3. Heat a griddle or large skillet over medium. Reduce heat to medium-low; lightly grease griddle with butter. Working in batches, pour about ¼ cup batter per pancake onto griddle. Cook until tops have a few bubbles and edges look dry and cooked, 3 to 4 minutes. Flip pancakes; cook until puffed and thoroughly cooked, 3 to 4 minutes. Transfer to a plate. Repeat process with remaining batter. Serve immediately with maple syrup and butter.

AUTUMN SALAD WITH
MAPLE-CIDER VINAIGRETTE

SLOW-COOKER
CHEDDAR SOUP

Halloween Hangout

Gather the gang for a cozy supper featuring soup, salad, and mulled cider

Slow-Cooker Cheddar Soup

ACTIVE 1 HOUR, 5 MIN. · TOTAL 4 HOURS, 5 MIN.
SERVES 8

- 4 cups chicken stock
- 2 cups chopped sweet onion (from 1 large onion)
- ½ cup chopped carrot (from 1 large carrot)
- ½ cup chopped celery (from 1 large stalk)
- ½ cup chopped red bell pepper (from 1 small pepper)
- ¼ cup unsalted butter
- 1½ tsp. kosher salt
- ½ tsp. black pepper
- ¼ tsp. crushed red pepper
- 12 oz. sharp cheddar cheese, shredded (about 3 cups)
- 1 (8-oz.) pkg. cream cheese
- 1¼ cups whole milk, divided
- ¼ cup cornstarch
- 8 soft pretzel burger buns (such as Pretzilla) or small round bakery bread loaves, warmed
  Crumbled cooked bacon and sliced scallions

1. Place stock, onion, carrot, celery, bell pepper, butter, salt, black pepper, and crushed red pepper in a 6-quart slow cooker. Cover and cook on HIGH until vegetables are tender, about 3 hours.
2. Whisk cheddar cheese, cream cheese, and 1 cup of the milk into mixture in slow cooker. Cover and cook on HIGH until cheese is melted and smooth, whisking occasionally, about 30 minutes.
3. Whisk together cornstarch and remaining ¼ cup milk in a small bowl until smooth. Whisk into soup in slow cooker. Cover and cook on HIGH, whisking occasionally, until thickened, about 15 minutes.
4. Slice ½ inch from the top of each pretzel bun using a serrated knife. Scoop out centers of bun bottoms, leaving a ¼-inch-thick shell. Ladle soup evenly into bun bottoms; garnish with bacon and scallions. Serve bun tops alongside.

Autumn Salad with Maple-Cider Vinaigrette

ACTIVE 20 MIN. · TOTAL 50 MIN.
SERVES 6

- 3 cups chopped peeled sweet potatoes (from 2 medium-size sweet potatoes)
- ¼ tsp. black pepper
- ½ cup olive oil, divided
- 1 tsp. kosher salt, divided
- 3 Tbsp. apple cider vinegar
- 1½ Tbsp. pure maple syrup
- 1 Tbsp. Dijon mustard
- 1 Tbsp. finely chopped shallot (from 1 shallot)
- 6 cups chopped stemmed Lacinato kale (from 2 bunches)
- 1 medium Honeycrisp apple, unpeeled and thinly sliced
- 4 oz. Manchego cheese, shaved (about 2 cups)

1. Preheat oven to 400°F. Toss together sweet potatoes, pepper, 2 tablespoons of the oil, and ½ teaspoon of the salt on a rimmed baking sheet until coated. Spread in an even layer. Roast until sweet potatoes are lightly browned and tender, about 25 minutes, stirring once halfway through cook time. Cool on baking sheet just until warm, about 10 minutes.
2. Meanwhile, whisk together vinegar, maple syrup, Dijon mustard, shallot, and remaining ½ teaspoon salt in a small bowl. Gradually whisk in remaining 6 tablespoons oil until combined.
3. Toss together kale and half of the vinaigrette (about 5 tablespoons) in a large bowl. Massage, using your hands, until kale is well coated and slightly tender, 3 to 5 minutes. Transfer mixture to a large serving platter; top evenly with sweet potatoes, apple slices, and cheese. Drizzle with remaining vinaigrette.

Big-Batch Mulled Cider

ACTIVE 10 MIN. · TOTAL 40 MIN.
SERVES 8

- 1 (½-gal.) bottle unfiltered apple cider
- ¼ cup packed light brown sugar
- 2 large navel oranges, unpeeled, ends removed, and oranges sliced into rounds
- 1 medium Honeycrisp apple, unpeeled and chopped
- 3 whole star anise
- 2 cinnamon sticks
  Optional garnishes: fresh cranberries, thin orange slices, cinnamon sticks, thin apple slices, whole star anise

Stir together cider, brown sugar, orange rounds, chopped apple, star anise, and cinnamon sticks in a large Dutch oven or heavy-bottom saucepan. Bring to a boil over high, stirring occasionally. Reduce heat to low. Simmer, covered, stirring occasionally, until fruits soften and mixture becomes aromatic, about 30 minutes. Pour through a fine-mesh strainer into a large heatproof bowl or drink dispenser; discard solids. Ladle cider into 8 heatproof mugs; garnish as desired.

Pan-Sauce Perfection
Four simple steps to add more flavor your favorite protein

1.
Season the meat well with salt and black pepper. Heat a cast-iron skillet over medium-high. Cook until browned on both sides and cooked through. Transfer meat from pan and set aside.

2.
Add aromatics (sliced garlic, onions, ginger, shallots, spices, etc.) to the pan. Cook until vegetables are softened and fragrant.

3.
Pour liquid (wine, stock, broth, water, canned tomatoes and their juices, or any combination) into the pan. Bring to a boil, then lower the heat until liquid is reduced by half. Stir constantly, scraping up browned bits from bottom of the pan.

4.
Whisk in a few pats of cold butter until melted and incorporated into the sauce. Continue whisking in any additional flavorings (fresh herbs, mustard, or capers). Season with salt and pepper to taste.

No Pumpkin? No Problem.

'Tis the season for fall leaves, cooler temperatures, and grocery stores selling out of canned pumpkin puree. If you find yourself staring at an empty space in the canned-fruit section, don't fret. Roasted butternut squash or sweet potatoes are excellent stand-ins. If you want a substitute that isn't sweet, defrosted frozen squash puree works well, too.

"For the most evenly browned nuts, **I prefer using an oven rather than a skillet.** Spread them on a baking sheet, and bake at 350°F for about 10 minutes, stirring every 3 minutes or so."

—Pam Lolley,
Test Kitchen professional

November

MULLED APPLE-
CRANBERRY CIDER

Cheers to Cider

Crisp and refreshing apple drinks to toast the season

Mulled Apple-Cranberry Cider

ACTIVE 10 MIN. - TOTAL 10 MIN.,
PLUS 1 HOUR COOKING

SERVES 8

Toast 10 **whole cloves**, 8 (3-inch) **cinnamon sticks**, 6 **whole star anise**, and 1 **whole nutmeg** in a large Dutch oven over medium, shaking pot often, until spices are fragrant, 3 to 4 minutes. Stir in 6 cups **filtered apple cider** and 2 cups **cranberry juice**. Reduce heat to low, and cook, uncovered, 1 hour. (Do not let mixture come to a simmer. If it begins to simmer, remove from heat for 30 seconds then return to heat.) During last 10 minutes of cooking, add 1 **orange**, thinly sliced; 2 cups **fresh or frozen, thawed cranberries**; and 1 each **Granny Smith** and **Honeycrisp apple**, thinly sliced crosswise. Serve warm with slices of fruit and cranberries in each mug. If desired, stir in ½ cup **brandy or bourbon** just before serving.

BOURBON-CIDER MULE

MAKE IT A MOCKTAIL
This light and fizzy drink is also delicious without the bourbon.

APPLE CIDER SHANDY

Apple Cider Shandy

ACTIVE 5 MIN. - TOTAL 5 MIN.

SERVES 2

Combine 6 oz. each of chilled **green apple hard cider** and chilled **sparkling apple cider** in each of 2 pilsner or pint glasses. Top each glass with 1 Tbsp. **fresh lemon juice**, and stir gently. Garnish with thin **lemon** wheels and **green apple** slices.

Bourbon-Cider Mule

ACTIVE 5 MIN. - TOTAL 5 MIN.

SERVES 1

Combine ¼ cup **bourbon**, ¼ cup **filtered apple cider**, and 2 Tbsp. **fresh lime juice** in a cocktail shaker filled with **ice**. Shake vigorously until chilled, about 30 seconds, then strain into a copper mug or rocks glass filled with **ice**. Top with ½ cup **ginger beer**, and garnish with a **lime** wheel and an **apple** slice.

Sweetie's Sweet Potatoes

Chef Kelsey Barnard Clark draws inspiration from a family matriarch

THANKSGIVING has never been a sit-down affair for chef and restaurateur Kelsey Barnard Clark. When she was growing up in Dothan, Alabama, her parents owned a beach house on the state's Gulf Coast, where both sides of the family would meet on the holiday weekend. "We didn't set a table. Instead, about 30 of us would eat on paper plates with our legs dangling off a dock," she says. "It was a loud, casual, fun, and absolutely magical potluck."

Those were also times to honor family matriarchs through food and memories, something Clark has held dear throughout her life. From when she attended culinary school in New York to when she opened her namesake restaurant, KBC, in Dothan, won season 16 of *Bravo's Top Chef,* published her first cookbook (*Southern Grit*), to raising two children (Monroe and Evelyn June) with her husband, Deavours—her constant inspiration has been these women. "So much of my life and business is informed by the example of my strong, hardworking female forebears, like my great-grandmother, Sweetie," Clark says. "She always did things differently and pushed for a life where women could have families and meaningful careers."

Mildred Rayford Buckhaults, better known as Sweetie, was a teacher who golfed, hunted, fished, and cooked every meal for her family of six during the early- to mid-20th century. "She was the epitome of the modern Southern woman, long before the region was ever considered modern," says Clark.

Sweetie's easy charm and generosity were reflected in her nickname, which came to be because her husband, Buck, greeted her with "Hey, Sweetie" every day. If there's a singular dish that yokes Clark's ancestral past to her accomplished present, it's Sweetie's Sweet Potatoes, a staple at every Thanksgiving meal.
—Brigid Ransome-Washington

MILDRED RAYFORD BUCKHAULTS (ABOVE) WAS CALLED SWEETIE BY HER FAMILY, INCLUDING HER GREAT-GRANDDAUGHTER KELSEY BARNARD CLARK (RIGHT).

Sweetie's Sweet Potatoes

"My great-grandmother made this every year, and we have all carried on the tradition. It actually tastes of sweet potatoes and is speckled with orange throughout—a refreshing contrast to the very sugary, more processed versions that many in the South typically dote on," says Clark.

ACTIVE 25 MIN. - TOTAL 1 HOUR, 10 MIN.
SERVES 12

- 4 lb. sweet potatoes (about 8 medium potatoes), peeled and cut into 1-inch chunks
- 1½ tsp. grated orange zest, plus ½ cup fresh juice (from 1 large orange)
- ½ cup unsalted butter, melted, plus more for baking dish
- 1 cup packed light brown sugar
- 2 tsp. ground cinnamon
- 2 tsp. ground nutmeg
- 2 tsp. kosher salt
- 2 cups pecan halves, toasted and chopped
- 20 marshmallows

1. Preheat oven to 350°F. Butter a 13- x 9-inch baking dish, and set aside.
2. Place sweet potato chunks in a large pot, and add water to cover. Bring to a boil over medium-high. Reduce heat to medium-low, and simmer until potatoes are tender when pierced with a fork, 15 to 20 minutes. Drain potatoes in a colander, and let cool 10 minutes.
3. Meanwhile, stir together orange zest and juice in a small bowl. Stir in melted butter until combined.
4. Stir together brown sugar, cinnamon, nutmeg, and salt in a separate small bowl.
5. Arrange half of the sweet potato chunks in an even layer in prepared baking dish. Sprinkle with half of the brown sugar mixture, and drizzle with half of the butter mixture. Sprinkle with half of the toasted pecans. Repeat process with remaining sweet potatoes, brown sugar mixture, butter mixture, and toasted pecans. Top evenly with marshmallows.
6. Bake in preheated oven until marshmallows are golden and casserole is bubbling around edges, 20 to 30 minutes. Serve hot.

MAKE IT AHEAD
Prepare the casserole through Step 5. Cover with aluminum foil and refrigerate up to 3 days. Let stand at room temperature at least 30 minutes or up to 1 hour before baking as directed in Step 6.

KABOCHA SQUASH PIZZA
WITH SAGE PESTO

It's Squash Season

Take advantage of all the varieties at the market with these colorful and creative dishes

Kabocha Squash Pizza with Sage Pesto

Green Kabocha: If you're a fan of acorn squash, give this variety a try. When cooked, the golden flesh has an earthy flavor and a texture that's starchy and a bit dry.

ACTIVE 45 MIN. - TOTAL 1 HOUR, 10 MIN.
SERVES 4

- 1 lb. fresh pizza dough
  All-purpose flour, for work surface and dusting
- 2 oz. sliced prosciutto
- ¾ cup, plus 2 Tbsp. olive oil, divided
- 1 small kabocha squash, peeled and seeds removed, cut into ½-inch pieces (about 3 cups)
- 2 Tbsp. chopped lightly salted shelled pistachios, toasted
- 1 oz. Parmesan cheese, grated with a Microplane grater (about ⅔ cup)
- 2 Tbsp. fresh lemon juice (from 1 lemon)
- 1 tsp. kosher salt
- 1 cup fresh flat-leaf parsley leaves, plus more for garnish
- 1 cup fresh sage leaves
- ½ cup sliced red onion (from 1 medium onion)
- 4 oz. goat cheese, crumbled (about 1 cup)
  Black pepper

1. Place pizza dough on a lightly floured work surface. Let rest at room temperature, covered with plastic wrap or a kitchen towel, until dough reaches room temperature, at least 30 minutes or up to 1 hour.
2. Meanwhile, heat a large nonstick skillet over medium. Add prosciutto slices to skillet. Cook until crispy, about 5 minutes per side, working in batches if necessary. Transfer prosciutto to a plate lined with paper towels; set aside. Reduce heat to low, and add 2 tablespoons of the oil to skillet. Place squash in skillet. Cook, stirring occasionally, until mostly tender and caramelized, about 20 minutes. Transfer squash to a plate lined with paper towels; set aside.
3. Preheat oven to 400°F. Process pistachios, cheese, lemon juice, salt, and remaining ¾ cup oil in a blender until smooth, about 1 minute. Add parsley and sage; process until smooth and well combined, about 1 minute. Set pesto aside.
4. Gently roll dough to a 14-inch circle on lightly floured work surface. Transfer dough to a 15-inch nonstick pizza pan lightly dusted with flour. Pierce holes in dough with a fork, leaving a ½-inch border unpierced. Bake dough in preheated oven until set, about 10 minutes. Carefully remove pan from oven. Spread pesto evenly over dough, leaving a 1-inch border. Arrange squash and red onion on pesto. Return pizza pan to oven; continue baking at 400°F until toppings are tender and slightly caramelized and crust is crisp and golden brown on edges and underneath, about 15 minutes. Sprinkle goat cheese on pizza; cut into 8 slices. Break prosciutto into bite-size pieces; sprinkle on pizza. Garnish with parsley leaves, and sprinkle with black pepper; serve immediately.

Cheesy Baked Grits with Blue Hokkaido Squash and Bacon

(Photo, page 268)
ACTIVE 35 MIN. - TOTAL 1 HOUR
SERVES 12

- 1 medium (4-lb.) Blue Hokkaido or kabocha squash
- 4 thick-cut bacon slices, chopped
- 8 cups whole milk
- 2 cups uncooked stone-ground yellow grits
- ¼ cup unsalted butter, cut into pieces, plus more for greasing
- ¼ cup crème fraîche
- 1 Tbsp. chopped fresh thyme leaves
- 1 tsp. chopped fresh sage leaves, plus whole leaves for garnish
- 1½ Tbsp. kosher salt
- 1½ tsp. black pepper
- 8 oz. sharp cheddar cheese, shredded (about 2 cups), divided

1. Using a sharp knife, remove and discard stem and base from squash. Slice squash in half lengthwise. Remove and discard seeds and pulp with a spoon. Using a vegetable peeler, remove and discard skin. Cut each squash half into 2 pieces. Grate, using large holes of a box grater, to yield 4 cups grated squash. Wrap grated squash in paper towels and squeeze out as much moisture as possible. Transfer grated squash to a medium bowl; set aside at room temperature.
2. Heat a nonstick skillet over medium. Add bacon. Cook, stirring occasionally, until crisp, about 6 minutes. Using a slotted spoon, transfer bacon to a plate lined with paper towels; set aside. Reserve 1 tablespoon drippings.
3. Preheat oven to 375°F. Bring milk to a gentle boil in a large saucepan over medium-high. Whisk in yellow grits and grated squash; return to a boil, whisking constantly. Reduce heat to low; simmer mixture, whisking often, until grits are mostly tender and thick, about 15 minutes. Whisk in butter, crème fraîche, thyme, chopped sage, kosher salt, pepper, 1½ cups of the cheese, and reserved bacon drippings. Continue simmering, stirring occasionally, over low until well combined and creamy, about 5 minutes more.
4. Grease a 13- x 9-inch baking dish with butter. Pour grits mixture into baking dish; smooth top with a spatula. Sprinkle bacon and remaining ½ cup cheese evenly over top; arrange sage leaves on surface. Bake in preheated oven until cheese is melted and golden brown and sage leaves are crisp, about 20 minutes. Remove from oven; cool 5 minutes before serving.

CHEESY BAKED GRITS WITH BLUE HOKKAIDO SQUASH AND BACON (PAGE 267)

SAUSAGE-STUFFED SQUASH

Sausage-Stuffed Squash

Delicata: Go ahead—you can eat this small squash skin and all. Flavorwise, it's sweet and creamy. Use it in place of acorn squash or sweet potatoes.

ACTIVE 20 MIN. - TOTAL 45 MIN.

SERVES 4

- 2 medium delicata squash, halved lengthwise, seeds and stems removed and discarded
- 2 Tbsp. olive oil, divided
- 1 tsp. kosher salt, divided
- ½ tsp. black pepper, divided
- 8 oz. ground hot Italian pork sausage
- ½ cup finely chopped red onion (from 1 medium onion)
- 2 garlic cloves, minced
- 1½ tsp. chopped fresh thyme leaves
- 1 tsp. chopped fresh oregano leaves
- 1 bunch rainbow chard, stems removed, leaves cut into 1-inch strips (about 4 cups)
- ¼ cup water or chicken stock
- ¼ cup crumbled day-old cornbread
- 2 Tbsp. finely chopped pecans, toasted
- ½ oz. Pecorino Romano cheese, grated with a Microplane grater (about ⅓ cup)

1. Preheat oven to 375°F. Brush squash with 1 tablespoon of the oil; season with ½ teaspoon of the salt and ¼ teaspoon of the pepper. Place squash, cut sides up, on a rimmed baking sheet lined with parchment paper. Bake, uncovered, until almost tender, about 30 minutes. Remove squash from oven; set aside at room temperature.

2. While squash roast, heat remaining 1 tablespoon oil in a large skillet over medium. Add sausage. Cook, using a spatula to break apart into small pieces, until browned, about 5 minutes. Add onion, garlic, thyme, and oregano. Cook, stirring often, until fragrant, about 2 minutes. Add chard, water, and remaining ½ teaspoon salt and ¼ teaspoon pepper. Cook, stirring occasionally, until chard is wilted and liquid is reduced by half, about 5 minutes. Remove skillet from heat.

3. Evenly spoon sausage mixture into squash halves. Stir together cornbread, pecans, and cheese in a small bowl

until well combined. Sprinkle evenly over pork mixture. Bake stuffed squash halves in preheated oven until squash are tender and topping is golden brown, about 10 minutes; cool 5 minutes before serving.

Penne with Squash and Italian Chicken Sausage

(Photo, page 271)

Red Kuri: This variety stands out for its bold color and teardrop shape. The nutty taste ("kuri" means chestnut in Japanese) makes it a good substitute for butternut squash.

ACTIVE 1 HOUR - TOTAL 1 HOUR, 40 MIN.

SERVES 4

- 2 medium-size red kuri squash or 2 small butternut squash, cut in half lengthwise, seeds removed
- 2½ Tbsp. olive oil, divided
- ¼ tsp. black pepper, plus more to taste and for serving
- 1½ tsp. kosher salt, divided, plus more to taste
- 1 lb. uncooked penne rigate pasta
- 1 lb. uncooked Italian chicken sausage
- 1 medium-size red bell pepper, finely chopped (1¼ cups)
- 1 medium-size yellow bell pepper, chopped (1¼ cups)
- 1 medium-size yellow onion, chopped (2 cups)
- 2 tsp. finely chopped garlic (from 2 garlic cloves)
- 1½ tsp. chopped fresh thyme leaves
- 1½ tsp. chopped fresh oregano leaves
- 2 cups chicken stock
- ½ cup heavy whipping cream
  Finely chopped fresh flat-leaf parsley leaves
  Parmesan cheese, grated with a Microplane grater

1. Preheat oven to 400°F. Brush cut sides of squash with 1 tablespoon of the oil, and season evenly with pepper and ½ teaspoon of the salt. Place squash halves, cut-side down, on a rimmed baking sheet lined with parchment paper. Roast until almost tender, about 30 minutes. Remove squash from oven; set aside until cool enough to handle, about 10 minutes. Using a spoon, scrape flesh from 2 squash halves into a medium bowl; discard skin. Add pan drippings from sheet pan. Cut each remaining half lengthwise into 2 equal pieces. Carefully cut away skin from flesh, and discard skin. Cut squash flesh into ½-inch cubes; set aside.

2. While squash roast, bring a large pot of salted water to a boil over high. Add pasta and cook until very al dente (about 2 minutes shorter than package directions call for); drain. Set aside.

3. Heat 1 tablespoon of the oil in a large deep nonstick skillet over medium-high. Add sausage. Cook, turning occasionally, until sausage is well browned and a thermometer inserted in sausage registers 165°F, about 10 minutes. Transfer sausage from skillet to a plate lined with paper towels. Add remaining ½ tablespoon oil to skillet. Add red bell pepper to skillet; cook, stirring occasionally, until tender, about 5 minutes. Using a slotted spoon, transfer cooked red bell pepper to a medium bowl. Set aside, reserving drippings in skillet. Add yellow bell pepper and onion to skillet. Cook, stirring occasionally, until tender, about 5 minutes. Add garlic, thyme, and oregano. Cook, stirring constantly, until fragrant, about 1 minute. Add scraped squash flesh and pan drippings, chicken stock, and remaining 1 teaspoon salt to skillet; bring to a boil over medium-high. Reduce heat to low. Simmer squash mixture, stirring occasionally, until thickened, about 15 minutes.

4. Working in batches if necessary, pour squash mixture into a blender. Secure lid on blender, and remove center piece to allow steam to escape. Place a clean towel over opening. Process until smooth, about 1 minute. Return pureed squash to deep skillet; whisk in heavy cream and bring to a simmer over low, whisking occasionally.

5. Add cooked pasta to sauce and cook over medium, stirring constantly, until sauce thickens and coats pasta, about 3 minutes. Slice sausage at an angle into ½-inch-thick pieces; stir sausage, cubed squash, and red bell pepper into pasta mixture. Add salt and black pepper to taste; remove from heat. Evenly divide pasta mixture among 4 bowls. Top with black pepper, parsley, and Parmesan cheese. Serve immediately.

Spicy Blue Hubbard Squash Soup

(Photo, page 271)

Blue Hubbard: Pale bluish-gray on the outside and bright orange on the inside. This heirloom gourd is semisweet and smooth, similar to sugar pumpkin or butternut squash.

ACTIVE 30 MIN. - TOTAL 2 HOURS

SERVES 6

- 1 medium Blue Hubbard or kabocha squash
- 4 Tbsp. olive oil, divided
- 1 Tbsp. kosher salt, divided
- ¾ tsp. black pepper, divided, plus more for serving
- 1 medium leek
- 1 medium-size yellow onion, thinly sliced (2 cups)
- 2 tsp. ground coriander
- 1 tsp. ground cumin
- 4 cups vegetable broth
- 1 tsp. chili powder
- ½ cup heavy whipping cream
  Mexican crema
  Queso fresco (fresh Mexican cheese)
  Thinly sliced serrano chiles
  Fresh cilantro leaves

1. Preheat oven to 400°F. Using a sharp knife, remove and discard stem from squash. Cut squash in half lengthwise. Remove seeds and pulp with a spoon, and transfer to a large bowl. Set aside. Brush cut sides of squash with 1 tablespoon of the oil, and season evenly with ½ teaspoon of the salt and ¼ teaspoon of the black pepper. Place squash halves, cut-side down, on a rimmed baking sheet lined with parchment paper. Roast until squash is tender, about 1 hour.

2. While squash is roasting, separate squash seeds from pulp. Transfer seeds to a small bowl and discard pulp. Cut greens from white part of leek; reserve greens for another use or discard. Cut white part in half lengthwise, and thinly slice to equal ¾ cup.

3. Remove squash from oven; let stand until cool enough to handle, about 10 minutes. Using a spoon, scrape flesh from skin and transfer flesh to a medium bowl, along with any pan drippings from

baking sheet. Discard skin. Set scraped squash aside. Reduce oven temperature to 300°F.

4. Heat 2 tablespoons of the oil in a large stockpot over medium. Add leek and onion to pot. Cook, stirring often, until tender and translucent, about 4 minutes. Add coriander, cumin, roasted squash and pan drippings, and vegetable broth to pot; bring to a boil over medium. Reduce heat to low. Simmer, stirring occasionally, until mixture is reduced and has thickened slightly, about 30 minutes.

5. Meanwhile, toss together squash seeds, chili powder, ½ teaspoon of the salt, and remaining 1 tablespoon oil in a medium bowl until well combined. Transfer seasoned squash seeds to a rimmed baking sheet lined with parchment paper. Roast at 300°F until fragrant and seeds begin to pop, about 15 minutes, stirring halfway through roasting. Set aside.

6. Remove pot from heat and pour half of squash mixture into a blender. Secure lid on blender, and remove center piece to allow steam to escape. Place a clean towel over opening. Process until smooth, about 1 minute. Transfer soup mixture to a clean saucepan. Repeat process until all squash mixture is pureed. Bring squash mixture to a simmer over low. Whisk heavy cream and remaining 2 teaspoons salt and ½ teaspoon black pepper into squash mixture; cook until heated through, about 2 minutes.

7. To serve, ladle soup into 6 bowls. Drizzle Mexican crema over each serving. Top with crumbled queso fresco, roasted squash seeds, thinly sliced serrano chiles, fresh cilantro leaves, and additional black pepper; serve immediately.

Roasted Acorn Squash Salad with Sorghum-Tahini Vinaigrette

ACTIVE 30 MIN. - TOTAL 30 MIN.
SERVES 4

- 2 medium acorn squash
- ¼ cup olive oil, divided
- 1 Tbsp. kosher salt, divided
- ½ tsp. black pepper, divided
- 1 shallot, peeled and thinly sliced crosswise into rings
- ½ cup, plus 3 Tbsp. apple cider vinegar, divided
- ¼ cup sorghum syrup or honey, divided
- 2 Tbsp. tahini (sesame paste)
- 1 Tbsp. finely chopped fresh flat-leaf parsley
- 1 tsp. finely chopped fresh thyme
- 10 cups packed chopped curly kale (from 1 to 2 bunches, stems removed)
- 1 Granny Smith apple, very thinly sliced
- ½ cup dried cranberries
- 3 Tbsp. salted roasted sunflower seed kernels

1. Preheat oven to 400°F. Using a sharp knife, slice each acorn squash in half lengthwise; remove and discard stems. Using a spoon, scoop out and discard seeds and pulp. Slice each squash half crosswise into ¾-inch-thick wedges. Toss squash wedges with 1 tablespoon of the oil, ½ teaspoon of the salt, and ¼ teaspoon of the pepper in a medium bowl. Arrange squash slices on a rimmed baking sheet lined with parchment paper; roast until tender, 30 to 35 minutes, flipping squash halfway through. Remove from oven; cool until ready to use.

2. While squash are roasting, place shallot slices in a medium-size heatproof bowl; set aside. Bring ½ cup water, ½ cup of the apple cider vinegar, 2 tablespoons of the sorghum syrup, and 1 teaspoon of the salt to a gentle boil in a small saucepan over medium-high. Carefully pour hot brine mixture over shallots; cover bowl tightly with plastic wrap. Let stand 10 minutes.

3. Meanwhile, whisk together tahini, parsley, thyme, ½ teaspoon of the salt, and remaining 2 tablespoons sorghum, 3 tablespoons apple cider vinegar, and ¼ teaspoon pepper until combined. Slowly drizzle remaining 3 tablespoons oil into tahini mixture, whisking until well combined.

4. Using tongs, toss together kale and remaining 1 teaspoon salt in a large bowl until well combined and tender, about 2 minutes. Add sorghum-tahini vinaigrette, apple slices, dried cranberries, and sunflower seeds; continue tossing until well combined. Divide salad among 4 plates; top with roasted squash wedges and drained pickled shallot rings.

Beef-and-Butternut Stew

ACTIVE 30 MIN. - TOTAL 3 HOURS, 30 MIN.
SERVES 6

- 2 Tbsp. olive oil
- 3 lb. boneless chuck roast, cut into 1½-inch pieces
- 3½ tsp. kosher salt, divided
- 1¼ tsp. black pepper, divided
- 2 Tbsp. all-purpose flour
- 1 medium-size yellow onion, finely chopped (2 cups)
- 3 medium carrots, peeled and cut into ½-inch-thick pieces (1 cup)
- 3 garlic cloves, finely chopped
- 2 Tbsp. tomato paste
- 2 cups dry red wine (such as Cabernet Sauvignon)
- 4 cups unsalted beef broth
- 2 fresh bay leaves
- 4 cups butternut squash, cut into ¾-inch cubes
- 1 Tbsp. chopped fresh thyme, divided
- 1 cup sour cream
- 2 tsp. grated orange zest, plus 2 Tbsp. fresh juice, divided (from 1 orange)
- Thinly sliced fresh chives

1. Heat oil in a large Dutch oven over medium. Season beef with 1 teaspoon of the salt and ½ teaspoon of the pepper. Working in batches if necessary, add beef to Dutch oven in an even layer. Cook, turning occasionally, until beef is well browned on all sides, about 10 minutes. Transfer beef to a plate; remove and reserve 1 tablespoon drippings.

2. Add flour to remaining drippings in Dutch oven. Cook, stirring constantly, until dark golden brown in color and nutty in aroma, about 4 minutes. Add onion, carrots, and garlic. Cook, stirring constantly, until aromatic, about 3 minutes. Add tomato paste. Cook, stirring constantly, until vegetable mixture is evenly coated, about 1 minute. Add red wine, stirring and scraping to loosen browned bits from bottom of Dutch oven, and bring to a boil over medium. Boil, stirring occasionally, until liquid bubbles and is reduced by half, about 7 minutes.

3. Add beef broth, bay leaves, and browned beef to Dutch oven; bring to a gentle boil over medium. Reduce heat to low. Simmer, covered, just until beef is tender, about 2 hours and 30 minutes. Add butternut squash and 1 teaspoon of the thyme. Continue simmering, uncovered, over low, skimming and discarding fat that rises to the surface, until squash is tender and liquid has thickened, about 30 minutes.

4. Meanwhile, whisk together sour cream, orange zest, reserved 1 tablespoon drippings, 1 teaspoon of the orange juice, ½ teaspoon of the salt, ¼ teaspoon of the black pepper, and remaining 2 teaspoons thyme in a medium bowl until well combined. Cover with plastic wrap; chill until ready to use.

5. Remove bay leaves from stew. Season stew with remaining 1 tablespoon plus 2 teaspoons orange juice, 2 teaspoons salt, and ½ teaspoon pepper. Divide among 6 bowls, and top each with 2 heaping tablespoons sour cream mixture. Garnish with chives; serve immediately.

SPICY BLUE HUBBARD
SQUASH SOUP (PAGE 269)

PENNE WITH SQUASH AND
ITALIAN CHICKEN SAUSAGE
(PAGE 268)

ROASTED ACORN SQUASH
SALAD WITH SORGHUM-TAHINI
VINAIGRETTE

BEEF-AND-BUTTERNUT STEW

For the Love of Pie

In Charlotte, writer Keia Mastrianni has built a bakery—and a sweet life—from scratch

HIGH PIE SEASON, the time of year that begins in October and spans through Thanksgiving and Christmas holidays, is a maelstrom of flour, butter, grit, and perseverance. It's the Super Bowl for bakers across the nation. At Milk Glass Pie, my farm-based bakery in western North Carolina, it's no different. The refrigerator is stacked with disks of tightly wrapped pastry dough. Skyscrapers of crimped pie shells inhabit the bulk of the freezer's real estate. Hundreds of eggs await cracking. The spreadsheet of orders, with its dizzying pattern of Xs running up and down multiple columns, eerily resembles The Matrix. The madness starts weeks before Thanksgiving and slowly builds into a crescendo of flour dust and recipe math. Days upon days at the baking table, just me and a rolling pin, culminate in the crowning feat of the year: racks and tables laden with neat white boxes, golden crusts, and another record holiday season well done.

I didn't come to baking from a long line of matriarchs steeped in Southern tradition, nor did I arrive by way of formal training. Baking was a hobby that emerged alongside a budding food-writing career. I had a notion to create

things by hand. I longed to acquire the fine skill of "whipping something up." Making pie felt Southern, domestic—two things that I was not.

Food writing introduced me to a roster of interesting people, including many bakers, and I soon found myself a student at those bakeries, taking workshops on pie and other pastries. At first, making an entire pie from start to finish was an all-day affair, a monumental and painstaking task that was worth it. I bumbled along, writing stories for work and baking when I could for no one in particular. Then in 2014, I wrote a story about a farmer, and that changed everything.

As I suspect is true with most good things, the twin gifts of baking and love came unexpectedly, like an anvil on the head. I fell in love with this art because, well, I fell in love.

At the time, I lived in a small rental in one of the old mill villages in Charlotte. The kitchen was adequate, the counter space was dismal, and there was a little oven that could barely fit two baking sheets. Adjacent to this galley was just enough room for an efficiency-size Ikea table and two chairs.

One Saturday, I set a slice of buttermilk chess pie on that table for one very specific person—the farmer I had written about who had made a habit of visiting me after market on the weekends. He enjoyed it, forkful by deliberate forkful, savoring each bite. When he finished, he looked up and said, "No one's ever made me a pie before."

The first holiday we shared, he got me a pie cookbook. The inscription was simple, appropriate for a relationship barely in bloom. It read: "Merry Christmas. Love is pie!"

Our second holiday together, he inscribed another cookbook, addressing it to "My Beautiful Baker..." This suggestion felt unfounded in my opinion, not to mention the fact that it nipped at my impostor syndrome. I didn't yet consider myself a baker and wouldn't dare call what I was doing a "business,"

but somehow this new love of mine knew something I didn't. It would be several more years before I would embrace the term myself. Nevertheless, I kept at it, fueled by new love and courage. Milk Glass Pie began as a series of small pop-ups, my courtship with baking a parallel companion to my new partnership. It grew into a modest holiday list out of that tiny kitchen and then into another home, the one I began sharing with this farmer.

One pie turned into 10, 20 into 50, and then a brand-new life on a farm in Cleveland County, where I make my home and bakery space today. I married that farmer, too. Maybe that's the highest we can hope for in love—for someone to see us, often before we see ourselves, and nurture our sweetest parts. –Keia Mastrianni

Five Tips from a Pie Pro
Tried-and-true advice for beginners

1. PRACTICE AS MUCH AS YOU CAN
The more you bake, the more understanding you will have. And until then, ugly pie is still delicious.

2. KEEP IT COLD
Temperature matters. Chilled ingredients ensure the alchemical magic of flaky pastry happens inside the oven.

3. BREAK IT INTO STEPS
If you're new to pie, try staggering the process. Make the dough one day and the filling the next. It's less cumbersome and feels more like a pleasure.

4. USE ALL YOUR SENSES
Look, listen, smell, taste, and touch. Essentially, be present while you bake.

5. PUT LOVE INTO IT
I swear, it makes any recipe taste better.

APPLE PIE WITH RYE
CRUST AND CIDER
CARAMEL (PAGE 276)

SORGHUM CUSTARD PIE
WITH CORNMEAL CRUST
(PAGE 277)

Apple Pie with Rye Crust and Cider Caramel

(Photo, page 273)

Apple molasses is the tart-sweet result of reducing apple cider down to a syrup. My husband uses it as a natural sweetener, but I like it as a base for a caramel in this apple pie. Paired with an earthy rye crust, this is a recipe for those who dig a dessert that's not too sweet but perfectly fruity.

ACTIVE 1 HOUR · TOTAL 3 HOURS, 45 MIN., PLUS 1 HOUR, 15 MIN. CHILLING

SERVES 8

CIDER CARAMEL

- 4 cups good-quality fresh-pressed apple cider
- ½ cup unsalted butter
- ¼ tsp. kosher salt
- ¼ cup heavy whipping cream
- 1 tsp. vanilla extract

RYE CRUST

- 1½ cups all-purpose flour, plus more for work surface
- 1 cup light rye flour
- 1 Tbsp. granulated sugar
- 1 tsp. kosher salt
- 1 cup cold unsalted butter, cut into ½-inch cubes
- 1 Tbsp. apple cider vinegar
  Ice water

FILLING

- 2½ lb. apples (about 8 medium apples), peeled and sliced (about 6 cups)
- ⅓ cup granulated sugar
- ¼ cup packed light brown sugar
- ¼ cup all-purpose flour
- ½ tsp. kosher salt
- ½ tsp. ground allspice
- ½ tsp. ground ginger
- ½ tsp. ground cinnamon
- ¼ tsp. freshly grated nutmeg

EGG WASH

- 1 egg yolk
- 2 Tbsp. heavy whipping cream

ADDITIONAL INGREDIENT

Demerara sugar, for sprinkling

1. At least 1 day ahead and up to 1 week ahead, prepare the Cider Caramel: Reduce apple cider in a large pot over medium-high until thick and syrupy, 1 hour to 1 hour, 30 minutes. You should have about ½ cup apple "molasses" when this is complete. Once the cider is reduced, add butter and salt. Stir until butter melts; boil 2 minutes more.

Remove from heat, and stir in cream and vanilla. Cool completely; store in a sealed container until ready to use.

2. Prepare the Rye Crust: Whisk together flours, sugar, and salt in a large bowl. Add cold butter, and toss to coat in flour mixture. Using a pastry blender, cut butter into flour mixture, breaking large pieces into smaller pebble-size pieces. Use your fingers to "snap" the butter, flattening it into large flakes. Continue working butter into flour until mixture is well blended. (It should look like grated Parmesan cheese with a few pebble-size pieces throughout.)

3. Place vinegar in a measuring cup; then pour in ice water to make ½ cup total liquid.

4. Make a well in center of flour mixture, and add half of the ice water mixture. Toss thoroughly, being sure to incorporate it evenly throughout entire bowl. Add remaining ice water mixture. Scoop mixture from bottom of bowl to top of dough mound, and press gently. Continue scooping and pressing (not kneading) until most of the dough holds together. Turn out onto a lightly floured work surface and shape into a round. Cut in half; shape each half into a disk. Wrap tightly in plastic wrap; chill at least 1 hour or up to overnight (12 hours).

5. Roll 1 chilled dough disk into a 13-inch round on a lightly floured work surface. Transfer dough to a 9½-inch deep-dish pie plate or a 10-inch pie plate, leaving a 1-inch overhang. Chill in refrigerator while working with remaining dough. Roll remaining dough into a rough rectangle (about 12 x 14 inches). Cut 6 strips of dough approximately 2½ inches wide (this will be the lattice). Place on a baking sheet lined with parchment paper; chill until ready to use.

6. Prepare the Filling: Toss together sliced apples, sugars, flour, salt, allspice, ginger, cinnamon, and nutmeg in a bowl. Pour in Cider Caramel then use a spatula to mix together. Working from the outside in, layer apple mixture tightly in prepared pie plate. Continue layering and stacking until apples reach top of piecrust. Mound remaining apples with any remaining juices in center.

7. Place 3 strips of lattice vertically on top of pie. Pull middle strip down, and lay 1 horizontal strip across. Replace middle strip over top of horizontal strip. Next, pull 2 outer strips down, and lay next horizontal strip across. Replace outer strips over horizontal strips, and repeat process for final horizontal strip

across bottom of pie. Trim all lattice pieces just to edge of pie plate, being sure to leave bottom overhang intact.

8. Fold up the overhang of the bottom crust to cover the edges of lattice pieces; press gently to seal. Crimp as desired, or use the tines of a fork to create a decorative edge. Chill assembled pie in freezer for 15 minutes.

9. Prepare the Egg Wash: Beat egg yolk and cream in a small bowl until well combined. Preheat oven to 425°F with rack in lower half of oven.

10. Brush Egg Wash over entire pie; sprinkle with demerara sugar. Place pie on a baking sheet lined with parchment paper. Bake in preheated oven until crust sets and begins to brown, about 25 minutes. Reduce oven temperature to 375°F, and rotate pie. Place on middle rack; bake until pie is deeply golden and filling is bubbling, 30 to 40 minutes, covering with aluminum foil during last 20 minutes, if desired, to prevent overbrowning.

Does Lattice Make You Nervous?

Try a Crumble Topping

If rolling out and weaving dough into a lattice feels too fussy, pull out your favorite deep baking dish and make an easy apple crisp. Follow the instructions for the Cider Caramel (left) and Filling (left). Transfer Filling to a 9½-inch deep-dish pie shell or 2½-quart baking dish, and top with Brown Sugar-Pecan Crumble (below). Bake at 375°F on the middle rack until edges are bubbly, 45 to 55 minutes, covering with aluminum foil during the last 20 minutes, if desired, to prevent overbrowning.

BROWN SUGAR-PECAN CRUMBLE: Stir together 1 cup all-purpose flour; 1 cup uncooked old-fashioned regular rolled oats; 1 cup packed light brown sugar; ½ cup toasted pecans, chopped; and ½ teaspoon salt in a bowl. Add ¾ cup unsalted butter, cubed, and begin working it into the mixture with your fingers. Keep working and mixing until ingredients come together in clumps and resemble wet sand. Refrigerate 20 minutes. Pile on top of your favorite pie or crisp, and bake as directed.

Gingered Sweet Potato Pie with Pecan-Crumb Crust and Ginger-Honey Whip

(Photo, page 274)

I get my sweet potatoes from a man named Loyd Lewis, who lives in the neighboring town of Fallston, North Carolina. He's 78 years old and has been growing sweet potatoes since he first turned the soil with a mule plow as a teenager. In this recipe, fresh ginger complements the filling, along with a salty-sweet pecan crust that becomes centerpiece-worthy once it meets the edges of a springform pan.

ACTIVE 25 MIN. - TOTAL 5 HOURS

SERVES 10

PECAN-CRUMB CRUST
- 1 cup toasted pecan halves
- 1 cup all-purpose flour
- ⅓ cup packed light brown sugar
- ¾ tsp. kosher salt
- 5 Tbsp. unsalted butter, melted

SWEET POTATO FILLING
- 1 lb. sweet potatoes (about 3 medium-size sweet potatoes), roasted and peeled
- 4 large eggs
- ½ cup packed light brown sugar
- 2 Tbsp. grated fresh ginger
- ½ tsp. ground cinnamon
- ¼ tsp. kosher salt
- ¼ tsp. ground nutmeg
- ¼ tsp. ground ginger
- ⅓ cup heavy whipping cream
- 3 Tbsp. unsalted butter, melted
- 2 tsp. vanilla extract

GINGER-HONEY WHIP
- 1½ cups heavy whipping cream
- ½ tsp. grated fresh ginger
- ¼ cup powdered sugar
- ¼ cup honey
- Pinch of kosher salt

CANDIED PECANS
- 1 Tbsp. unsalted butter
- 1 Tbsp. sorghum syrup
- ⅛ tsp. kosher salt
- ⅛ tsp. ground cinnamon
- ½ cup pecan halves

1. Prepare the Pecan-Crumb Crust: Cut out a parchment paper circle fitted to line the bottom of a 9-inch springform pan. Coat with cooking spray, and set aside. Pulse pecans in a food processor until finely ground, 10 to 15 pulses. Scrape sides of bowl with a small spatula to loosen any pecans stuck to the side. Add flour, sugar, and salt, and pulse to combine, about 5 pulses. With food processor running, slowly pour in melted butter, and process until thoroughly incorporated. Pour crumbs into prepared pan. Press firmly against bottom and 1½ inches up sides of pan. Use a measuring cup to smooth bottom crust. Use a circular motion rather than a stamping motion to keep crust from lifting off. Freeze 10 to 15 minutes. Preheat oven to 350°F. Once crust is frozen, bake until set, 10 to 12 minutes. Remove from oven, and let cool completely.

2. Prepare the Sweet Potato Filling: Preheat oven to 375°F. Process roasted sweet potatoes in a food processor until smooth, about 1 minute. Add eggs, brown sugar, fresh ginger, cinnamon, salt, nutmeg, and ground ginger; process until combined, about 30 seconds. With processor running, pour in cream, melted butter, and vanilla, stopping to scrape sides of bowl if needed. Pour filling through a fine-mesh strainer into a medium bowl; discard solids. Spoon strained filling into cooled crust. Bake 30 minutes. Rotate and bake until filling is set and slightly puffed, 10 to 15 minutes. Let cool completely before removing from springform pan.

3. Prepare the Ginger-Honey Whip: Combine cream and ginger in the bowl of a stand mixer fitted with a whisk attachment. Beat on medium-high speed until mixture begins to thicken, about 1 minute. Add powdered sugar and beat until soft peaks form, about 1 minute. Carefully add honey, pouring slowly down side of bowl, and beat on medium until smooth peaks form, 1 to 2 minutes. With mixer running, add salt. Do not overbeat.

4. Prepare the Candied Pecans: Preheat oven to 325°F. Line a baking sheet with parchment paper, and coat paper lightly with cooking spray.

5. Combine butter and sorghum syrup in a small saucepan over medium-low. Cook, stirring constantly, until melted, 1½ to 2 minutes. Stir in salt and cinnamon. Remove from heat. Add pecans; stir to coat. Pour onto prepared baking sheet. Bake in preheated oven until pecans are toasted and glazed, 8 to 10 minutes. Let cool completely, about 30 minutes. (Candied Pecans can be stored in an airtight container up to 3 days until ready to use.)

6. Chop half of the pecans and leave remaining pecans whole. Serve pie with Ginger-Honey Whip and sprinkle with chopped Candied Pecans.

Sorghum Custard Pie with Cornmeal Crust

(Photo, page 275)

Sorghum syrup is the currency of the mountains, and this product bears the signature of the land from which it came as well as the hand of its maker. This pie captures the essence of sorghum, with notes of grass and cane in a delicate custard filling. Top slices with whipped cream and a drizzle of sorghum for a fancy finish.

ACTIVE 30 MIN. - TOTAL 2 HOURS, 15 MIN., PLUS 1 HOUR CHILLING

SERVES 8

CORNMEAL CRUST
- 1 cup all-purpose flour, plus more for work surface
- ¼ cup yellow cornmeal
- 2 tsp. granulated sugar
- ½ tsp. kosher salt
- ½ cup cold unsalted butter, cut into ½-inch cubes
- ¼ cup ice water

FILLING
- ½ cup unsalted butter
- 1 vanilla bean, split and seeds scraped
- ¼ cup granulated sugar
- ¼ cup packed light brown sugar
- ¼ cup fine yellow cornmeal
- ½ tsp. kosher salt
- ½ tsp. ground cinnamon
- ½ cup sorghum syrup
- 3 large eggs
- 1 egg yolk
- 1 cup heavy whipping cream

1. Prepare the Cornmeal Crust: Whisk together flour, cornmeal, sugar, and salt in a large bowl. Add cold butter and toss to coat in flour mixture. Using a pastry blender, cut butter into flour mixture, breaking large pieces into small, pebble-size pieces. Use your fingers to "snap" the butter, flattening it into large flakes. Continue working butter into flour until

Continued on page 278

Continued from page 277

mixture is well blended. (It should look like grated Parmesan cheese with a few pebble-size pieces.)

2. Make a well in center of flour mixture, and add ice water; toss thoroughly. Turn out onto a lightly floured work surface; bring dough together into a single mass. Shape into a disk. Wrap tightly in plastic wrap, and chill at least 1 hour or up to overnight (12 hours).

3. Roll dough into a 12-inch circle on a lightly floured work surface. Transfer to a 9-inch pie plate. Trim any excess dough, leaving a 1-inch overhang. Roll overhanging dough under itself to create piecrust. Crimp as desired; place in freezer for 20 minutes. Preheat oven to 425°F with rack in lower half of oven. Line frozen pie shell with parchment paper; fill completely with pie weights to top of crust. Bake until set and very lightly browned, about 20 minutes. Remove pie weights and parchment; bake until light golden, 3 to 5 minutes. Remove from oven; cool completely, 30 minutes.

4. Prepare the Filling: Preheat oven to 325°F. Cook butter, vanilla bean, and scraped seeds in a small saucepan over medium, stirring often, until butter is melted, about 1 minute. Whisk together granulated sugar, brown sugar, cornmeal, salt, and cinnamon in a medium bowl. Remove vanilla bean pod from melted vanilla butter; discard pod. Whisk in melted vanilla butter. Add sorghum syrup, eggs, and egg yolk, whisking until thoroughly combined. Whisk in the cream. Pour into prepared pie shell.

5. Bake until filling is just set, 40 to 50 minutes, rotating pie halfway through and covering edges with aluminum foil during the last 20 minutes, if needed, to prevent overbrowning.

Black Walnut-Buttermilk Pie with Hibiscus-Cranberry Relish

In this recipe, buttermilk is perfumed with the almost fruity umami of black walnuts and balanced with the Hibiscus-Cranberry Relish. Hibiscus, grown by my farmer husband, is a mouth-puckering stand-in for cranberries, which don't grow in our region. I like to mix the two in this holiday relish, but you can use all cranberries just the same.

ACTIVE 40 MIN. · TOTAL 3 HOURS, PLUS 1 HOUR CHILLING

SERVES 8

ALL-BUTTER CRUST

- 1¼ cups all-purpose flour, plus more for work surface
- 2 tsp. granulated sugar
- ½ tsp. kosher salt
- ½ cup cold unsalted butter, cut into ½-inch cubes
- ¼ cup cold water

FILLING

- 1¼ cups granulated sugar
- ⅓ cup black walnuts, finely ground
- ¼ cup all-purpose flour
- ½ tsp. kosher salt
- 3 large eggs
- ¾ cup whole buttermilk
- 1 tsp. fresh lemon juice (from 1 lemon)
- ¼ cup butter, melted
- 1 tsp. vanilla bean paste (or vanilla extract)

HIBISCUS-CRANBERRY RELISH

- 1 cup water
- ½ cup dried hibiscus
- 1 cup fresh or frozen cranberries
- ½ cup packed light brown sugar
  Zest of 1 lemon (about 2 tsp.)
- ¼ tsp. kosher salt
- 1 cinnamon stick
- 1 to 2 dried bay leaves
- 5 grinds of black pepper
- 1 (4-inch) fresh rosemary sprig (optional)

1. Prepare the All-Butter Crust: Whisk together flour, sugar, and salt in a large bowl. Add cold butter, and toss to coat in flour mixture. Using a pastry blender, cut butter into flour mixture, breaking large pieces into smaller, pebble-size pieces. Use your fingers to "snap" the butter, flattening it into large flakes. Continue working butter into flour until mixture is well blended. (It should look like grated Parmesan cheese with a few pebble-size pieces.)

2. Make a well in center of flour mixture and add ¼ cup cold water; toss thoroughly, making sure to incorporate it evenly throughout entire bowl. Turn out onto a lightly floured work surface, and bring dough together into a single mass. Shape into a disk. Wrap tightly in plastic wrap and chill at least 1 hour or up to overnight (12 hours).

3. Roll dough into a 12-inch circle on a lightly floured work surface. Transfer dough to a 9-inch pie plate. Trim any excess dough to just barely skim work surface. Roll dough under itself to create piecrust. Crimp as desired then place in freezer for 20 minutes. Preheat oven to 425°F with rack in lower half of oven. Line frozen pie shell with parchment paper; fill completely with pie weights to top edge of crust. Bake 20 minutes. Remove pie weights and parchment; bake 3 to 5 minutes. Remove and cool completely.

4. Prepare the Filling: Preheat oven to 350°F. Whisk together sugar, black walnuts, flour, and salt in a bowl. Add eggs 1 at a time, whisking until incorporated. Stir in buttermilk and lemon juice. Add melted butter and vanilla, and whisk until combined. Pour into prepared pie shell. Cover edges of pie shell with aluminum foil to prevent overbrowning. Bake just until set, 35 to 45 minutes. Remove to a wire rack; cool completely.

5. Prepare the Hibiscus-Cranberry Relish: Combine 1 cup water and the dried hibiscus in a saucepan then bring to a boil. Remove from heat; cover and steep 5 minutes. Pour mixture through a fine-mesh strainer over a bowl; discard solids. Return strained hibiscus water to saucepan. Add cranberries, brown sugar, lemon zest, salt, cinnamon stick, bay leaf, pepper, and (if desired) rosemary sprig to saucepan. Simmer over medium until thickened and jammy, about 15 minutes. Let cool; discard bay leaf. Serve with Black Walnut-Buttermilk Pie.

BLACK WALNUT- BUTTERMILK PIE
WITH HIBISCUS-CRANBERRY RELISH

From Our Table to Yours

Test Kitchen pros and contributors share recipes for their must-have holiday dishes

JOHN SOMERALL
Test Kitchen Professional

"I took over cooking the family Thanksgiving about 10 years ago. We typically do two turkeys every year, one smoked and the other roasted. I like to smoke one for two reasons: I just love the flavor, and it gives me an excuse to be outside and escape the family for a little bit while everything is baking in the ovens. We have a huge whiskey-and-bourbon tasting after lunch. Everybody brings a bottle, and we all share them and talk about what we're thankful for."

John's Sweet Tea-Brined Smoked Turkey

The aromatic wet brine (made with black tea, citrus, herbs, and sorghum) infuses the entire bird with flavor.

ACTIVE 20 MIN. - TOTAL 5 HOURS, 50 MIN., PLUS 24 HOURS BRINING

SERVES 6 TO 8

BRINE
- 3 cups kosher salt
- 3 cups sorghum syrup
- 4 large lemons, thinly sliced (about 5 cups)
- 1 large orange, thinly sliced (about 2 cups)
- ½ cup whole black peppercorns, toasted
- 1 oz. fresh thyme sprigs
- 1 oz. fresh sage sprigs
- 1 oz. fresh rosemary sprigs
- 32 regular-size black tea bags or 8 (1-oz.) gallon-size black tea bags
- 10 lb. ice
- 1 (10- to 12-lb.) fresh or thawed, frozen whole turkey

RUB
- ¼ cup kosher salt
- 3 Tbsp. ground black tea leaves (from 1 [1-oz.] black tea bag)
- 2 Tbsp. light brown sugar
- 2 Tbsp. ground black pepper
- 2 Tbsp. chili powder
- 1 Tbsp. paprika
- ½ tsp. cayenne pepper

MOPPING SAUCE
- 1½ cups ketchup
- 1¼ cups sorghum syrup
- ½ cup apple cider vinegar
- 2 Tbsp. chili powder
- 2 Tbsp. Dijon mustard
- 2 Tbsp. Worcestershire sauce
- 2 tsp. kosher salt
- 1½ tsp. ground black pepper
- 1 tsp. cayenne pepper

ADDITIONAL INGREDIENTS:
Hickory wood chunks, for smoking

1. Prepare the Brine: Combine salt, sorghum syrup, lemon and orange slices, peppercorns, herb sprigs, and tea bags in an extra-large container, such as a food-safe 5-gallon bucket. Bring 2 gallons water to a boil in a large stockpot over high. Pour boiling water into large container with aromatics. Stir to dissolve salt and sorghum, about 2 minutes. Let steep at room temperature 30 minutes; remove and discard tea bags. Add ice to warm mixture; stir gently until all ice is melted and Brine is cool, about 5 minutes.

2. Place turkey on a large cutting board, breast-side down, legs toward you. Using kitchen shears, cut parallel along each side of backbone; remove and discard backbone (or save for stock). Simultaneously press down both sides of turkey toward cutting board, using your body weight, until you hear a pop or crack. Flip turkey over to ensure it lays flat, applying additional pressure to breastbone, if needed, to flatten it. (A butcher can also do this step.) Completely submerge turkey in Brine.

Cover container with a lid or plastic wrap; transfer to a refrigerator to chill for 24 hours.

3. Prepare the Rub: Stir together all ingredients in a medium bowl until well combined; set aside. Store, covered, at room temperature up to 1 week.

4. Prepare the Mopping Sauce: Whisk together all ingredients in a medium saucepan until well combined. Bring sauce to a gentle boil over medium, whisking often. Remove from heat and cover to keep warm.

5. Remove turkey from Brine. Transfer to a large sheet pan lined with paper towels; discard Brine. Pat turkey with paper towels until completely dry, then evenly sprinkle both sides with Rub (do not massage Rub into turkey). Tuck wing tips behind breasts, then place turkey (skin-side up) on sheet pan. Let stand at room temperature 1 hour.

6. Meanwhile, prepare a grill at least 22 inches in diameter for smoking. Open bottom vent of grill completely. Light charcoal chimney starter filled with briquettes. When briquettes are covered with gray ash, evenly pour them onto bottom grate of grill. (Never use charcoal lighter fluid to start a charcoal fire; it will give grilled or smoked foods a chemical taste.) Place a few hickory wood chunks on hot coals, then place top grate on grill. Maintain internal temperature at 225°F for 15 to 20 minutes. Place turkey, skin-side up, on unoiled grate. Smoke, covered, until a thermometer inserted in thickest portion registers 145°F, 2 hours to 2 hours, 30 minutes.

7. Remove 1 cup Mopping Sauce; set aside for serving. Mop remaining 1½ cups Mopping Sauce on skin side of turkey. Cover grill; continue cooking until a thermometer inserted in thickest portion of the breast registers 160°F, 45 minutes to 1 hour.

8. Transfer turkey to a large cutting board. Cover loosely with aluminum foil; let rest 30 minutes before carving. Serve with reserved 1 cup Mopping Sauce, if desired.

ANN'S KALE-CITRUS SALAD WITH BACONY PECANS

KAREN'S ITALIAN SAUSAGE DRESSING WITH MARSALA-MUSHROOM GRAVY (PAGE 287)

JESSICA'S HARVARD BEETS

IVY'S LACY CORNBREAD

PAIGE'S CALABACITAS (PAGE 284)

ANN TAYLOR PITTMAN
Contributing Editor

"This kale salad is designed to fit this time of year—it has enough little indulgences to feel right for the holiday. It's pretty and it offers a fresh, crisp respite from the heavy dishes. Center-cut bacon doesn't overpower like other varieties might, and the drippings impart smoky goodness to the salted nuts."

___

Ann's Kale-Citrus Salad with Bacony Pecans

Watermelon radishes add a pop of color. If you can't find them at your grocery store or farmers market, use regular radishes.
ACTIVE 25 MIN. · TOTAL 30 MIN.
SERVES 8

- 6 center-cut bacon slices, cut crosswise into ½-inch-thick slices
- 1 cup pecan halves
- ¾ tsp. kosher salt, divided
- 6 Tbsp. extra-virgin olive oil
- 3 Tbsp. apple cider vinegar
- 2 Tbsp. minced shallots
- 2 tsp. honey
- 2 tsp. Dijon mustard
- ½ tsp. black pepper
- 2 large navel oranges
- 5 cups baby arugula
- 5 cups thinly sliced, stemmed Lacinato kale (about 4½ oz. from 1 [7-oz.] bunch)
- 2 medium watermelon radishes, very thinly sliced

1. Heat a medium skillet over medium. Add bacon to skillet. Cook, stirring occasionally, until browned and crisp, 6 to 7 minutes. Transfer bacon with a slotted spoon to a paper towel–lined plate, reserving drippings in skillet.
2. Add pecans to drippings. Cook, stirring occasionally, until pecans are browned and toasted, 4 to 5 minutes. Transfer pecans with slotted spoon to a paper towel–lined plate; sprinkle with ¼ teaspoon of the salt. Reserve drippings for another use or discard.

3. Combine oil, vinegar, shallots, honey, mustard, pepper, and remaining ½ teaspoon salt in a small jar with lid; shake well until emulsified.
4. Cut off top and bottom of each orange. Stand each one upright. Following the curve of the fruit, cut off the peel and pith. Cut orange segments away from membranes.
5. Combine arugula, kale, and radishes in a large serving bowl. Drizzle with dressing; toss well to coat. Add oranges, and toss to combine. Sprinkle with pecans and bacon.

JESSICA B. HARRIS
Contributing Editor

"There was never a Thanksgiving when sweet-and-sour Harvard beets—which my mother prepared using canned beets—did not appear on the table. It was the only time of year that we had this dish."

___

Jessica's Harvard Beets

Made with just a few ingredients, these tangy beets have a rich, glossy sauce.
ACTIVE 10 MIN. · TOTAL 35 MIN.
SERVES 6

- ¾ cup granulated sugar
- ⅓ cup apple cider vinegar
- 4 tsp. cornstarch
- 2 (15-oz.) cans sliced beets, drained, reserving ⅓ cup beet liquid
- 3 Tbsp. butter
- ¼ tsp. kosher salt
- ¼ tsp. black pepper

Whisk together sugar, vinegar, cornstarch, and ⅓ cup beet liquid (or water) in a medium saucepan. Bring to a boil over medium-high. Reduce heat to medium-low and cook, whisking occasionally, about 5 minutes. Gently stir beets into sugar-vinegar mixture. Reduce heat to low and simmer about 30 minutes, gently stirring occasionally.

Stir in butter, salt, and pepper until butter is melted. Remove from heat. Serve beets warm or chilled.

IVY ODOM
Hey Y'all Host and Test Kitchen Professional

"These crispy, golden rounds of cornbread go by many other names, like hoecakes, hot-water cornbread, lacy hoecakes, johnnycakes, and more. Although they are delicious on their own, they're best served as an accompaniment to casseroles or side dishes. I spoon the perfect bite of green bean casserole, cornbread dressing, turkey, and cranberry sauce on a piece of lacy cornbread."

___

Ivy's Lacy Cornbread

For extra flavor, substitute bacon drippings for some or all of the oil.
ACTIVE 35 MIN. · TOTAL 35 MIN.
SERVES 10

- ¾ cup canola oil
- 1 cup buttermilk self-rising white cornmeal mix
- ½ tsp. kosher salt
- ¾ cup hot tap water

1. Heat oil to 375°F in a 10-inch nonstick skillet over medium-high. Meanwhile, whisk together cornmeal mix, salt, and hot water in a medium bowl. (Batter will be very thin.)
2. Carefully pour 2 tablespoons batter into hot oil. Batter will immediately spread to about a 4-inch circle and appear lacy. Fry until golden on first side, 1 minute to 1 minute, 30 seconds. Flip and fry until golden on second side, 1 minute to 1 minute, 30 seconds. Place on a paper towel–lined plate to drain. Repeat procedure with remaining batter, stirring batter before each batch.

PAIGE GRANDJEAN
Test Kitchen Professional

"My aunt and uncle live in Hatch, New Mexico (the Chile Capital of the World), and my family goes there every fall to roast green chiles and make red chile sauce to stock our freezers for the year. Our Thanksgiving wouldn't be complete without green chiles. They usually make an appearance in multiple dishes: calabacitas, cornbread, and mac and cheese. Calabacitas (which means little squash) is made of sautéed squash, onion, and corn and has a smoky, slightly sweet flavor from the chiles. It feels like a New Mexico take on succotash."

Paige's Calabacitas

(Photo, page 282)

If possible, use frozen roasted green chiles rather than canned, which can have a metallic taste.

ACTIVE 25 MIN. - TOTAL 25 MIN.

SERVES 8

- 4 Tbsp. unsalted butter
- 1 large yellow onion, roughly chopped (2½ cups)
- 5 garlic cloves, chopped (about 1½ Tbsp.)
- 1½ lb. yellow squash (about 4 small), cut into ¼-inch-thick half-moons (about 5 cups)
- 1½ lb. zucchini (about 4 small), cut into ¼-inch-thick half-moons (about 5 cups)
- 2 tsp. kosher salt, plus more to taste
- 1½ tsp. ground cumin
- 1 tsp. dried Mexican oregano leaves
- ¾ tsp. black pepper, plus more to taste
- 2 cups (10 oz.) fresh or thawed, frozen yellow corn kernels (from 3 ears)
- 1½ cups (10 oz.) roasted, peeled, and chopped medium-heat Hatch green chiles, drained well (from fresh or thawed, frozen chiles)
- 6 oz. shredded Mexican cheese blend (about 1½ cups)

- 4 oz. crumbled queso fresco (about 1 cup)
  Fresh cilantro leaves, for garnish

1. Melt butter in a large (12-inch) cast-iron skillet over medium. Add onion. Cook, stirring often, until slightly softened, about 5 minutes. Add garlic. Cook, stirring constantly, until fragrant, about 1 minute. Add yellow squash, zucchini, salt, cumin, Mexican oregano, and black pepper. Cook, stirring often, until softened, 10 to 14 minutes. Stir in corn and green chiles. Cook, stirring occasionally, until corn is tender and flavors meld, 5 to 8 minutes.
2. Reduce heat to low. Add the Mexican cheese blend, stirring until melted and well combined, about 2 minutes. Season to taste with additional salt and black pepper, if desired. Sprinkle with queso fresco and garnish with cilantro before serving.

LISA CERICOLA
Senior Food Editor

"I'm not big on mashed potatoes throughout the year, but they are required at Thanksgiving. This recipe is ultrarich thanks to butter, half-and-half, cream cheese, and a generous swirl of Herbed Brown Butter on top. It is guaranteed to upstage the other sides on the buffet."

Lisa's Mashed Potatoes with Herbed Brown Butter

When cooking the potatoes, start them in cold (not boiling) water for the most even, tender results.

ACTIVE 20 MIN. - TOTAL 45 MIN.

SERVES 12

MASHED POTATOES

- 3 lb. Yukon Gold potatoes (about 7 medium potatoes), peeled and cut into 1-inch pieces (about 8 cups)
- 2 medium-size garlic cloves, smashed

- 2 tsp. kosher salt, divided
- ½ cup softened cream cheese or sour cream
- 5 Tbsp. half-and-half or whole milk, plus more to taste
- 3 Tbsp. butter
- ¾ tsp. coarsely ground black pepper

HERBED BROWN BUTTER

- ½ cup butter, cubed
- 15 small fresh sage leaves, rosemary sprigs, or thyme sprigs (or any combination), patted dry

1. Prepare the Mashed Potatoes: Bring 2 quarts cold water, the potatoes, garlic, and 1 teaspoon of the salt to a boil in a large Dutch oven over medium-high. Reduce heat to medium-low. Cook until potatoes are fork-tender, 15 to 20 minutes; drain well.
2. Return potatoes to Dutch oven. Stir in cream cheese, half-and-half, butter, pepper, and remaining 1 teaspoon salt. Heat over low until butter is melted and potato mixture is heated through, 1 to 2 minutes. Remove from heat.
3. Beat potato mixture with an electric mixer on medium speed until desired smoothness, 30 seconds to 1 minute, gradually stirring in 1 tablespoon half-and-half at a time to reach desired consistency. Do not overbeat. Keep warm.
4. Prepare the Herbed Brown Butter: Melt butter in a medium skillet over medium, stirring constantly, until butter begins to turn golden brown, 5 to 6 minutes. Add herbs; cook until crisp, 30 seconds to 1 minute. (Do not let the butter overbrown.) Immediately remove skillet from heat. Use a fork to carefully transfer the fried herbs to a paper towel-lined plate, reserving brown butter in skillet.
5. Transfer warm potatoes to a serving dish. Drizzle with Herbed Brown Butter and top with fried herbs.

LISA'S MASHED POTATOES
WITH HERBED BROWN BUTTER

JASMINE'S RICE
AND BEANS

JASMINE SMITH

Test Kitchen Professional

"My dad always makes this twist on Caribbean rice and beans for the holidays. Usually, these types of recipes call for coconut milk instead of canned diced tomatoes. Dad's version is way better because it's lighter and more versatile. The spices and tomatoes give it a Creole vibe."

Jasmine's Rice and Beans

For the fluffiest rice, don't be tempted to stir. Leave it undisturbed as it cooks on low.

ACTIVE 15 MIN. - TOTAL 30 MIN.

SERVES 8

- 2   Tbsp. olive oil
- 1   medium-size yellow onion, chopped (about 1 cup)
- 1   Tbsp. minced garlic (from 3 cloves)
- 1   Tbsp. minced fresh ginger
- ¾   tsp. ground cumin
- 1½ cups uncooked basmati rice
- 1   tsp. kosher salt
- ½   tsp. black pepper
- ¼   tsp. cayenne pepper
- 1   (15.5-oz.) can dark kidney beans, drained and rinsed
- 1   (14.5-oz.) can diced tomatoes, undrained
- 1   Tbsp. chopped fresh thyme leaves
- ½   Tbsp. chopped fresh oregano leaves, plus more for garnish

1. Heat oil in a medium pot over medium–high. Add onion. Cook, stirring occasionally, until onion begins to brown, about 5 minutes. Add garlic, ginger, and cumin. Cook, stirring often, until fragrant, 1 minute. Add rice, and cook, stirring constantly, 1 minute.
2. Stir in 2½ cups water, the salt, black pepper, cayenne pepper, kidney beans, and tomatoes. Bring rice mixture to a simmer over medium–high. Cover and reduce heat to low. Cook, undisturbed, until rice is tender, 20 minutes.
3. Remove from heat, and stir in thyme and oregano. Transfer to a serving dish. Garnish with additional oregano.

KAREN SCHROEDER-RANKIN

Test Kitchen Professional

"This dressing smells like Thanksgiving heaven—there's nothing better than butter, sausage, onion, celery, and thyme. If I don't make this recipe, my children feel like we have not done our part to be thankful. And it's even better the next day. My absolute favorite way to enjoy it is on a turkey sandwich with mayo and cranberry sauce on toasted wheat bread, eaten while sitting at the table late at night with my daddy."

Karen's Italian Sausage Dressing with Marsala-Mushroom Gravy

(Photo, page 282)

You can assemble the dressing the day before and chill it overnight. Let the pan rest at room temperature for 30 minutes before baking.

ACTIVE 45 MIN. - TOTAL 1 HOUR, 55 MIN.

SERVES 12

- 2   (12-oz.) French bread loaves, cut into 1-inch cubes
- 2   lb. bulk mild Italian sausage
- ½   cup, plus 6 Tbsp. unsalted butter, divided
- 2   cups chopped sweet onion
- 2   cups chopped celery
- 3   Tbsp. chopped fresh thyme leaves and tender stems, divided
- 2   tsp. kosher salt, divided
- 1   tsp. black pepper, divided
- 2   eggs
- ½   cup chopped fresh flat-leaf parsley
- 8   cups low-sodium chicken stock, divided
- 1   lb. sliced cremini mushrooms (from 2 [8-oz.] pkg.)
- ¼   cup chopped shallot (from 1 shallot)
- ¼   cup all-purpose flour
- ¼   cup dry Marsala
- 3   Tbsp. heavy whipping cream

1. Preheat oven to 375°F. Lightly spray a 13- x 9-inch baking pan with cooking spray.

2. Place bread cubes on a large rimmed baking sheet. Bake in preheated oven 25 minutes, stirring halfway through to toast bread cubes evenly. They should be crispy on the outside and semitender on the inside.
3. Meanwhile, heat a large skillet over medium–high. Add sausage. Cook, stirring often with a wooden spoon or spatula to break into small pieces, until it begins to brown and is cooked through, 7 to 9 minutes. Remove from skillet with a slotted spoon; place in a large bowl, reserving drippings in skillet.
4. Add ½ cup of the butter to drippings in skillet; cook over medium–high until butter melts. Add sweet onion, celery, 2 tablespoons of the thyme, 1 teaspoon of the salt, and ½ teaspoon of the pepper. Cook, stirring often, until vegetables are softened, 6 to 8 minutes. Add vegetable mixture to bowl with sausage. Add toasted bread cubes to sausage mixture; stir to blend ingredients.
5. Whisk eggs in a medium bowl until smooth. Add parsley and 5 cups of the stock to eggs; whisk to combine. Pour egg mixture over sausage-and-bread mixture in bowl. Stir with hands or a wooden spoon, gently turning mixture over until ingredients are well combined. Let stand until liquid is absorbed, about 30 minutes, stirring 2 or 3 times. Spoon dressing mixture into prepared baking pan, pressing lightly to pack into pan. Melt 2 tablespoons of the butter, and drizzle over top of dressing mixture. Bake in preheated oven until top is golden brown and dressing is moist but not wet in the center, 50 to 55 minutes. Let dressing stand 5 to 6 minutes before serving.
6. To make gravy, heat remaining 4 tablespoons butter in a large saucepan over medium–high. Add mushrooms, shallot, and remaining 1 teaspoon salt and ½ teaspoon pepper to saucepan. Cook, stirring often, until mushrooms are golden brown and most of the liquid has evaporated, 8 to 10 minutes. Add flour, stirring to incorporate completely. Add Marsala, stirring until alcohol evaporates and a thick paste forms on mushrooms. Add remaining 3 cups stock, stirring until mixture comes to a boil and liquid thickens, 4 to 6 minutes. Stir in cream and remaining 1 tablespoon thyme. Remove from heat. Serve gravy with dressing.

MELISSA GRAY
Test Kitchen Professional

"My Aunt Terry is admittedly not a great baker, so she makes this cranberry granita. I'm from Florida, and November can be rather hot there. Granita is a cooling dessert. It's perfectly tart and sweet; plus, it's so light that it saves room for that second plate from the buffet!"

Melissa's Cranberry Granita

This treat can be made a week ahead and stored in the freezer.
ACTIVE 20 MIN. - TOTAL 20 MIN.,
PLUS 12 HOURS FREEZING
SERVES 16

- 1 lb. fresh or thawed, frozen cranberries (about 3½ cups)
- 4 cups cold water, divided
- 2 cups granulated sugar
- 1 (3-oz.) pkg. lemon-flavor gelatin (such as Jell-O)
- 2 cups hot water
- ½ cup fresh orange juice (from 1 large orange)
- ½ cup fresh lemon juice (from 2 large lemons)

1. Combine cranberries and 2 cups of the cold water in a saucepan. Bring to a boil over medium-high. Cook, stirring occasionally, until cranberries burst, about 10 minutes. Place a strainer over a large bowl; strain mixture, gently pressing cranberries with back of a spoon. Discard cranberries. Add sugar to cranberry juice; stir until dissolved, 1 minute. Pour into a 13- x 9-inch (3-quart) baking dish. Set aside to cool at room temperature.
2. Meanwhile, whisk together gelatin and 2 cups hot water in a large bowl until dissolved, 1 minute. Stir in orange and lemon juices and remaining 2 cups cold water until combined. Add gelatin mixture to cranberry juice, stirring until combined. Freeze, covered, until solid, about 12 hours or overnight. Scrape with a fork; serve immediately.

PAM LOLLEY
Test Kitchen Professional

"This was my mom's go-to pie for the holidays. She was notorious for leaving it in the oven too long. As far as I know, she never owned a timer. We all had a lot of fun teasing her—saying, 'It must be Thanksgiving when you smell pecans and sugar burning!' Her first reply would always be, 'Well, I just don't know what went wrong.'"

Pam's Pecan Pie

Fresh pecans, not the ones from the back of the freezer, make all the difference in this simple pie.
ACTIVE 20 MIN. - TOTAL 2 HOURS, 40 MIN.,
PLUS 3 HOURS COOLING
SERVES 8

CRUST
- 1½ cups all-purpose flour
- 1 Tbsp. granulated sugar
- ½ tsp. kosher salt
- 6 Tbsp. cold butter, cubed
- 3 Tbsp. cold shortening, cubed
- 4 to 5 Tbsp. ice water

FILLING
- 1 cup dark corn syrup
- ¾ cup granulated sugar
- 3 Tbsp. butter, melted
- 2 Tbsp. plain white cornmeal
- 1 tsp. vanilla extract
- ½ tsp. kosher salt
- 3 large eggs, lightly beaten
- 2 cups pecan halves
  Vanilla ice cream or whipped cream (optional)

1. Prepare the Crust: Pulse flour, sugar, and salt in a food processor until combined, 3 or 4 pulses. Add cubed butter and shortening; pulse until mixture resembles coarse meal, 8 to 10 pulses. Drizzle 4 tablespoons ice water over mixture. Pulse until dough clumps together, 4 or 5 pulses, adding up to 1 tablespoon ice water, 1 teaspoon at a time, if necessary. Gently shape dough into a flat disk. Wrap in plastic wrap, and chill 30 minutes.
2. Preheat oven to 400°F. Roll dough into a 12-inch circle (about ⅛ inch thick) on a floured surface. Fit into a lightly greased (with cooking spray) 9-inch pie plate, and crimp edges. Prick bottom and sides with a fork. Line pastry with parchment paper; fill with pie weights or dried beans.
3. Bake in preheated oven 10 minutes. Remove weights and parchment; bake until lightly browned, about 8 minutes. Transfer Crust to a wire rack; cool completely, 30 minutes.
4. Prepare the Filling: Reduce oven temperature to 325°F. Whisk together corn syrup, sugar, melted butter, cornmeal, vanilla, salt, and eggs in a medium bowl until combined. Stir in pecans. Pour into Crust.
5. Bake on middle rack of preheated oven until Filling is set, 1 hour to 1 hour, 10 minutes, shielding edges with aluminum foil during the last 10 to 15 minutes of bake time to prevent overbrowning. Transfer to a wire rack; cool completely, 3 hours. Top slices with ice cream or whipped cream, if desired.

MELISSA'S
CRANBERRY GRANITA

PAM'S PECAN PIE

Day-After Dumplings

This tasty slow-cooker soup is an easy way to make the most out of leftover turkey

Slow-Cooker Turkey and Dumplings

ACTIVE 10 MIN. · TOTAL 10 MIN.,
PLUS 6 HOURS, 30 MIN. SLOW-COOKING
SERVES 6

- 8 cups lower-sodium chicken broth
- 4 cups shredded cooked turkey (about 1 lb.)
- 1 cup chopped sweet onion (from 1 small onion)
- 1 cup chopped carrots (from 3 medium carrots)
- 1 cup chopped celery (from 2 large stalks)
- 1 Tbsp. minced garlic (from 3 large cloves)
- 1 Tbsp. dried thyme
- ¼ cup cornstarch
- ¾ tsp. kosher salt
- 1½ cups self-rising flour
- ¼ tsp. black pepper
- ¾ cup whole buttermilk
- 1 large egg
- 2 Tbsp. unsalted butter, melted
  Chopped fresh flat-leaf parsley

1. Place chicken broth, cooked turkey, onion, carrots, celery, garlic, and dried thyme in a 6-quart slow cooker. Cover; cook on LOW until turkey and vegetables are tender, 6 to 7 hours.

2. Whisk together ¼ cup water, the cornstarch, and salt in a small bowl. Stir cornstarch mixture into turkey mixture. Cover and cook on HIGH until mixture begins to simmer, about 10 minutes.

3. Whisk together self-rising flour and black pepper in a medium bowl. Whisk together buttermilk and egg in a small bowl. Whisk buttermilk mixture into flour mixture until combined. Stir in melted butter just until combined. Drop heaping tablespoonfuls of batter into simmering soup. Cover and cook on HIGH until a wooden pick inserted in center of dumplings comes out clean, 20 to 25 minutes. Sprinkle with parsley.

GOOD GRAVY
Before adding the dumpling batter, stir up to ½ cup leftover turkey gravy into the soup to make it thicker and richer.

Comfort for a Crowd

This hearty hash feeds a full house

Cheesy Sausage Hash

Refrigerated (not frozen) diced potatoes make this hash come together fast because they're parcooked and don't need to thaw.
ACTIVE 35 MIN. · TOTAL 50 MIN.
SERVES 6

- 3 Tbsp. olive oil, divided
- 8 oz. ground pork sausage
- 1 sweet onion, diced (2 cups)
- 1 poblano chile, seeded and chopped (1 cup)
- 1 red bell pepper, seeded and chopped (1 cup)
- 1½ tsp. kosher salt, divided
- 2 cups refrigerated diced potatoes (such as Simply Potatoes)
- ¾ tsp. garlic powder
- 4 oz. Gruyère cheese, shredded (about 1 cup), divided
- 4 oz. extra-sharp cheddar cheese, shredded (about 1 cup), divided
- 5 large eggs
- ¼ cup heavy whipping cream
- 1 Tbsp. minced fresh chives

1. Preheat oven to 425°F with oven rack about 6 inches from heat. Heat 1 tablespoon of the oil in a 10-inch cast-iron skillet over medium-high. Add sausage. Cook, breaking up sausage into pieces with a wooden spoon, until golden brown and just cooked through, about 4 minutes. Remove sausage to a medium bowl with a slotted spoon; set aside. Do not wipe skillet clean.
2. Add onion, chile, bell pepper, and ½ teaspoon of the salt to skillet. Cook over medium-high, stirring occasionally, until onion is tender and pepper pieces have charred in spots, about 8 minutes. Remove with slotted spoon to bowl with sausage. Wipe skillet clean.
3. Heat remaining 2 tablespoons oil in skillet over medium-high. Add diced potatoes to skillet in an even layer. Cook, undisturbed, until browned on bottom, about 5 minutes. Add ½ teaspoon of the salt. Continue cooking, stirring occasionally, until golden brown and crispy on most sides, about 5 minutes. Remove from heat. Return sausage and pepper mixture to skillet, and add garlic powder. Stir to combine. Stir in ½ cup each of the Gruyère and cheddar cheeses just until combined.
4. Whisk together eggs, cream, and remaining ½ teaspoon salt in a medium bowl. Pour over mixture in skillet, then tilt pan to allow eggs to distribute. Top with remaining ½ cup each Gruyère and cheddar cheeses. Bake in preheated oven until eggs have set and cheese has melted, about 8 minutes. Increase oven temperature to broil, and broil until cheese has turned golden brown, 2 to 3 minutes. Remove; let stand 5 minutes. Sprinkle with chives. Slice and serve immediately.

COOKING SCHOOL

TIPS AND TRICKS FROM THE SOUTH'S MOST TRUSTED KITCHEN

Must-Have Multitasking Ingredients
Take recipes from good to great, or save a dish from disaster

1. ORANGES

This fruit's juice adds zing to cranberry sauce, glazed carrots, sweet potatoes, and pumpkin pie. If you are brining the turkey, add orange slices to the soaking liquid or add zest to the dry rub. A pinch of zest can also be a sunny addition to whipped cream.

2. FRESH HERBS

The dried kind is fine, but fresh herbs bring color and vibrancy to almost every dish. Dress up the most humble-looking casserole with a sprinkle of leaves, or infuse homemade stock with flavor from a simple bouquet of parsley, rosemary, and thyme sprigs. Herbs also make a pretty garnish on the turkey platter.

3. PECANS

Keep a stash of these nuts on hand to top desserts and vegetable sides and to add texture to dressing. Chop them finely, and roll them into pie dough for a nutty crust. Toast them in butter and sprinkle with your favorite spice blend to serve as an easy predinner nibble.

4. HEAVY CREAM

It's more than adding richness to casseroles, mashed potatoes, and gravy. A fluffy dollop of lightly sweetened whipped cream can camouflage a cracked or less-than-perfect pie. It also lightens and flavors evening tea or coffee.

Southern Staple
Sister Schubert's Dinner Yeast Rolls

These puffy, golden, bake-and-serve rolls are the next best thing to homemade. Back in 1989, Alabama native Patricia "Sister" Barnes (formerly Patricia Schubert) sold frozen pans of her grandmother's dinner rolls at a church fair. They were such a hit that she started a business to keep up with demand. Little did she know that her family recipe would later become a staple on tables across the South, especially during the holidays. Here are more ways to use them beyond the bread basket.

■ Bake a savory bread pudding.

■ Make a French toast casserole.

■ Use for leftover turkey sandwiches.

■ Cube and toast to make croutons.

December

Darling Clementines

'Tis the season for these juicy, easy-to-peel citrus fruits. Although clementines are sold year-round, now is the time for peak flavor. (Hint: The smaller the size, the sweeter they are.) Use them to make an easy edible gift that will brighten anyone's holiday

Clementine-Vanilla Bean Marmalade

ACTIVE 30 MIN. - TOTAL 2 HOURS, 15 MIN., PLUS 1 DAY CHILLING

MAKES 6 CUPS

- 3 lb. seedless clementines (mandarin oranges)
- 2 lemons
- 3 Tbsp. minced crystallized ginger
- ½ tsp. kosher salt
- 4½ cups granulated sugar
- 2 tsp. vanilla bean paste

1. Slice ends off clementines and lemons. Slice each piece of fruit in half from end to end. Thinly slice each half into ¼-inch-thick half-moons. Cut each half-moon in half so each piece is a quarter of a slice. Discard lemon seeds. Bring clementines, lemons, and 6 cups water to a boil in a large Dutch oven over medium-high; reduce heat to medium, and simmer 5 minutes. Remove from heat; let stand 30 minutes. Cover; chill 12 to 24 hours.

2. Prepare a boiling-water canner. Heat 6 half-pint glass jars in simmering water until ready to use. Do not boil. Wash lids in warm, soapy water, and set bands aside.

3. Uncover clementine mixture; bring to a simmer over medium. Stir in ginger and salt; cook, stirring occasionally, until citrus rinds are very soft, about 30 minutes.

4. Stir in sugar and vanilla paste. Bring mixture to a boil over medium-high. Reduce heat to medium; attach a candy thermometer to side of Dutch oven. Cook, stirring every 3 to 4 minutes, until thermometer registers 220°F, about 45 minutes. (A spoon dragged across bottom of pot should briefly leave a clean line.)

5. Remove mixture from heat; carefully ladle into hot sterilized jars, filling to ¼ inch from top. Remove air bubbles; wipe jar rims. Center lids on jars, and apply bands; adjust to fingertip tight. Lower jars into boiling water canner, and process, covered, for 10 minutes. Turn off heat, uncover, and let jars stand 5 minutes. Remove jars from canner; cool 12 to 24 hours. Check lids for seal (lids should not flex when center is pressed). Store in a cool, dark, dry place for up to 18 months. Or store in refrigerator in airtight jars up to 2 months.

A Caribbean Celebration

U.S. Army veteran and chef Nicola Blaque brings her Jamaican holiday traditions to the Lone Star State

FOR CHEF AND TEXAS RESTAURATEUR, Nicola Blaque, Christmastime smells like slow-simmering goat curry and spiced punch on the stovetop and sounds like spirited Jamaican carols and the glug of rum being poured over a freshly baked cake. Blaque was born in Jamaica and lived there until she was 5. "For us, Christmas was big, and it was all about the food."

Blaque's Christmases could be spent anywhere from New Hampshire to Texas to Hawaii, depending where her stepfather was stationed. Her mother always made sure their family's Caribbean traditions were upheld.

Typical Christmas meals throughout Jamaican culture include vibrant, piquant dishes such as braised oxtails, fried sweet plantains, ackee and saltfish, and sweet potato pudding. The twinkling star on top of the Yuletide festivities? Rum cake. The classic, spiked dessert hides out for hours before the merrymaking begins, soaking up rum. Kindred to a fruitcake, it calls for dried fruits, citrus peels, cozy spices, and a bit of booze. The dessert tops off the savory feast and keeps the party ticking further into the night.

During the 10 years Blaque served in the army, she'd cook comforting meals in the barracks for her fellow soldiers during the holidays, before later going to culinary school and opening two successful Caribbean restaurants in San Antonio. She lives there now with her two young children, stepson, and husband Cornelius Massey. Her flagship restaurant, The Jerk Shack, quickly became recognized nationally for its jerk chicken, while her newer concept, Mi Roti, offers build-your-own wraps and bowls inspired by Caribbean street food.

Now, when the holiday season comes around and a busy schedule keeps Blaque and her family in Texas, she celebrates in a familiar way: inviting over anyone who needs a place to go and serving up the nostalgic dishes of her heritage with a touch of Southern flair.

Nicola's Rum Cake
ACTIVE 25 MIN. - TOTAL 3 HOURS, 20 MIN., PLUS 8 HOURS STANDING
SERVES 12

Baking spray with flour
1¼ cups cane sugar
1 cup unsalted butter, softened
2 Tbsp. burnt sugar or molasses
1 tsp. vanilla extract
4 large eggs
1½ cups all-purpose flour
1 tsp. baking powder
1 tsp. ground cinnamon
½ tsp. mixed spice (British baking spice blend) or ¼ tsp. each ground allspice and nutmeg
½ tsp. kosher salt
1 cup port or brandy
2 cups raisins
½ cup pitted dried dates
¼ cup chopped orange peel (from 1 orange),
¼ cup chopped lemon peel (from 1 lemon)
½ cup drained maraschino cherries (from 1 [7-oz.] jar), plus more for serving (optional)
½ cup dried pitted plums
½ cup light rum
Whipped cream, for serving

1. Preheat oven to 325°F. Coat a 9-inch springform pan with baking spray; set aside. Beat cane sugar, butter, burnt sugar, and vanilla in a stand mixer fitted with a paddle attachment on medium-high speed until soft and fluffy, about 4 minutes. Reduce mixer speed to medium; beat in eggs 1 at a time, beating after each addition, stopping to scrape down sides as needed.
2. Sift together flour, baking powder, cinnamon, mixed spice, and salt in a medium bowl; stir to combine. Add flour mixture and port alternately to butter mixture, beginning and ending with flour mixture, beating on low speed until fully blended after each addition, about 2 minutes total. Set aside.

3. Process raisins, dates, orange peels, lemon peels, cherries, and dried plums in a food processor almost until a smooth paste forms, about 2 minutes, stopping to scrape down sides after 1 minute. Fold raisin mixture into batter; spoon into prepared springform pan.
4. Bake in preheated oven until cake top is firm to the touch and a wooden pick inserted into center comes out clean, 55 minutes to 1 hour, 5 minutes. Transfer springform pan to a wire rack, and let cake cool completely, about 2 hours.
5. Pour rum over cake; cover with plastic wrap. Let stand at room temperature at least 8 hours or up to 24 hours. Unwrap cake, and remove sides of springform pan. Serve with whipped cream and cherries, if desired.

Tastes Like Home

Three chefs from across the South share favorite dishes that are full of special meaning

CHRIS WILLIAMS
Houston, TX
Chef/owner, Lucille's and Late August

I fell in love with cooking at a very young age and devoured cookbooks the way other people ate Tic Tac candies. When I was still a teenager, I realized that the best way to understand a culture was through food. I traveled throughout Europe for years, cooking and learning and cooking some more. When I came back Stateside, I knew that my love of food, culture, and people was always going to be my bread and butter. But it wasn't until I opened up my first restaurant—named after my great-grandmother Lucille—that I fully embraced how much meaning my family recipes carried for me, and by extension, for our guests.

Wassail was always a Christmas tradition when I was growing up and was one of my great-grandmother's favorites. We served the drink to the traveling circus of friends and family who filled our home every December. And now at Lucille's, the wassail is offered with the same spirit of joy behind it. We serve it warm in a coupe glass, garnished with a dehydrated lemon slice and a cinnamon stick.

Our version shows a little of my own touch, too, by incorporating a couple of unexpected ingredients that truly make it sing: nutmeg and vodka. The nutmeg gives the drink a palpable but not overpowering zing of spice. We use Highway vodka, a hemp-based product of my brother's Houston distillery. The spirit is incredibly clean and imparts a velvety viscosity to any cocktail. Clearly we like to keep things in the family, especially at Christmas.

Williams Family Wassail

ACTIVE 10 MIN. · TOTAL 1 HOUR
SERVES 6

- 4 cups unfiltered apple cider
- 1½ cups fresh-squeezed orange juice (from 3 large oranges)
- ½ cup pineapple juice
- 2½ Tbsp. fresh lemon juice (from ½ lemon)
- 2 Tbsp. honey
- 1 Tbsp. brown sugar
- ¼ tsp. ground ginger
- ¼ tsp. ground nutmeg
- 2 (3-inch) cinnamon sticks, plus more for garnish
- ¾ cup vodka
  Lemon slices, for garnish

1. Bring apple cider, orange juice, pineapple juice, and lemon juice to a simmer in a saucepan or stockpot over medium.
2. Stir in honey, brown sugar, ginger, nutmeg, and cinnamon sticks; reduce heat to medium-low, and simmer 35 to 45 minutes. Stir in vodka; serve warm.

PAOLA VELEZ
Washington, D.C.
Pastry chef and cofounder of
Bakers Against Racism

In Latin cultures, Christmas Eve is
known as Noche Buena, and it's a night
for big meals, big celebrations, and big
gatherings. For our family, a honey
baked ham was always part of the feast.
This recipe for a ham-stuffed empanada
finds its inspiration from those lively
holiday traditions as well as key
moments from my upbringing.

I grew up in the Bronx in New York
City, but every summer, my mother
made sure I experienced a part of my
heritage in the Dominican Republic.
For three or four months, I stayed with
my extended family in the countryside,
or what we fondly called "El Campo"
(the camp). That place always had
such a rich sense of community.
Spending time on my family's land
made me extraordinarily appreciative
of fresh herbs (like achiote, oregano,
and cilantro), fruits (such as passion
fruit, mangoes, and guavas), and other
tropical produce (like cacao, tamarind,
and avocado) because they all grew at
El Campo. Those summers shaped the
person I am and the way I cook and
bake now, blending my culture with
classic techniques in a way that's fun
and playful.

These empanadas repurpose holiday
leftovers in an inventive way. I take
that traditional ham and cocoon pieces
of it in a light and airy dough to make
empanadas that hit on all the right notes
of savory and sweet. After Noche Buena,
I pair them with rice and beans for an
easy lunch. They are a delicious way to
bring core memories to life, especially
when I'm not able to see my family.

Paola Velez's Ham-and-Cheese Empanadas

ACTIVE 40 MIN. · TOTAL 1 HOUR, 20 MIN.

MAKES 18 EMPANADAS

- 2 cups all-purpose flour, plus more
  for work surface
- 1 tsp. baking powder
- 1 tsp. kosher salt
- ¾ cup water, at room temperature,
  plus more as needed
- 3 Tbsp. vegetable oil, plus more for
  frying
- 3 oz. leftover fully cooked spiral-cut
  ham, cut into ½-inch cubes (about
  ⅔ cup)
- 3 oz. low-moisture cheese such as
  mozzarella, cheddar, or queso
  blanco, cut into ¼-inch cubes or
  shredded (about ⅔ cup)

1. Whisk together flour, baking powder,
and salt in a large mixing bowl until
well combined. Make a well in middle
of flour mixture. Add ¾ cup water and
3 tablespoons vegetable oil to the well in
mixing bowl.

2. Using hands, mix ingredients together
until dough is tacky but not sticky. If
dough is dry, add water (in 1-teaspoon
increments) until dough comes together.

Form dough into a ball, and place in
bowl. Cover with a dish towel, and let
rest at room temperature 30 minutes
to an hour.

3. Meanwhile, combine ham and cheese
in a medium bowl; set aside.

4. Lightly flour countertop. Divide dough
into 18 (1-ounce) balls. Using a rolling
pin, roll out each ball into a 4-inch disk.
Spoon 1 tablespoon ham mixture onto
half of each disk, making sure not to
overfill. Dab a finger or pastry brush
in a small bowl of water, tap off excess
moisture, and run around outside
edge of empanada dough on the half
containing filling. Fold dough edges over
to form half-circles; crimp with a fork to
seal. Place on a lightly floured rimmed
baking sheet, and repeat process with
remaining dough. If empanadas are too
soft when you pick them up from the
tray, chill 10 minutes before frying.

5. Pour oil to a depth of 2 inches in a
large Dutch oven; heat oil over medium
to 350°F. Working in 4 or 5 batches, fry
empanadas until golden, 90 seconds
to 2 minutes per side. Place on a paper
towel-lined plate or baking sheet. Serve
immediately, or cool completely and
chill in an airtight container for up to
5 days. Reheat in oven.

CYNTHIA WONG
**Charleston, S.C.
Chef/owner, Life Raft Treats**

When I was a child growing up in South Carolina, I was always turning fruit and other produce into baked goods. And so, later in life, I followed the path I loved and attended a culinary school on the outskirts of Paris called École Lenôtre.

While traveling through Europe, I met my husband, John David Harmon, a fellow Southerner, at a free Spanish class in Barcelona. We returned to the States after a very meaningful stint in London where I worked for restaurants in various leadership roles. While I enjoyed it, the grueling schedule was not the life I wanted, especially with two toddlers in tow. I quite literally needed a life raft to get out, and that's when Life Raft Treats, my specialty ice cream business, was born.

I've always loved the process of inventing, and it's likely why this English pudding means so much to me—it was unlike anything I'd ever made. I remember seeing the recipe for the first time when we lived in London with our first newborn son and thinking to myself, "I've never steamed a whole cake before!" It's quite remarkable how it bubbles along on the stove, with its gooey, buttery texture taking form to resemble a hot and fluffy pound cake.

Although this pudding isn't traditionally made for the holidays in England, I make it for my family every Christmas Eve. The way it comes together still has me rapt all these years later. I serve it with a marmalade made from pink grapefruits off our backyard tree in Charleston. The dessert reminds us of the first Christmas we spent together as a family across the pond. It's the most delicious keepsake of the joy that slowing down brings, especially during the holidays.

Cynthia Wong's Steamed Pudding

ACTIVE 15 MIN. - TOTAL 2 HOURS, 25 MIN.
SERVES 4 TO 6

- ¾ **cup unsalted butter, softened, plus more for greasing**
- 2 **Tbsp. golden syrup, honey, sorghum, or cane syrup**
- 1¼ **cups unbleached all-purpose flour**
- 1¾ **tsp. baking powder**
- ½ **tsp. kosher salt**
- 1 **cup packed light brown sugar**
- 3 **large eggs**
- 1 **tsp. vanilla paste**
- 1 **tsp. grated lemon zest (from 1 lemon)**
- **Vanilla Custard (recipe follows)**

1. Grease a 1-quart ceramic pudding bowl or 4 (8-ounce) ceramic ramekins with butter. Cut a circle of parchment paper to fit bottom of bowl or ramekins. Place parchment in bottom of bowl/ramekins. Drizzle golden syrup into bottom of bowl or divide among ramekins.

2. Stir together flour, baking powder, and salt in a bowl; set aside. Beat butter and sugar at medium speed in a stand mixer with a whisk attachment until light and fluffy, 2 minutes. Add eggs, 1 at a time, beating well after each addition, 45 seconds total. Add vanilla and lemon zest until combined, 15 seconds. Gradually add flour mixture on low speed until just combined, 30 seconds. Scrape batter into prepared bowl or ramekins; gently tap on a towel to remove any air bubbles.

3. Cover top of bowl or ramekins with a piece of buttered aluminum foil large enough for overhang and loose enough to allow space for pudding to rise. Crimp foil tightly just below outer rim. Secure foil with kitchen twine, running it all the way around bowl or ramekins, just below rim. Tie another length of twine to the twine wrapped around rim; run it over the top and tie to twine on other side to form a handle to lift pudding out of the steamer. (Make sure twine on top is long enough to allow space for pudding to rise.)

4. Place a steamer rack or a heatproof bowl turned upside-down into a pot large enough to hold pudding with room for it to rise covered with lid. Place bowl or ramekins with pudding on top. Fill pot with boiling water to halfway up the side of the upside-down bowl. Steam over low, keeping water at a simmer, until a cake tester inserted in center comes out clean, about 2 hours (8-ounce ramekins will cook in 45 minutes). Lift pudding out of steamer with twine handle. Cool on a kitchen towel 10 minutes.

5. Carefully unwrap pudding; place a large plate over bowl or a small plate over each ramekin. Invert pudding onto plate. Serve warm with Vanilla Custard.

Vanilla Custard Whisk 4 large egg yolks vigorously in a medium bowl until eggs start to turn light pale. Combine 1½ cups heavy cream, ¼ cup granulated sugar, and 1 vanilla bean, scraped and seeded (or 1 tsp. vanilla), in a small saucepan; bring to a simmer over medium-low. Cook, stirring occasionally, until sugar is dissolved. Gradually add half of the cream mixture into yolks, whisking constantly. Pour yolk mixture back into saucepan. Cook over low, whisking constantly, until custard is thick enough to coat the back of a spoon, 15 to 18 minutes.

Nutcracker Tales

Even the most festive times can turn frantic. For one family, a few hours
in the kitchen put everything into perspective—and created
memories for a lifetime

BEFORE ALABAMA RECORDED "Why Can't Christmas Day Last All Year Long," I might have warned them to be careful what they wish for. Starting at age 8, my holidays began in August with auditions for *The Nutcracker* at the Tanglewood Mall in Roanoke, Virginia. My sister, Jordan-Elizabeth, and I would spend the rest of summer playing the score to the Christmas ballet as we discussed what parts we would dance that December.

Two years older and remarkably focused, my sister accepted the challenge of elegant roles involving a tutu or at least a party dress. Always looking for a laugh, I crossed my fingers for a character part, and Fight Scene Mouse remains one of my greatest hits.

Once rehearsals began in September, every family member contributed. Pink tulle and green organza leaves covered the living room as Mom made tutus for the "Waltz of the Flowers." Our dad spent Saturdays driving us through the Blue Ridge Mountains to the Roanoke Civic Center, an hour each way.

By the time the holidays finally arrived, we were starting to lose steam. An expert at making the ordinary feel magical, Mom suggested we whip up a batch of Christmas Mice, inspired by my onstage persona. While this recipe didn't require a mixer, an oven, or a hint of flour, it allowed us to slow down and reminisce on the joy of the past few months as we prepared for the celebrations ahead. —Brennan Long

Christmas Mice
ACTIVE 25 MIN. - TOTAL 45 MIN.
MAKES 20

- 1 cup chocolate candy coating disks (from 1 [10-oz.] pkg., such as Ghirardelli Dark Chocolate Flavored Melting Wafers)
- 20 stemmed maraschino cherries (from 2 [10-oz.] jars), blotted dry
- 20 milk chocolate kisses (such as Hershey's Kisses)
- 40 almond slices
  Black decorating gel
  White decorating gel

1. Line a baking sheet with parchment paper; set aside. Microwave chocolate disks in a small microwavable bowl on MEDIUM (50% power) until melted and smooth, 60 to 90 seconds, stirring every 30 seconds.

2. Working with 1 cherry at a time, hold by the stem, and dip in melted chocolate. Working quickly, and still holding cherry by the stem, attach flat bottom of 1 chocolate kiss to rounded bottom of dipped cherry; hold together for about 20 seconds. Place on prepared baking sheet. Place 2 almond slices in groove where cherry and chocolate kiss meet, using more melted chocolate if needed. Add 2 dots black decorating gel in front of almonds for eyes. Add 1 drop white decorating gel on the tip of each chocolate kiss for nose. Repeat process with remaining ingredients. Chill until set, about 20 minutes. Store, covered, in refrigerator up to 2 days.

Pass the Cheese, Please

Skip the usual grazing board and go all out with these irresistible appetizers

Baked Brie Bites

These pretty appetizers have it all: gooey cheese, crunchy nuts, flaky pastry, and a hit of tangy sweetness from cranberries. Pair with a dry sparkling wine for the ultimate bite.

ACTIVE 30 MIN. - TOTAL 1 HOUR, 15 MIN.

SERVES 12

- 1½ tsp. grated orange zest, plus 2 Tbsp. fresh juice (from 1 medium orange), divided
- 4 Tbsp. honey
- 1 cup fresh or frozen cranberries
- 2 tsp. chopped fresh sage, plus small leaves for garnish
- ¼ tsp. kosher salt
- 1 (17.3-oz.) pkg. frozen puff pastry sheets (2 sheets), thawed
- 2 (8-oz.) Brie rounds
- ¼ cup chopped pecans, toasted

1. Preheat oven to 400°F. Bring orange juice, 1 tablespoon water, and 4 tablespoons honey to a boil in a medium saucepan over medium-high, stirring occasionally. Add cranberries, and reduce heat to medium-low. Simmer, stirring occasionally, until cranberries have burst and mixture has

thickened slightly and reduced to about ¾ cup, about 10 minutes. Remove from heat, and stir in orange zest, chopped sage, and salt. Cool to room temperature, about 30 minutes.

2. Meanwhile, spray 2 (12-cup) mini muffin pans with cooking spray. Place puff pastry sheets on a lightly floured surface, and roll into 2 (12- x 9-inch) rectangles. Generously prick each rectangle with a fork. Cut each dough rectangle into 12 (3-inch) squares. Press squares into muffin pan cavities, crimping edges of dough together as needed to fit, leaving a ½-inch overhang. Chill 10 minutes.

3. Meanwhile, trim rind edges from Brie rounds (there is no need to trim rind from top and bottom of rounds). Discard rind edges. Cut each round into 12 (about ½-ounce, ¾-inch-wide) wedges.

4. Place a Brie wedge in each pastry cup, folding in half if needed for a better fit. Bake in preheated oven until pastry has puffed and is golden brown and Brie has melted, 24 to 30 minutes. Remove pans from oven, and cool slightly on wire racks, about 5 minutes. Remove Brie bites from pans, and top each with about 1 teaspoon cranberry sauce, ½ teaspoon pecans, and sage leaves. Reserve remaining cranberry sauce for another use. Serve immediately, or let cool to room temperature, about 20 minutes.

Hot Cheesy Crab Dip

Jumbo lump crabmeat makes this dip absolutely decadent—and a bit pricey—but you can keep costs down with crab claw meat. Either way, make sure the crab is fresh, not canned.

ACTIVE 15 MIN. - TOTAL 50 MIN.

SERVES 12

- 4 medium scallions (about 3¼ oz. total)
- 8 oz. cream cheese, at room temperature

- ¾ cup mayonnaise
- ⅓ cup sour cream
- 1 tsp. kosher salt
- 2 tsp. Worcestershire sauce
- 1 tsp. hot sauce (such as Tabasco)
- 1 tsp. sherry vinegar
- ½ tsp. celery salt
- 5 oz. extra-sharp cheddar cheese, shredded (about 1¼ cups), divided
- 5 oz. creamy Havarti cheese, shredded (about 1¼ cups), divided
- 1 lb. fresh jumbo lump crabmeat, drained and picked over
- 4 medium-size Belgian endive heads (about 12 oz. total), leaves separated

1. Preheat oven to 375°F. Thinly slice scallions, separating dark green parts from white and light green parts; set aside.

2. Beat cream cheese, mayonnaise, sour cream, salt, Worcestershire sauce, hot sauce, vinegar, and celery salt in the bowl of a stand mixer fitted with a paddle attachment on medium speed until creamy and smooth, 30 seconds to 1 minute, stopping to scrape down sides of bowl as needed. Add 1 cup each of the cheddar and Havarti, and beat on medium-low speed until incorporated, about 10 seconds. Remove bowl from stand mixer, and fold in crabmeat and white and light green parts of scallions.

3. Transfer crab mixture to a 2-quart baking dish, and top with remaining ¼ cup each cheddar and Havarti. Bake in preheated oven until edges are bubbly and cheese is melted, about 20 minutes. Turn oven to broil, and continue baking until cheese is browned, 3 to 5 minutes. Remove from oven, and set aside to cool slightly, about 10 minutes. Top with reserved dark green parts of scallions, and serve with endive leaves.

BAKED BRIE BITES

Spicy Cheese Twists

This recipe is a creative use of that forgotten box of puff pastry in the back of the freezer (and a few pantry staples) into an impressive appetizer, or edible gift when packaged in a cookie tin.

ACTIVE 20 MIN. - TOTAL 55 MIN.

SERVES 12

- 6 oz. aged Gouda cheese, grated in a food processor (about 1 cup)
- 1 Tbsp. fresh thyme leaves
- ½ (17.3-oz.) pkg. frozen puff pastry sheets (1 sheet), thawed
  All-purpose flour, for work surface
- 1 large egg, beaten
- ½ tsp. kosher salt
- ½ tsp. garlic powder
- ½ tsp. cayenne pepper

1. Preheat oven to 425°F. Line 2 baking sheets with parchment paper, and set aside. Mix together Gouda and thyme in a small bowl; set aside.

2. Roll puff pastry sheet into a 14-inch square on a lightly floured work surface. Thoroughly prick all over with a fork. Whisk together egg and 1 tablespoon water in a small bowl. Brush pastry lightly with egg mixture. Sprinkle evenly with salt, garlic powder, and cayenne pepper. Cut pastry in half lengthwise to form 2 (14- x 7-inch) rectangles. Spread about ¾ cup of the Gouda mixture evenly over one of the rectangles, and press with palms of hands to bind cheese to pastry. Place remaining pastry sheet, egg wash side up, directly onto pastry sheet with cheese. Sprinkle remaining ⅓ cup Gouda mixture evenly over top pastry, pressing with palms of hands to bind cheese to pastry. (Alternatively, gently roll a rolling pin over both sheets to bind cheese.) Cut pastry stack lengthwise into 2 (14- x 3½-inch) rectangles. Cut each rectangle into 12 (about 3½- x 1-inch) strips.

3. Working with 1 strip at a time, twist the ends in opposite directions so that each end is cheese side up, resembling a bow tie. Arrange bow ties on prepared baking sheets, at least ½ inch apart. Press ends down gently to adhere to parchment. Pinch middle of each strip with fingers to create center of bow tie. Bake in preheated oven, 1 baking sheet at a time, until crispy and golden brown, about 12 to 16 minutes. Cool on baking sheet at least 5 minutes. Serve warm or at room temperature.

PISTACHIO-CHEDDAR
SHORTBREAD

BACON-CHEESE
GOUGÈRES

CREAMY SPINACH-
RICOTTA CROSTINI

Pistachio-Cheddar Shortbread

If you can make slice-and-bake cookies, you can bake these savory, buttery homemade crackers. Serve them as-is, or top with your favorite pepper jelly.

ACTIVE 20 MIN. - TOTAL 1 HOUR, PLUS 1 HOUR CHILLING

SERVES 12

- 1½ cups all-purpose flour
- ⅓ cup roasted, salted shelled pistachios
- 2 tsp. granulated sugar
- 1½ tsp. kosher salt
- ¾ tsp. dry mustard
- ½ tsp. black pepper
- ½ cup unsalted butter, chilled and cut into ½-inch cubes
- 7 oz. aged Irish white cheddar cheese (such as Kerrygold Aged Cheddar), shredded (about 1¾ cups)
- 1 oz. Parmesan cheese, shredded (about ⅓ cup)
- ¼ cup ice water
  Hot pepper jelly, for serving

1. Combine flour, pistachios, sugar, salt, dry mustard, and black pepper in a food processor. Pulse until pistachios are finely chopped, 15 to 20 times. Add butter, and pulse until butter is the size of peas, about 15 times. Add cheddar and Parmesan; pulse until combined, about 5 times. Add ¼ cup ice water, and pulse until mixture sticks together when pinched with fingers, about 5 times. Transfer mixture to a clean work surface, and knead gently to bring together. Divide mixture in half (about 11 ounces each), and roll and shape each piece into a 6-inch log (about 1¾-inch diameter). Wrap each log in plastic wrap, and refrigerate until firm, at least 1 hour or up to 1 day.
2. Place oven racks in upper and bottom thirds of oven. Preheat oven to 375°F. Line two baking sheets with parchment paper. Remove shortbread logs from refrigerator, and slice into ¼-inch-thick rounds. Arrange rounds on prepared baking sheets, spacing at least ½ inch apart. Bake until golden brown and crispy, 20 to 25 minutes, rotating pans and switching racks halfway through. Remove from oven, and carefully transfer crackers to wire racks to cool completely, about 20 minutes. Top with pepper jelly.

Bacon-Cheese Gougères

Two types of cheese and bacon make this party classic even more delicious. While they're best when fresh, they can be baked ahead, frozen, and reheated in the oven at 350°F.

ACTIVE 25 MIN. - TOTAL 1 HOUR, 30 MIN.

SERVES 12

- 2 oz. Gruyère cheese, shredded (about ½ cup), divided
- 2 oz. aged white cheddar cheese, shredded (about ½ cup), divided
- ½ cup half-and-half
- ½ cup unsalted butter
- 1 cup all-purpose flour
- ¾ tsp. kosher salt
- ⅛ tsp. ground nutmeg
- 4 large eggs
- 3 slices bacon, cooked and finely chopped (about ¼ cup)

1. Preheat oven to 425°F. Line two baking sheets with parchment paper, and set aside. Toss together Gruyère and cheddar in a small bowl, and set aside. Heat half-and-half, ½ cup water, and butter in a small saucepan over medium. Bring to a boil, stirring occasionally. Immediately add flour, salt, and nutmeg, and cook, stirring constantly with a wooden spoon, until mixture forms a ball and bottom of pan has developed a thin film, about 2 minutes. Remove from heat, and transfer dough to a stand mixer fitted with a paddle attachment. Beat on medium-high for 30 seconds to release steam and cool slightly. Decrease speed to medium. With mixer running, add eggs, 1 at a time, beating well after each addition. Continue beating on medium until batter is stiff and glossy, about 5 minutes. Reduce speed to medium-low, and add bacon and 3 ounces of cheese mixture.
2. Transfer dough mixture to a large piping bag fitted with a ½-inch pastry tip. Pipe 1½-inch mounds of dough (about 2 tablespoons) onto prepared baking sheets, spacing at least 1 inch apart. Tap tops of dough with a lightly moistened finger to flatten slightly. (Alternatively, use a 1¾-inch ice cream scoop to scoop dough onto baking sheet.) Sprinkle dough with remaining cheese mixture (about ½ teaspoon each).
3. Bake 1 pan in preheated oven 10 minutes. Reduce oven temperature to 375°F, and continue baking until golden brown, risen, and puffed, 15 to 18 minutes. Cool gougères on baking sheet for at least 10 minutes. Increase oven temperature to 425°F, and repeat baking procedure with remaining pan of dough. Serve gougères while still warm.

Creamy Spinach-Ricotta Crostini

This bright green ricotta spread adds a pop of color to your buffet table and is a tasty match for prosciutto. Or pair with pita chips for an easy take on spinach dip.

ACTIVE 15 MIN. - TOTAL 15 MIN.

SERVES 8

- 5 oz. baby spinach
- ½ cup roughly chopped fresh parsley
- ½ cup roughly chopped fresh chives
- 1 medium garlic clove, chopped
- ⅔ cup whole-milk ricotta cheese
- 5 oz. goat cheese, softened
- 1½ oz. Pecorino Romano, finely shredded (about ½ cup)
- 1 Tbsp. fresh lemon juice (from 1 lemon), plus zest for garnish
- 1 tsp. kosher salt
- ½ tsp. black pepper
- 3 Tbsp. olive oil
- 16 (½-inch-thick) baguette slices, toasted
- 3 oz. thinly sliced prosciutto, torn

1. Bring a large pot of water to a boil over medium-high. Add spinach, and cook, stirring occasionally, until bright green and wilted, about 45 seconds. Transfer to a large bowl of ice water to cool 3 minutes. Drain. Squeeze spinach between paper towels to remove as much moisture as possible.
2. Combine spinach, parsley, chives, and garlic in a food processor. Pulse until finely chopped, about 12 times. Add ricotta, goat cheese, Pecorino Romano, lemon juice, salt, and pepper; process until smooth, about 25 seconds, stopping to scrape down sides of bowl as needed. Add olive oil, and process until incorporated, 5 to 10 seconds. Spinach-ricotta mixture can be chilled in an airtight container for up to 2 days.
3. Spread about 2 tablespoons spinach-ricotta mixture over each baguette slice. Top with prosciutto; garnish with zest.

CAROLINA GOLD
RICE MIDDLINS
(PAGE 306)

LOWCOUNTRY FISH
STEW (PAGE 306)

ROASTED OYSTERS
WITH MUSHROOMS
AND WATERCRESS

GRAMMY ROLLS
(PAGE 307)

A Whole Lata Christmas

Across the harbor from Charleston, South Carolina, the holiday means dinner on the front porch, oysters all around, and a game plan that leaves time to savor the season

WE'RE NOT CUCKOO for Christmas decorations," explains chef Mike Lata, the owner and culinary force behind FIG and The Ordinary restaurants in Charleston, South Carolina. "We have friends who go deep, but that's not us." These are not the words of a grinch. While it's true that Lata and his wife, Jenni Ridall, can fit their combined ornaments in one box, they wholeheartedly embrace the season in their own style. As you might imagine, that means devoting abundant attention to their menu.

After all, it was a passion for the pleasures of the table that brought them together. Lata moved to Charleston as a young chef in 1998, and then opened FIG in 2003 and The Ordinary in 2012. Ridall came to the industry later in life, after studying art history and then culinary technique at Le Cordon Bleu. They met when she applied for a job at FIG in February 2015. "Even before then, I was drawn to Mike's food and aesthetic," Ridall says.

Ridall worked at FIG as a culinary administrator, transcribing recipes written on napkins and notebooks, documenting endless variations of dishes, and planning events. In 2018, she struck out on her own to create TK Test Kitchen, a culinary consulting business. The couple married in 2019, so their holiday rituals are new and evolving. "Jenni brings strong family traditions to our relationship," Lata says, "She ignited my desire to play along and start creating our own Christmases that our children would remember."

The fragrant greens and a few simple adornments inspire a welcoming table on the front porch, where they'll serve a feast on Christmas Eve. Planning is everything, Lata emphasizes. That means when Ridall's family arrives from Atlanta, there's nothing to do but uncork a bottle of cold white Burgundy, watch the happy chaos unfold, and toast to a job well done. "We celebrate the real blessing that is our family," Lata says.

Winter Greens Salad with Creamy Walnut Vinaigrette

"The nice thing about heartier winter greens is that they hold up after they've been dressed," Lata says. "I'm a huge fan of fresh mint. You can get the herb year-round, and it makes the salad taste alive and fresh."

ACTIVE 15 MIN. - TOTAL 45 MIN.

SERVES 6

- ¾ cup walnuts
- ½ cup canola oil
- 1½ Tbsp. finely chopped shallot (from 1 shallot)
- 2½ Tbsp. sherry vinegar
- 2 Tbsp. mayonnaise
- 1 Tbsp. cold water
- ½ Tbsp. Dijon mustard
- ¼ tsp. coarse kosher salt
- ⅛ tsp. freshly ground black pepper
- 8 cups torn hearty greens (such as escarole, radicchio, or endive)
- ¼ cup lightly packed fresh flat-leaf parsley leaves, roughly chopped
- ¼ cup lightly packed fresh mint leaves, torn
- 1 oz. Pecorino Romano or Parmesan cheese, shaved (about ½ cup)

1. Preheat oven to 300°F. Spread walnuts in an even layer on a baking sheet; toast in oven until golden and fragrant, about 20 minutes. Remove from oven; cool about 15 minutes. Combine canola oil and ¼ cup of the cooled walnuts in a blender; pulse until well incorporated (a few chunks are fine), 4 to 5 times. Set aside.
2. Whisk together shallot, vinegar, mayonnaise, cold water, and mustard in a medium bowl until well combined. Slowly whisk in walnut-canola oil mixture until emulsified. Season with salt and pepper.
3. Combine greens, parsley, and mint in a large mixing bowl. Add ½ cup of the vinaigrette; toss to combine. Mound salad into a serving bowl; drizzle with remaining ¼ cup vinaigrette. Top with cheese and reserved walnuts.

Roasted Oysters with Mushrooms and Watercress

Oysters might seem intimidating, but a bit of advance prep makes this appetizer easy. "The mushroom stuffing can be prepared and refrigerated a couple of days ahead," Lata says. "Then it's easy to finish them off."

ACTIVE 30 MIN. - TOTAL 40 MIN.

SERVES 8

- 1 Tbsp. olive oil
- 2 oz. diced pancetta
- 1 cup finely chopped shallots (about 4 small shallots)
- ¼ cup finely chopped garlic (about 10 cloves)
- 8 oz. shiitake mushrooms, stems removed and roughly chopped (about 4 cups)
- ½ tsp. crushed red pepper
- 2 oz. dry sherry
- 1 (4-oz.) pkg. watercress (about 4 cups)
- ¼ cup chopped fresh basil
- ¼ cup thinly sliced fresh chives
- 1 Tbsp. fresh thyme leaves
- 1 tsp. kosher salt
- 4 Tbsp. unsalted butter, divided
- ½ cup panko breadcrumbs
- 2 oz. Parmigiano-Reggiano cheese, grated (about ½ cup)
- 1 (4-lb.) box rock salt
- 2 dozen deep cup East Coast oysters
- 3 (1- x 1½-inch) lemon peel strips, thinly sliced
- Lemon wedges, for serving

1. Heat a large skillet or Dutch oven over medium-low. Add olive oil and pancetta, and cook, stirring often, until pancetta is browned and fat has rendered, about 5 minutes. Add shallots and garlic; cook, stirring often, until lightly brown and toasted, about 5 minutes. Add mushrooms and crushed red pepper; cook, stirring often, until tender, 5 to 7 minutes. Add sherry; cook until reduced by half, about 1 minute. Stir in

Continued on page 306

Continued from page 305

watercress, basil, chives, and thyme; stir until wilted, 1 to 2 minutes. Remove from heat; season with kosher salt. Add 2 tablespoons of the butter; stir until melted. Transfer to the bowl of a food processor. Pulse until finely chopped but not pureed, 4 to 5 pulses.

2. Melt remaining 2 tablespoons butter in a medium skillet. Add panko; cook, stirring constantly, until deep golden, about 4 minutes. Transfer to a medium bowl; cool slightly, about 5 minutes. Stir in Parmigiano-Reggiano.

3. Preheat oven to 400°F. Line a rimmed baking sheet with rock salt. Shuck oysters; loosen adductor muscles so oysters float freely in liquor in bottom cup. Gently remove any dirt or debris, taking care not to spill the briny liquor. Top each oyster with about 1 tablespoon mushroom mixture and 2 teaspoons panko mixture. Nestle oysters into rock salt on prepared pan. Roast until bubbly and hot, 8 to 10 minutes. Remove from oven; garnish with lemon peel strips. Serve hot with lemon wedges.

Lowcountry Fish Stew

(Photo, page 304)

A version of this stew, a Lowcountry riff on French bouillabaisse, has been on the menu at FIG since 2003. If the broth is made in advance, this dish is quick to assemble. Lata says to simmer the fish until it's just done to preserve the delicate textures and flavors.

ACTIVE 30 MIN. - TOTAL 1 HOUR, 30 MIN.

SERVES 6

AÏOLI

- 2 pasteurized egg yolks, at room temperature
- 1 Tbsp. white wine vinegar
- 1 tsp. coarse kosher salt, plus more to taste
- 1 tsp. fresh lemon juice
- 1 cup olive oil
- 1 to 2 large garlic cloves

STEW

- 5 Tbsp. olive oil, plus more for garnish
- 1½ cups chopped red onion (from 1 onion)
- 1 cup chopped fennel (from 1 bulb)
- 1 cup chopped celery (about 3 stalks)
- 1 cup chopped leeks, white and light green parts only (from 2 leeks)
- 1 cup chopped shallots (from 3 shallots)
- 6 garlic cloves, crushed
- 2 fresh bay leaves
- 3½ Tbsp. tomato paste
- 1 lb. large (21-25 count) peeled, deveined raw white shrimp, shells reserved
- 1 lb. (1- to 1½-inch-thick) firm white fish fillet (such as flounder, grouper, snapper, or bass), cut into (2- x 1-inch) strips, fish bones reserved
- 2 cups crisp unoaked white wine (such as Pinot Grigio or Sauvignon Blanc)
- 2 oz. anise-flavor liqueur (such as Pernod) (optional)
- ⅛ tsp. saffron threads (optional)
- 2 (3- x 1-inch) orange peel strips (from 1 orange)
- 2 medium carrots, sliced diagonally into ¼-inch-thick slices
- 2 cups (1-inch) cubed green cabbage (from 1 small cabbage)
- 1½ tsp. kosher salt, plus more to taste
- 18 to 24 little neck clams (1 lb.), scrubbed
- 1 lb. mussels, scrubbed and debearded
- 4 Tbsp. unsalted butter, softened
- ¼ tsp. cayenne pepper
- 1 Tbsp. fresh lemon juice, plus lemon wedges for serving
- Finely chopped fresh flat-leaf parsley, for garnish
- Cooked Carolina Gold Rice Middlins (recipe follows) or white rice
- Toasted or grilled sourdough bread

1. Prepare the Aïoli: Combine egg yolks, vinegar, salt, and lemon juice in a medium bowl, and whisk vigorously until pale yellow and foamy. Slowly drizzle in olive oil, whisking constantly until thick and emulsified. Scrape down sides of bowl with a spatula. Using a Microplane grater, finely grate 1 garlic clove into Aïoli. Taste; add more garlic and salt, if desired. Cover; chill until ready to use.

2. Prepare the Stew: Heat olive oil in a large heavy-duty pot or Dutch oven over medium. Add onion, fennel, celery, leeks, shallots, garlic, and bay leaves. Reduce heat to medium-low, and cook, stirring occasionally, until vegetables are softened but do not take on any color, 5 to 8 minutes. Stir in tomato paste; cook, stirring often, until mixture darkens slightly, about 2 minutes. Add shrimp shells and fish bones; cook, stirring often, 5 minutes. Add wine and liqueur (if using), and bring to a boil over medium. Once it reaches a boil, add 6 cups water, saffron (if using), and orange peel. Return to a boil; reduce heat to low, and simmer 45 minutes. Strain through a fine-mesh sieve into a bowl; discard solids. (At this point, the broth can be frozen. I highly recommend making this ahead. Feel free to double the batch and freeze it, as this is the majority of the work in the recipe.)

3. Bring broth to a simmer in a 6-quart pot over medium. Add carrots, cabbage, salt, and clams; simmer, covered, until clams start to open (some might not be completely open yet) and vegetables are tender, 8 to 10 minutes. Add fish, mussels, and shrimp. Cover; simmer gently over medium until just cooked through, 5 to 7 minutes. Using a slotted spoon, divide seafood and vegetables evenly among serving bowls. Remove pot from heat, and whisk in butter, cayenne pepper, and lemon juice. Season with additional salt as needed.

4. Ladle broth over seafood and vegetables in bowls. Garnish with parsley and a few drizzles of olive oil. Serve with warm rice, toasted bread, and Aïoli.

Carolina Gold Rice Middlins

(Photo, page 304)

ACTIVE 10 MIN. - TOTAL 45 MIN.

SERVES 8

- 2 cups Carolina Gold rice grits or middlins
- 2 bay leaves
- 1½ tsp. kosher salt, plus more to taste
- 1½ Tbsp. unsalted butter
- Toasted benne seeds
- Thinly sliced scallions

1. Place rice in a large bowl, and fill bowl with cold water. Stir thoroughly or massage rice with your hands, and drain. Repeat this procedure 3 or 4 times, until water is crystal clear. Cover rice with fresh cold water, and soak 30 minutes; drain.

2. Meanwhile, add 2 cups water, bay leaves, and salt to a medium saucepan. Bring to a boil over medium-high. Add soaked rice to boiling water, and stir well. Return to a boil, and stir again. Reduce heat to low, and stir one more time. Cover and simmer, undisturbed, until all liquid is absorbed, 10 to 12 minutes. Remove from heat, and let stand, covered, 7 minutes. Add butter, and fluff rice with a fork until butter is melted. Discard bay leaves. Season with additional salt to taste.

3. Transfer to a serving bowl. Garnish rice with toasted benne seeds and scallions.

Chopped Chicken Livers on Toast

This easy make-ahead dish is basically chicken salad made with livers. "We convert a lot of our guests on livers," Lata says. "It's one of those things people think they don't like ... so we serve them at dinner parties, and everyone really enjoys them."

ACTIVE 30 MIN. · TOTAL 45 MIN.

SERVES 10

- 2 lb. chicken livers
- 2 tsp. kosher salt, divided, plus more to taste
- 1½ tsp. freshly ground black pepper, divided, plus more to taste
- 8 center-cut bacon slices (8 oz.), chopped
- 1½ cups mayonnaise
- ¼ cup minced red onion
- ¼ cup chopped fresh flat-leaf parsley
- 2½ Tbsp. whole-grain mustard
- 2 Tbsp. fresh lemon juice
- 4 large hard-cooked eggs, peeled and roughly chopped (1½ cups)
- 2 to 3 dashes hot sauce (such as Tabasco), plus more to taste
- 2 Tbsp. unsalted butter, at room temperature
- 1 (12-oz.) artisanal sourdough bread loaf, cut into ½-inch-thick slices (about 10 slices), toasted
  Thinly sliced radish
  Mustard microgreens (optional)
  Grated fresh horseradish

1. Clean chicken livers of any bruises, membranes, and connective tissue, leaving livers as whole as possible, and pat dry. Season with 1½ teaspoons of the salt and 1¼ teaspoons of the black pepper on both sides, and set aside.
2. Heat a large cast-iron or nonstick skillet over medium. Add bacon, and cook, stirring occasionally, until bacon

is crisp and fat is rendered, about 5 minutes. Using a slotted spoon, transfer bacon to a plate lined with paper towels, and set aside.
3. Working in batches, add chicken livers to skillet with bacon fat. Cook over medium until browned on both sides and pink in the center, 3 to 5 minutes total. Transfer livers to a baking sheet lined with parchment paper, scraping all browned bits on top. Let cool to room temperature, about 15 minutes.
4. Stir together mayonnaise, red onion, parsley, mustard, lemon juice, and remaining ½ teaspoon salt and ¼ teaspoon black pepper in a large bowl. Cut cooked livers into ½-inch cubes, and add to mayonnaise mixture. Add hard-cooked eggs and cooked bacon. Gently fold everything together with a rubber spatula until just combined. Season with hot sauce, and add additional salt and black pepper, if desired.
5. Spread butter over toasted bread, and top slices evenly with chopped chicken liver mixture. Garnish evenly with thinly sliced radish, mustard microgreens (if using), and freshly grated horseradish. Serve immediately.

Grammy Rolls

(Photo, page 304)

Prepared the night before the holiday and baked first thing the next morning, Grammy Rolls, one of Ridall's most cherished recipes, fill the house with cinnamon-scented cheer.

ACTIVE 40 MIN. · TOTAL 1 HOUR, 20 MIN., PLUS 1 HOUR RISING AND 1 HOUR STANDING

SERVES 8

- 2 cups warm whole milk (about 95°F)
- 9 Tbsp. unsalted butter, melted and divided
- 1 cup granulated sugar, divided
- 1 (¼-oz.) envelope active dry yeast (2¼ tsp.)
- 1 tsp. coarse kosher salt
- 5¼ cups, plus 2 Tbsp. all-purpose flour, plus more as needed
- 1 Tbsp. unsalted butter, softened
- 1½ Tbsp. ground cinnamon
  Powdered sugar, for topping

1. Stir together milk, 4 tablespoons of the melted butter, and ¼ cup of the granulated sugar in the bowl of a stand mixer. Whisk by hand until sugar is dissolved. Sprinkle yeast over top, and

let stand until active and foamy, about 5 minutes. Whisk in salt.
2. Attach dough hook to stand mixer, and place bowl on mixer. With mixer on low speed, add 5 cups of the flour, 1 cup at a time, until a shaggy dough starts to come together. Increase speed to medium, and mix until dough is smooth and tacky but will pull away cleanly from sides of bowl, about 5 minutes. Add additional flour, 1 tablespoon at a time, to achieve this texture.
3. Butter a large mixing bowl with softened butter. Form dough into a ball, and place in prepared bowl; cover with plastic wrap. Let rise at a warm room temperature until doubled in size, 1 to 1½ hours.
4. Pour remaining 5 tablespoons melted butter in a medium bowl. Whisk together cinnamon and remaining ¾ cup granulated sugar in a medium shallow bowl.
5. Transfer dough to a clean work surface. Portion into roughly 45 (1-ounce) pieces. Cup your hand on top of 1 piece of dough. Gently press it against the counter, moving in a tight circular motion until you have a smooth ball. Repeat with remaining dough pieces.
6. Dip each ball of dough in melted butter; then roll in cinnamon sugar to coat. Arrange dough in two or three layers in a 10-inch tube pan greased with butter. Sprinkle any remaining cinnamon sugar over dough in pan. Cover with plastic wrap; let stand at room temperature until doubled in volume, about 1 hour, or chill dough overnight.
7. If dough was chilled overnight, allow it to sit at room temperature for 30 minutes. Preheat oven to 375°F. Bake rolls until puffy and golden brown, 25 to 30 minutes. Let rest in pan 10 minutes before unmolding. While still warm, invert pan onto a serving platter or cake stand; tap to gently release rolls. Dust with powdered sugar, and serve warm.

Absolutely Ambrosial

One of the South's sweetest traditions gets all dolled up for the holidays in these reimagined desserts

AMBROSIA CHEESECAKE

COCONUT-CITRUS BARS

AMBROSIA TRIFLE
(PAGE 310)

COCONUT PANNA COTTA
WITH BLOOD ORANGE GRANITA
(PAGE 310)

AMBROSIA MEANS "FOOD OF THE GODS."
In Greek and Roman mythology, it referred to magical victuals with the power to bestow immortality on anyone who tasted them. Today, as most food historians agree, ambrosia belongs to the South. When it is mentioned, many think of the holiday table and a serving dish filled to the brim with a fluffy, fruit-studded concoction rather than visions of eternal life. Or they go even further back in time to a crystal bowl containing a vivid, sweet mélange of oranges and coconut.

Recipes for this original version—layers of fresh citrus, sugar, and coconut—began appearing in cookbooks in the late 19th century. How ambrosia became a beloved dish in the South remains vague. Many believe that the completion of the transcontinental railroad, which made it easier to obtain fresh coconuts and winter oranges practically anywhere, had a lot to do with it becoming a special treat during the winter holidays.

Since then, the old-fashioned dish has been bedazzled with maraschino cherries and pineapple—and made richer with whipped cream, mayonnaise, and sour cream. Which may be why some people consider it to be a salad and others a dessert. In the 1920s, Whitman's Marshmallow Whip, a jarred marshmallow creme, hit shelves. Recipes using the product soon followed, including one for ambrosia.

If you ask a native Southerner of a certain age, they'll tell you about the ritual of cracking, peeling, and grating the coconut. "You must not use canned cocoanut," wrote Mary D. Pretlow in her 1930 book *Old Southern Recipes*. But in 1949, the towering American culinary figure James Beard wrote in *The Fireside Cook Book*: "The moist canned coconut is the best for [ambrosia]."

However you like your ambrosia—a simple showcase of fresh citrus; a fruit-filled cloud; or in one of these sophisticated desserts—it has earned its spot on the Southern sideboard.

Ambrosia Cheesecake

North meets South in this New York-style cheesecake with an ambrosia-inspired citrus topping and coconut-graham cracker crust. It's a make-ahead dessert, too. Prepare and chill the cheesecake up to four days in advance, then add citrus just before serving.

ACTIVE 35 MIN. - TOTAL 4 HOURS, 20 MIN., PLUS 12 HOURS CHILLING

SERVES 12

- 2 cups finely ground honey graham crackers (from 17 cracker sheets)
- 1½ cups unsweetened desiccated coconut
- 1¾ cups, plus 2 Tbsp. granulated sugar, divided
- 1½ tsp. kosher salt, divided
- ½ cup unsalted butter, melted
- 3 (8-oz.) pkg. cream cheese, at room temperature
- ⅔ cup unsweetened coconut cream (from 1 [13½-oz.] can)
- 3 large eggs, at room temperature
- 1 large egg yolk, at room temperature
- 1 Tbsp. vanilla extract
- 2 cups assorted citrus segments and rounds (such as Ruby Red grapefruit, navel oranges, blood oranges, and kumquats, from about 2 lb. citrus fruits)

1. Preheat oven to 350°F with rack in lower-third position. Coat bottom and sides of a 9-inch round springform pan with cooking spray. Wrap outside of springform pan with a double layer of aluminum foil. Set aside.
2. Place graham crackers, desiccated coconut, 2 tablespoons of the sugar, and 1 teaspoon of the salt in a food processor; pulse until combined, about 5 pulses. Add melted butter; pulse until evenly combined, about 10 pulses. Press crust evenly into bottom and all the way up sides of prepared springform pan. Bake in preheated oven until crust is lightly browned, 14 to 18 minutes. Transfer crust in springform pan to a wire rack; let cool completely, about 30 minutes. Do not turn oven off.
3. Beat cream cheese, coconut cream, and remaining 1¾ cups sugar and ½ teaspoon salt with a stand mixer fitted with a paddle attachment on medium speed until smooth, about 4 minutes, stopping occasionally to scrape down sides of bowl. Reduce speed to medium-low; beat in eggs and egg yolk 1 at a time, beating well after each addition. Stir in vanilla. Pour filling into prepared crust, and smooth top.
4. Place cheesecake in springform pan in a large roasting pan. Add boiling water to roasting pan to reach halfway up sides of springform pan. Bake at 350°F until cheesecake is lightly browned on top and set around edges but still slightly jiggly in middle, 1 hour to 1 hour, 15 minutes. Remove cheesecake from roasting pan, and transfer to a wire rack; let cool in springform pan completely, about 2 hours. Remove foil from springform pan, and discard. Cover cheesecake in springform pan with plastic wrap. Chill at least 12 hours or up to 4 days.
5. To serve, uncover cheesecake, and carefully remove edges of springform pan. Top cheesecake with assorted citrus.

Coconut-Citrus Bars

Made with tangerine juice, cherry syrup, and a coconut crust, these cookies have the texture of lemon bars without the puckery tartness. It's important to chill the bars thoroughly before removing them from the pan, or the crust will be soft and bend. Bars can be chilled in an airtight container for up to five days. Top with citrus wedges just before serving.

ACTIVE 30 MIN. - TOTAL 3 HOURS, 40 MIN., PLUS 6 HOURS CHILLING

SERVES 24

- 1 cup coconut flour
- 2 cups all-purpose flour, divided
- 1½ cups unsweetened desiccated coconut, divided
- 3 cups granulated sugar, divided
- ¾ tsp. kosher salt, divided
- 1 cup unsalted butter, chilled and cut into ½-inch pieces
- 6 large eggs
- 1 Tbsp. syrup from jarred maraschino cherries
- 1 Tbsp. grated lemon zest, plus ½ cup fresh juice (from about 3 lemons)
- 2 tsp. grated tangerine or satsuma zest, plus ½ cup fresh juice (from about 3 tangerines)
- Orange food coloring gel
- 4 (1-inch-thick) sliced citrus rounds, each cut into 6 wedges (such as tangerine, satsuma, Ruby Red grapefruit, or blood orange)

Continued on page 310

Continued from page 309

1. Preheat oven to 350°F. Line bottom and sides of a 13- x 9-inch baking dish with heavy-duty aluminum foil, leaving 2 to 3 inches overhang on all sides. Lightly coat foil with cooking spray.

2. Pulse coconut flour, 1 cup of the all-purpose flour, ¾ cup of the desiccated coconut, ½ cup of the sugar, and ¼ teaspoon of the salt in a food processor until well combined, about 5 pulses. Add butter; pulse until mixture is crumbly, about 12 pulses. Press mixture evenly into bottom of prepared pan. Bake in preheated oven until lightly browned, 18 to 22 minutes. Let cool completely on a wire rack, about 30 minutes. Do not turn oven off.

3. Whisk eggs in a large bowl until smooth. Add cherry syrup, lemon zest and juice, tangerine zest and juice, and remaining 1 cup all-purpose flour, 2½ cups sugar, and ½ teaspoon salt; whisk together until well combined and smooth. Using a wooden pick, add a small amount of orange food coloring gel. Stir until evenly incorporated, adding more food coloring until desired color. Pour mixture over crust. Return to oven, and bake at 350°F until filling is set, 25 to 30 minutes. Transfer loaf in pan to a wire rack, and let cool completely, about 2 hours. Cover and chill until firm, at least 6 hours or up to 24 hours.

4. Remove loaf from pan using foil overhang as handles. Cut loaf into 24 (about 2-inch) bars. Cut a small square (about 4 inches) of parchment paper. Sprinkle remaining ¾ cup desiccated coconut over bars, covering half of each bar at a diagonal, using parchment square as a guide to form a straight line. Top each bar with 1 citrus wedge.

Ambrosia Trifle

(Photo, page 308)

Toasted peaks of Italian meringue stand in for marshmallow fluff on the top of this showstopping dessert. Save a step by replacing the meringue with piles of sweetened whipped cream.

ACTIVE 30 MIN. - TOTAL 50 MIN., PLUS 6 HOURS CHILLING

SERVES 12

COCONUT PASTRY CREAM
- 2 (13½-oz.) cans unsweetened coconut milk, well shaken and stirred
- 5 large egg yolks
- 1¼ cups granulated sugar
- ⅓ cup all-purpose flour
- ½ tsp. kosher salt
- ¼ cup coconut oil
- 2 tsp. vanilla extract

ITALIAN MERINGUE
- ¾ cup granulated sugar
- ⅛ tsp. kosher salt
- 3 large egg whites, at room temperature
- ¼ tsp. cream of tartar

ADDITIONAL INGREDIENTS
- 7 cups cubed (1-inch pieces) store-bought angel food cake
- 3 cups assorted citrus segments (such as navel orange, blood orange, or Ruby Red grapefruit) (from about 3 lb. citrus fruits)
- 1½ cups chopped fresh pineapple (from 1 small [2½-lb.] pineapple)
- 1 cup unsweetened shaved coconut
- ⅔ cup drained maraschino cherries (from 1 [13½-oz.] jar)

1. Prepare the Coconut Pastry Cream: Whisk together coconut milk and egg yolks in a medium bowl until well combined. Whisk together sugar, flour, and salt in a large saucepan; whisk in coconut milk mixture. Bring to a boil over medium, whisking constantly. Boil, whisking constantly, until mixture is thick and pudding-like, about 1 minute. Remove from heat. Add coconut oil and vanilla; whisk until smooth. Transfer mixture to a large bowl; press a piece of plastic wrap directly onto the surface. Cool at room temperature 30 minutes. Transfer to refrigerator; chill until cold, at least 6 hours or up to 2 days.

2. Just before assembling, prepare the Italian Meringue: Cook sugar, ¼ cup water, and the salt in a small saucepan over medium-high, stirring often, until sugar is dissolved and mixture registers 240°F on an instant-read thermometer, 6 to 8 minutes. Remove from heat. While sugar mixture is cooking (after it reaches about 225°F), beat egg whites with a stand mixer fitted with a whisk attachment on medium speed until foamy, about 30 seconds. Add cream of tartar to egg whites; continue beating on medium speed until soft peaks form, 1 to 2 minutes. (The goal is for the sugar mixture to reach 240°F at the same time the egg whites reach soft peaks.) Gradually drizzle in sugar mixture,

beating on medium speed. Increase mixer speed to medium-high; beat until glossy and stiff peaks form, 1 minute, 30 seconds to 2 minutes. Set aside.

3. Assemble the trifle: Spoon half of the Coconut Pastry Cream (about 2 cups) in an even layer in a 3½- to 4-quart trifle dish. Top with 3½ cups angel food cake cubes, 1½ cups citrus segments, ¾ cup chopped pineapple, ½ cup shaved coconut, and ⅓ cup cherries. Repeat layers once. Top trifle with Italian Meringue. Brown meringue using a kitchen torch, holding torch 1 to 2 inches from meringue and moving torch back and forth. Serve immediately, or chill, uncovered, up to 6 hours.

Coconut Panna Cotta with Blood Orange Granita

(Photo, page 308)

A tangy, icy citrus granita is perfectly balanced by the rich and creamy coconut custard. When shopping, look for canned unsweetened coconut cream, not cream of coconut or coconut milk.

ACTIVE 30 MIN. - TOTAL 30 MIN., PLUS 8 HOURS CHILLING

SERVES 6

- 1 (¼-oz.) pkg. unflavored gelatin
- ⅔ cup, plus 3 Tbsp. cold water, divided
- 1¾ cups heavy whipping cream
- 1 tsp. vanilla bean paste
- ¼ tsp. coconut extract
- 1¼ cups granulated sugar, divided
- ¾ tsp. kosher salt, divided
- 1 (13½-oz.) can unsweetened coconut cream
- 2¼ cups fresh blood orange juice (from 8 blood oranges)
  Peeled blood orange rounds

1. Stir together gelatin and 3 tablespoons of the cold water in a small bowl; let stand 5 minutes.

2. Meanwhile, whisk together whipping cream, vanilla, coconut extract, ½ cup of the sugar, and ½ teaspoon of the salt in a small saucepan. Cook over medium, whisking often, until sugar dissolves and mixture is hot, 4 to 5 minutes (do not boil). Remove from heat.

3. Add gelatin mixture to whipping cream mixture; whisk until fully dissolved. Whisk in coconut cream. Pour mixture through a fine-mesh strainer into a large measuring cup with a spout; discard solids. Pour strained mixture

evenly into 6 (6-ounce) ramekins or straight-sided glasses (about ⅔ cup each). Chill, uncovered, until set, at least 8 hours or up to 2 days.

4. Meanwhile, stir together remaining ⅔ cup water, ¾ cup sugar, and ¼ teaspoon salt in a small saucepan. Cook over medium-high, stirring often, until sugar is dissolved, about 4 minutes. Pour into a 9-inch square baking pan. Stir in blood orange juice. Freeze, uncovered, until just set but not completely frozen, about 2 hours. Rake through granita using a fork, breaking up any large chunks. Return to freezer, and freeze 1 hour. Repeat raking process. If granita is still slightly slushy, repeat freezing and raking process once more. Transfer to an airtight container and store in freezer up to 2 weeks. Rake using a fork just before serving.

5. To serve, carefully run an offset spatula around edges of 1 panna cotta. Dip bottom half of ramekin into hot water for 10 seconds. Invert panna cotta onto a serving plate. Repeat process with remaining panna cottas. Top each with about ⅓ cup granita. (Reserve remaining granita for another use.) Garnish with blood orange rounds. Serve immediately.

Tropical Coconut-Citrus Pie

Crisp coconut cookies make a special crust for this creamy riff on Key lime pie. The crust will feel soft after it has been parbaked, but it will firm up when cool.
ACTIVE 30 MIN. · TOTAL 3 HOURS, 25 MIN., PLUS 8 HOURS, 30 MIN. CHILLING

SERVES 8

- 2 cups finely ground crisp coconut cookies (from about 14 cookies)
- 3 Tbsp. granulated sugar
- 1 tsp. kosher salt, divided
- ¼ cup unsalted butter, melted
- 4 large egg yolks
- 2 tsp. grated lime zest (from 2 limes)
- 1 (14-oz.) can sweetened condensed milk
- ⅔ cup bottled Key lime juice
- 1 (8-oz.) pkg. cream cheese, softened
- 1 (7-oz.) jar marshmallow creme
  Garnishes: Thinly sliced pineapple wedges and citrus slices

1. Lightly coat a 9-inch pie plate with cooking spray. Pulse cookies, sugar, and ½ teaspoon of the salt in a food processor until well combined, about 5 pulses. Add butter; pulse until evenly incorporated, about 10 pulses. Pour mixture into prepared pie plate; press evenly into bottom and up sides. Freeze pie shell, uncovered, until hardened, at least 30 minutes or up to 24 hours.

2. Preheat oven to 350°F. Bake pie shell until lightly browned, 12 to 16 minutes. Let cool completely on a wire rack, about 30 minutes. Do not turn oven off.

3. Beat egg yolks, lime zest, and remaining ½ teaspoon salt with a stand mixer fitted with a whisk attachment on medium-high speed until pale and fluffy, 5 minutes. Add condensed milk; beat until thick, 3 minutes, stopping occasionally to scrape down sides of bowl. Reduce mixer speed to low, and gradually add lime juice, beating until just combined. Pour into cooled pie shell. Bake at 350°F until just set (center will be slightly jiggly), 9 to 11 minutes. Transfer to a wire rack; cool completely, about 1 hour. Chill, uncovered, until cold, at least 8 hours or up to 2 days.

4. Beat cream cheese and marshmallow creme with a stand mixer fitted with a paddle attachment on medium-high speed until light and fluffy, 1 to 2 minutes, stopping to scrape down sides of bowl as needed. Spread mixture over top of pie. Chill until topping firms up slightly, at least 30 minutes or up to 12 hours. Garnish with pineapple and citrus. Serve immediately.

Ambrosia Cupcakes

These cupcakes are made with five types of coconut and topped with marshmallow-orange frosting. Cake flour makes the crumb tender, and coconut flour adds extra flavor. If you can't find coconut sugar, use an equal amount of granulated sugar.
ACTIVE 30 MIN. · TOTAL 1 HOUR, 25 MIN.

SERVES 24

COCONUT CUPCAKES
- ¾ cup unsalted butter, softened
- ¼ cup coconut oil, solid at room temperature
- 1½ cups granulated sugar
- ½ cup coconut sugar
- 4 large eggs
- 2 cups bleached cake flour
- 1 cup coconut flour
- 1 Tbsp. baking powder
- ¾ tsp. kosher salt
- 1 cup unsweetened coconut milk
- 1 cup sweetened shredded coconut
- 1 tsp. vanilla extract

FROSTING
- 2 cups unsalted butter, softened
- 2 (7-oz.) jars marshmallow creme
- 2 tsp. finely grated orange zest, plus 4 to 6 Tbsp. fresh juice (from 2 oranges), divided
- 4 cups powdered sugar

ADDITIONAL INGREDIENTS
Orange peel twists
Maraschino cherries

1. Prepare the Coconut Cupcakes: Preheat oven to 350°F. Line 2 (12-cup) muffin pans with paper baking cups; set aside. Beat butter and coconut oil with a stand mixer fitted with a paddle attachment on medium speed until creamy, about 2 minutes. Add granulated sugar and coconut sugar; beat until fluffy, about 3 minutes. Add eggs 1 at a time, beating well after each addition.

2. Whisk together cake and coconut flours, baking powder, and salt in a medium bowl. Add to butter mixture alternately with coconut milk in 3 additions, beginning and ending with flour mixture, beating on low speed until just combined after each addition. Stir in shredded coconut and vanilla.

3. Divide batter between prepared muffin cups (about ¼ cup batter each). Bake in preheated oven until golden and a wooden pick inserted into centers comes out clean, 18 to 22 minutes. Transfer pans to wire racks; cool 5 minutes. Remove cupcakes from pans; cool completely on wire racks, about 30 minutes.

4. Prepare the Frosting: Beat butter, marshmallow creme, and orange zest with a stand mixer fitted with a paddle attachment on medium-high speed until light and fluffy, about 3 minutes. Reduce mixer speed to low; beat in 4 tablespoons orange juice. Gradually add powdered sugar, beating on low speed, until creamy and smooth. Beat in remaining 2 tablespoons orange juice, 1 tablespoon at a time, as needed to thin frosting. Increase mixer speed to medium-high; beat until light and fluffy, about 1 minute.

5. Transfer buttercream to a piping bag fitted with a ½-inch closed-star piping tip. Frost cooled cupcakes. Garnish with orange peel twists and cherries.

Grandmother's Wreath

For Cassandra King, every time she bakes these warm, sweet, pillowy rolls,
she's reminded of her last Christmas with Big Mama

SOMEHOW WE'VE COME TO BELIEVE that all Christmas memories must be happy ones or they don't count. In my case, I can look back and say that, regardless of what else might have been going on, the magic that is Christmas made the majority of my holidays good ones. I hold recollections in my heart with joy and gratitude, as treasures to be cherished.

I was 17 the year my paternal grandmother, who we called Big Mama, died. She was plump with a sweet face and her white-streaked hair often pinned in two braids on top of her head. As the oldest granddaughter, I spent my time with her in the kitchen, learning the secrets of the unique recipes she brought from her Swiss heritage. At Christmas, though, she baked all of the requisite Southern cakes and pies.

That year, I'd learned to cook and wanted to surprise her with something different. Because my family lived close by, we always had a Christmas Eve supper of oyster stew with my grandparents. Before adjourning to the dining room, we gathered around the tree to open our presents. I couldn't wait to show off the treat I'd made: a cinnamony sweet bread that was shaped and decorated like a wreath and had a cranberry-pecan filling.

I knew Big Mama had been sick, and I'd heard the word "cancer" whispered among the grown-ups. Such things weren't discussed then. When dinner was over, Mother got up to serve ambrosia and fruitcake. I hurried to get the Christmas wreath I'd hidden under a dishcloth. I slipped out of the kitchen with it on one of Mother's silver platters. Big Mama's face lit up when I brought it to her and uncovered it with a flourish. "Oh, my," she said with a smile. "Don't tell me you made that!" When I admitted I'd done it to surprise her, she declared it too pretty to cut and said, "But you made it to eat, so let's you and me try it."

It would be years before I baked that wreath again. One year, when my children were little, they wanted stories of my holidays growing up. I told them about the grandmother they never knew and the year I made her a special wreath. "Make us one, Mommy!" they begged, and I knew the time had come. Since then, I've made it every year. I always have gratitude that, whether joyful or sad, our sweetest memories live on. –Cassandra King

Christmas Sweet Roll Wreath

ACTIVE 45 MIN. - TOTAL 3 HOURS, 55 MIN., PLUS 4 HOURS CHILLING

SERVES 20

DOUGH
- 1 cup whole milk
- ½ cup unsalted butter
- ½ cup granulated sugar
- 1 (¼-oz.) envelope active dry yeast
- 4 cups unbleached bread flour, divided, plus more for work surface
- 1 large egg, at room temperature
- 1 tsp. fine sea salt

FILLING
- 1 cup fresh or thawed frozen cranberries
- 1 cup pecan halves
- ¾ cup chopped unpeeled orange (from 1 orange)
- ¾ cup packed dark brown sugar
- ¼ tsp. fine sea salt

ADDITIONAL INGREDIENTS
- 1 large egg yolk, at room temperature
- ½ cup powdered sugar
- 2 to 3 tsp. whole milk, as needed

1. Prepare the Dough: Stir together milk, butter, and ¼ cup water in a small saucepan. Cook over medium-low, stirring often, just until butter is melted. Remove from heat. Let stand, stirring occasionally, until mixture cools to 120°F, 10 to 15 minutes.

2. Stir together sugar, yeast, and 1¼ cups of the flour in the bowl of a stand mixer fitted with a paddle attachment. Add warm butter mixture, and beat on medium-low speed until well combined, about 1 minute. Add egg and ¼ cup of the flour. Beat until incorporated, about 2 minutes. With mixer running, gradually add salt and remaining 2½ cups flour, beating until mixture forms a stiff and

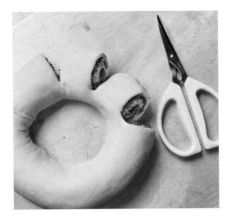

sticky batter, about 1 minute. Cover bowl tightly with plastic wrap. Chill at least 4 hours or up to 12 hours.

3. Prepare the Filling: Pulse cranberries, pecans, and chopped unpeeled orange in a food processor until finely chopped, 10 to 12 pulses. Transfer to a small saucepan; stir in brown sugar and salt. Cook over medium, stirring often, until mixture begins to bubble around pan edges, 3 to 5 minutes. Reduce heat to medium-low; cook, stirring often, until thick and jammy, about 5 minutes. Remove from heat. Cool completely, about 1 hour.

4. Turn Dough out onto a very lightly floured work surface. Divide evenly into 2 pieces (about 1 pound, 2 ounces each). Working with 1 Dough piece at a time, roll into a 14- x 7-inch rectangle. Spread half of the cooled Filling (about 1 cup) on top of Dough rectangle, spreading to edges. Starting with 1 long side, roll up jelly-roll style, and pinch each end to seal. Shape into a ring (about 7 inches in diameter), and pinch ends together to seal. Place ring, seam-side down, on a baking sheet coated with cooking spray. Repeat process using remaining Dough and Filling, placing ring on a separate greased baking sheet.

5. Using kitchen shears and keeping Dough ring on baking sheet, make cuts around 1 ring at 1½-inch intervals, cutting from outer edge and in toward center, leaving about ¾ inch attached at the center. Turn each cut section, in the same direction, to lie on its side with the Filling side exposed. Repeat process with remaining Dough ring. Cover rings loosely with plastic wrap. Let rise in a warm place (75°F to 85°F) until doubled in volume, about 1 hour.

6. About 30 minutes before Dough is finished rising, preheat oven to 350°F with racks in the top third and lower-third positions. Meanwhile, whisk together egg yolk and 1 tablespoon water in a small bowl. Brush Dough rings lightly with egg mixture. Bake until golden brown, 25 to 30 minutes, rotating baking sheets between top and bottom racks halfway through bake time. Do not remove from oven. Cool completely on baking sheets in oven, about 30 minutes.

7. Whisk together powdered sugar and 2 teaspoons of the milk in a small bowl. Add remaining 1 teaspoon milk, ¼ teaspoon at a time, if needed to thin glaze to a pourable consistency. Drizzle glaze over rings; let stand 10 minutes.

The Gift of Chocolate

Whether they prefer milk, dark, or white, give them what they really want
this year—cookie tins and platters filled with tasty treats they won't be able to resist

Triple-Chocolate Sandwich Cookies

Inspired by MoonPies, these no-bake treats start with a homemade chocolate-marshmallow filling that gets sandwiched between two store-bought chocolate wafers. Then the whole cookie is covered with melted chocolate.

ACTIVE 20 MIN. - TOTAL 35 MIN.

MAKES 1½ DOZEN

- 4 tsp. dark cocoa
- ½ cup, plus 2 Tbsp. powdered sugar, sifted
- 1¼ cups marshmallow creme (from 1 [7-oz.] jar)
- 6 Tbsp. unsalted butter, softened
- ¼ tsp. vanilla extract
- 36 chocolate wafer cookies (from 1 [9-oz.] box)
- 1 (10-oz.) pkg. 60% cacao bittersweet chocolate chips
- 1 Tbsp. canola oil
  Assorted holiday candy sprinkles
- 1 cup vanilla-flavor melting wafers

1. Stir together cocoa and powdered sugar in a medium bowl. Beat marshmallow creme, butter, and vanilla in a stand mixer fitted with a paddle attachment on medium speed until thoroughly blended, about 2 minutes. Add cocoa mixture, and beat until fluffy, about 3 minutes. Spread about 1 tablespoon marshmallow mixture onto half of wafers, and top with remaining wafers to make 18 sandwich cookies.
2. Line a baking sheet with parchment paper. Melt chocolate chips according to package directions; stir in oil until thoroughly combined. Place 1 sandwich cookie on a fork, and spoon melted chocolate over top of cookie, spreading chocolate so it spills over edges and covers sides completely. Transfer to prepared baking sheet, and top with desired sprinkles. Repeat procedure with remaining sandwich cookies, melted chocolate, and sprinkles. Refrigerate 15 minutes before serving.

3. If using vanilla melting wafers, allow cookies covered with melted chocolate to chill for 15 minutes. Melt wafers according to package directions, then place in a piping bag fitted with a small round tip. Pipe onto cookies in a zigzag pattern or as desired.

Striped Slice-and-Bake Shortbread

(Photo, page 316)

If you're planning to make lots of cookies this year for giveaways or gatherings, this slice-and-bake option is a great idea. You can make the dough a day ahead, and then bake and decorate them when needed.

ACTIVE 25 MIN. - TOTAL 1 HOUR, PLUS 2 HOURS CHILLING AND 30 MIN. STANDING

MAKES 4 DOZEN

- 2½ cups all-purpose flour, plus more for work surface
- ¼ tsp. kosher salt
- 1 cup, plus 2 Tbsp. unsalted butter, softened
- ½ cup powdered sugar
- ¼ cup granulated sugar
- 1¼ tsp. vanilla extract
- 2 Tbsp. dark cocoa
  Gold and silver metallic candy sprinkles
- 1¼ cups semisweet chocolate chips (from 1 [12-oz.] pkg.)
- 1 tsp. canola oil

1. Whisk together flour and salt in a small bowl. Beat butter, powdered sugar, and granulated sugar with a stand mixer fitted with a paddle attachment on medium speed until light and fluffy, about 3 minutes. Add vanilla, and beat until blended, about 10 seconds. Reduce speed to low, and gradually add flour mixture, one-third at a time, beating just until blended after each addition, about 1 minute.
2. Turn dough out onto a lightly floured surface, and knead a few times until dough comes together. Halve dough,

and set 1 portion aside for plain dough. Return remaining dough to mixer, and add cocoa, beating on medium speed until blended, about 2 minutes. Divide chocolate dough and plain dough each into thirds, and roll each piece into a 15-inch rope. Stack ropes alternately on top of each other, flattening each slightly into a strip to cover previous layer. Roll dough into an even log by gently pushing each end toward center of log and rolling as needed. Wrap in plastic wrap, and refrigerate 2 hours.
3. Preheat oven to 350°F. Line 2 baking sheets with parchment paper. Trim log so ends are flat, and slice half of log crosswise into ¼-inch-thick slices. Arrange cookies on prepared baking sheets, spacing them 2 inches apart. Place remaining unsliced log of dough and 1 baking sheet of cookies in refrigerator.
4. Bake remaining baking sheet of cookies in preheated oven until set and lightly golden on bottoms, about 14 minutes, rotating baking sheet from front to back halfway through bake time. Let cool on baking sheet 5 minutes; transfer cookies to a wire rack to cool completely, about 30 minutes. Meanwhile, bake remaining baking sheet of cookies as directed. Repeat slicing and baking procedure with remaining dough log in refrigerator, lining baking sheets with a new sheet of parchment paper for each batch. Reserve baking sheets, and line each with a new sheet of parchment paper.
5. Place sprinkles in small bowls. Melt semisweet chocolate chips according to package directions, and stir in oil. To decorate, dip edge of each cookie in chocolate mixture, and top immediately with sprinkles. Place on prepared baking sheets, and let stand until chocolate sets, about 30 minutes. Store in an airtight container until ready to serve.

CHOCOLATE GINGERBREAD WREATHS (PAGE 319)

RED VELVET CAKE CRINKLE COOKIES (PAGE 317)

TRIPLE-CHOCOLATE SANDWICH COOKIES

CORNMEAL-LIME COOKIES (PAGE 318)

EARL GREY TEA CAKES (PAGE 317)

MINT MERINGUE
CHRISTMAS TREES

CHOCOLATE-
ALMOND
THUMBPRINTS
(PAGE 320)

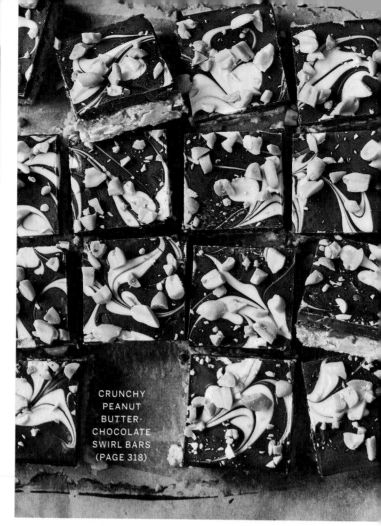

CRUNCHY
PEANUT
BUTTER-
CHOCOLATE
SWIRL BARS
(PAGE 318)

BOURBON-ORANGE
BISCOTTI (PAGE 320)

CHERRY-WALNUT
RUGELACH (PAGE 319)

STRIPED SLICE-AND-
BAKE SHORTBREAD
(PAGE 314)

COCONUT-
PECAN
TRUFFLES
(PAGE 318)

Red Velvet Cake Crinkle Cookies

(Photo, page 315)

These festive treats are coated in a snowy layer of powdered sugar just like a conventional crinkle cookie, but inside they're more like a velvety chocolate cake. To ensure your cookies have a deep hue, use gel food coloring rather than liquid.

ACTIVE 25 MIN. - TOTAL 1 HOUR, 45 MIN.

MAKES ABOUT 2½ DOZEN

- 2½ cups all-purpose flour
- ¼ cup dark cocoa
- 1½ tsp. baking soda
- ½ tsp. kosher salt
- ½ cup unsalted butter, softened
- 1 cup packed light brown sugar
- 2 large eggs, at room temperature
- 1 tsp. vanilla extract
- 2 to 3 tsp. red food coloring gel
- 3 Tbsp. whole milk
- ¾ cup white chocolate chips
- 1 cup powdered sugar

1. Preheat oven to 350°F, and line 2 baking sheets with parchment paper. Whisk together flour, cocoa, baking soda, and salt in a small bowl. Beat butter and brown sugar with a stand mixer fitted with a paddle attachment on medium speed until light and fluffy, about 3 minutes. Add eggs, 1 at a time, beating until blended after each addition. Add vanilla and 2 teaspoons food coloring gel, and beat until well blended, adding more food coloring to reach desired shade.
2. Add half of flour mixture, and beat on low speed until well blended. Add milk, and beat until blended. Add remaining flour mixture, and beat until blended. Fold in white chocolate chips. Refrigerate dough for 15 minutes.
3. Place powdered sugar in a small bowl. Roll dough into 1-inch balls; roll dough balls in powdered sugar. Place on prepared baking sheets, spacing 2 inches apart.
4. Place 1 baking sheet of cookies in refrigerator until ready to bake. Bake remaining baking sheet of cookies in preheated oven until cookies are set in center and lightly browned on bottoms, about 16 to 18 minutes, rotating baking sheet from front to back halfway through bake time. Transfer cookies to a wire rack to cool completely, about 30 minutes. Meanwhile, repeat with remaining baking sheet of cookies.

Mint Meringue Christmas Trees

These chocolate-dipped peppermint tree cookies are the stuff of holiday fairy tales. Because not all metallic sprinkles are oven-safe, add the adornment after baking.

ACTIVE 30 MIN. - TOTAL 2 HOURS, PLUS 1 HOUR COOLING AND 30 MIN. STANDING

MAKES 1½ DOZEN

- 2 large egg whites
- ¼ tsp. cream of tartar
- ⅛ tsp. peppermint extract
- ½ cup superfine sugar (caster sugar)
  Green food coloring gel
  Rainbow candy sprinkles
- 1 cup 60% cacao bittersweet chocolate chips
- 1 tsp. canola oil
- 1 Tbsp. ready-to-spread vanilla frosting
  Gold star-shape candy sprinkles

1. Preheat oven to 200°F. Line a baking sheet with parchment paper.
2. Beat egg whites with an electric mixer on medium speed until frothy, about 1 minute. Add cream of tartar, peppermint extract, and 1 tablespoon sugar. Beat well, about 30 seconds. Continue adding remaining sugar, 1 tablespoon at a time, beating well after each addition. Increase speed to medium-high, and beat until stiff peaks form, about 8 minutes. Beat in desired amount of green food coloring gel.
3. Spoon egg white mixture into a piping bag fitted with a large star tip. Pipe a 1½-inch dollop of egg white mixture onto prepared baking sheet, and then pipe 2 slightly smaller dollops on top to create a tree shape, taking care not to let stacked dollops separate as you work. Repeat with remaining egg white mixture, spacing trees 2 inches apart. Top trees with rainbow sprinkles. Bake meringue trees in preheated oven 2 hours. Turn oven off; let trees cool completely in oven, undisturbed, 1 hour. Transfer meringues to a plate; reserve baking sheet, and line with a new sheet of parchment paper.
4. Melt chocolate chips according to package directions, and stir in oil until thoroughly combined. Dip bottom of each meringue tree in chocolate mixture, and place on prepared baking sheet. Use a wooden pick to apply a small dot of frosting to each star-shape sprinkle, and attach one star to top of each meringue tree. Let stand until

chocolate and frosting are set, about 30 minutes. Store tree cookies (standing upright) in an airtight container until ready to serve.

Earl Grey Tea Cakes

(Photo, page 315)

A dash of tea leaves gives these dainty, diamond-shape cookies their sophisticated taste. If you can't find loose tea at the grocery store, you can also use the leaves from 2 or 3 individually packaged bags. To make extra-tender tea cakes, don't roll out the dough too thin, and be sure to take them out of the oven as soon as they're light golden on the edges.

ACTIVE 30 MIN. - TOTAL 1 HOUR, 20 MIN., PLUS 30 MIN. STANDING

MAKES 2 DOZEN

- 2 cups all-purpose flour, plus more for work surface
- ¾ tsp. baking powder
- 1 Tbsp. loose Earl Grey tea leaves
- ¼ tsp. kosher salt
- ½ cup unsalted butter, softened
- ½ cup granulated sugar
- 1 large egg, at room temperature
- 1 tsp. vanilla extract
- 2 (4-oz.) white chocolate bars, finely chopped
- 1 tsp. canola oil
  Assorted candy sprinkles

1. Preheat oven to 375°F. Line 2 baking sheets with parchment paper. Whisk together flour, baking powder, tea leaves, and salt in a small bowl. Beat butter and sugar with a stand mixer fitted with a paddle attachment on medium speed until light and fluffy, about 3 minutes. Add egg and vanilla, and beat until fully combined. Reduce speed to low, and gradually add flour mixture, one-third at a time, beating just until blended after each addition.
2. Turn dough out onto a lightly floured surface, and roll to ¼-inch thickness. Cut dough into diamond-shape cookies using a 2½- to 3-inch cookie cutter. Transfer to prepared baking sheets. Gather and reroll dough as needed.
3. Place 1 baking sheet of cookies in refrigerator until ready to bake. Bake remaining baking sheet in preheated oven until light golden around edges, about 10 to 12 minutes, rotating baking sheet from front to back halfway

Continued on page 318

Continued from page 317

through bake time. Transfer cookies to a wire rack to cool completely, about 30 minutes. Meanwhile, repeat procedure with remaining baking sheet of cookies. Reserve baking sheets, and line each with a new sheet of parchment paper.

4. Melt white chocolate according to package directions, and stir in oil until thoroughly combined. Place sprinkles in a small bowl. Dip each cookie in melted chocolate, and top immediately with sprinkles; place on prepared baking sheets. Let stand until chocolate sets, about 30 minutes.

Crunchy Peanut Butter-Chocolate Swirl Bars

(Photo, page 316)

These sliceable squares feature a winning combination of white and dark chocolate swirls atop a rich peanut buttery base. The bars get their crunch from crisp rice cereal and a sprinkling of roasted peanuts.

ACTIVE 20 MIN. - TOTAL 20 MIN., PLUS 2 HOURS CHILLING

MAKES 16

10	Tbsp. unsalted butter, melted
1¼	cups creamy peanut butter
	Pinch of kosher salt
1½	cups crisp rice cereal
1¾	cups powdered sugar
1	cup bittersweet chocolate chips (from 1 [10-oz.] pkg.)
6	tsp. refined coconut oil, divided
½	cup white chocolate chips (from 1 [11-oz.] pkg.)
½	cup roasted, salted peanuts, roughly chopped (optional)

1. Line an 8-inch square baking pan with parchment paper, allowing 4 inches to extend over sides. Whisk together melted butter, peanut butter, and salt in a large bowl. Carefully stir in cereal and powdered sugar until well blended, taking care not to crush cereal. Scatter clumps of cereal mixture in prepared pan, and use a sheet of parchment paper to smooth and flatten mixture into an even layer.

2. Melt bittersweet chocolate chips according to package directions, and stir in 4 teaspoons of the oil until thoroughly combined. Pour bittersweet chocolate over cereal mixture, spreading chocolate evenly over top. Melt white chocolate

according to package directions, and stir in remaining 2 teaspoons oil until thoroughly combined. Spoon large dollops of white chocolate on top of bittersweet chocolate layer. Use a wooden pick to make a swirl pattern in white and bittersweet chocolates, blending slightly. Sprinkle top with chopped peanuts, if desired.

3. Refrigerate until set and sliceable, about 2 hours. Cut into 16 squares. Store cookies in refrigerator in an airtight container until ready to serve.

Cornmeal-Lime Cookies

(Photo, page 315)

The subtle vanilla notes of white chocolate are the perfect complement to these not-too-sweet cookies made with yellow cornmeal and a hint of lime. We used a cookie stamp for the tops—a quick way to dress up any sturdy dough.

ACTIVE 40 MIN. - TOTAL 1 HOUR, 15 MIN., PLUS 30 MIN. CHILLING AND 30 MIN. STANDING

MAKES 2 DOZEN

1½	cups all-purpose flour, plus more for work surface and dusting
½	cup, plus 2 Tbsp. fine yellow cornmeal
¼	tsp. kosher salt
10	Tbsp. unsalted butter, softened
¼	cup powdered sugar
¼	cup granulated sugar
1	large egg, at room temperature
½	tsp. grated lime zest (from 1 lime)
2	cups white chocolate chips (from 2 [11-oz.] pkg.)
1	tsp. canola oil
	Gold edible luster dust and sparkling sugar (optional)

1. Whisk together flour, cornmeal, and salt in a small bowl. Beat butter, powdered sugar, and granulated sugar with a stand mixer fitted with a paddle attachment on medium speed until light and fluffy, about 3 minutes. Add egg and lime zest, and beat until incorporated. Reduce speed to low, and gradually add flour mixture, one-third at a time, beating just until incorporated after each addition.

2. Turn dough out onto a lightly floured surface, and knead until dough is smooth and comes together, a few times. Flatten into a disk, wrap in plastic wrap, and refrigerate 30 minutes.

3. Preheat oven to 350°F. Line 2 baking sheets with parchment paper. Scoop 1 rounded tablespoon of dough, and roll into a ball. Place on prepared baking sheets, dust a cookie stamp with flour, and use stamp to press dough into a flat round. Repeat with remaining dough, dusting stamp with flour between each cookie and spacing them 2 inches apart.

4. Place 1 baking sheet of cookies in refrigerator until ready to bake. Bake remaining baking sheet in preheated oven until cookies are set and light golden around edges, about 12 minutes, rotating baking sheet from front to back halfway through bake time. Transfer cookies to a wire rack to cool completely, about 20 minutes. Meanwhile, repeat procedure with remaining baking sheet of cookies. Reserve baking sheets; line each with a new sheet of parchment paper.

5. Melt white chocolate chips according to package directions. Stir in oil until thoroughly combined. Spoon and spread about 1 to 2 teaspoons white chocolate mixture onto bottom of each cookie. Place them, white chocolate-side down, on prepared baking sheets. If desired, transfer remaining white chocolate mixture to a piping bag fitted with a small round tip, and pipe chocolate mixture into grooves of cookies. Brush cookies with gold luster dust or top with sparkling sugar, if desired. Let stand until chocolate is set, about 30 minutes. Store in an airtight container at room temperature.

Coconut-Pecan Truffles

(Photo, page 316)

These two-bite confections have an irresistible combination of nuts, coconut, and chocolate. Seek out chocolate that is at least 60% cacao, and use unsweetened coconut that's shredded extra fine so it blends effortlessly into the ganache.

ACTIVE 25 MIN. - TOTAL 25 MIN., PLUS 5 HOURS CHILLING

MAKES 2 DOZEN

8	oz. high-quality bittersweet chocolate, finely chopped
⅔	cup heavy whipping cream
1	Tbsp. unsalted butter
¼	tsp. vanilla extract
½	tsp. ground cinnamon
	Pinch of kosher salt

6 Tbsp. unsweetened finely shredded coconut

1¼ cups toasted pecans, finely chopped

1. Place chopped chocolate in a heatproof bowl. Bring cream and butter to a simmer in a small saucepan over medium, stirring occasionally. (Do not let mixture boil.) Pour hot cream mixture over chopped chocolate, and let stand 1 minute; whisk until smooth and shiny. Add vanilla, cinnamon, salt, and coconut to chocolate mixture, and stir to combine, scraping down sides as necessary.

2. Tap bowl on work surface so chocolate mixture has a smooth top surface; cover and refrigerate until firm, about 4 hours.

3. Place chopped pecans in a small bowl. Scoop a heaping teaspoon of chocolate mixture, and use hands to quickly roll it into a ball. Gently roll in pecans to coat; place on a baking sheet or plate. Repeat with remaining chocolate mixture and pecans. Refrigerate about 1 hour. Store truffles in an airtight container in refrigerator.

Chocolate Gingerbread Wreaths

(Photo, page 315)

Rich, dark chocolate cocoa powder and a circular shape give this classic a new twist. We recommend applying the royal icing with a piping bag fit with a writing tip, but if you don't have one, a plastic sandwich bag with a tiny corner snipped off will do.

ACTIVE 45 MIN. - TOTAL 1 HOUR, 15 MIN., PLUS 1 HOUR CHILLING, 1 HOUR COOLING, AND 6 HOURS STANDING

MAKES 2½ DOZEN

2½ cups all-purpose flour, plus more for work surface

⅔ cup dark cocoa

1½ tsp. ground ginger

½ tsp. ground cinnamon

⅛ tsp. ground cloves

½ tsp. baking soda

½ tsp. baking powder

½ tsp. kosher salt

½ cup unsalted butter, softened

¾ cup granulated sugar

1 large egg, at room temperature

¾ tsp. vanilla extract

⅓ cup unsulphured molasses

1¼ cups powdered sugar

2 Tbsp. meringue powder
Green food coloring gel
Pearl candy sprinkles

1. Whisk together flour, cocoa, ginger, cinnamon, cloves, baking soda, baking powder, and salt in a small bowl. Beat butter and sugar in a stand mixer fitted with a paddle attachment on medium speed until light and fluffy, about 3 minutes. Add egg and vanilla, and beat until incorporated. Beat in molasses. Reduce speed to low, and gradually add flour mixture, one-third at a time, beating just until blended after each addition.

2. Turn dough out onto a lightly floured surface, and knead a few times until smooth. Roll dough into a ball, and flatten into a disk. Wrap in plastic wrap, and chill 1 hour.

3. Preheat oven to 350°F. Line 2 baking sheets with parchment paper. Roll dough to ¼-inch thickness on a lightly floured surface. Cut dough into circles using a 2½- to 3-inch round cookie cutter. Cut middle out of each dough circle using a 1-inch round cookie cutter. Arrange cookies on prepared baking sheets, spacing 2 inches apart. Gather and reroll dough as needed.

4. Place 1 baking sheet of cookies in refrigerator until ready to bake. Bake remaining baking sheet in preheated oven until cookies are set and lightly browned on bottom, about 12 minutes, rotating baking sheet from front to back halfway through bake time. Let cool on baking sheet on wire rack 5 minutes; transfer cookies to wire rack to cool completely, about 1 hour. Meanwhile, repeat procedure with remaining baking sheet of cookies.

5. Beat powdered sugar, meringue powder, and 3 tablespoons water with stand mixer fitted with a whisk attachment on medium-high speed until fluffy and slightly stiff. Add more water, 1 teaspoon at a time, if needed, for desired consistency. Stir in desired amount of food coloring, and spoon into a piping bag fitted with a writing tip.

6. Decorate 1 cookie at a time. Pipe icing on each in a spiral pattern, and top with desired amount of sprinkles. Repeat with remaining cookies, icing, and sprinkles. Let stand until icing is set, about 6 hours. Store in an airtight container at room temperature.

Cherry-Walnut Rugelach

(Photo, page 316)

These tasty rolled cookies feature a tender cream cheese dough and walnuts but otherwise break from tradition. They're filled with cherry jam and milk chocolate—a scrumptious substitute for the usual cinnamon sugar and apricot preserves.

ACTIVE 30 MIN. - TOTAL 1 HOUR, 20 MIN., PLUS 1 HOUR CHILLING

MAKES 2 DOZEN

¾ cup unsalted butter, softened

6 oz. cream cheese, softened

1½ cups all-purpose flour, plus more for work surface

1 Tbsp. granulated sugar
Pinch of kosher salt

⅔ cup cherry jam or cherry preserves with larger pieces removed

½ cup chopped walnuts, finely chopped

24 milk chocolate rectangles (from 2 [2.6-oz.] milk chocolate candy bars)

1 large egg

2 Tbsp. sparkling sugar

1. Beat butter and cream cheese in a stand mixer fitted with a paddle attachment on medium speed until creamy, about 1 minute. Reduce speed to low, and add flour, granulated sugar, and salt; beat until blended, about 2 minutes. Turn dough out onto a lightly floured surface, and knead gently until smooth, 4 or 5 times. Divide dough into 2 equal portions; roll each into a ball, and press into a disk. Wrap each disk in plastic wrap, and chill 1 hour.

2. Preheat oven to 350°F. Line 2 baking sheets with parchment paper. Roll 1 portion of dough into a 16-inch round on a lightly floured surface. Spread half of jam evenly over dough, and sprinkle evenly with half of chopped walnuts. Use a pizza cutter to cut dough into 12 even wedges.

3. Place a chocolate rectangle at the wide end of 1 wedge, and carefully roll up; place wedge, point side down, on prepared baking sheet. Repeat with 11 more pieces of chocolate and remaining wedges, spacing cookies 2 inches apart on baking sheet. Repeat procedure with remaining dough, jam, walnuts, and chocolate pieces.

4. Whisk together egg and 1 tablespoon water in a small bowl. Brush top of each

Continued on page 320

Continued from page 319

cookie with egg wash, and sprinkle with sparkling sugar.

5. Place 1 baking sheet of cookies in refrigerator until ready to bake. Bake remaining baking sheet in preheated oven until golden, about 20 to 25 minutes, rotating baking sheet from front to back halfway through bake time. Transfer cookies to a wire rack to cool completely, about 30 minutes. Meanwhile, repeat procedure with remaining baking sheet of cookies.

Chocolate-Almond Thumbprints

(Photo, page 316)

Filled with whipped chocolate ganache and topped with a stemmed maraschino cherry, these embellished cookies would be a sweet finish to any celebratory meal. The cookie base can be made ahead, but we suggest filling and decorating them no more than a few hours before serving.

ACTIVE 40 MIN. - TOTAL 2 HOURS, 15 MIN.

MAKES ABOUT 3 DOZEN

- 2¼ cups all-purpose flour, plus more for work surface
- ½ tsp. baking soda
- ¼ tsp. kosher salt
- ¾ cup, plus 2 Tbsp. unsalted butter, softened
- ⅔ cup granulated sugar
- 1 large egg, at room temperature
- ¾ tsp. vanilla extract
- 1 cup whole raw almonds, finely chopped
- 12 oz. semisweet chocolate, finely chopped
- ¾ cup heavy whipping cream
- 36 whole maraschino cherries with stems, patted dry (from 2 [10-oz.] jars)

1. Preheat oven to 350°F. Line 2 baking sheets with parchment paper. Whisk together flour, baking soda, and salt in a small bowl. Beat butter and sugar in a stand mixer fitted with a paddle attachment on medium speed until light and fluffy, about 3 minutes. Add egg and vanilla, and beat until incorporated. Reduce speed to low, and gradually add flour mixture, one-third at a time, beating just until blended after each addition.

2. Place chopped almonds in a small bowl. Turn dough out onto a lightly floured surface, and knead a few times until dough is smooth and comes together. Scoop a level tablespoon of dough, and roll it into a ball. Roll ball in chopped almonds. Place on prepared baking sheet. Repeat with remaining dough, spacing balls 2 inches apart on baking sheets.

3. Use back of a teaspoon to make a deep indentation in center of each dough ball.

4. Place 1 baking sheet of cookies in refrigerator until ready to bake. Bake remaining baking sheet in preheated oven 8 minutes. Remove from oven, and use teaspoon to redo indentation in center of each ball. Return to oven, and bake until set and lightly golden on bottom, about 6 to 8 minutes. Cool 5 minutes on baking sheet; transfer cookies to a wire rack to cool completely, about 30 minutes. Repeat with remaining baking sheet of cookies.

5. Place chopped chocolate in a heatproof bowl. Heat cream in a small saucepan over low until just beginning to bubble around edges, about 2 to 3 minutes. (Do not let cream boil, or it will be too hot for chocolate.) Pour hot cream over chocolate, and let stand 1 minute; whisk until smooth. Refrigerate chocolate mixture, stirring often so mixture cools evenly, about 15 to 20 minutes.

6. Beat chocolate mixture with an electric mixer on medium speed until light and fluffy. Transfer ganache to a piping bag fitted with a star tip. Pipe ganache in indentation in center of each cookie. Top each with a cherry. Refrigerate in an airtight container until ready to serve.

Bourbon-Orange Biscotti

(Photo, page 316)

Homemade biscotti have a more pleasing and delicate crunch than the cookies you'll find in your local coffee shop. A light drizzle of white chocolate adds a finishing touch, but you can double the amount of chocolate and dip them.

ACTIVE 35 MIN. - TOTAL 1 HOUR, 30 MIN., PLUS 30 MIN. COOLING AND 30 MIN. STANDING

MAKES 2 DOZEN

- 2½ cups all-purpose flour, plus more for work surface
- 2 tsp. baking powder
- ¼ tsp. kosher salt
- ½ cup unsalted butter, softened
- ¾ cup granulated sugar
- 2 large eggs
- 1 tsp. vanilla extract
- 2 Tbsp. (1 oz.) bourbon
- ¾ tsp. grated orange zest (from 1 orange)
- ½ cup whole raw almonds, roughly chopped
- 6 Tbsp. white chocolate chips (from 1 [11-oz.] pkg.)
- 1 tsp. canola oil

1. Preheat oven to 350°F, and line a baking sheet with parchment paper. Whisk together flour, baking powder, and salt in a small bowl.

2. Beat butter and sugar in a stand mixer fitted with a paddle attachment on medium speed until light and fluffy, about 3 minutes. Add eggs, 1 at a time, beating until blended after each addition. Add vanilla, bourbon, and orange zest, and continue beating until incorporated. (Mixture may separate slightly.)

3. Reduce speed to medium-low; gradually add flour mixture, one-third at a time, and beat until well blended. Fold in chopped almonds using a rubber spatula. With floured hands, scoop dough onto a lightly floured surface. (Dough will be very sticky.)

4. Roll dough into a 15-inch-long log. Carefully transfer log to prepared baking sheet, and gently press top to shape log into a ½-inch-thick rectangle (about 4 inches wide).

5. Bake in preheated oven until golden and puffy, about 25 to 30 minutes, rotating baking sheet from front to back halfway through bake time. Transfer baked rectangle to a wire rack, and let cool 15 minutes. Reserve parchment paper-lined baking sheet.

6. With a sharp serrated knife, cut rectangle crosswise into ¾-inch-thick slices. Arrange cookies, standing upright (not on cut sides), on reserved baking sheet, and return to oven. Bake at 350°F until lightly dried, deep golden, and crisp on the outside, about 15 to 20 minutes. Transfer cookies to a wire rack, and cool completely, about 30 minutes. Cover baking sheet with a new sheet of parchment paper.

7. Arrange biscotti, cut side up, on prepared baking sheet. Melt white chocolate chips according to package directions, and stir in oil until thoroughly combined. Drizzle melted white chocolate mixture over biscotti. Let stand until chocolate sets, about 30 minutes. Store in an airtight container at room temperature.

Welcome Home

This sweet cottage–topped cake celebrates the joy of the season and reconnecting with family and friends

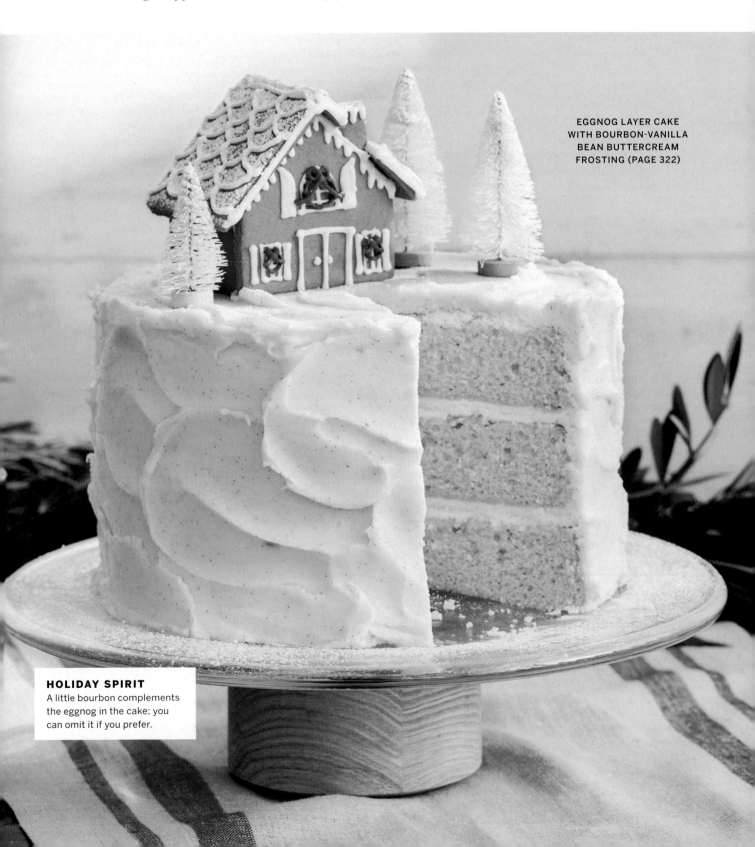

EGGNOG LAYER CAKE
WITH BOURBON-VANILLA
BEAN BUTTERCREAM
FROSTING (PAGE 322)

HOLIDAY SPIRIT
A little bourbon complements
the eggnog in the cake; you
can omit it if you prefer.

Eggnog Layer Cake with Bourbon-Vanilla Bean Buttercream Frosting

(Photo, page 321)

ACTIVE 30 MIN. · TOTAL 2 HOURS, 10 MIN.

SERVES 12

CAKE LAYERS

Baking spray with flour

1¾ cups granulated sugar

1 cup butter, softened

4 large eggs

3 cups all-purpose flour

1 Tbsp. baking powder

½ tsp. kosher salt

½ tsp. ground nutmeg

2 cups refrigerated eggnog, divided

2 Tbsp. (1 oz.) bourbon

1 tsp. vanilla extract

FROSTING

1 cup butter, softened

1 (32-oz.) pkg. powdered sugar

¾ cup heavy whipping cream

1 vanilla bean pod, split

2 Tbsp. (1 oz.) bourbon

FOR DECORATING

Gingerbread House and Paver, Cookies (recipe follows)

Powdered sugar, for sprinkling

Bottle brush trees, for decoration

1. Prepare the Cake Layers: Preheat oven to 350°F. Coat 3 (8-inch) round cake pans with baking spray. Line each pan bottom with a circle of parchment paper; coat parchment with baking spray.

2. Beat sugar and butter with a stand mixer fitted with a paddle attachment on medium speed until mixture is light and fluffy, about 4 minutes. Add eggs 1 at a time, beating until combined.

3. Stir together flour, baking powder, salt, and nutmeg in a separate bowl. Add flour mixture to sugar-butter mixture alternately with 1 cup of the eggnog in 3 additions, beginning and ending with flour mixture. Beat on low speed until blended after each addition, about 1 minute total. Beat in bourbon and vanilla extract until smooth. Divide batter evenly among prepared pans (1⅔ cups per pan).

4. Bake on center rack in preheated oven until a wooden pick inserted in center of each layer comes out clean, 22 to 25 minutes. Poke each hot Cake Layer with a fork, and evenly drizzle each layer with ⅓ cup eggnog.

Let cool in pans 20 minutes. Run an offset spatula around edges of each layer; remove from pans, and cool completely on a wire rack, about 1 hour.

5. Meanwhile, prepare the Frosting: Beat butter with an electric mixer on medium speed until creamy, about 2 minutes. Reduce mixer speed to low. Gradually beat in powdered sugar alternately with cream, beating until blended after each addition, about 2 minutes total. Scrape seeds from split vanilla bean pod using dull edge of a paring knife; add scraped vanilla seeds and bourbon to butter mixture (discard scraped vanilla bean pod). Beat on high speed until smooth and fluffy, about 2 minutes.

6. Place 1 Cake Layer, soaked side up, on a platter; spread 1 cup Frosting over top. Top with second Cake Layer, soaked side up, and 1 cup Frosting. Top with remaining Cake Layer, soaked side down. Frost top and sides of cake with remaining Frosting.

7. Place Gingerbread House Cookie and Gingerbread Paver Cookies on top of cake. Sprinkle roof of house and paver cookies with a small amount of powdered sugar to resemble snow. Top with bottle-brush trees.

Gingerbread Cookies

ACTIVE 1 HOUR · TOTAL 2 HOURS, PLUS 2 HOURS CHILLING AND 3 HOURS STANDING

MAKES 1 GINGERBREAD HOUSE, 12 GINGERBREAD DOORS, AND 3 OR 4 GINGERBREAD PAVERS

COOKIES

¾ cup packed dark brown sugar

½ cup unsalted butter, at room temperature

½ cup unsulphured molasses

1 large egg

2 tsp. vanilla extract

3 cups all-purpose flour, plus more for work surface

1 Tbsp. ground ginger

2 tsp. ground cinnamon

1 tsp. kosher salt

ROYAL ICING

1 lb. powdered sugar

6 Tbsp. warm water

3 Tbsp. meringue powder

Red and green food coloring gel (optional)

1. Prepare the Cookies: Preheat oven to 350°F. Line 2 baking sheets with parchment paper; set aside. Beat brown sugar, butter, and molasses with a stand mixer fitted with a paddle attachment on medium speed until smooth, about

1 minute. Add egg and vanilla, and beat just until combined, about 10 seconds, stopping to scrape down sides of bowl as needed.

2. Whisk together flour, ginger, cinnamon, and salt in a medium bowl until well combined. Gradually add flour mixture to brown sugar mixture, beating on low speed until dough begins to come together, about 3 minutes total. Place dough on a lightly floured work surface; shape dough into a disk, and wrap with plastic wrap. Chill at least 2 hours or up to 2 days.

3. Unwrap dough disk. Place on a lightly floured work surface, and roll into a ⅓-inch-thick rectangle. Using House Templates, cut out pieces from dough for Gingerbread House using a sharp paring knife. Cut remaining dough into 12 (2- x 3-inch) rectangles to use for doors and 3 or 4 (¾-inch) squares for pavers. Arrange cutouts 1 inch apart on prepared baking sheets, keeping house and door Cookies and pavers on separate baking sheets.

4. Bake in 2 batches on middle rack in preheated oven until edges start to darken slightly, 10 to 12 minutes for house and door Cookies and 7 to 8 minutes for pavers. Let cool on baking sheets 5 minutes; transfer to a wire rack, and let cool completely, about 30 minutes. Use a sharp paring knife to cut a small notch (about 1 inch long and ½ inch deep) on one side of one roof panel Cookie to accommodate chimney.

5. Prepare the Royal Icing: Beat powdered sugar, water, and meringue powder with a stand mixer fitted with a whisk attachment on medium speed until fully combined and smooth, about 1 minute, stopping to scrape down sides of bowl as needed. Increase mixer speed to high, and beat until Royal Icing is no

longer glossy, about 1 minute. Transfer ¼ cup Royal Icing to a small bowl; stir in red food coloring to tint to desired shade. Repeat with an additional ¼ cup Royal Icing and green food coloring in a separate bowl. Cover bowls with plastic wrap, and set aside at room temperature until ready to use.

6. Spoon remaining Royal Icing into a piping bag fitted with a small round tip (such as Wilton #2 or #3). Pipe Royal Icing along edges of cooled Cookie house, side, and roof pieces, 1 at a time, and hold each piece in place for 1 minute to set before moving on to the next. Let Gingerbread House stand 1 hour before decorating.

7. Transfer red and green Royal Icings to piping bags fitted with small round tips (such as Wilton #2 or #3), or cut a small corner from bottom of each bag. Decorate house and door Cookies as desired with white, red, and green Royal Icing. Let stand until set, about 2 hours.

HOUSE TEMPLATES

ENLARGE 200%

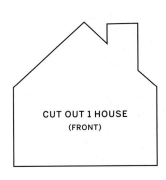

CUT OUT 1 HOUSE
(FRONT)

CUT OUT 1 HOUSE
(BACK)

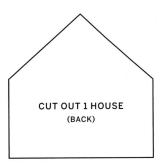

CUT OUT
2 SIDES
(LEFT AND RIGHT)

CUT OUT 2 ROOFS
(LEFT AND RIGHT)

Eight Golden, Delicious Nights

Southerners never need a reason to enjoy fried foods, but Hanukkah calls
for something extra special, like these fancied-up snacks

Mini Sweet Potato Latkes

ACTIVE 30 MIN. · TOTAL 30 MIN.
SERVES 8

- 1 large (1-lb.) sweet potato, peeled
- 2 medium scallions, finely chopped (about ¼ cup), plus more thinly sliced scallions for garnish
- ½ cup potato flour
- 2 large eggs, lightly beaten
- 1 tsp. kosher salt, plus more to taste
- 1 tsp. black pepper, plus more to taste
- Canola oil
- Sour cream

1. Grate sweet potato using the largest holes of a box grater (4 cups). Gently stir together grated sweet potato, finely chopped scallions, potato flour, eggs, 1 teaspoon salt, and 1 teaspoon pepper in a large bowl until well combined. Divide and shape sweet potato mixture into 16 (3-inch) thin patties (about ¼ cup sweet potato mixture per patty). Place patties (latkes) on a baking sheet lined with parchment paper until ready to cook.
2. Pour oil to a depth of ¼ inch in a large skillet, and heat over medium to 325°F. Working in 4 batches, add latkes to hot oil, and cook until golden brown and crispy, about 1 minute and 30 seconds per side. Transfer to a baking sheet lined with paper towels, and immediately season to taste with salt and black pepper. Keep warm in a 200°F oven. Allow hot oil to return to 325°F between batches. Serve hot latkes immediately with sour cream; garnish with thinly sliced scallions.

Crispy Spiced Chickpeas

ACTIVE 20 MIN. · TOTAL 20 MIN.
SERVES 4

- 6 Tbsp. olive oil
- 2 (15½-oz.) cans chickpeas (garbanzo beans), drained, rinsed, and dried on paper towels
- 2 tsp. za'atar seasoning blend
- ½ tsp. kosher salt

Heat oil in a large skillet over medium. Add chickpeas, and cook, stirring occasionally, until deep golden brown and crispy, about 16 to 20 minutes. Using a slotted spoon, transfer chickpeas to a medium bowl, and toss with za'atar and salt; serve immediately. (Chickpeas can be stored in an airtight container at room temperature for up to 3 days.)

Cheesy Potato Croquettes

ACTIVE 1 HOUR · TOTAL 3 HOURS, 10 MIN.
SERVES 8

- 3 medium russet potatoes (about 3 lb. total), peeled and quartered
- 1 large egg, lightly beaten
- 2 Tbsp. potato flour
- ¾ oz. Parmesan cheese, grated with a Microplane grater (about ½ cup)
- 2 oz. mozzarella cheese, shredded (½ cup)
- 2 oz. sharp cheddar cheese, shredded (½ cup)
- 1 tsp. kosher salt, plus more to taste
- ½ tsp. black pepper, plus more to taste
- 1½ cups panko breadcrumbs
- Canola oil
- Thinly sliced chives

1. Bring a large pot of salted water to a boil over high. Add potatoes, and cook until fork-tender, about 18 to 20 minutes. Drain potatoes, and let stand until cool enough to handle, about 10 minutes. Press potatoes through a potato ricer into a large bowl (or mash thoroughly with a potato masher); chill, uncovered, until cold, about 1 hour. Using your hands, gently stir in egg, potato flour, cheeses, 1 teaspoon salt, and ½ teaspoon pepper until well combined. Scoop potato mixture, and shape into 20 (3-inch) patties (about ¼ cup per patty).
2. Place panko in a medium bowl. Working with 1 patty at a time, gently press into panko to coat completely, and transfer to a baking sheet lined with parchment paper. Chill, uncovered, for 30 minutes (this will help the panko stick to the patties).
3. Pour canola oil to a depth of ½ inch in a large skillet; heat oil over medium to 350°F. Working in 5 batches, add croquettes to hot oil, and fry until golden brown and crispy, about 2 minutes per side. Drain on a baking sheet lined with paper towels, and immediately season to taste with salt and pepper. Keep warm in a 200°F oven. Allow oil to return to 350°F between batches. Garnish hot croquettes with chives.

Arancini with Pomodoro Dipping Sauce

ACTIVE 1 HOUR, 35 MIN. · TOTAL 2 HOURS, 35 MIN.
SERVES 4

POMODORO DIPPING SAUCE
- 1 (28-oz.) can whole peeled San Marzano plum tomatoes
- 1 Tbsp. chopped fresh oregano
- 1 Tbsp. finely chopped garlic (from 4 small garlic cloves)
- 2 tsp. granulated sugar
- ½ tsp. kosher salt

ARANCINI
- 3½ cups chicken or vegetable stock
- 2 Tbsp. olive oil
- 2 garlic cloves, finely chopped (about 1 tsp.)
- ½ cup finely chopped yellow onion (from 1 small onion)
- 1 cup uncooked Arborio rice
- ½ cup dry white wine
- ¼ cup heavy whipping cream
- 2 Tbsp. sour cream
- 1½ oz. Parmesan cheese, grated with a Microplane grater (about 1 cup)
- 1 Tbsp. finely chopped fresh thyme
- 1 tsp. kosher salt, plus more to taste

Continued on page 326

CLOCKWISE FROM TOP LEFT:

- MINI SWEET POTATO LATKES

- CRISPY SPICED CHICKPEAS

- CHEESY POTATO CROQUETTES

- ARANCINI WITH POMODORO DIPPING SAUCE

- OVEN-FRIED "EVERYTHING" CHICKEN DRUMETTES (PAGE 327)

- FRIED OLIVES WITH BLUE CHEESE AÏOLI (PAGE 326)

- HOMEMADE POTATO CHIPS WITH FRIED HERBS (PAGE 326)

- FRIED ARTICHOKE HEARTS WITH ROASTED RED PEPPER AÏOLI (PAGE 327)

Continued from page 324

- ½ tsp. black pepper, plus more to taste
  Canola oil
- ⅓ cup all-purpose flour
- 2 large eggs
- 1 cup panko breadcrumbs

1. Prepare the Pomodoro Dipping Sauce: Process tomatoes in a blender until smooth, about 10 seconds. Transfer tomato puree to a large saucepan, and stir in oregano, garlic, and sugar. Bring to a simmer over medium-low. Simmer, stirring occasionally, until thickened, about 45 minutes. Stir in salt, and remove from heat; cover to keep warm.
2. Prepare the Arancini: Line a rimmed baking sheet with parchment paper. Bring chicken stock to a simmer in a small saucepan over medium-low. Meanwhile, heat olive oil in a large saucepan over medium. Add garlic and onion, and cook, stirring often, until onion is translucent, about 4 minutes. Add rice, and cook, stirring constantly, until rice is lightly toasted, about 2 minutes. Add white wine, and cook, stirring often, until wine is completely absorbed, about 3 minutes. Add hot chicken stock to rice mixture, ½ cup at a time, and cook, stirring often, until stock is completely absorbed before adding more, about 15 minutes total. Add heavy cream and sour cream, and cook, stirring constantly, until mixture is creamy and rice is tender, about 3 minutes. Remove from heat, and stir in cheese, thyme, 1 teaspoon salt, and ½ teaspoon pepper. Pour rice mixture onto prepared baking sheet, and spread in an even layer. Chill rice mixture, uncovered, until cold, about 1 hour.
3. Pour canola oil to a depth of 2 inches in a large Dutch oven; heat oil over medium to 350°F. Line a sheet pan with paper towels; set aside. Place flour in a medium bowl. Whisk together eggs in a separate medium bowl until well combined. Place panko in a third medium bowl. Remove rice mixture from refrigerator, and shape into 16 (1¼-inch) balls (about ¼ cup each). Working with 1 rice ball at a time, place ball in flour, and toss to coat. Transfer to whisked eggs, and toss to coat. Place in panko, and toss again until well coated. Transfer breaded rice ball to a plate; repeat process with remaining rice balls.

4. Carefully add rice balls to hot oil in 3 or 4 batches, and fry, stirring occasionally, until rice balls are deep golden brown, about 3 minutes. Drain on a rimmed baking sheet lined with paper towels, and immediately season to taste with salt and pepper. Keep warm in a 200°F oven. Allow oil to return to 350°F between batches. Serve hot with Pomodoro Dipping Sauce.

Fried Olives with Blue Cheese Aïoli

(Photo, page 325)
ACTIVE 35 MIN. - TOTAL 35 MIN.
SERVES 4

BLUE CHEESE AÏOLI

- 1 cup mayonnaise
- ¼ cup sour cream
- 2 medium garlic cloves, grated (½ tsp.)
- 2 oz. blue cheese, crumbled (about ½ cup)
- 2 tsp. fresh lemon juice (from 1 lemon)
- ½ tsp. kosher salt
- ½ tsp. black pepper
  Thinly sliced chives

FRIED OLIVES

  Canola oil
- 1 cup all-purpose flour, divided
- ½ cup whole buttermilk
- ½ cup corn flour
- ½ cup medium-ground cornmeal
- 1 Tbsp. kosher salt
- 1 tsp. black pepper
- 1 tsp. smoked paprika
- ¼ tsp. cayenne pepper
- 1 (19-oz.) jar pimiento-stuffed green olives, drained and thoroughly patted dry (about 32 olives)

1. Prepare the Blue Cheese Aïoli: Combine mayonnaise, sour cream, garlic, blue cheese, lemon juice, salt, and black pepper in a food processor, and process until smooth, about 1 minute; chill until ready to serve. (Blue Cheese Aïoli can be stored in an airtight container in the refrigerator for up to 1 week.)
2. Prepare the Fried Olives: Pour oil to a depth of 2 inches in a large Dutch oven; heat oil over medium to 350°F. Place ½ cup of the all-purpose flour in a medium bowl. Pour buttermilk into a separate medium bowl. Stir together

corn flour, cornmeal, salt, black pepper, paprika, cayenne pepper, and remaining ½ cup all-purpose flour in a third medium bowl. Working in batches, toss olives in all-purpose flour until well coated. Transfer olives to buttermilk, and toss to coat. Place olives in cornmeal mixture, and toss again to coat; transfer to a baking sheet lined with parchment paper.
3. Working in 3 batches, fry olives in hot oil, stirring occasionally, until golden brown, about 1 minute and 30 seconds; drain on a baking sheet lined with paper towels. Keep warm in a 200°F oven. Allow oil to return to 350°F between batches. Sprinkle chives over Blue Cheese Aïoli. Serve with hot olives.

Homemade Potato Chips with Fried Herbs

(Photo, page 325)
ACTIVE 25 MIN. - TOTAL 40 MIN.
SERVES 4

- 2 medium russet potatoes (about 8 oz. each), sliced crosswise with a mandoline into 1/32-inch-thick rounds
  Canola oil
- 4 (6-inch) fresh rosemary sprigs
- 4 (4-inch) fresh sage sprigs
  Fine sea salt

1. Place potato slices in a large bowl, and add water to cover. Gently agitate potatoes to release their starches. When water is cloudy, pour off water and discard, leaving potato slices in bowl. Repeat process 3 times or until water pours off clear. Pat potato slices dry with paper towels.
2. Pour oil to a depth of 3 inches in a large Dutch oven; heat oil over medium to 350°F. Add rosemary and sage sprigs to hot oil, and fry until leaves are crisp, about 30 to 45 seconds. Drain on a baking sheet lined with paper towels until herb sprigs are cool enough to handle, about 3 minutes. Carefully separate leaves from stems, discarding stems. Set fried herb leaves aside.
3. Reduce heat to low, and allow oil temperature to drop to 275°F to 300°F. Working in batches, add potato slices to hot oil, and fry, stirring gently and constantly to keep chips separated, until slices begin to turn a very light golden brown, about 2 to 3 minutes. Drain chips on a baking sheet lined with

paper towels, and immediately season to taste with sea salt. Allow oil to return to 275°F to 300°F between batches. Transfer seasoned chips to a large bowl, and toss with fried herb leaves; serve immediately, or store in an airtight container at room temperature for up to 3 days.

Oven-Fried "Everything" Chicken Drumettes

(Photo, page 325)
ACTIVE 10 MIN. - TOTAL 1 HOUR
SERVES 6

- 1 cup potato flour
- 1 tsp. kosher salt
- ½ tsp. black pepper
- 24 chicken drumettes (about 3 lb.)
- 3 Tbsp. everything bagel seasoning

1. Preheat oven to 450°F on the convection setting. (If oven does not have a convection setting, preheat to 450°F.) Line a rimmed baking sheet with aluminum foil, and place a wire rack on top of foil; spray rack generously with cooking spray. Stir together potato flour, salt, and pepper in a medium bowl. Working in batches, toss chicken in potato flour mixture until completely coated, and transfer to wire rack on prepared baking sheet.
2. Bake chicken in preheated oven until skin is golden brown, about 45 to 50 minutes. (If not using convection setting, flip chicken pieces over halfway through bake time.)
3. Remove chicken from oven, and transfer to a large bowl; do not turn oven off. Sprinkle chicken with everything bagel seasoning, and toss until chicken is well coated. Return chicken to baking sheet, and bake chicken at 450°F until skin is golden brown and crispy and a thermometer inserted into thickest portion registers at least 165°F, about 5 minutes; serve immediately.

Fried Artichoke Hearts with Roasted Red Pepper Aïoli

(Photo, page 325)
ACTIVE 35 MIN. - TOTAL 35 MIN.
SERVES 6

ROASTED RED PEPPER AÏOLI
- 1 cup mayonnaise
- ¼ cup sour cream
- 2 Tbsp. tomato paste
- 2 tsp. fresh lemon juice (from 1 lemon)
- ¾ tsp. kosher salt
- ½ tsp. black pepper
- 2 garlic cloves, grated (½ tsp.)
- 1 (12-oz.) jar roasted red bell peppers, drained and thoroughly patted dry
- 2 Tbsp. finely chopped fresh parsley

FRIED ARTICHOKE HEARTS
- Canola oil
- ½ cup all-purpose flour
- 2 large eggs, lightly beaten
- 2 Tbsp. whole buttermilk
- 1½ cups dry breadcrumbs
- 1 tsp. kosher salt, plus more to taste
- ½ tsp. black pepper, plus more to taste
- 1 (24-oz.) jar marinated quartered artichoke hearts, drained and thoroughly patted dry

1. Prepare the Roasted Red Pepper Aïoli: Combine mayonnaise, sour cream, tomato paste, lemon juice, salt, black pepper, garlic, and roasted red peppers in a food processor, and process until smooth, about 1 minute. Stir in parsley. Cover; chill until ready to serve. (Roasted Red Pepper Aïoli can be stored in an airtight container in the refrigerator for up to 1 week.)
2. Prepare the Fried Artichoke Hearts: Pour oil to a depth of 2 inches in a large Dutch oven; heat oil over medium to 350°F. Place flour in a medium bowl. Stir together eggs and buttermilk in a separate medium bowl until well combined. Stir together breadcrumbs, 1 teaspoon salt, and ½ teaspoon black pepper in a third medium bowl. Working in batches, toss artichoke heart quarters in flour until well coated. Transfer to egg mixture, and toss to coat. Place in breadcrumb mixture, and toss again to coat; place on a baking sheet lined with parchment paper.
3. Working in 3 batches, fry artichoke hearts in hot oil, stirring occasionally, until golden brown, about 1 minute and 30 seconds; drain on a baking sheet lined with paper towels, and immediately season to taste with salt and black pepper. Keep warm in a 200°F oven. Allow oil to return to 350°F between batches. Serve hot Fried Artichoke Hearts immediately alongside Roasted Red Pepper Aïoli for dipping.

The Golden Rules of Frying

Start with a Thermometer
Use a frying or candy thermometer that attaches to the side of a pot or skillet so you are hands-free.

Choose Your Oil
Vegetable, peanut, and canola oils are great options for frying with high smoke points (400°F to 450°F) and neutral flavors.

Pick the Right Pan (Or Pot)
For deep-frying, a heavy Dutch oven with a large diameter gives you a wider cooking area. Cast iron retains heat longer than other materials, allowing for better temperature control and uniform results. A fully clad stainless-steel pot is another good option. For pan-frying, look for heavy-bottom skillets or sauté pans that will ensure even and consistent heating.

Watch the Temperature
Make sure the oil temperature is consistent throughout the cooking process, especially when frying multiple batches. If the oil isn't hot enough, the outer crust will cook too slowly and become soggy and greasy. If it's too hot, the crust will darken and burn before the inside has had a chance to cook adequately.

Get Organized
Frying is a quick cooking method, so have the ingredients and equipment in place before you get started. Bread all of the ingredients before putting anything in the fryer to avoid slowing down the entire process. As you cook, remove impurities (like breadcrumbs) from the oil with a small strainer before they build up, burn, and add an unappealing flavor.

Dispose Carefully
After frying, let the hot oil return to room temperature, then carefully pour it back into its original container, and discard.

ANY-SEASON
SUCCOTASH

PECAN-COATED
ROAST LOIN OF PORK

Joyous Kwanzaa!

For many African Americans, this holiday is a time to honor the past,
look toward the present, and feast with loved ones.

I CAME LATE to Kwanzaa, celebrating it first in the 1980s. I remember the effect it had on the starry-eyed children present, who watched the ceremony with rapt interest. In 1995, I wrote a book about the holiday: *A Kwanzaa Keepsake,* which presented it in the context of the African diaspora.

Many people are astonished to learn that Kwanzaa was established only recently, in 1966 by African American activist and professor Maulana Karenga. It was created to counteract the commercialization of Christmas, year–end holidays, and to provide a way to celebrate African cultural values.

Kwanzaa, which runs from the day after Christmas through New Year's, uses Swahili as its language. Seven is an important number for the holiday, with seven days, seven principles, and seven symbols used on the centerpiece that celebrates Kwanzaa. (Those items are the mat on which the centerpiece is built; the ears of corn, which symbolize the children in the household; the arrangement of fruit; the chalice of unity; the seven-branched kinara, or candleholder; the red, black, and green candles; and the gifts, which should be handmade or educational and (if purchased) obtained from African American or African diaspora sources.

I led Kwanzaa ceremonies for almost two decades at the university where I taught. Over the years, the college events grew in importance and came to include things such as African fashion shows, dance performances, poetry readings, choral singing, drumming, and more. There was a buffet loaded with foods from the African diaspora. It featured everything from American fried chicken and collard greens to Jamaican jerk chicken and rice and peas to Trinidadian curries and rotis.

I reveled in the drumming, dancing, and feasting, and I was always moved by watching how the holiday and the ceremony and its celebration of our cultural heritage helped empower the African American faculty and students. We left with spines straighter, minds clearer, and hearts lighter for having shared a bit of ourselves with all.
—Jessica B. Harris

Pecan-Coated Roast Loin of Pork

This elegant roast is rubbed with a mixture of dark brown sugar and herbs, then marinated overnight for an extra-rich flavor. A crust of chopped pecans adds a little crunch that balances the tender meat beautifully.
ACTIVE 15 MIN. - TOTAL 1 HOUR, 25 MIN., PLUS 12 HOURS CHILLING
SERVES 8

- 4 lb. boneless pork center-cut loin roast, trimmed
- ¼ cup olive oil, divided
- 1 Tbsp. dark brown sugar
- 2 tsp. dried sage
- 1½ tsp. kosher salt
- 1 tsp. dried thyme
- 1 tsp. minced garlic (from 1 clove)
- 1 tsp. black pepper
- 1 cup pecan halves

1. Rub pork loin all over with 3 tablespoons of the oil. Pulse brown sugar, sage, salt, thyme, garlic, and pepper in a food processor or blender until finely ground, 8 to 10 pulses. Drizzle in remaining 1 tablespoon oil, pulsing until mixture forms a thick paste, 8 to 10 pulses. Slather mixture all over pork. Wrap pork with plastic wrap, and refrigerate overnight (or 12 hours).
2. Preheat oven to 400°F. Pulse pecans in a food processor or blender until finely chopped, 10 to 12 pulses. Remove pork from refrigerator, and unwrap. Roll pork in chopped pecans, and place in a roasting pan. Tent with aluminum foil, being sure to completely cover pecans to prevent burning.
3. Roast in preheated oven 20 minutes. Reduce oven temperature to 350°F (do not remove pork from oven), and continue to roast until a thermometer inserted into thickest portion of meat registers 140°F, about 40 minutes, removing foil after 30 minutes. Remove from oven; let pork rest 10 minutes (temperature will rise to 145°F as pork stands). Slice and serve.

Any-Season Succotash

This colorful and easy side dish can be made year-round. Use frozen or fresh vegetables, depending on what's available.
ACTIVE 30 MIN. - TOTAL 30 MIN.
SERVES 6

- 6 large (10 oz. each) tomatoes, peeled, seeded, and coarsely chopped (about 3 cups) or 1 (28-oz.) can diced tomatoes and green chiles
- 1 Tbsp. canola oil
- 1½ cups chopped yellow onion (from 1 medium [9-oz.] onion)
- 1 fresh habanero chile, seeded and minced (about 2 Tbsp.)
- 2 tsp. minced garlic (about 2 cloves)
- 1 lb. fresh or frozen okra, trimmed and cut into ½-inch rounds
- 2 cups fresh or frozen corn kernels
- 1 Tbsp. white wine vinegar
- 1 Tbsp. unsalted butter
- ¾ tsp. kosher salt
- ½ tsp. black pepper

1. If using canned tomatoes, drain into a large bowl and reserve ¾ cup liquid.
2. Heat oil in a large cast-iron skillet over medium–high. Add onion; cook, stirring occasionally, until softened, about 4 minutes. Add habanero and garlic; cook, stirring constantly, until fragrant, about 1 minute. Add okra and corn; cook, stirring occasionally, until starting to blister, about 6 minutes. Stir in chopped tomatoes (or canned tomatoes with reserved ¾ cup liquid); cook, stirring occasionally, until thickened, about 4 minutes.
3. Add vinegar, butter, salt, and black pepper, stirring until butter melts.

Merry Mocktails

Austin bar owner Chris Marshall holds the booze on these buzz worthy seasonal sippers

Berry Juniper Fizz

ACTIVE 5 MIN. - TOTAL 5 MIN.
SERVES 1

- ¼ cup refrigerated pomegranate juice
- 2 Tbsp. Juniper Syrup (recipe follows)
- 1 Tbsp. fresh orange juice
- 2 Tbsp. (1 oz.) nonalcoholic gin alternative (optional)
  Ice
- ¼ cup (2 oz.) chilled nonalcoholic cranberry-flavor sparkling beverage
- 1 (4- x 1-inch) orange peel strip
  Fresh cranberries

Combine pomegranate juice, Juniper Syrup, orange juice, and (if using) gin alternative in a cocktail shaker filled with ice. Shake vigorously until cold and frothy, about 30 seconds. Strain into a coupe glass; top with cranberry-flavor sparkling beverage. Garnish with orange peel strip and cranberries.

Juniper Syrup

ACTIVE 5 MIN. - TOTAL 35 MIN.
MAKES 1½ CUPS

Bring 1 cup **granulated sugar** and 1 cup **water** to a simmer in a small saucepan over medium, stirring occasionally, until sugar is dissolved, about 1 minute. Remove from heat; stir in 2 Tbsp. crushed **dried juniper berries**; cool to room temperature, about 30 minutes. Pour through a fine-mesh strainer into a glass or jar, discarding berries. Store syrup in an airtight glass jar in refrigerator for up to 1 month.

Rosemary and Ginger Mule

ACTIVE 5 MIN. - TOTAL 5 MIN.
MAKES 1

- 1 (7½-oz.) can ginger beer
- 2 Tbsp. Rosemary Syrup (recipe follows)
- 1 Tbsp. fresh lime juice
  Ice
  Fresh rosemary sprig
  Fresh lime wheel

Stir together ginger beer, Rosemary Syrup, and lime juice in a copper mug filled with ice until mug is frosty, about 30 seconds. Lightly smack rosemary sprig against palm to release natural oils. Garnish with rosemary and lime wheel.

Rosemary Syrup

ACTIVE 5 MIN. - TOTAL 35 MIN.
MAKES 1½ CUPS

Bring 1 cup **granulated sugar**, 1 cup **water**, and 1 cup loosely packed fresh **rosemary sprigs** to a boil in a small saucepan over medium-high, stirring occasionally. Boil, stirring occasionally, until sugar is dissolved, about 1 minute. Remove from heat, cover, and steep 30 minutes. Pour through a fine-mesh strainer into a glass or jar, discarding rosemary. Store in an airtight glass jar in refrigerator for up to 3 weeks.

Comfort and Joy

ACTIVE 5 MIN. - TOTAL 5 MIN.
SERVES 1

- 1 cup unfiltered mulled apple cider
- 3 Tbsp. (1½ oz.) nonalcoholic whiskey alternative
- 2 Tbsp. honey or pure maple syrup
- 1 Tbsp. fresh lemon juice
  Ice (optional)
  Cinnamon stick or lemon wheel

To serve chilled: Combine cider, whiskey alternative, honey, and lemon juice in a cocktail shaker filled with ice; shake vigorously until chilled, 30 seconds. Strain into a highball glass filled with ice; garnish with cinnamon stick or lemon wheel.

To serve warm: Heat cider and honey in a small saucepan over medium-high until gently simmering, stirring occasionally, about 2 minutes. Remove from heat; stir in lemon juice and whiskey alternative. Transfer to a mug. Garnish with cinnamon stick or lemon wheel.

BERRY JUNIPER FIZZ

Morning Glory

When served with coffee, this make–ahead spice cake is just the thing to eat while unwrapping presents

Christmas Morning Coffee Cake

ACTIVE 15 MIN. - TOTAL 1 HOUR, 50 MIN.
SERVES 12

CAKE

Baking spray with flour
- 3 cups all-purpose flour
- 1 tsp. kosher salt
- ½ tsp. baking powder
- ½ tsp. baking soda
- 2 cups granulated sugar
- 1 cup unsalted butter, softened
- 2 tsp. vanilla extract
- 4 large eggs
- 2 cups sour cream (from 1 [24-oz.] container)
- 1 cup dried tart cherries, chopped (from 1 [5-oz.] pkg.)

TOPPING

- ¾ cup shelled roasted, salted pistachios, chopped
- ½ cup all-purpose flour
- ½ cup firmly packed light brown sugar
- 1 tsp. ground cinnamon
- ½ tsp. fresh ground nutmeg
- ¼ tsp. kosher salt
- ⅓ cup unsalted butter, melted
- 1 cup powdered sugar
- 5 Tbsp. heavy cream

1. Preheat oven to 325°F. Grease a 10-inch tube pan with baking spray.
2. Prepare the Cake: Whisk together flour, salt, baking powder, and baking soda in a bowl. Beat together sugar and butter on medium-high speed with a stand mixer fitted with the paddle attachment until light and fluffy, about 4 minutes. With mixer on low speed, add vanilla and eggs, 1 at a time, beating well after each addition. Add flour mixture and sour cream alternately to butter mixture, beginning and ending with flour mixture. Fold in dried cherries. Pour batter into tube pan.

3. Prepare the Topping: Stir together pistachios, flour, brown sugar, cinnamon, nutmeg, and salt. Stir in butter. Sprinkle over batter.
4. Bake in preheated oven until a wooden pick inserted in center comes out clean, 65 to 70 minutes. Cool in pan 30 minutes. Remove from pan; place streusel-side up on a platter. Whisk together powdered sugar and cream until smooth. Drizzle over cake.

QUICK TIP
Trade the pistachios for pecans or walnuts, or leave the nuts out if you prefer.

Tasty Traditions

Hey Y'all host Ivy Odom celebrates the holidays with a delicious mix of old and new recipes

DURING THE MONTH of December, my kitchen never closes. From family gatherings to cookie exchanges with friends, I host and attend more parties than at any other time of year. Like most people, I have my tried-and-true Christmas favorites that always make a comeback. Some are intensive baking projects like intricate iced cookies or fancy cakes, and others are quick, crowd-pleasing dishes that I can throw together at a moment's notice. While these recipes will remain staples for me during the holidays, I still find myself looking for easy new meals to serve to hungry houseguests.

This recipe for Slow-Cooker Short Ribs with Pork Rind Gremolata checks every box for my dinner party menu. It's a fresh take on a comforting classic that looks impressive without being too fussy. And best of all, it's made in a slow cooker, which gives me plenty of time to entertain without standing over a stove. It can even be made a day or two in advance.

Even though good food is always at the center of every Southern holiday gathering, it's getting to spend extra time with the ones we love that matters most.

Slow-Cooker Short Ribs with Pork Rind Gremolata

ACTIVE 35 MIN. - TOTAL 35 MIN., PLUS 7 HOURS SLOW-COOKING

SERVES 4

- 3 lb. beef chuck short ribs (about 8 [7-oz.] short ribs)
- 1 tsp. black pepper
- 2¾ tsp. kosher salt, divided
- 2 Tbsp. canola oil
- 4 cups sliced yellow onions (from 2 medium onions)
- 1½ cups beef stock
- 1 tsp. grated orange zest, plus ½ cup fresh juice (from 1 large orange)
- 1 (2-inch) piece fresh ginger, unpeeled and sliced
- 1 garlic head, halved crosswise and loose, papery skins discarded
- 1 Tbsp. cornstarch
- 1 Tbsp. warm water
- ½ cup crumbled pork rinds (from about 6 pork rinds)
- 2 Tbsp. chopped fresh flat-leaf parsley
  Hot cooked grits or polenta, for serving

1. Sprinkle ribs evenly with pepper and 2 teaspoons of the salt. Heat oil in a large (12-inch) cast-iron skillet over high. When oil is very hot, add ribs to skillet, working in batches if needed. Cook until well browned on all sides, about 10 minutes. Transfer ribs, bone-sides up, to a 5- or 6-quart slow cooker.
2. Reduce heat under skillet to medium-high. Add onions and ½ teaspoon of the salt to skillet, and cook, stirring often, until softened, about 8 minutes. Using a slotted spoon, transfer onions to slow cooker; discard drippings in skillet. Add beef stock, orange juice, ginger, and garlic to slow cooker. Cover and cook on LOW until meat is very tender and falling off the bones, about 7 hours.

3. Remove ribs from slow cooker, and set aside. Pour remaining mixture in slow cooker through a fine-mesh strainer into a medium saucepan; discard solids. Cook liquid in pan over medium-high until reduced by half (about 1 cup), 10 to 12 minutes. Stir together cornstarch and warm water in a small bowl; whisk into liquid in pan, and cook until sauce simmers, 2 to 3 minutes. Remove from heat.
4. Stir together pork rinds, parsley, orange zest, and remaining ¼ teaspoon salt in a small bowl. Spoon sauce onto a plate, and place ribs on sauce. Garnish with pork rind mixture, and serve with grits.

The Case for Crab Cake

Senior Food Editor Lisa Cericola has made seafood an annual tradition, and she might convince you to do it too

EVERY HOLIDAY SPREAD needs a grand centerpiece. Usually it takes the form of a massive roast or a shiny glazed ham. These impressive (and often expensive) proteins are a treat–it's not every day that you sit down to a prime rib supper–which is why they're seasonal mainstays. At my house, though, it's crab cakes that bring everyone to the table.

I'm a Florida native, so it's not that surprising that I'd choose seafood for Christmas dinner over beef or pork. My Italian roots may also play a part, though my family is so small that we've never been able to justify a Feast of the Seven Fishes celebration. (Way too many leftovers.)

There are many reasons why I love crab cakes: You can assemble them ahead, and dress them up with sauces, and they pair well with just about any side dish. You don't have to take their temperature, they won't smoke up your kitchen, and you don't have to go through that nerve-racking internal debate over whether to carve them in the kitchen or at the table. They feel just as special as any large cut of meat and require way less angst.

I've learned a few things about them over the years. The best ones are made with a mix of fresh-picked jumbo lump and regular lump crab. Don't bother with the stuff in cans–it's Christmas, after all. These two types work together to form patties that hold their shape and still have decadent chunks of seafood throughout. Keep the flavorings simple. You've paid good money for that crab, so let its delicate sweetness shine. Cook the patties in a mixture of butter and olive oil. (Again, it's a holiday.)

My last piece of advice is to make a few extra, if you can, and hide them in the back of the fridge. That way, you can enjoy crab cakes topped with poached eggs for breakfast the next morning or inside a soft, squishy potato bun for lunch. Consider it a Christmas gift to yourself.

Christmas Crab Cakes

(Photo, page 6)
ACTIVE 25 MIN. - TOTAL 25 MIN.,
PLUS 1 HOUR CHILLING
SERVES 10

- 12 oz. fresh jumbo lump crabmeat, drained and picked over
- 12 oz. fresh lump crabmeat, drained and picked over
- 1¼ cups panko breadcrumbs
- 2 large eggs, beaten
- 3 Tbsp. mayonnaise
- 1 tsp. Dijon mustard
- 1 tsp. Worcestershire sauce
- ¼ tsp. salt
- ¼ tsp. black pepper
- 1 Tbsp. chopped fresh flat-leaf parsley, plus more for garnish
- 1 Tbsp. grated lemon zest, plus 2 tsp. fresh juice (from 1 lemon)
- 2 Tbsp. butter
- 2 Tbsp. olive oil
- Herbed Crème Fraîche (recipe follows)
- Spicy Pepper Sauce (recipe follows)
- Creamy Dijonnaise (recipe follows)

1. Combine crab, panko, eggs, mayonnaise, mustard, Worcestershire sauce, salt, pepper, parsley, and lemon zest and juice in a large bowl. Using your hands or a rubber spatula, gently fold the ingredients until combined, being careful not to break up the crab. Cover and chill at least 1 hour or up to overnight.
2. Preheat oven to 200°F. Place a wire rack inside a large rimmed baking sheet; set aside.
3. Heat butter and oil in a large nonstick skillet over medium. Gently form the chilled crab mixture into 10 (2-inch) balls. Do not squeeze mixture. Place balls in skillet in batches. Do not overcrowd the pan. Cook until golden brown on one side, about 4 minutes. Flatten slightly with a spatula before gently flipping over; cook until golden brown, about 5 minutes. Transfer cooked crab cakes to the prepared rack, and place in preheated oven to keep warm. Repeat procedure with remaining crab mixture.
4. Transfer hot crab cakes to a serving plate; sprinkle with additional parsley. Serve with desired sauces.

Herbed Crème Fraîche

ACTIVE 5 MIN. - TOTAL 5 MIN.
MAKES 1¼ CUPS

Stir together 1 cup **crème fraîche**, 1 Tbsp. chopped fresh **parsley**, 1 Tbsp. fresh **lemon juice**, 2 tsp. chopped fresh **dill**, 2 tsp. chopped fresh **tarragon**, 1 tsp. minced **scallion** (light green part only), and ¼ tsp. **kosher salt** in a bowl until combined. Cover; chill 30 minutes before serving.

Spicy Pepper Sauce

ACTIVE 5 MIN. - TOTAL 5 MIN.
MAKES 1½ CUPS

Combine 1 drained (7.5-oz.) jar **roasted red peppers**, 1 tsp. **hot sauce**, 1 tsp. fresh **lemon juice**, 1 tsp. **Worcestershire** sauce, ¼ tsp. **kosher salt**, and 1 small smashed **garlic** clove in a food processor. Process until smooth, 1 minute. Transfer to a bowl; cover. Chill 30 minutes before serving.

Creamy Dijonnaise

ACTIVE 5 MIN. - TOTAL 5 MIN.
MAKES 1¼ CUPS

Stir together ½ cup **mayonnaise,** ½ cup **sour cream,** 1 Tbsp. **country-style Dijon** mustard, 1 tsp. **Dijon** mustard, and ¼ tsp. **kosher salt** in a bowl. Transfer to a bowl. Cover; chill 30 minutes before serving.

SWEET SPIN-OFFS

1.
LEMON-ROSEMARY SQUARES
Add 4 tsp. **lemon zest** and 2 tsp. minced **fresh rosemary** to dough. Cut chilled dough into 2½-inch squares using a fluted cutter. Bake as directed.

2.
PISTACHIO THUMBPRINTS
Form chilled dough into 1 Tbsp. balls; roll in chopped **pistachios.** Indent centers with thumb; fill each with ½ tsp. **raspberry jam.** Chill 30 minutes. Bake 12 to 15 minutes.

3.
SPICED RAISIN PINWHEELS
Roll chilled dough into a 10- x 13-inch rectangle. Combine ⅓ cup each **brown sugar** and **chopped walnuts** and **raisins;** 2 Tbsp. melted **butter;** and 2 tsp. **cinnamon.** Sprinkle over dough. Roll tightly into a log. Wrap; chill 1 hour. Slice ⅓ inch thick. Bake 12 to 15 minutes.

4.
CHOCOLATE-TAHINI CRISPS
Replace ¼ cup of the butter with ¼ cup **tahini;** add 3 Tbsp. **dark cocoa** to dough. Shape chilled dough into a log; roll in **sesame seeds.** Wrap; chill 1 hour. Slice ¼ inch thick. Bake as directed.

5.
CRAN-ORANGE SHORTBREAD
Add 2 tsp. **orange zest,** ⅓ cup chopped **dried cranberries,** and ¼ cup **cornstarch** to dough. Roll chilled dough into a ½-inch-thick square; cut into 3-inch rectangles. Bake 18 minutes. Dip cooled cookies into melted **white chocolate;** top with chopped **dried cranberries.**

Make Some Dough
Get your cookie tins ready: This easy recipe can make five different treats

All-Purpose Cookie Dough
ACTIVE 30 MIN. - TOTAL 45 MIN., PLUS 2 HOURS, 15 MIN. CHILLING
MAKES ABOUT 24 COOKIES

Beat 1 cup softened **butter** and ¾ cup granulated **sugar** with an electric mixer on medium speed until light and fluffy. Beat in 2 large **eggs** and 1 tsp. **vanilla extract.** Set aside. Combine 2½ cups all-purpose **flour** and ½ tsp. each **baking powder** and **salt;** gradually add to butter mixture, beating on low until combined. Shape dough into a disk; wrap in plastic wrap. Chill 2 hours. Roll dough on a floured surface to ¼-inch thickness; cut cookies using a 2½-inch round cutter, rerolling scraps as needed. Place on parchment-lined baking sheets; chill 15 minutes. Bake at 350°F for 10 to 12 minutes.

"Before you bake cutout cookies, pop them in the refrigerator for 30 minutes. Chilling the dough helps it hold its shape when baked."

Jasmine Smith,
Test Kitchen professional

Our Favorite Appetizer Recipes

Whether you're bringing a dish to a party or hosting a party yourself, this selection of tempting nibbles, hearty dips, delicious spreads, savory sliders, and mouthwatering wings offers up fare for celebrating. Our picks include Loaded Brisket Nachos (page 343), Spicy-Sweet Pecans (page 348), Warm Turnip Green Dip (page 335), Simple Blue Cheese Spread (page 338), Nashville Hot Chicken Sliders (page 344), and Grilled Salt-and-Pepper Chicken Wings (page 340). Complete an appetizer buffet with a refreshing glass of punch, lemonade, or sweet tea.

Dips & Spreads

Baked Vidalia Onion Dip

ACTIVE 15 MIN. - TOTAL 50 MIN.

MAKES 6 CUPS

- 2 Tbsp. butter or margarine
- 3 large Vidalia onions, coarsely chopped
- 8 oz. Swiss cheese, shredded (1½ cups)
- 2 cups mayonnaise
- 1 (8-oz.) can sliced water chestnuts, drained and chopped
- ¼ cup dry white wine
- 1 garlic clove, minced
- ½ tsp. hot sauce
  Tortilla chips and/or crackers, for serving

1. Preheat oven to 375°F. Melt butter in a large skillet over medium-high; add onion. Cook, stirring occasionally, until onion is tender, about 10 minutes.
2. Stir together shredded cheese, mayonnaise, water chestnuts, wine, garlic, and hot sauce in a large bowl; stir in onion. Spoon mixture into a lightly greased 2-quart baking dish.
3. Bake in preheated oven until center is hot and edges are bubbly, about 25 minutes. Let stand 10 minutes. Serve with tortilla chips and/or crackers.

Warm Turnip Green Dip

ACTIVE 35 MIN. - TOTAL 40 MIN.

MAKES 4 CUPS

- 5 bacon slices, chopped
- ½ medium yellow onion, chopped
- 2 garlic cloves, chopped
- ¼ cup dry white wine
- 1 (16-oz.) pkg. frozen chopped turnip greens, thawed
- 12 oz. cream cheese, cut into pieces
- 1 (8-oz.) container sour cream
- ½ tsp. crushed red pepper
- ¼ tsp. salt
- ¾ cup freshly grated Parmesan cheese
  Crushed red pepper, for garnish (optional)
  Crackers, for serving

1. Preheat oven to broil. Cook bacon in a Dutch oven over medium-high until crisp, 5 to 6 minutes. Transfer bacon to paper towels; reserve 1 tablespoon drippings in Dutch oven.
2. Cook onion and garlic in hot drippings until softened, 3 to 4 minutes. Add wine, and cook 1 to 2 minutes, stirring to loosen bits from bottom of Dutch oven. Stir in turnip greens, cream cheese, sour cream, crushed red pepper, salt, and ½ cup of the Parmesan cheese. Cook, stirring often, until cream cheese is melted and mixture is heated through, 6 to 8 minutes. Transfer to a lightly greased broiler-safe 1½-quart baking

dish. Sprinkle with remaining ¼ cup Parmesan cheese.
3. Broil about 6 inches from heat 4 to 5 minutes or until cheese is lightly browned. Sprinkle with bacon. Sprinkle with crushed red pepper, if desired. Serve with crackers.
Note: To make ahead, prepare recipe as directed through Step 2. Cover and chill up to 8 hours. Bake, covered, at 350°F for 30 minutes or until heated through. Uncover; continue with recipe as directed in Step 3.

Layered Crabmeat Spread

ACTIVE 20 MIN. - TOTAL 40 MIN.

MAKES 12 TO 15 SERVINGS

- 1 (8-oz.) pkg. cream cheese, softened
- 2 Tbsp. lemon juice
- 1 Tbsp. mayonnaise
- ½ tsp. seasoned salt
- ½ tsp. lemon pepper
- ¼ tsp. Worcestershire sauce
- ¾ cup cocktail sauce
- 1 (16-oz.) container lump crabmeat, drained
- 8 oz. Monterey Jack cheese, shredded (2 cups)
- 3 scallions, chopped
- ½ green bell pepper, chopped
- ½ cup sliced ripe olives
  Crackers and/or cut-up vegetables, for serving

Recipe continued on page 336

Recipe continued from page 335

1. Beat cream cheese on medium speed with an electric mixer until smooth. Add lemon juice, mayonnaise, seasoned salt, lemon pepper, and Worcestershire, beating until blended. Spoon mixture into a 9-inch serving dish. Cover and chill at least 20 minutes.

2. Spread cocktail sauce evenly over cream cheese mixture. Top with crabmeat; sprinkle with cheese, scallions, bell pepper, and ripe olives. Serve with crackers and vegetables.

Hot Spinach-Artichoke Dip

ACTIVE 15 MIN. - TOTAL 45 MIN.
MAKES 8 SERVINGS

- 1 cup freshly grated Parmesan cheese
- 1 cup reduced-fat sour cream
- ½ cup mayonnaise
- 4 scallions, sliced
- 3 Tbsp. fresh lemon juice
- 1 garlic clove, pressed
- 1¼ cups (5 oz.) shredded pepper Jack cheese
- 1 (10-oz.) pkg. frozen chopped spinach, thawed and well drained
- 1 (14-oz.) can artichoke hearts, drained and chopped
  Freshly ground black pepper
  Crackers and/or cut-up vegetables, for serving

1. Preheat oven to 350°F. Stir together first 6 ingredients and 1 cup of the pepper Jack cheese. Fold in spinach and artichokes. Spoon into a lightly greased 1-quart baking dish. Sprinkle with remaining ¼ cup pepper Jack cheese.

2. Bake in preheated oven 30 minutes or until center is hot and edges are bubbly. Sprinkle with freshly ground pepper to taste. Serve with crackers and/or vegetables.

Hot Spinach-Artichoke Dip with Crab: Increase mayonnaise to 1 cup and Parmesan cheese to 1¼ cups. Prepare recipe as directed in Step 1, folding in 1 pound fresh jumbo lump crabmeat, drained and picked, with spinach and artichokes. Spoon into a 2-quart baking dish. Bake at 350°F for 40 minutes or until center is hot and edges are bubbly.

Bacon-Leek Dip

ACTIVE 35 MIN. - TOTAL 1 HOUR, 35 MIN.
MAKES 2½ CUPS

- 1 large leek
- 6 bacon slices
- 1 large yellow onion, minced
- 1 (8-oz.) pkg. cream cheese, softened
- 1 cup sour cream
- ½ tsp. salt
- 1 (2-lb.) acorn squash
  Assorted multigrain and vegetable chips
  Chopped fresh chives, for garnish

1. Remove and discard root ends and dark green top of leek. Cut in half lengthwise and rinse thoroughly under cold running water to remove grit and sand. Thinly slice leek.

2. Cook bacon in a large skillet over medium-high 6 to 8 minutes or until crisp; remove bacon and drain on paper towels, reserving 1 tablespoon drippings in skillet. Crumble bacon.

3. Sauté onion and leek in hot drippings 15 minutes or until tender and golden. Stir together onion mixture, bacon, cream cheese, sour cream, and salt. Cover and chill 1 hour.

4. Cut about ½ to 1 inch from side of squash; remove and discard seeds.

5. Heat a small skillet over medium-high. Place squash, cut-side down, in skillet and cook 3 to 5 minutes or until cut side is golden brown and caramelized. Serve dip in squash with assorted chips. Garnish, if desired.

Bacon-Onion Dip

ACTIVE 10 MIN. - TOTAL 10 MIN.
MAKES 1¾ CUPS

- 1 (8-oz.) container sour cream
- ½ cup cooked and crumbled bacon
- 2 Tbsp. sliced scallion
- 3 Tbsp. buttermilk
- 1 Tbsp. horseradish
- 2 tsp. fresh lemon juice
- ¼ tsp. black pepper
- ½ tsp. salt
  Chopped fresh chives, for garnish (optional)
  Freshly ground black pepper, for garnish (optional)
  Crackers, torn bread, or cut-up vegetables, for serving

Stir together the first 8 ingredients. Cover and chill until ready to serve or up to 24 hours. Garnish, if desired. Serve with crackers, bread, or vegetables

Blue Cheese-Bacon-Onion Dip: Fold 1 (4-ounce) package crumbled blue cheese into dip.

Crab and Corn Dip

ACTIVE 10 MIN. - TOTAL 25 MIN.
SERVES 8

- 1½ (8-oz.) pkg. cream cheese, softened
- ½ cup sour cream
- ¼ cup mayonnaise
- 2 tsp. Dijon mustard
- 1 tsp. lemon zest, plus 1 Tbsp. fresh juice (from 1 lemon)
- 1 tsp. kosher salt
- ½ tsp. black pepper
- 1 lb. fresh jumbo lump crabmeat, drained and picked over
- 1 cup fresh corn kernels (from 2 ears)
- 2 Tbsp. chopped fresh chives, plus more for garnish (optional)
- 2 Tbsp. chopped fresh flat-leaf parsley
- 1 Tbsp. chopped fresh tarragon
- 1 cup panko (Japanese-style breadcrumbs)
- ¼ cup (2 oz.) unsalted butter, melted
  Buttery crackers, for serving

1. Preheat oven to 425°F. Stir together cream cheese, sour cream, mayonnaise, mustard, lemon zest and juice, salt, and pepper in a large bowl until combined. Fold crabmeat, corn, chives, parsley, and tarragon into the cream cheese mixture. Spoon into a 2-quart baking dish.

2. Stir together panko and butter in a small bowl; sprinkle over dip. Bake in preheated oven until bubbly and golden, about 15 minutes. Garnish with additional chives, if desired. Serve with crackers.

Sausage-Cheese Dip

ACTIVE 15 MIN. - TOTAL 1 HOUR, 5 MIN.
SERVES 10

- 1 lb. hickory-smoked sausage, chopped
- ½ cup thinly sliced scallions (about 6)
- 24 oz. processed cheese (such as Velveeta)
- 1 (10-oz.) can diced tomatoes and green chiles (such as Ro-Tel)
  Corn chips, for serving

1. Cook sausage in a large skillet over medium-high, stirring often, until browned, 8 to 10 minutes. Add scallions and cook, stirring often, until softened, about 2 minutes. Drain any fat.
2. Place sausage mixture, cheese, and diced tomatoes in a 3½- or 4-quart slow cooker; stir. Cover and cook on HIGH until cheese is melted and dip is bubbly, 45 to 50 minutes. Serve with corn chips.

Sloppy Joe Dip

ACTIVE 30 MIN. - TOTAL 45 MIN.
SERVES 12

- 2 tsp. vegetable oil
- 1½ lb. lean ground beef
- ½ cup chopped yellow onion (from 1 onion)
- 2 garlic cloves, minced (about 1 Tbsp.)
- 1 (15-oz.) can fire-roasted diced tomatoes
- ¼ cup ketchup
- 2 Tbsp. Dijon mustard
- 2 Tbsp. dark brown sugar
- 2 Tbsp. tomato paste
- 1 Tbsp. Worcestershire sauce
- 1 Tbsp. white vinegar
- 1 tsp. paprika
- 1 tsp. crushed red pepper
- ½ tsp. kosher salt
- 1 (8-oz.) pkg. shredded cheddar cheese (about 2 cups)
  Corn chips, for serving

1. Preheat oven to 400°F. Heat oil in a large skillet over medium-high. Add beef and cook, stirring often, until meat is no longer pink, 5 to 7 minutes. Add onion and garlic; cook until softened, about 3 minutes. Stir in tomatoes, ketchup, Dijon, brown sugar, tomato paste, Worcestershire, vinegar, paprika, crushed red pepper, and salt.
2. Reduce heat to low and simmer, stirring occasionally, until the sauce is slightly thickened, about 15 minutes. Stir in 1 cup of the cheese.
3. Spoon mixture into a 2-quart baking dish. Sprinkle with remaining 1 cup cheese. Bake in preheated oven until cheese is melted, about 15 minutes. Serve with corn chips.

Cheesy Vidalia Onion Dip

This hot dip is comfort food for cold game days. The onions are caramelized in the slow cooker, which heightens sweetness, before mixing with the cheeses.

ACTIVE 10 MIN. - TOTAL 6 HOURS, 30 MIN.
MAKES 6 CUPS

- 8 cups chopped sweet onions (such as Vidalia) (about 4 large onions)
- 2 Tbsp. apple cider vinegar
- 2 Tbsp. unsalted butter
- ¾ tsp. kosher salt
- ½ tsp. black pepper
- 1 (8-oz.) pkg. cream cheese, cut into cubes
- 4 oz. Gruyère cheese, shredded (about 1 cup)
- 4 oz. white cheddar cheese, shredded (about 1 cup)
- 2 Tbsp. finely chopped fresh chives, plus more for garnish
  Kettle-cooked potato chips, pretzels, and/or crudités, for serving

1. Combine onions, vinegar, butter, salt, and pepper in a 3½- or 4-quart slow cooker coated with cooking spray. Cover and cook on LOW until onions are tender and golden, about 6 hours. Drain and discard liquid.
2. Stir cream cheese, Gruyère and cheddar cheeses, and chives into onions in slow cooker. Cook, covered, on LOW until melted, stirring occasionally, about 20 minutes. Serve warm with chips, pretzels, and/or crudités.

Black-Eyed Pea Dip

Prepare this dip ahead and chill. When ready to serve, briefly microwave the dip until heated through.

ACTIVE 15 MIN. - TOTAL 15 MIN.
MAKES 12 TO 15 SERVINGS

- ¼ cup butter
- 2 (15.8-oz.) cans black-eyed peas, undrained
- 1 cup (4 oz.) shredded cheddar cheese
- ½ cup (2 oz.) shredded mozzarella cheese
- 2 Tbsp. blackened seasoning
- 3 scallions, chopped
- ¼ cup chopped green bell pepper
- ¾ cup chopped cooked ham
  Tortilla chips, for serving

1. Microwave butter in a 2-quart microwave-safe bowl on HIGH 30 seconds or until melted. Stir in peas and next 5 ingredients; microwave on HIGH 7 to 8 minutes or until cheese is melted, stirring every 2 minutes.
2. Stir ham into dip; spoon into a serving dish. Serve warm with tortilla chips.

Goat Cheese Spread

ACTIVE 30 MIN. - TOTAL 30 MIN., PLUS 8 HOURS CHILLING
MAKES 12 TO 16 SERVINGS

- 2 (8-oz.) pkg. cream cheese, softened
- 8 oz. goat cheese
- 2 garlic cloves, minced
- 4 tsp. chopped fresh oregano or 1¼ tsp. dried oregano
- ⅛ tsp. freshly ground black pepper
- ¼ cup basil pesto
- ½ cup dried tomatoes in oil, drained and chopped
  Dried tomato slivers and fresh oregano sprigs, for garnish
  Sliced French bread or crackers, for serving

1. Process cream cheese, goat cheese, garlic, oregano, and pepper in a food processor until smooth. Spread one-third of the cheese mixture in the bottom of an 8- x 4-inch loaf pan lined with plastic wrap. Spread pesto on cheese mixture. Spread another one-third of the cheese mixture on pesto. Sprinkle with dried tomatoes, then spread with remaining cheese mixture. Cover and chill 8 hours.
2. Invert spread onto a serving plate; discard plastic wrap. For the garnish, gently press tomato slivers and fresh oregano sprigs in a decorative pattern on top. Serve with bread or crackers.

Layered Cheese Torta

Layer the torta according to directions for three even ribbons of color. Chill the torta well to ensure its shape.

ACTIVE 25 MIN. - TOTAL 25 MIN., PLUS 9 HOURS CHILLING
MAKES 3 CUPS

- 1 (8-oz.) pkg. cream cheese, softened
- ¼ cup crumbled blue cheese
- 1 (8-oz.) can crushed pineapple, drained

Recipe continued on page 338

Recipe continued from page 337

⅛ tsp. ground ginger

½ cup chopped pecans

1 (3-oz.) pkg. cream cheese, softened

⅓ cup milk

8 oz. cheddar cheese, shredded (2 cups)

6 bacon slices, cooked and crumbled

1 tsp. grated onion

¼ tsp. hot sauce

Chopped pecans and fresh parsley sprigs, for garnish (optional)

Crackers, for serving

1. Combine the 8-ounce package cream cheese, the blue cheese, pineapple, and ginger in a bowl. Beat with an electric mixer on medium speed until blended; stir in pecans.
2. Line a lightly greased 7⅜- x 3⅝-inch loaf pan with plastic wrap, allowing edges to extend over sides of pan. Spread one-third of the blue cheese mixture into mold; chill 1 hour.
3. Combine the 3-ounce package cream cheese and milk in a large bowl. Beat with an electric mixer on medium speed until blended. Add cheddar cheese, bacon, onion, and hot sauce, and stir until well combined. Spread over chilled blue cheese layer. Top with remaining two-thirds blue cheese mixture, spreading evenly. Cover with plastic wrap.
4. Chill at least 8 hours or up to 3 days. Unmold onto a serving platter. Remove and discard plastic wrap. Garnish, if desired. Serve with crackers.

Pimiento Cheese

ACTIVE 15 MIN. - TOTAL 15 MIN.
MAKES 4 CUPS

1¼ cups mayonnaise

1 (4-oz.) jar diced pimientos, drained

1 tsp. Worcestershire sauce

1 tsp. finely grated onion

¼ tsp. cayenne pepper

8 oz. extra-sharp cheddar cheese, finely shredded

8 oz. sharp cheddar cheese, shredded

Celery sticks or assorted crackers

Stir together mayonnaise, pimientos, Worcestershire, onion, and cayenne pepper in a large bowl. Stir in cheeses.

Cover and refrigerate up to 1 week. Serve with celery sticks or crackers.
Jalapeño Pimiento Cheese: Prepare recipe as directed, except add 2 jalapeño peppers, seeded and minced.
Cream Cheese-and-Olive Pimiento Cheese: Stir together ¾ cup mayonnaise, the pimientos, Worcestershire, onion, and cayenne pepper in a large bowl. Stir in 1 (8-ounce) package cream cheese, softened, and 1 (5¾-ounce) jar drained sliced pimiento-stuffed Spanish olives.
Pecan Pimiento Cheese: Prepare recipe as directed, stirring in ¾ cup toasted chopped pecans.

Simple Blue Cheese Spread

Fans of blue cheese will enjoy this three-ingredient spread.
ACTIVE 10 MIN. - TOTAL 10 MIN., PLUS 1 HOUR CHILLING
MAKES 1 CUP

1 (4-oz.) pkg. blue cheese

1 (3-oz.) pkg. cream cheese, softened

3 Tbsp. brandy

Crackers, pumpernickel or rye bread, and/or apple or pear slices, for serving

Crumble and mash blue cheese with a fork in a medium bowl. Add cream cheese; beat with an electric mixer on medium speed until smooth. Add brandy, and beat until mixture is blended. Cover and chill at least 1 hour or up to 4 hours. Serve with crackers, bread, or fruit slices.

Warm Nacho Dip

ACTIVE 20 MIN. - TOTAL 25 MIN.
MAKES 12 APPETIZER SERVINGS

2 (16-oz.) cans refried beans

1 (4.5-oz.) can chopped green chiles, drained

1 (1.25-oz.) pkg. taco seasoning

8 oz. Monterey Jack cheese with jalapeño peppers, shredded (2 cups)

1 (7.5-oz.) container avocado dip

1 (8-oz.) container sour cream

1 cup chopped tomato

6 scallions, thinly sliced

1 (4.5-oz.) can sliced ripe olives, drained

1. Preheat oven to 350°F. Stir together refried beans, chiles, and taco seasoning in a medium bowl. Spread mixture in a lightly greased 11- x 7-inch baking dish.
2. Bake 20 minutes or until heated through. Sprinkle with cheese; bake 5 minutes more or until cheese is melted.
3. Spread avocado dip over warm bean mixture; spread sour cream over avocado dip. Top with tomato, scallions, and olives. Serve warm with tortilla chips or corn chips.

Hot Appetizers

Broiled Tomatoes with Feta Cheese

ACTIVE 5 MIN. - TOTAL 8 MIN.
SERVES 6

6 plum tomatoes

Salt and black pepper, to taste

½ tsp. Italian seasoning

⅔ cup crumbled feta cheese

¼ cup Italian dressing

1. Cut tomatoes in half lengthwise, and place, cut-sides up, on a baking sheet. Sprinkle evenly with salt and pepper, Italian seasoning, and feta cheese. Drizzle evenly with Italian dressing.
2. Broil 3 inches from heat just until cheese starts to brown, 2 to 3 minutes.

Cocktail Meatballs

ACTIVE 40 MIN. - TOTAL 1 HOUR
MAKES 4 DOZEN

1½ lb. ground chuck

¼ cup seasoned breadcrumbs

2 tsp. prepared horseradish

2 garlic cloves, crushed

¾ cup tomato juice

2 tsp. kosher salt

¼ tsp. freshly ground black pepper

2 medium-size yellow onions, chopped (about 1½ cups), divided

2 Tbsp. butter

2 Tbsp. all-purpose flour

1½ cups beef broth

½ cup dry red wine

2 Tbsp. light brown sugar
2 Tbsp. ketchup
1 Tbsp. fresh lemon juice

1. Preheat oven to 450°F. Gently stir together ground chuck, breadcrumbs, horseradish, garlic, tomato juice, salt, pepper, and ¾ cup of the chopped onions. Shape into 1-inch balls; place in a lightly greased (with cooking spray) 13- x 9-inch baking dish. Bake 20 minutes. Remove from oven, and drain any fat.
2. Heat butter in a large skillet over medium; add remaining onions, and cook, stirring often, until tender, 4 to 6 minutes. Whisk in flour; cook, whisking constantly, 1 minute. Gradually whisk in broth and cook, whisking constantly, until smooth. Stir in wine, brown sugar, ketchup, and lemon juice. Reduce heat to low; cook, stirring often, 15 minutes. Add meatballs; simmer, stirring occasionally, until heated through, about 5 minutes.

Hot Roast Beef Party Sandwiches

ACTIVE 25 MIN. - TOTAL 50 MIN.
SERVES 12 TO 16

½ cup finely chopped walnuts
2 (9.25-oz.) pkg. dinner rolls
⅔ cup peach preserves
½ cup mustard-mayonnaise blend
¾ lb. thinly sliced deli roast beef, chopped
½ lb. thinly sliced Havarti cheese
Salt and black pepper, to taste (optional)

1. Preheat oven to 325°F. Heat walnuts in a small nonstick skillet over medium-low, stirring occasionally, 5 to 6 minutes or until lightly toasted.
2. Remove rolls from packages. (Do not separate rolls.) Cut rolls in half horizontally, creating 1 top and 1 bottom per package. Spread peach preserves on cut sides of top of rolls; sprinkle with walnuts. Spread mustard-mayonnaise blend on cut sides of bottom of rolls; top with beef and cheese. Sprinkle with salt and pepper, if desired. Cover with top halves of rolls, preserves sides down, and wrap in aluminum foil.
3. Bake in preheated oven until cheese is melted, 20 to 25 minutes. Slice into individual sandwiches.

Note: To make ahead, prepare recipe as directed through Step 2. Freeze up to 1 month. Thaw overnight in refrigerator; bake as directed in Step 3.

Okra Fritters

ACTIVE 25 MIN. - TOTAL 25 MIN., PLUS 45 MIN. CHILLING
SERVES 6

1 lb. fresh okra
2 cups buttermilk
1 cup self-rising cornmeal
1 cup self-rising flour
1 tsp. salt
¼ tsp. cayenne pepper
Vegetable oil
¼ cup bacon drippings

1. Cut off and discard tip and stem ends from okra; cut okra into ½-inch slices. Stir into buttermilk; cover and chill 45 minutes.
2. Combine cornmeal and next 3 ingredients in a bowl. Remove okra from buttermilk with a slotted spoon, and discard buttermilk. Dredge okra, in batches, in the cornmeal mixture.
3. Pour oil to a depth of 2 inches into a Dutch oven or cast-iron skillet; add bacon drippings, and heat to 375°F. Fry okra, in batches, 4 minutes or until golden; drain on paper towels.

Beer-Battered Pumpkin with Dipping Sauce

ACTIVE 40 MIN. - TOTAL 40 MIN.
SERVES 4 TO 6

Vegetable oil
1⅓ cups all-purpose flour
¼ cup cornstarch
1 Tbsp,. plus ½ tsp. kosher salt, divided, plus more to taste
1 (12-oz.) bottle cold light beer (such as Corona Light)
½ (3-lb.) sugar pumpkin, peeled, seeded, and cut into ½-inch-thick wedges
15 large fresh sage leaves
1 garlic clove, peeled
½ cup low-fat Greek yogurt
¼ cup buttermilk
¼ tsp. hot sauce (such as Tabasco)
¼ tsp. freshly ground black pepper

1. Pour oil to a depth of 1½ inches in a Dutch oven; heat over medium-high to 350°F.
2. Whisk together flour, cornstarch, and 1 tablespoon salt in a large bowl; whisk in beer. Dip pumpkin wedges in batter, allowing excess batter to drip off. (Pumpkin should be very lightly coated.)
3. Gently lower pumpkin into hot oil, using tongs. Fry pumpkin, in 3 batches, 3 to 4 minutes or until tender inside and light brown outside, turning once. Place fried pumpkin on a wire rack in a jelly-roll pan; season with salt. Repeat procedure with sage leaves, frying 1 minute on each side.
4. Place peeled garlic clove on a cutting board; smash garlic, using flat side of knife, to make a paste. Whisk together garlic, yogurt, buttermilk, hot sauce, black pepper, and remaining ½ teaspoon salt. Serve yogurt sauce with fried pumpkin and sage leaves.

Chicken-and-Black-Bean Chimichangas

ACTIVE 20 MIN. - TOTAL 20 MIN.
SERVES 4

1 lb. shredded deli-roasted chicken
1 (15-oz.) can black beans, drained and rinsed
1 (4-oz.) can mild chopped green chiles
¼ cup salsa verde
½ tsp. kosher salt
¼ tsp. freshly ground black pepper
¼ cup chopped fresh cilantro
4 (10-inch) flour tortillas
1 cup (4 oz.) shredded Monterey Jack cheese
⅓ cup canola oil
Guacamole, sour cream, chopped tomatoes, for topping

1. Stir together the first 7 ingredients in a large bowl. Spoon chicken mixture among tortillas just below center of each tortilla. Sprinkle with cheese. Fold sides of tortilla over filling, and roll up.
2. Fry chimichangas, in 2 batches, in hot oil in a large skillet over medium-high until browned and crispy, 3 to 4 minutes on each side. Drain on paper towels. Serve with desired toppings.

Grilled Salt-and-Pepper Chicken Wings

Broiler option: Broil on a foil-lined jelly-roll pan 8 inches from heat 20 minutes or until done, turning halfway through.

ACTIVE 10 MIN. - TOTAL 35 MIN., NOT INCLUDING DRIZZLE

SERVES 6 TO 8

- 2 lb. chicken wings
- 2 Tbsp. olive oil
- 1½ tsp. kosher salt
- ½ tsp. black pepper
  Honey Drizzle (recipes follow)

Preheat a gas grill to medium-high (350°F to 400°F). Toss together wings and oil in a large bowl. Sprinkle with salt and pepper; toss to coat. Grill wings, covered, until skin is crisp and wings are cooked through, turning occasionally, 25 to 30 minutes. Toss with Honey Drizzle.

Cider Vinegar-Brown Butter Honey Drizzle

ACTIVE 10 MIN. - TOTAL 15 MIN.

MAKES ABOUT ¾ CUP

Cook ¼ cup **butter** in a saucepan over medium-high until browned and fragrant, about 5 minutes. Transfer to a small bowl; cool 5 minutes. Heat ½ cup **honey** and 1 Tbsp. **apple cider vinegar** in a saucepan over medium, stirring often, until heated through, about 2 minutes. Whisk in browned butter.

Horseradish-Honey Mustard Drizzle

ACTIVE 5 MIN. - TOTAL 5 MIN.

MAKES ABOUT ¾ CUP

Heat ½ cup **honey**, 3 Tbsp. prepared **horseradish**, and 2 Tbsp. **coarse-grain mustard** in a small saucepan over medium, stirring often, 2 minutes or until heated through.

Cracked Pepper-Rosemary Honey Drizzle

ACTIVE 5 MIN. - TOTAL 5 MIN.

MAKES ABOUT ½ CUP

Heat ½ cup **honey**, 2 Tbsp. **water**, 1 tsp. **cracked black pepper**, and 1 (3-inch) **fresh rosemary sprig** in a saucepan over medium, stirring often, 2 minutes or until heated through. Discard rosemary.

Chili-Lemon Honey Drizzle

ACTIVE 5 MIN. - TOTAL 5 MIN.

MAKES ABOUT 1 CUP

Heat ½ cup **honey**, ¼ cup bottled **chili sauce**, and 2 Tbsp. fresh **lemon juice** over medium, stirring often, 2 minutes or until heated through.

Party-Perfect Meatballs

ACTIVE 35 MIN. - TOTAL 50 MIN.

SERVES 20

- 1 cup pitted Kalamata olives
- ½ small red onion, coarsely chopped
- ¾ cup coarsely chopped fresh mint leaves
- ½ cup coarsely chopped fresh parsley
- 2 tsp. lemon zest
- ¾ cup panko (Japanese-style breadcrumbs)
- ½ cup ricotta cheese
- 2 large eggs
- 1½ tsp. kosher salt
- ½ tsp. freshly ground black pepper
- 1 lb. ground beef
- 1 lb. mild Italian sausage, casings removed
- 1 (6-oz.) can tomato paste
- 3 cups beef broth
- ⅓ cup hot pepper jelly

1. Preheat oven to 450°F. Pulse olives, onion, mint, parsley, and lemon zest in a food processor until chopped, 8 to 10 times. Stir together panko, ricotta, eggs, salt, pepper, ground beef, sausage, and olive mixture in a large bowl until well combined. Shape mixture into 1-inch balls, and place 1 inch apart on aluminum jelly-roll pans lined with foil.
2. Bake in preheated oven 12 minutes. Cool 5 minutes.
3. Meanwhile, heat a large saucepan over medium 2 minutes. Add tomato paste to dry pan; cook, stirring occasionally, until paste begins to brown and coat bottom of pan, about 3 minutes. Increase heat to high and add beef broth, stirring to loosen bits from bottom of pan. Whisk until smooth. Whisk in hot pepper jelly until combined. Reduce heat to low. Add cooked meatballs. Serve warm.
Note: Sauce may be refrigerated in an airtight container up to 3 days.

Make Ahead: Prepare meatballs through Step 2. Freeze in zip-top plastic freezer bags for up to 1 month. To reheat from frozen, pick up with Step 3 and warm the meatballs in the sauce over low. To serve, keep meatballs warm in a slow cooker, Dutch oven over low, or fondue pot.

Pork Tenderloin Sliders

ACTIVE 25 MIN. - TOTAL 55 MIN., NOT INCLUDING SAUCES

MAKES 20 SLIDERS

- 2 pork tenderloins (about 2½ lb.), trimmed
- 3 Tbsp. olive oil, divided
- 2 tsp. kosher salt
- 1 tsp. freshly ground black pepper
- ¼ cup firmly packed dark brown sugar
- 2 Tbsp. Dijon mustard
- 3 Tbsp. fresh thyme leaves
- 2 Tbsp. chopped fresh rosemary
- 20 slider buns or dinner rolls, split
  Italian-Style Salsa Verde, Blackberry-Honey Mustard Sauce, or Bacon-and-Sweet Onion Jam (recipes follow)

1. Preheat oven to 400°F. Rub tenderloins with 1 tablespoon of the oil, and sprinkle with salt and pepper. Stir together sugar, mustard, thyme, and rosemary; rub over tenderloins
2. Cook tenderloins in remaining 2 tablespoons hot oil in a skillet over medium-high, browning on all sides, about 5 minutes. Place tenderloins on a wire rack in a jelly-roll pan.
3. Bake in preheated oven until a meat thermometer inserted in thickest portion registers 145°F, about 15 minutes. Remove from oven. Let stand, covered, 5 minutes. Slice and serve on slider buns with sauces. Or wrap unsliced tenderloins in plastic wrap, and refrigerate up to 3 days.

Italian-Style Salsa Verde

ACTIVE 30 MIN. - TOTAL 1 HOUR, 5 MIN.

MAKES ABOUT 1 CUP

- 1 small jalapeño pepper
- 2 medium-size banana peppers
- ½ cup extra-virgin olive oil
- ⅓ cup finely chopped fresh flat-leaf parsley

4½ teaspoons chopped fresh chives
1 Tbsp. minced fresh oregano
2 garlic cloves, minced
1 tsp. kosher salt

1. Preheat broiler with oven rack
6 inches from heat. Broil jalapeño on a
small baking pan until blackened, 3 to
4 minutes on each side. Place blackened
jalapeño in a small bowl; cover with
plastic wrap and let stand 10 minutes.
Meanwhile, broil banana peppers just
until blistered and slightly softened, 1 to
2 minutes on each side. Cool banana
peppers completely (about 10 minutes);
chop. Peel jalapeño, then slice in
half, remove and discard seeds, and
finely chop.
2. Stir together oil, parsley, chives,
oregano, garlic, salt, and chopped
peppers in a small bowl. Cover and
let stand 30 minutes. Serve at room
temperature, or cover and refrigerate up
to 1 week.

Blackberry-Honey Mustard Sauce

ACTIVE 20 MIN. - TOTAL 1 HOUR, 20 MIN.
MAKES ABOUT 1¼ CUPS

⅓ cup sugar
1 (6-oz.) container fresh
   blackberries
¼ cup honey
1 Tbsp. dry mustard
3 Tbsp. Dijon mustard
2 Tbsp. fresh lemon juice
1 tsp. kosher salt
⅓ cup extra-virgin olive oil

1. Bring sugar and blackberries to a
boil in a small saucepan over medium-
high, stirring occasionally and mashing
berries with the back of a wooden
spoon. Reduce heat to medium. Simmer,
stirring often and mashing berries,
until slightly thickened, 2 to 3 minutes.
Remove from heat. Pour mixture
through a fine-mesh strainer into a
blender, pressing with spoon to release
juices; discard solids.
2. Add honey, mustards, lemon juice,
and salt to blender; process on low
20 seconds. Increase blender speed
to high, and process 30 seconds. With
blender running, add oil in a slow,
steady stream, processing until smooth.
Transfer sauce to a small bowl; cover
and chill 1 hour or up to 12 hours.

Bacon-and-Sweet Onion Jam

ACTIVE 35 MIN. - TOTAL 1 HOUR, 15 MIN.
MAKES 1½ CUPS

4 uncooked thick applewood-
  smoked bacon slices, chopped
1 Tbsp. butter
2 medium-size sweet onions,
  chopped
4 large shallots, chopped
½ cup balsamic vinegar
3 Tbsp. light brown sugar
2½ tsp. kosher salt
2 tsp. chopped fresh chives
2 tsp. chopped fresh thyme

1. Cook bacon in a medium skillet over
medium-low, stirring occasionally, until
crisp, 8 to 10 minutes. Remove bacon,
and drain on paper towels, reserving
drippings in skillet.
2. Add butter to drippings, and stir
until butter is melted. Increase heat to
medium; add onions, and cook, stirring
frequently, 10 to 12 minutes or until
tender. Add shallots, vinegar, sugar,
and salt; cook, stirring constantly,
1 to 2 minutes more or until sugar is
dissolved.
3. Reduce heat to low; cook, stirring
occasionally, until onions are very
tender and brown, 20 to 25 minutes.
Remove from heat; stir in chives, thyme,
and bacon. Cool completely (about
20 minutes), or refrigerate in an airtight
container up to 3 days.

Ham-and-Dijon Biscuits with Caramelized Onion Butter

ACTIVE 20 MIN. - TOTAL 20 MIN., PLUS 8 MIN.
PER BATCH
MAKES 4 DOZEN

9 cups all-purpose baking mix
2 cups milk
½ cup Dijon mustard
¼ cup honey
  Caramelized Onion Butter
  (recipe follows)
2 lb. boneless ham, cut into slivers

1. Preheat oven to 450°F. Make a well in
center of baking mix in a large bowl.
2. Whisk together milk, mustard, and
honey. Add milk mixture to baking mix,
stirring just until moistened.
3. Turn out soft dough onto a floured
surface; knead 3 or 4 times.

4. Roll dough, half at a time, to ½-inch
thickness; cut with a 2-inch round
cutter, and place on lightly greased
baking sheets. Reroll dough scraps and
cut more biscuits.
5. Bake in preheated oven 8 minutes
or until lightly browned. Split warm
biscuits. Spread with Caramelized Onion
Butter, and fill with slivers of ham. Cover
biscuits loosely with aluminum foil.
6. Reduce oven temperature to 350°F.
Bake biscuit sandwiches just until
heated through, 5 to 7 minutes.
Make Ahead: Place assembled biscuits
in an airtight container. Chill up to
8 hours or freeze up to 3 weeks. Thaw
frozen biscuits in refrigerator. To reheat,
place biscuits on baking sheets, and
cover loosely with aluminum foil. Bake
at 350°F until heated through, 10 to
12 minutes.

Caramelized Onion Butter

ACTIVE 5 MIN. - TOTAL 25 MIN.
MAKES 2½ CUPS

1¾ cups butter, softened and divided
2 large sweet onions, finely chopped
¼ cup firmly packed brown sugar
1 Tbsp. balsamic vinegar

Melt ¼ cup of the butter over medium-
high in a large skillet. Add onions and
brown sugar; cook, stirring often, until
a deep caramel color, 15 to 20 minutes.
Remove from heat; cool slightly. Stir
in remaining 1½ cups butter and
the vinegar.

Blue Cheese-Pecan Apples

ACTIVE 10 MIN. - TOTAL 20 MIN.
MAKES 6 SERVINGS

¼ cup chopped pecans
1 Gala apple, thinly sliced
1 Granny Smith apple, thinly sliced
1 (5-oz.) soft blue cheese wedge,
  rind removed
  Salt and black pepper, to taste
  Fresh parsley sprigs, for garnish
  (optional)

1. Preheat oven to 350°F. Bake pecans
in a single layer in a shallow pan until
toasted and fragrant, stirring halfway
through, 8 to 10 minutes. Increase oven
temperature to 425°F.

Recipe continued on page 342

Recipe continued from page 341

2. Arrange apples on a parchment-paper–lined baking sheet. Pinch blue cheese into small pieces; arrange on apples.

3. Bake at 425°F just until cheese is melted, 2 to 3 minutes. Sprinkle with pecans and season with salt and pepper to taste. Garnish, if desired.

Monster Meatball Sandwiches

ACTIVE 10 MIN. - TOTAL 40 MIN.

MAKES 16 SERVINGS

- 32 bite-size frozen meatballs
- 1 (9-oz.) jar mango chutney
- 1 cup chicken broth
- 16 fresh dinner rolls
- 1 (16-oz.) jar sweet-hot pickle sandwich relish

1. Stir together meatballs, chutney, and broth in a medium saucepan. Bring to a boil over medium-high; reduce heat to low and simmer, stirring occasionally, 25 to 30 minutes.

2. Cut rolls vertically through top, cutting to, but not through, bottom. Place 2 meatballs in each roll. Top with relish.

Make Ahead: Prepare meatballs as directed through Step 1. Store in an airtight container in refrigerator 3 to 4 days. To reheat, combine the meatballs and sauce in a medium saucepan and cook over low until meatballs are warmed through.

Mummy Dogs

ACTIVE 15 MIN. - TOTAL 35 MIN.

MAKES 12 SERVINGS

- 1 (11-oz.) can refrigerated breadstick dough
- 12 bun-length hot dogs

1. Preheat oven to 400°F. Unroll breadstick dough and separate into 12 strips at perforations. Gently stretch each strip to a length of 8 inches.

2. Wrap 1 dough strip lengthwise around each hot dog. Secure with wooden picks, if necessary. Lightly coat with cooking spray. Place on a lightly greased baking sheet.

3. Bake in preheated oven until golden brown, 15 minutes. Let stand 5 minutes. (If using wooden picks, remove before serving.)

Garlic Mummy Dogs: Substitute 1 (11-oz.) can refrigerated garlic breadstick dough. Prepare recipe as directed.

Parmesan-Garlic Mummy Dogs: Substitute 1 (11-oz.) can refrigerated Parmesan-garlic breadstick dough. Prepare recipe as directed.

Garlic-Herb Mummy Dogs: Substitute 1 (11-oz.) can refrigerated garlic-herb breadstick dough. Prepare recipe as directed.

Sweet Potato Squares with Lemon-Garlic Mayonnaise

Serve this appetizer warm or at room temperature. If you prefer warm, prepare the Lemon-Garlic Mayonnaise first.

ACTIVE 36 MIN. - TOTAL 1 HOUR, INCLUDING MAYONNAISE

MAKES 8 APPETIZER SERVINGS

- 2 lb. sweet potatoes, peeled and cut into 32 (1-inch) cubes
- 2 Tbsp. olive oil
- ¼ tsp. salt
- ½ tsp. black pepper
- ½ lb. spicy smoked sausage, cut into 32 (½-inch) pieces
- 32 wooden picks
- Lemon-Garlic Mayonnaise (recipe follows)
- Fresh thyme sprigs, for garnish (optional)

1. Preheat oven to 450°F. Place sweet potato cubes on a lightly greased 15- x 10-inch jelly-roll pan. Drizzle potatoes with oil and sprinkle with salt and pepper. Toss to coat.

2. Bake in preheated oven 15 to 20 minutes, turning cubes twice.

3. Cook sausage in a large nonstick skillet over medium-high until browned on each side, 3 to 4 minutes. Drain on paper towels.

4. Place 1 sausage slice on 1 sweet potato cube; secure with a wooden pick. Repeat with remaining sausage slices and potato cubes. Serve with Lemon-Garlic Mayonnaise. Garnish, if desired.

Lemon-Garlic Mayonnaise

ACTIVE 10 MIN. - TOTAL 10 MIN.

MAKES ABOUT ½ CUP

- 1 cup mayonnaise
- 2 Tbsp. chopped fresh flat-leaf parsley
- 2 tsp. minced garlic
- 1 tsp. lemon zest
- 2 Tbsp. fresh lemon juice
- ½ tsp. black pepper
- ¼ tsp. salt

Stir together all ingredients in a small bowl. Refrigerate in an airtight container up to 7 days.

Creamy Lemon-Garlic Dressing: Stir together ⅓ cup **Lemon-Garlic Mayonnaise**, ¼ cup **buttermilk**, and a pinch of **salt**.

BBQ Chicken Drumsticks

ACTIVE 30 MIN. - TOTAL 1 HOUR, 10 MIN.

SERVES 8

- 1 Tbsp. vegetable oil
- 1 cup finely chopped white onion (8 oz.)
- 4 garlic cloves, minced (about 1 Tbsp.)
- 2 cups ketchup
- ½ cup packed dark brown sugar
- 3 Tbsp. Worcestershire sauce
- 3 Tbsp. apple cider vinegar
- 1 tsp. smoked paprika
- ½ tsp. cayenne pepper
- 1 Tbsp. kosher salt
- 1 Tbsp. black pepper
- 16 chicken drumsticks (about 4 lb.)

1. Heat the oil in a large heavy-bottom saucepan over medium. Add onion and cook, stirring often, until tender, about 5 minutes. Add garlic and cook until fragrant, about 1 minute. Stir in ketchup, brown sugar, Worcestershire, vinegar, paprika, cayenne pepper, and 1 teaspoon each of the salt and black pepper; bring to a boil. Remove from heat. Process with an immersion blender until smooth; reserve ½ cup.

2. Preheat 1 side of a grill to medium-low (300°F to 350°F). Sprinkle drumsticks with the remaining 2 teaspoons each salt and black pepper. Place drumsticks over the unlit side of the grill; grill, covered, 20 minutes. Turn drumsticks, and brush with ½ cup barbecue sauce; grill, covered, 20 minutes. Turn drumsticks, and brush with another

½ cup barbecue sauce; grill, covered, until cooked through, 30 to 40 minutes. Transfer drumsticks to the lit side of the grill; grill until skin is crispy, 2 to 3 minutes. Serve with reserved ½ cup sauce.

Grilled Jalapeño Poppers
ACTIVE 20 MIN. · TOTAL 30 MIN.
SERVES 12

- 1 (8-oz.) pkg. cream cheese, softened
- 4 oz. sharp cheddar cheese, grated (about 1 cup)
- 2 Tbsp. finely chopped scallions
- 2 tsp. Worcestershire sauce
- 1 garlic clove, grated
- ¼ tsp. kosher salt
- ⅛ tsp. black pepper
- 12 green jalapeño chiles or mini sweet peppers, halved lengthwise and seeded

Preheat grill to medium-high (about 450°F). Stir together cream cheese, cheese, scallions, Worcestershire, garlic, salt, and black pepper. Spoon 1 to 2 tablespoons of the cheese mixture into each jalapeño half. Place the jalapeño halves, cut-sides up, on lightly greased grill grates. Grill, covered, until jalapeños are charred and cheese is melted, about 8 minutes.

Ham-and-Cheddar Pinwheels
ACTIVE 10 MIN. · TOTAL 35 MIN.
MAKES 12 PINWHEELS

- 1 (8-oz.) can refrigerated crescent dough sheet
- 2 Tbsp. Dijon mustard
- 1 Tbsp. honey
- 1 tsp. hot sauce
- 1 tsp. black pepper
- 8 oz. smoked ham, thinly sliced (about 12 slices)
- 6 oz. sharp cheddar cheese, thinly sliced (10 to 12 slices)
- 2 Tbsp. salted butter, melted

1. Preheat oven to 375°F. Roll crescent dough sheet into a 16- x 12-inch rectangle on a lightly floured surface.
2. Whisk together Dijon, honey, hot sauce, and pepper in a small bowl; spread mustard mixture on dough sheet. Top with ham and cheese.

3. Roll up dough rectangle from 1 short side; press the seam to seal. Cut the roll into 12 (1-inch) slices. Place 1 slice into each greased cup of a 12-cup muffin pan. Drizzle melted butter evenly over the top of each pinwheel.
4. Bake in preheated oven until golden brown, 20 to 25 minutes. Cool in pan on a wire rack, about 5 minutes. Transfer pinwheels to wire rack. Serve warm or cool completely.

Loaded Brisket Nachos
ACTIVE 25 MIN. · TOTAL 25 MIN.
SERVES 10

- 1½ cups cherry tomatoes, halved
- ¾ cup thinly sliced red onion (from 1 onion)
- 2 tsp. fresh lime juice (from 1 lime)
- 1 tsp. chili powder
- ¼ tsp. kosher salt
- ¼ tsp. black pepper
- 1 jalapeño chile, thinly sliced (about 1 Tbsp.)
- ¼ cup chopped fresh cilantro, plus more for garnish (optional)
- 1 (13-oz.) bag tortilla chips
- 4 cups shredded cooked beef brisket, warmed (about 1 lb.)
- 4 oz. sharp cheddar cheese, shredded (about 1 cup)
- 4 oz. Monterey Jack cheese, shredded (about 1 cup)
- ¾ cup sour cream
- 1 ripe avocado, diced
  Hot sauce (optional)

1. Toss together tomatoes, onion, lime juice, chili powder, salt, black pepper, jalapeño slices, and ¼ cup of the cilantro in a large bowl.
2. Preheat broiler with rack 6 inches from heat. Line a large rimmed baking sheet with aluminum foil; lightly coat the foil with cooking spray. Arrange tortilla chips in a single layer on prepared baking sheet. Top chips evenly with shredded beef and tomato mixture. Sprinkle with cheeses. Broil, rotating baking sheet often, until cheese is melted and bubbly, about 1 minute.
3. Top nachos with sour cream and avocado. Garnish with additional cilantro and a few dashes of hot sauce, if desired.

Loaded Potato Skins
To get a jump-start on this popular appetizer, prepare the recipe through Step 2. Cover and chill the potato wedges up to 24 hours. Uncover and continue as directed in Step 3.
ACTIVE 45 MIN. · TOTAL 1 HOUR, 45 MIN.
SERVES 8

- 8 medium-size russet potatoes
- 1 Tbsp. canola oil
- 6 Tbsp. (3 oz.) salted butter, melted
- 1¼ tsp. kosher salt
- 1 tsp. black pepper
- 1 cup finely chopped country ham (about 4 oz.)
- ½ cup finely chopped red onion (from 1 small onion)
- 8 oz. white cheddar cheese, shredded (about 2 cups)
- 1 cup diced tomato (from 2 medium plum tomatoes)
- ½ cup sour cream
- 1 cup barbecue sauce
- 3 Tbsp. chopped fresh chives

1. Preheat oven to 400°F. Pierce potatoes all over with a fork; rub all over with oil. Place on a foil-lined baking sheet. Bake in preheated oven until tender when pierced with a fork, about 1 hour. Let cool on baking sheet about 10 minutes. Place oven rack in center of oven; turn oven to broil.
2. Cut potatoes in quarters lengthwise and scoop out flesh, leaving ¼-inch layer of potato next to skin. (Reserve removed potato flesh for another use, if desired.) Brush potato quarters all over with melted butter; sprinkle with salt and pepper, and place on baking sheet, skin-side up.
3. Broil until browned and crisp, about 5 minutes. Remove from oven and turn potato skins over. Top evenly with ham, red onion, and cheese. Broil until cheese is melted and browned, 3 to 4 minutes. Top with tomatoes, sour cream, barbecue sauce, and chives; serve hot.

Mini Potato and Onion Frittatas

ACTIVE 30 MIN. - TOTAL 45 MIN.
MAKES 12 MINI FRITTATAS

- 2 Tbsp. salted butter
- 4 Tbsp. olive oil
- 1 large yellow onion, thinly sliced vertically (about 2 cups)
- 1 tsp. kosher salt
- ½ tsp. black pepper
- 8 oz. frozen shredded hash browns, thawed
- ½ cup chopped fresh chives
- 12 large eggs, lightly beaten

1. Preheat oven to 350°F. Grease a standard 12-cup muffin pan with butter, about ½ teaspoon per muffin cup; set aside.
2. Heat 2 tablespoons of the olive oil in a large nonstick skillet over medium-high. Add onion, salt, and pepper; cook, stirring often, 1 minute. Reduce heat to medium-low; cook, stirring often, until onions are tender and caramelized, 12 to 15 minutes. Transfer to a large bowl.
3. Meanwhile, squeeze thawed hash browns between paper towels to remove as much water as possible; set aside. Heat remaining 2 tablespoons oil in the same skillet over medium-high. Add hash browns and cook, stirring often, until tender and starting to brown, 6 to 8 minutes. Remove from heat.
4. Add hash browns and chives to the onions; stir to combine. Let stand to cool slightly, about 5 minutes. Add beaten eggs to hash brown mixture, and stir to incorporate.
5. Spoon the frittata mixture into prepared muffin cups. Bake in preheated oven until the eggs are set, 12 to 15 minutes. Serve hot or at room temperature.

Nashville Hot Chicken Sliders

ACTIVE 40 MIN. - TOTAL 1 HOUR, 40 MIN., INCLUDES 1 HOUR CHILLING
SERVES 8

- 3 cups whole buttermilk
- 3 Tbsp. cayenne pepper
- 3 Tbsp. kosher salt
- 2 Tbsp. black pepper
- 16 chicken breast tenders (about 2 lb.)
- 2 Tbsp. light brown sugar
- 6 cups peanut oil
- 3 cups self-rising flour

- 1 Tbsp. cornstarch
- 1 tsp. garlic powder
- 2 Tbsp. unsalted butter, softened
- 16 slider buns
- 16 dill pickle slices

1. Combine buttermilk, 1½ tablespoons of the cayenne, and 1 tablespoon each of the salt and black pepper in a large bowl. Add chicken; toss to coat. Chill 1 hour.
2. Combine brown sugar and remaining 1½ tablespoons cayenne in a bowl. Heat oil in a large Dutch oven over medium to 200°F. Whisk 1 cup of the hot oil into the brown sugar mixture; set aside. Continue heating remaining oil in Dutch oven to 350°F over medium.
3. Combine flour, cornstarch, garlic powder, and remaining 2 tablespoons salt and 1 tablespoon pepper in a shallow baking dish. Remove chicken from buttermilk; let excess drip off. Dredge in flour mixture; shake off excess.
4. Fry chicken in hot oil until golden brown and cooked through, 5 to 6 minutes.
5. Preheat broiler on low with rack 6 inches from heat. Spread butter on cut sides of each bun, then place buns on a rimmed baking sheet. Broil until lightly toasted, about 4 minutes. Remove from oven.
6. Toss hot chicken in the reserved brown sugar-oil mixture. Place 1 chicken tender and 1 pickle on bottom of each slider bun. Top with bun tops.

Wonder Wings

ACTIVE 25 MIN. - TOTAL 1 HOUR, NOT INCLUDING SAUCES
SERVES 6 TO 8

- 3 lb. chicken wings
- 2 tsp. vegetable oil
- 1 tsp. kosher salt
- ½ tsp. freshly ground black pepper
  Classic White Sauce or Buttery Hot Sauce (recipes follow)

1. Light 1 side of the grill, heating to medium-high (350°F to 400°F); leave the other side unlit. Dry each wing well with paper towels. Toss together the wings and oil in a large bowl. Sprinkle with the salt and pepper, and toss to coat.
2. Place the chicken over the unlit side of the grill, and grill, covered, 15 minutes on each side. Transfer the chicken to the lit side of the grill, and grill, uncovered,

10 to 12 minutes or until the skin is crispy and lightly charred, turning every 2 to 3 minutes. Toss the wings immediately with the desired sauce. Let stand, tossing occasionally, 5 minutes before serving.

Classic White Sauce

This tangy sauce is so good that you could pair it with all sorts of meats—from pork tenderloin to cuts of beef to lamb shanks.
ACTIVE 10 MIN. - TOTAL 10 MIN.
MAKES ABOUT ⅔ CUP

- ⅓ cup mayonnaise
- 3 Tbsp. chopped fresh chives, plus more for garnish
- 1 Tbsp. prepared horseradish
- 4 tsp. apple cider vinegar
- 2 tsp. Creole mustard
- 1 tsp. coarsely ground black pepper
- ¼ tsp. granulated sugar
- 1 finely grated garlic clove

Whisk together all ingredients in a small bowl. Garnish with additional chives, if desired.

Buttery Hot Sauce

ACTIVE 5 MIN. - TOTAL 5 MIN.
MAKES ABOUT ⅓ CUP

- ¼ cup (2 oz.) butter, melted
- 3 to 4 tsp. cayenne pepper
- 2 tsp. dark brown sugar
- ¾ tsp. kosher salt
- ½ tsp. smoked paprika
- ½ tsp. garlic powder
- 1 Tbsp. apple cider vinegar

Cook melted butter, cayenne, sugar, salt, paprika, and garlic powder in a small saucepan over medium, stirring constantly, 1 minute or until fragrant. Remove from heat and stir in apple cider vinegar.

Shrimp Boil Kabobs

ACTIVE 30 MIN. - TOTAL 1 HOUR
MAKES 24 SERVINGS

- 24 (6-inch) wooden skewers
- 2 Tbsp. butter
- ¾ cup finely chopped red bell pepper
- ½ cup finely chopped sweet onion
- 1 garlic clove, minced

2 cups fresh corn kernels (about 4 medium ears)

½ to ¾ tsp. Creole seasoning

¼ cup chopped fresh flat-leaf parsley

1 Tbsp. red wine vinegar

¼ cup Old Bay seasoning

24 baby red potatoes (about 1 lb.)

½ lb. smoked sausage, cut into 24 slices

24 extra-large peeled, deveined raw shrimp (about 1¼ lb.)

1. Melt butter in a medium skillet over medium; add bell pepper, onion, and garlic; cook, stirring occasionally, 4 minutes. Stir in corn and Creole seasoning; cook, stirring occasionally, 3 minutes. Remove from heat and stir in parsley and vinegar.

2. Bring Old Bay seasoning and 5 quarts water to a boil, covered, in a large stockpot. Add potatoes and cook, uncovered, 10 minutes. Add sausage and cook 3 minutes. Add shrimp; cook 3 minutes or just until shrimp turn pink and potatoes are tender. Drain.

3. Thread 1 potato, 1 shrimp, and 1 sausage piece onto each skewer. Arrange on serving plates or a long shallow platter. Spoon corn mixture over kabobs.

Grilled Watermelon with Blue Cheese and Prosciutto

ACTIVE 20 MIN. - TOTAL 20 MIN.

MAKES 12 SERVINGS

3 (½-inch-thick) watermelon rounds, quartered

1 Tbsp. olive oil

⅛ tsp. kosher salt

½ tsp. freshly ground black pepper

2 oz. thinly sliced prosciutto

2 oz. blue cheese, crumbled
Fresh basil leaves

2 tsp. bottled balsamic glaze

1. Preheat grill to 350°F to 400°F (medium-high). Brush both sides of each watermelon quarter with olive oil; season with salt and pepper. Cut prosciutto into thin strips.

2. Grill watermelon quarters, uncovered, 1 minute on each side or until grill marks appear.

3. Transfer watermelon to a serving plate; top with blue cheese, prosciutto strips, and fresh basil. Drizzle with balsamic glaze. Serve immediately.

Chicken and Mini Waffles with Spiced Honey

ACTIVE 10 MIN. - TOTAL 1 HOUR, 10 MIN.

MAKES 24 SERVINGS

12 chicken breast tenders, each cut in half crosswise (1 lb., 10 oz.)

¾ cup fat-free buttermilk

1½ cups panko (Japanese breadcrumbs)

½ tsp. garlic powder

¼ tsp. smoked paprika

¼ tsp. freshly ground black pepper

¼ tsp. salt

24 whole-grain mini waffles

¾ cup honey

¾ tsp. ground cinnamon

½ tsp. grated fresh ginger

½ tsp. hot sauce

1. Stir together chicken and buttermilk in a medium bowl. Chill 30 minutes. Place a large baking sheet in oven; preheat oven to 450°F.

2. Place panko in a shallow bowl. Stir together garlic powder, smoked paprika, pepper, and salt. Remove chicken from buttermilk and pat dry; discard buttermilk.

3. Sprinkle chicken evenly with spice mixture; dredge in panko. Remove baking sheet from oven; coat with cooking spray. Immediately place chicken on hot baking sheet; coat chicken with cooking spray.

4. Bake in preheated oven until chicken is crisp and lightly browned, 20 to 25 minutes.

5. Arrange waffles on a wire rack in a jelly-roll pan. Bake 3 minutes on each side or until toasted.

6. Meanwhile, stir together honey, cinnamon, ginger, and hot sauce in a small microwave-safe bowl. Microwave on HIGH 30 seconds or until warm.

7. Place waffles on a serving platter; top waffles with chicken and drizzle with spiced honey.

Fried Green Tomato Sliders

ACTIVE 30 MIN. - TOTAL 40 MIN.

MAKES ABOUT 20 SLICES

1½ cups shredded red cabbage

1½ cups shredded napa cabbage

1 cup matchstick-cut carrots

⅓ cup thinly sliced red onion

2 Tbsp. olive oil

2 Tbsp. fresh lime juice

½ cup chopped fresh cilantro, divided

½ tsp. salt

¼ tsp. black pepper

¼ cup canola mayonnaise

2 to 3 tsp. Asian hot chili sauce (such as Sriracha)

12 slider buns or dinner rolls, warmed and split

12 Fried Green Tomatoes

1. Stir together cabbages, carrots, onion, oil, lime juice, and ¼ cup of the cilantro in a medium bowl. Season with salt and pepper. Let stand 10 minutes.

2. Stir together mayonnaise, chili sauce, and remaining ¼ cup cilantro. Spread mixture on buns. Divide tomatoes and cabbage mixture evenly among bun bottoms. Top with bun tops.

Fried Green Tomatoes: Cut 4 medium-size green tomatoes (about 1⅓ lb.) into ½-inch slices; sprinkle with ½ tsp. salt and ½ tsp. black pepper. Let stand 10 minutes. Combine 1 cup self-rising white cornmeal mix and ½ cup panko (Japanese breadcrumbs) in a shallow dish or pie plate. Place ½ cup all-purpose flour in a second shallow dish. Whisk 4 large egg whites in a medium bowl until foamy. Dredge tomato slices in flour, shaking off excess. Dip in egg whites, then dredge in cornmeal mixture. Half at a time, cook tomato slices in 3 Tbsp. olive oil in a nonstick skillet over medium 4 to 5 minutes on each side or until golden brown. Season with salt to taste. Place on a wire rack in a jelly-roll pan and keep warm in a 225°F oven.

Baby Hot Browns

This appetizer is hors d'oeuvre-size servings of this famous Kentucky sandwich.

ACTIVE 35 MIN. - TOTAL 55 MIN.

MAKES 16 APPETIZERS

16 pumpernickel rye party bread slices

2 Tbsp. butter

2 Tbsp. all-purpose flour

½ cup (2 oz.) shredded sharp cheddar cheese

1½ cups milk

¼ tsp. salt

¼ tsp. cayenne pepper

Recipe continued on page 346

Recipe continued from page 345

- 2 lb. thinly sliced turkey
- ½ cup freshly grated Parmesan cheese
- 6 bacon slices, cooked and crumbled

1. Preheat oven to 500°F. Arrange bread slices on a lightly greased baking sheet; bake until toasted, 3 to 4 minutes.
2. Melt butter in a saucepan over low; add flour and cook, whisking constantly, until smooth. Add cheddar cheese, whisking until cheese is melted. Gradually whisk in milk; cook over medium, whisking constantly, until mixture is thick and bubbly. Stir in salt and cayenne pepper.
3. Top bread slices evenly with turkey. Top each with about 1½ tablespoons cheese sauce. Sprinkle evenly with Parmesan cheese and bacon.
4. Bake in preheated oven 7 minutes or until Parmesan is melted.
Make Ahead: Prepare recipe through Step 2. Cover and refrigerate. When ready to serve, continue with Steps 3 and 4.

Chicken Cakes with Rémoulade Sauce

This recipe delivers the quality of crab cakes at a friendly price, and the chicken cakes are easy to make ahead. Also make, bite-size portions by forming 16 patties.
ACTIVE 20 MIN. - TOTAL 35 MIN.
MAKES 8 APPETIZER CAKES

- 2 Tbsp. butter
- ½ medium-size red bell pepper, diced
- 4 scallions, thinly sliced
- 1 garlic clove, pressed
- 3 cups chopped cooked chicken
- 1 cup soft breadcrumbs
- 1 large egg, lightly beaten
- 2 Tbsp. mayonnaise
- 1 Tbsp. Creole mustard
- 2 tsp. Creole seasoning
- ¼ cup vegetable oil, divided
  Fresh parsley sprigs, for garnish
  Rémoulade Sauce (recipe follows)

1. Melt butter in a large skillet over medium. Add bell pepper, scallions, and garlic, and cook, stirring occasionally, until vegetables are tender, 3 to 4 minutes.

2. Stir together bell pepper mixture, chicken, breadcrumbs, egg, mayonnaise, mustard, and seasoning. Shape mixture into 8 (3½-inch) patties.
3. Fry 4 patties in 2 tablespoons hot oil in a large skillet over medium 3 minutes on each side or until golden brown. Drain on paper towels. Repeat procedure with remaining patties and 2 tablespoons oil. Garnish, if desired. Serve immediately with Rémoulade Sauce.

Rémoulade Sauce
ACTIVE 10 MIN. - TOTAL 10 MIN.
MAKES ABOUT 1¼ CUPS

- 1 cup mayonnaise
- 3 scallions, sliced
- 2 Tbsp. Creole mustard
- 2 garlic cloves, pressed
- 1 Tbsp. chopped fresh parsley
- ¼ tsp. cayenne pepper

Stir together all ingredients in small bowl until well blended.

Corncakes with Tomato-Lima Bean Relish
ACTIVE 35 MIN. - TOTAL 1 HOUR, 20 MIN., INCLUDING RELISH
MAKES ABOUT 2 DOZEN

- 1⅔ cups fresh corn kernels (3 large ears)
- ½ cup low-fat buttermilk
- 2 Tbsp. butter, melted
- 2 large eggs
- 2 garlic cloves
- 3 oz. reduced-fat jalapeño-cheddar cheese, shredded (about ¾ cup)
- ½ cup all-purpose flour
- ½ cup plain yellow cornmeal
- 1 tsp. freshly ground black pepper
- ¾ tsp. salt
  Tomato-Lima Bean Relish (recipe follows)

1. Pulse corn, buttermilk, butter, eggs, and garlic in a food processor 4 to 5 times or just until corn is coarsely chopped.
2. Stir together cheese, flour, cornmeal, black pepper, and salt in a large bowl; add corn mixture, stirring just until dry ingredients are moistened.
3. Pour 2 tablespoons batter for each corncake onto a hot, lightly greased

griddle or large nonstick skillet to form 2-inch cakes (do not spread or flatten cakes). Cook corncakes over medium heat 2 to 3 minutes, until edges start to brown. Turn and cook 2 to 3 minutes or until golden brown and edges look dry.
4. Spoon Tomato-Lima Bean Relish onto corncakes.

Tomato-Lima Bean Relish
ACTIVE 10 MIN. - TOTAL 45 MIN.
MAKES 1½ CUPS

Place 1 cup frozen **baby lima beans** and 1 cup **water** in a medium microwave-safe bowl. Cover bowl tightly with heavy-duty plastic wrap; fold back a small edge to allow steam to escape. Microwave on HIGH 15 to 18 minutes or just until beans are tender. Drain; return beans to bowl. Add ½ cup sliced **grape tomatoes**, 3 tablespoons chopped **red onion**, 1 tablespoon **extra-virgin olive oil**, 2 teaspoons **red wine vinegar**, 1 teaspoon minced fresh **garlic**, ½ teaspoon **salt**, and ¼ teaspoon freshly ground **black pepper** to bowl; toss gently. Add 2 tablespoons chopped fresh **dill**; toss gently. Cover and chill until ready to serve.

Hot Ham-and-Cheese Rollups

For lunch, reheat a rollup in the microwave on HIGH 1 minute or until heated through.
ACTIVE 20 MIN. - TOTAL 1 HOUR
MAKES 4 SERVINGS

- 1 (13.8-oz.) refrigerated pizza crust dough
- 2 Tbsp. chopped fresh basil or 2 tsp. dried basil
- 6 oz. thinly sliced maple-glazed ham
- 4 oz. part-skim mozzarella cheese, shredded (1 cup)
  Pasta sauce or mustard (optional)

1. Preheat oven to 400°F. Roll dough into a 12-inch square. Sprinkle with basil to ½ inch from edges. Top with ham slices, and sprinkle with cheese to ½ inch from edges.
2. Roll up dough, beginning at 1 end; place, seam-side down, on an foil-lined baking sheet coated with cooking spray.
3. Bake in preheated oven until golden brown, 20 to 25 minutes. Cool 5 minutes. Cut into 1½-inch slices. Serve with pasta sauce or mustard, if desired.

Hot Mushroom Turnovers

ACTIVE 45 MIN. - TOTAL 55 MIN.,
PLUS 1 HOUR CHILLING

MAKES 3½ DOZEN

- 1 (8-oz.) pkg. cream cheese, softened
- ½ cup butter, softened
- 1¾ cups all-purpose flour
- 3 Tbsp. butter
- 1 (8-oz.) pkg. fresh mushrooms, minced
- 1 large onion, minced
- ½ cup sour cream
- 2 Tbsp. all-purpose flour
- 1 tsp. salt
- ¼ tsp. dried thyme
- 1 large egg, lightly beaten

1. Preheat oven to 450°F. Beat cream cheese and ½ cup butter with an electric mixer on medium speed until creamy; gradually add 1¾ cups of the flour, beating well.
2. Divide dough in half, and shape each portion into a ball; cover and chill 1 hour. Melt 3 tablespoons butter in a large skillet. Add mushrooms and onion; cook, stirring occasionally, until tender. Stir in sour cream flour, salt, and thyme; set aside.
3. Roll 1 dough portion to ⅛-inch thickness on a lightly floured surface; cut with a 2½-inch round cutter, and place on greased baking sheets. Repeat with remaining dough.
4. Spoon 1 teaspoon mushroom mixture onto half of each dough circle. Moisten edges with beaten egg, and fold dough over filling. Press edges with a fork to seal; prick tops. Brush turnovers with beaten egg.
5. Bake in preheated oven until golden, 8 to 10 minutes.

Miniature Cheese Quiches

ACTIVE 5 MIN. - TOTAL 30 MIN.

MAKES 2 DOZEN

- 2 large eggs, lightly beaten
- ½ cup milk
- 1½ Tbsp. butter, melted
- 1 cup (4 oz.) shredded cheddar cheese or Monterey Jack cheese with peppers
  Pastry Shells (recipe follows)
  Cayenne pepper or paprika (optional)

Preheat oven to 350°F. Combine eggs, milk, butter, and cheese in a small bowl; stir well. Spoon filling into Pastry Shells. Sprinkle with cayenne pepper, if desired. Bake until set and golden, 25 minutes.

Pastry Shells

ACTIVE 20 MIN. - TOTAL 20 MIN.

MAKES 2 DOZEN

- 1¼ cups all-purpose flour
- 1 tsp. salt
- 3 Tbsp. butter, melted
- 1 egg yolk
- 3 to 4 Tbsp. ice water

1. Combine flour and salt, stirring well; add butter, mixing well. Add egg yolk and ice water; stir with a fork just until dry ingredients are moistened.
2. Shape dough into 24 (1-inch) balls. Place in lightly greased 1¾-inch miniature muffin pans, shaping each into a shell. Chill until ready to bake.

Spicy Party Meatballs

Serve these meatballs from a slow cooker or chafing dish.
ACTIVE 5 MIN. - TOTAL 50 MIN.

MAKES 8 DOZEN

- 1 (12-oz.) jar cocktail sauce
- 1 (10.5-oz.) jar jalapeño pepper jelly
- ½ small yellow onion, minced
- ½ (3-lb.) pkg. frozen cooked meatballs

1. Cook cocktail sauce, pepper jelly, and onion in a Dutch oven over medium, stirring until jelly is melted and mixture is smooth.
2. Stir in meatballs. Reduce heat and simmer, stirring occasionally, until heated through, 35 to 40 minutes.

Tomato Tart

ACTIVE 45 MIN. - TOTAL 2 HOURS, 30 MIN.

MAKES 4 TO 6 APPETIZER SERVINGS

- ½ (15-oz.) pkg. refrigerated piecrusts (1 crust)
- 1 garlic bulb
- ½ tsp. olive oil
- 1½ cups (6 oz.) shredded fontina cheese, divided
- 4 large tomatoes
- ½ tsp. salt
- ¼ tsp. black pepper

1. Preheat oven to 450°F. Press refrigerated piecrust on bottom and up sides of a 9-inch square tart pan. Bake until piecrust is lightly browned, about 9 minutes. Set aside. Reduce oven temperature to 425°F.
2. Cut off pointed ends of garlic bulb. Place bulb on a piece of foil and drizzle with olive oil. Fold foil to enclose and seal bulb.
3. Bake garlic at 425°F until softened, about 30 minutes; cool until easy to handle. Squeeze pulp from garlic cloves onto baked piecrust. Reduce oven temperature to 350°F.
4. Sprinkle ½ cup of the cheese over garlic. Slice tomatoes and sprinkle evenly with salt and pepper. Place on folded paper towels and let stand 10 minutes. Arrange tomato slices on shredded cheese. Sprinkle with remaining 1 cup cheese.
5. Bake at 350°F until tart is lightly browned, 45 minutes.

Warmed Cranberry Brie

Double this recipe for a crowd.
ACTIVE 10 MIN. - TOTAL 15 MIN.

MAKES 8 APPETIZER SERVINGS

- 1 (15-oz.) round Brie
- 1 (16-oz.) can whole-berry cranberry sauce
- ¼ cup firmly packed brown sugar
- 2 Tbsp. spiced rum*
- ½ tsp. ground nutmeg
- ¼ cup chopped pecans, toasted
  Crackers and apple and pear slices, for serving

1. Preheat oven to 500°F. Trim rind from top of Brie, leaving a ⅓-inch border of rind on top. Place Brie on a baking sheet.
2. Stir together cranberry sauce, sugar, rum, and nutmeg; spread mixture evenly on top of Brie. Sprinkle evenly with pecans.
3. Bake in preheated oven 5 minutes. Serve with crackers and apple and pear slices.
*Note: Substitute 2 tablespoons orange juice for spiced rum, if desired.

Snacky Appetizers

Caramel-Peanut-Popcorn Snack Mix

ACTIVE 30 MIN. - TOTAL 50 MIN.

MAKES ABOUT 18 CUPS

- 15 cups popped popcorn (about ¾ cup kernels)
- 1 cup, plus 2 Tbsp. firmly packed dark brown sugar
- ½ cup butter
- ½ cup dark corn syrup
- ¼ tsp. kosher salt
- 1 cup lightly salted dry-roasted peanuts
  Waxed paper
- 1 (10.5-oz.) pkg. candy-coated peanut butter pieces (such as Reese's Pieces)

1. Preheat oven to 325°F. Evenly spread popcorn on a lightly greased (with cooking spray) heavy-duty foil-lined 13- x 18-inch pan. Stir together brown sugar, butter, corn syrup, and salt in a small saucepan over medium-low; bring to a simmer. Simmer, stirring constantly, 1 minute. Pour over popcorn, and stir gently to coat.
2. Bake in preheated oven 25 minutes, stirring every 5 minutes. Add peanuts during last 5 minutes. Remove from oven. Spread on lightly greased (with cooking spray) waxed paper. Cool completely, about 20 minutes. Break apart large pieces, and stir in candy pieces. Store in an airtight container up to 1 week.
Note: To cook popcorn kernels without oil in microwave, place ¼ cup kernels in a 2½-quart microwave-safe bowl; completely cover bowl with a microwave-safe plate. Cook on HIGH 3 to 4 minutes or until kernels have popped. Repeat with remaining kernels.

Spicy-Sweet Pecans

Egg white helps the spice mixture adhere evenly and gives the pecans a crisp, glossy coating.

ACTIVE 10 MIN. - TOTAL 1 HOUR, 30 MIN.

MAKES 4 CUPS

- ¾ cup granulated sugar
- 1 Tbsp. light brown sugar
- 2 tsp. chopped fresh rosemary
- 1 tsp. kosher salt
- 1 tsp. ground cinnamon
- ½ tsp. ground ginger
- ¼ tsp. ground nutmeg
- ¼ tsp. cayenne pepper
- 1 large egg white
- 4 cups pecan halves

1. Preheat oven to 275°F. Stir together sugars, rosemary, salt, cinnamon, ginger, nutmeg, and cayenne pepper in a medium bowl.
2. Whisk together egg white and 1 tablespoon water in a separate medium bowl until foamy. (No liquid should remain.) Add pecans, stirring to coat.
3. Add pecan mixture to sugar mixture, stirring until evenly coated. Spread pecans in a single layer on a large lightly greased (with cooking spray) foil-lined rimmed baking sheet.
4. Bake in preheated oven 50 to 55 minutes or until sugar mixture hardens and nuts are toasted, stirring every 15 minutes. Spread immediately in a single layer on waxed paper. Cool completely, about 30 minutes. Store in an airtight container up to 7 days.

Chili-Lime Pecans

ACTIVE 10 MIN. - TOTAL 55 MIN.

MAKES 3 CUPS

- 2 Tbsp. lime juice
- 1 Tbsp. olive oil
- 1 tsp. paprika
- 1 tsp. chili powder
- 1 tsp. salt
- ½ tsp. cayenne pepper
- 3 cups pecan halves

Preheat oven to 350°F. Stir together lime juice, oil, paprika, chili powder, salt, and cayenne pepper. Add pecans; toss to coat. Spread mixture in a lightly greased foil-lined jelly-roll pan. Bake until pecans are toasted and dry, stirring occasionally, 12 to 14 minutes. Cool completely, about 30 minutes.

Caramel-Walnut Snack Mix

ACTIVE 15 MIN. - TOTAL 1 HOUR

SERVES 8

- 5 cups popped popcorn
- 3 cups corn cereal squares (such as Corn Chex)
- 2 cups pretzel squares
- 1 cup walnut pieces
- ¾ cup packed light brown sugar
- 6 Tbsp. (3 oz.) salted butter, softened
- 3 Tbsp. light corn syrup
- 1 tsp. vanilla extract
- ½ tsp. baking soda
- 1 cup candy-coated chocolate-covered peanuts (such as Peanut M&M's)

1. Preheat oven to 300°F. Combine popcorn, cereal, pretzels, and walnuts in a large bowl.
2. Place sugar, butter, and syrup in a small saucepan over medium. Cook, stirring occasionally, until the mixture comes to a boil, 3 to 4 minutes. Reduce heat to medium-low; cook, stirring often, until the sugar is completely dissolved, 1 to 2 minutes. Remove from heat. Stirring constantly, add vanilla and baking soda. Pour syrup over popcorn mixture, stirring gently until well combined and evenly coated.
3. Spread coated popcorn mixture in a single layer on a rimmed baking sheet lined with parchment paper. Bake in preheated oven, stirring after 15 minutes, until golden and caramelized, 25 to 30 minutes. Remove from oven. Cool completely, about 15 minutes. Transfer to a serving bowl, and stir in candies.

Deviled Eggs

ACTIVE 10 MIN. - TOTAL 10 MIN.

MAKES 10 DEVILED EGGS

- 5 hard-cooked eggs, peeled
- 1½ Tbsp. Dijon mustard
- 1½ Tbsp. mayonnaise
- 5 pimiento-stuffed olives, halved
- 1 tsp. Cajun seasoning

1. Cut eggs in half lengthwise; carefully remove yolks. Mash yolks, then stir in mustard and mayonnaise; blend well.
2. Spoon yolk mixture evenly into egg white halves. Place an olive half in the center of each; sprinkle with Cajun seasoning.

Marinated Olives

ACTIVE 10 MIN. - TOTAL 10 MIN.,
PLUS 8 HOURS CHILLING

MAKES 8 SERVINGS

- 1 lb. drained kalamata olives
- 12 drained pimiento-stuffed Spanish olives
- 12 drained pickled jalapeño peppers
- ¼ cup tequila
- ¼ cup lime juice
- 2 Tbsp. orange liqueur
- ¼ cup minced fresh cilantro
- 1 tsp. orange zest
- 1 tsp. olive oil

Stir together all ingredients in a medium bowl. Chill, covered, 8 hours.

Swedish Nuts

ACTIVE 15 MIN. - TOTAL 1 HOUR, 5 MIN.

MAKES 5 CUPS

- 1 cup whole blanched almonds
- ½ cup butter
- 2 egg whites
- ¾ cup sugar
  Dash salt
- 1 cup walnut halves
- 1 cup pecan halves

1. Preheat oven to 325°F. Spread almonds evenly on an ungreased baking sheet. Roast until lightly browned, stirring occasionally, 15 minutes. Transfer to a wire rack to cool. Place butter in a 13- x 9-inch pan; place in oven to melt butter.
2. Beat egg whites in a large bowl with an electric mixer on high speed until stiff peaks form. Gradually add sugar and salt; beat until mixture is stiff (2 to 4 minutes). Gently fold in almonds, walnuts, and pecans; spread nut mixture evenly over melted butter in pan.
3. Bake in preheated oven until nuts are browned and butter is absorbed, stirring every 10 minutes, about 35 minutes. Cool completely.

Chilled & Room Temp.

Mini Muffulettas

ACTIVE 25 MIN. - TOTAL 25 MIN.

MAKES 12 SERVINGS

- 2 (16-oz.) jars mixed pickled vegetables
- ¾ cup pimiento-stuffed Spanish olives, chopped
- 2 Tbsp. bottled olive oil-and-vinegar dressing
- 12 small dinner rolls, cut in half
- 6 Swiss cheese slices, cut in half
- 12 thin deli ham slices
- 12 Genoa salami slices
- 6 provolone cheese slices, cut in half

1. Pulse pickled vegetables in food processor 8 to 10 times or until finely chopped. Stir in olives and dressing.
2. Spread 1 heaping tablespoon pickled vegetables over cut side of each roll bottom. Top each with 1 Swiss cheese slice half, 1 ham slice, 1 salami slice, 1 provolone cheese slice half, and roll tops. Cover with plastic wrap. Serve immediately or chill until ready to serve.

Smoky Pimiento Cheese Sandwiches

ACTIVE 15 MIN. - TOTAL 15 MIN.

SERVES 7

- 1 (3-oz.) pkg. cream cheese, softened
- ½ cup mayonnaise
- 1 tsp. paprika
- ¼ tsp. salt
- 2 cups (8 oz.) shredded smoked cheddar cheese
- 2 cups (8 oz.) shredded smoked Gouda cheese
- ½ (8.5-oz.) jar sun-dried tomatoes in oil, drained and chopped
- 14 bread slices (sourdough and dark wheat)

1. Stir together cream cheese, mayonnaise, paprika, and salt in a large bowl until blended. Stir in cheeses and sun-dried tomatoes until combined.
2. Spread cheese mixture on half the bread slices (about ⅓ cup on each); top with remaining bread slices.

Tex-Mex Deviled Eggs

ACTIVE 15 MIN. - TOTAL 45 MIN.

MAKES 1 DOZEN

- 6 hard-cooked eggs, peeled
- 1 Tbsp. diced scallions
- 1 Tbsp. chopped fresh cilantro
- 1 small serrano or jalapeño pepper, seeded and finely chopped
- ¼ cup mayonnaise
- 1 tsp. yellow mustard
- ½ tsp. salt
- ¼ cup (1 oz.) shredded cheddar cheese
  Chili powder

1. Cut eggs in half lengthwise; carefully remove yolks, and place in a small bowl.
2. Mash egg yolks; stir in scallions, cilantro, serrano pepper, mayonnaise, mustard, and salt.
3. Spoon yolk mixture into egg white halves; sprinkle with cheese and chili powder. Serve immediately, or cover and chill until ready to serve.

Cream-Cheese-and-Olive Pecan Bites

ACTIVE 20 MIN. - TOTAL 20 MIN.

MAKES 40

- 80 large pecan halves
- 1 (3-oz.) pkg. cream cheese, softened
- ½ cup finely chopped pimiento-stuffed Spanish olives
- 1 Tbsp. chopped fresh chives
- ¼ tsp. black pepper

1. Preheat oven to 350°F. Bake pecans in a single layer in a shallow pan until toasted and fragrant, stirring halfway through, 8 to 10 minutes.
2. Stir together cream cheese, olives, chives, and pepper. Spread onto flat side of 40 pecans; top with remaining 40 pecans.

Goat Cheese-Pecan Finger Sandwiches

ACTIVE 10 MIN. - TOTAL 20 MIN.
MAKES ABOUT 12 SERVINGS

- ½ cup finely chopped pecans
- 1 (4-oz.) goat cheese log, softened
- 1 (3-oz.) pkg. cream cheese, softened
- 2 Tbsp. chopped fresh parsley
- 14 wheat bread slices
- ⅓ cup red pepper jelly

1. Preheat oven to 350°F. Bake pecans in a single layer in a shallow pan until toasted and fragrant, stirring halfway through, 8 to 10 minutes.
2. Stir together pecans, cheeses, and parsley in a small bowl. Spread on 1 side of 7 bread slices. Spread remaining 7 bread slices with pepper jelly; top with cheese-covered bread slices. Remove crusts; cut into desired shapes.

Italian Kabobs

ACTIVE 20 MIN. - TOTAL 8 HOUR, 20 MIN.
MAKES 16 SERVINGS

- 1 (8-oz.) block mozzarella cheese
- 16 (4-inch) Genoa salami slices
- 1 (14-oz.) can small artichoke hearts, drained and halved
- 1 pt. grape tomatoes
- 1 (6-oz.) jar large pitted Spanish olives, drained
- 16 (6- to 12-inch) wooden skewers
- 1 (16-oz.) bottle balsamic-basil vinaigrette
- 1 Tbsp. fresh lemon juice
  Fresh parsley sprigs, for garnish (optional)

1. Cut cheese into 16 cubes. Wrap salami slices around cheese cubes. Alternately thread cubes, artichoke hearts, tomatoes, and olives onto skewers. Place kabobs in a large plastic container or baking dish.
2. Stir together vinaigrette and lemon juice; pour over kabobs. Cover tightly, and chill 8 hours. Remove kabobs from marinade before serving, discarding marinade. Garnish, if desired.

Guacamole-Goat Cheese Toasts

ACTIVE 15 MIN. - TOTAL 50 MIN.
MAKES ABOUT 10 SERVINGS

- 2 ripe avocados
- 3 Tbsp. finely chopped red onion, divided
- ½ medium-size jalapeño pepper, seeded and chopped
- 1 garlic clove, pressed
- 2½ tsp. fresh lime juice
- ¼ tsp. salt
- ¼ tsp. coarsely ground black pepper
- ½ cup crumbled goat cheese
- 1 fresh tomatillo, husk removed
- 1 (7-oz.) pkg. miniature white pita rounds*
- 2 Tbsp. olive oil
- 1 plum tomato, seeded and finely chopped

1. Cut avocados in half. Scoop pulp into a bowl and mash with a potato masher or fork until slightly chunky. Stir in 2 tablespoons of the red onion, the jalapeño, garlic, lime juice, salt, and black pepper. Gently fold in cheese. Place plastic wrap directly on surface of avocado mixture, and let stand at room temperature 30 minutes.
2. Meanwhile, preheat oven to 375°F. Finely chop tomatillo.
3. Separate pita rounds lengthwise into two halves. Arrange in a single layer on a baking sheet; drizzle with olive oil.
4. Bake in preheated oven until toasted, 6 to 8 minutes. Top each with 1 rounded teaspoonful avocado mixture. Stir together tomatillo, tomato, and remaining 1 tablespoon red onion. Top avocado mixture with tomatillo mixture. Sprinkle with additional black pepper to taste.
*Note: 1 (8.5-oz.) French bread baguette may be substituted. Cut bread diagonally into 42 (½-inch) slices, discarding ends.

Pecan-Stuffed Pickled Jalapeños

ACTIVE 20 MIN. - TOTAL 30 MIN.
MAKES 6 SERVINGS

- ⅔ cup chopped pecans
- 1 (12-oz.) jar pickled jalapeño peppers, drained
- 1 (4-oz.) container garlic-and-herb spreadable cheese, softened

1. Preheat oven to 350°F. Bake pecans in a single layer in a shallow pan until toasted and fragrant, stirring halfway through, 8 to 10 minutes.
2. Cut peppers in half lengthwise; remove and discard seeds and membranes.
3. Pipe cheese into each pepper half. Press peppers, cheese-sides down, into chopped pecans. Serve immediately, or cover and chill up to 1 day.

Roasted Grape Chutney

ACTIVE 15 MIN. - TOTAL 1 HOUR, 10 MIN.
MAKES 1⅓ CUPS

- 1 cup seedless red grapes, halved
- 1 cup seedless green grapes, halved
- 1 Tbsp. olive oil
- 1 Tbsp. red wine vinegar
- 1 tsp. dried thyme
- ½ tsp. kosher salt
- ¼ tsp. black pepper
- 1 round Brie cheese

1. Preheat oven to 425°F. Stir together grapes, oil, vinegar, thyme, salt, and pepper. Spread grape mixture on a baking sheet lined with foil. Bake until grapes begin to shrivel, 20 minutes. Remove from oven; let cool 30 minutes. Reduce oven temperature to 400°F.
2. Trim rind from top of Brie. Place Brie on a lightly greased (with cooking spray) baking sheet.
3. Bake Brie at 400°F until warmed, 7 to 9 minutes. Top with grape chutney.

Tomato-and-Feta Cheese Crostini

ACTIVE 20 MIN. - TOTAL 20 MIN.
MAKES 20 APPETIZER SERVINGS

- 2 large tomatoes, seeded and diced
- ⅛ tsp. salt
- 2 Tbsp., plus 1 tsp. olive oil, divided
- 6 oz. herb-flavored feta cheese, crumbled
- 2 Tbsp. chopped fresh basil
- ¼ tsp. black pepper
- 1 (12-oz.) French bread baguette
- 2 garlic cloves, halved
  Fresh basil, oregano, and/or parsley sprigs, for garnish

1. Preheat grill to medium (300°F to 350°F). Stir together tomatoes, salt, and 1 teaspoon oil in a bowl. Stir together cheese, basil, and pepper in another bowl.

2. Cut bread diagonally into 20 (½-inch) slices. Brush both sides of bread with remaining 2 tablespoons oil. Grill bread 2 minutes on each side or until golden. Remove from grill.

3. Rub cut sides of garlic on bread slices. Top bread slices with tomato mixture, and sprinkle with feta mixture. Garnish, if desired.

Sausage and Cheddar Deviled Eggs

ACTIVE 25 MIN. - TOTAL 1 HOUR
SERVES 8

- 8 large eggs
- ½ (1-lb.) pkg. ground pork breakfast sausage, cooked and crumbled (such as Jimmy Dean)
- 2 oz. cheddar cheese, shredded (about ½ cup)
- ¼ cup mayonnaise
- 1½ Tbsp. pickle relish
- 1 Tbsp. apple cider vinegar
- 2 tsp. yellow mustard
- 1 tsp. paprika
- ¾ tsp. kosher salt
- ¼ tsp. cayenne pepper
- ¼ cup thinly sliced fresh scallions (green parts only)
- 2 Tbsp. hot sauce (optional)

1. Bring a large pot of water to a boil over high. Add eggs with a slotted spoon, and boil 12 minutes. Immediately plunge cooked eggs into a bowl of ice water. Cool completely. Peel eggs; discard shells.

2. Halve eggs lengthwise. Carefully remove yolks, leaving whites intact. Place yolks in a medium bowl, and mash with a fork until crumbled. Reserve 2 tablespoons each of the sausage and cheese. Add mayonnaise, relish, vinegar, mustard, paprika, salt, cayenne, and remaining sausage and cheese to yolks; stir until combined.

3. Spoon filling into egg white halves; place on a platter. Sprinkle each with reserved sausage and cheese; top with scallions and, if desired, hot sauce.

BBQ Peach Summer Rolls

ACTIVE 35 MIN. - TOTAL 45 MIN.
MAKES 16 SERVINGS

- Hot water
- 16 (8- to 9-inch) round rice paper sheets
- 2 small peaches, peeled and thinly sliced
- 16 Bibb lettuce leaves
- 1 English cucumber, cut into thin strips
- 1 large ripe avocado, thinly sliced
- 1 lb. shredded barbecued pork (without sauce), warm
- 1 Granny Smith apple, peeled and cut into thin strips
- 1½ cups torn fresh mint, cilantro, and basil
- Sweet Pepper-Peanut Sauce (recipe follows)

1. Pour hot water to depth of 1 inch into a large shallow dish. Dip 1 rice paper sheet in hot water briefly to soften (about 15 to 20 seconds). Pat dry with paper towels.

2. Place softened rice paper on a flat surface. Place 1 or 2 peach slices in center of rice paper; top with 1 lettuce leaf, 2 cucumber strips, 1 avocado slice, about 3 tablespoons pork, 3 or 4 apple strips, and 1½ to 2 tablespoons herbs. Fold sides over filling, then roll up, burrito-style. Place roll, seam-side down, on a serving platter. Cover with damp paper towels to keep from drying out. Serve with Sweet Pepper-Peanut Sauce.

Sweet Pepper-Peanut Sauce

ACTIVE 10 MIN. - TOTAL 10 MIN.
MAKES 16 SERVINGS

Stir together ½ cup **sweet pepper relish**, ¼ cup **salted cocktail peanuts**, 1½ Tbsp. fresh **lime juice**, 2 tsp. **light soy sauce**, 2 tsp. **toasted sesame oil**, 1½ tsp. grated fresh **ginger**, 1 finely chopped **green onion**, 1 minced **garlic clove**, and 1 tsp. **Asian hot chili sauce** (such as Sriracha). Cover and chill until ready to serve.

Pepper Jelly and Goat Cheese Cakes

ACTIVE 15 MIN. - TOTAL 2 HOURS, 45 MIN.
MAKES 24 SERVINGS

- Miniature paper baking cups
- ¼ cup Italian-seasoned breadcrumbs
- ¼ cup ground toasted pecans
- 2 Tbsp. grated Parmesan cheese
- 2 Tbsp. butter, melted
- 6 oz. ⅓-less-fat cream cheese, softened
- 1 (3-oz.) goat cheese log, softened
- 2 Tbsp. milk
- 1 Tbsp. Asian hot chili sauce (such as Sriracha)
- 1 large egg
- ¼ cup green pepper jelly
- ¼ cup red pepper jelly

1. Preheat oven to 350°F. Place paper baking cups in 2 (12-cup) miniature muffin pans, and coat with cooking spray. Stir together breadcrumbs, pecans, cheese, and butter in a small bowl; firmly press about 1 teaspoon mixture in bottom of each baking cup.

2. Beat cream cheese and goat cheese with an electric mixer on medium speed until light and fluffy. Add milk, chili sauce, and egg, beating just until blended. Spoon cheese mixture into baking cups, filling three-fourths full.

3. Bake in preheated oven until set, 10 minutes. Remove from oven to a wire rack, and cool completely (about 20 minutes). Remove from pans; place on a serving platter. Cover and chill 2 to 12 hours.

4. Microwave green pepper jelly in a small microwave-safe bowl on HIGH 20 to 25 seconds or until melted. Repeat procedure with red pepper jelly in another small microwave-safe bowl. Spoon 1 teaspoon melted green pepper jelly over each of 12 cheesecakes, and 1 teaspoon melted red pepper jelly over each of 12 remaining cheesecakes just before serving.

Feta-Stuffed Tomatoes

Use other cheeses of similar texture, such as goat cheese, in this easy side dish.
ACTIVE 15 MIN. - TOTAL 30 MIN.
MAKES 8 SERVINGS

- 4 large red tomatoes
- 4 oz. crumbled feta cheese
- ¼ cup fine dry breadcrumbs
- 2 Tbsp. chopped scallions
- 2 Tbsp. chopped fresh parsley
- 2 Tbsp. olive oil
- ¼ tsp. salt
- ¼ tsp. black pepper
- Fresh parsley sprig, for garnish

1. Preheat oven to 350°F. Cut tomatoes in half horizontally. Scoop out pulp from each tomato half, leaving shells intact. Discard seeds and coarsely chop pulp.
2. Stir together pulp, feta cheese, breadcrumbs, scallions, parsley, oil, salt, and pepper. Spoon mixture evenly into tomato shells; place in a 13- x 9-inch baking dish.
3. Bake in preheated oven 15 minutes. Transfer to a serving dish. Garnish, if desired.

Four-Cheese Pâté

This snowy white pâté makes an impressive appetizer. Toasty pecans enhance the blend of mild cheeses.
ACTIVE 30 MIN. - TOTAL 30 MIN.,
PLUS 4 HOURS CHILLING
MAKES 4½ CUPS

- 3 (8-oz.) pkg. cream cheese, softened
- 2 Tbsp. milk
- 1 cup chopped pecans, toasted
- 2 (8-oz.) pkg. cream cheese, softened
- 1 (4½-oz.) pkg. Camembert cheese, softened
- 1 (4-oz.) pkg. blue cheese
- 1 cup (4 oz.) shredded Swiss cheese
- Red and green grapes, for garnish (optional)
- Apple wedges, gingersnaps, and/or crackers, for serving

1. Line a lightly greased 8-inch round cake pan with plastic wrap; set aside. Combine 1 package cream cheese and the milk in a medium bowl; beat with an electric mixer on medium speed until smooth. Spread mixture into prepared pan; sprinkle evenly with chopped pecans. Cover and chill.
2. Combine remaining 2 packages cream cheese, Camembert cheese (including rind), blue cheese, and Swiss cheese in a bowl; beat until blended. Spoon mixture over pecan layer, spreading to edge of pan. Cover and chill at least 4 hours or up to 1 week.
3. To serve, invert pâté onto a serving plate; carefully remove plastic wrap. Garnish, if desired. Serve with apple wedges, gingersnaps, and/or crackers.

Roasted Pepper-Tomato Bruschetta

Seeding the tomatoes enhances the appearance of these appetizers.
ACTIVE 15 MIN. - TOTAL 15 MIN.
MAKES 2 DOZEN

- 1 (7-oz.) jar roasted red bell peppers, drained and chopped
- 6 ripe tomatoes, seeded and diced
- 3 Tbsp. shredded Parmesan cheese
- 2 Tbsp. chopped fresh basil
- 1 garlic clove, minced
- ½ tsp. coarse-grain sea salt or kosher salt
- ¼ tsp. freshly ground black pepper
- 24 French bread slices, toasted

Combine all ingredients except bread in a medium bowl. Spoon 1 heaping tablespoon topping over each toasted bread slice.

Swiss Cheese Crostini

ACTIVE 15 MIN. - TOTAL 25 MIN.
MAKES 3 DOZEN

- 1 French baguette
- 4 cups (16 oz.) shredded Swiss cheese
- ¼ cup beer
- 2 Tbsp. tomato paste
- 1 Tbsp. spicy brown mustard
- ¼ tsp. garlic powder
- ⅛ tsp. hot sauce

1. Preheat oven to 400°F. Cut baguette into ¼-inch slices, and place on a foil-lined baking sheet. Bake until lightly browned, about 5 minutes.
2. Combine cheese, beer, tomato paste, mustard, garlic powder, and hot sauce in a medium bowl; spread on bread slices.
3. Bake in preheated oven until cheese is melted, about 5 minutes. Serve immediately.

Shrimp Tarts

Asiago cheese updates the pastry in these rich appetizer tarts.
ACTIVE 15 MIN. - TOTAL 25 MIN.,
PLUS 2 HOURS CHILLING
MAKES 3 DOZEN

- 2 lb. large unpeeled fresh shrimp
- ⅔ cup finely chopped scallions
- ½ cup finely chopped fresh parsley
- ⅔ cup mayonnaise
- 2 Tbsp. capers
- 1 tsp. lemon juice
- ½ tsp. salt
- ¼ tsp. cayenne pepper
- 1 garlic clove, minced
- Tart Shells (recipe follows)
- Diagonally sliced scallions, for garnish

1. Bring 6 cups water to a boil; add shrimp and cook 3 to 5 minutes or until shrimp turn pink. Drain; rinse with cold water. Cover and chill 2 hours. Peel, devein, and coarsely chop shrimp.
2. Combine chopped shrimp, scallions, parsley, mayonnaise, capers, lemon juice, salt, cayenne pepper, and garlic in a large bowl. Spoon filling evenly into baked Tart Shells. Garnish, if desired.

Tart Shells

ACTIVE 15 MIN. - TOTAL 30 MIN., PLUS 1 HOUR CHILLING
MAKES 3 DOZEN

- ½ cup butter, softened
- ½ (8-oz.) pkg. cream cheese, softened
- 1¼ cups all-purpose flour
- ¼ cup grated Asiago cheese
- ¼ tsp. salt

1. Combine butter and cream cheese; stir until blended. Add flour, cheese, and salt, blending well. Cover and chill dough 1 hour. Divide dough into 3 portions. Shape each portion into 12 balls.

2. Preheat oven to 350°F. Press dough onto bottom and up sides of lightly greased 1¾-inch miniature muffin pans. Bake until golden, 15 to 17 minutes. Cool. Remove from pans.

Marinated Southwestern Cheese

As interest in Southwestern fare increased in the late 1980s, our Test Kitchens offered this variation. Serve on skewers for easy party pickups.
ACTIVE 30 MIN. - TOTAL 30 MIN., PLUS 8 HOURS CHILLING
MAKES 16 SERVINGS

- ½ cup olive oil
- ½ cup white wine vinegar
- ¼ cup fresh lime juice
- ½ (7.5-oz.) jar roasted sweet red peppers, drained and diced
- 3 scallions, minced
- 3 Tbsp. chopped fresh parsley
- 3 Tbsp. chopped fresh cilantro
- 1 tsp. granulated sugar
- ½ tsp. salt
- ½ tsp. freshly ground black pepper
- 1 (8-oz.) block sharp cheddar cheese, chilled
- 1 (8-oz.) block Monterey Jack cheese with peppers, chilled
- 1 (8-oz.) pkg. cream cheese, chilled
  Crackers, for serving

1. Whisk together oil, vinegar, and lime juice until blended. Stir in red peppers, scallions, parsley, cilantro, sugar, salt, and black pepper.
2. Cube cheeses, then place in a shallow dish; pour marinade over cheeses. Cover and chill 8 hours.
3. Transfer marinated cheese to a large glass jar or serving dish. Spoon marinade over top. Serve with crackers.

Breads & Crackers

Cheese Snappy Wafers

ACTIVE 20 MIN. - TOTAL 35 MIN.
MAKES 32 WAFERS

- 1 cup butter, cubed
- 2 cups all-purpose flour
- 8 oz. sharp cheddar cheese, grated
- ½ tsp. cayenne pepper
- ½ tsp. table salt
- 2 cups crisp rice cereal

Preheat oven to 350°F. Cut butter into flour until mixture resembles coarse meal. Stir in cheese, cayenne pepper, and salt. Fold in cereal. Shape into 1-inch balls; place 2 inches apart on ungreased baking sheets. Flatten each dough ball. Bake until lightly browned, about 15 minutes.

Sally's Cheese Straws

ACTIVE 15 MIN. - TOTAL 15 MIN., PLUS 10 MIN. BAKING PER BATCH
MAKES ABOUT 8 DOZEN

- 1 (16-oz.) block sharp cheddar cheese, shredded (not preshredded), at room temperature
- 1½ cups all-purpose flour
- ¼ cup butter, softened
- 1 tsp. salt
- ¼ tsp. cayenne pepper
- ⅛ tsp. dry mustard

1. Process all ingredients in a food processor about 30 seconds or until mixture forms a ball.
2. Preheat oven to 375°F. Fit a cookie press with a bar-shape disk, and, following manufacturer's instructions, shape dough into straws on ungreased baking sheets. Cut ribbons crosswise with a knife to make individual straws.
3. Bake in preheated oven until lightly browned, 8 to 10 minutes. Transfer to wire racks to cool.

Caramelized Onion Flatbread

ACTIVE 25 MIN. - TOTAL 45 MIN.
MAKES 8 SERVINGS

- 1 large sweet onion, sliced
- 3 Tbsp. olive oil, divided
- 1 lb. purchased pizza dough
- 1¼ tsp. kosher salt
- 1 tsp. chopped fresh rosemary

1. Preheat oven to 425°F with oven rack in lowest. Cook onion 1 tablespoon hot oil in a large nonstick skillet over medium-high 15 minutes or until golden brown.
2. Press dough into a 15- x 10-inch jelly-roll pan, pressing to about ¼-inch depth. Press a wooden spoon handle into dough to make indentations at 1-inch intervals; drizzle with remaining 2 tablespoons oil, and sprinkle with salt, rosemary, and caramelized onions.
3. Bake in preheated oven until lightly browned, 20 minutes.

Blue Cheese Thumbprints

ACTIVE 15 MIN. - TOTAL 15 MIN., PLUS 2 HOURS CHILLING AND 15 MIN. BAKING PER BATCH
MAKES ABOUT 5 DOZEN

- 2 (4-oz.) pkg. crumbled blue cheese
- ½ cup butter, softened
- 1⅓ cups all-purpose flour
- 3 Tbsp. poppy seeds
- ¼ tsp. cayenne pepper
- ⅓ cup cherry preserves

1. Beat blue cheese and butter in a medium bowl with an electric mixer on medium speed until fluffy. Add flour, poppy seeds, and cayenne pepper, beating just until combined. Roll dough into ¾-inch balls; cover and chill 2 hours.
2. Preheat oven to 350°F. Arrange balls on ungreased baking sheets; press thumb into each ball of dough, making an indentation.
3. Bake in preheated oven until golden, about 15 minutes. Transfer to wire racks to cool completely. Place about ¼ teaspoon preserves in each indentation.

Blue Cheese-Walnut Wafers

Don't substitute margarine for butter in this recipe. The butter makes the dough easy to handle and results in wonderfully tender wafers.

ACTIVE 10 MIN. - TOTAL 25 MIN., PLUS 1 HOUR, 5 MIN. CHILLING

MAKES 4 DOZEN

- 1 (4-oz.) pkg. blue cheese, softened
- ½ cup butter, softened
- 1¼ cups all-purpose flour
- ⅓ cup finely chopped walnuts

1. Process cheese, butter, and flour in a food processor until smooth, stopping to scrape down sides. (Dough will be sticky.) Spoon dough into a bowl; stir in walnuts. Cover and chill 5 minutes.
2. Divide dough in half. Shape each portion into an 8-inch log. Wrap in heavy-duty plastic wrap; chill 1 hour.
3. Preheat oven to 350°F. Slice dough into ¼-inch slices; place on ungreased baking sheets.
4. Bake until lightly browned, about 12 minutes. Store in an airtight container up to 1 week.

Salsa

Cowboy Caviar

Kick up the heat by including jalapeño seeds, or remove for a mild dip. Also serve with grilled meats or top baked potatoes.

ACTIVE 20 MIN. - TOTAL 35 MIN.

SERVES 10

- 3 Tbsp. olive oil
- 2 Tbsp. fresh lime juice (from 1 lime)
- 1½ tsp. red wine vinegar
- 1 tsp. ground cumin
- 1 tsp. kosher salt
- ½ tsp. smoked paprika
- ½ tsp. honey
- 1 (15-oz.) can black beans, drained and rinsed
- 1 (15-oz.) can black-eyed peas, drained and rinsed
- 1 cup fresh corn kernels (from 2 ears)

- 1 cup chopped yellow bell pepper (from 1 pepper)
- 1 cup chopped plum tomatoes (from 2 tomatoes)
- ½ cup finely chopped red onion (from 1 small onion)
- ½ cup chopped fresh cilantro
- 2 Tbsp. finely chopped jalapeño chile or serrano chile
- Tortilla chips, for serving

Whisk together the oil, lime juice, vinegar, cumin, salt, paprika, and honey in a large bowl. Add beans, peas, corn, bell pepper, tomatoes, onion, cilantro, and jalapeño; stir to coat well. Let stand 15 minutes, stirring occasionally. Serve with tortilla chips.

Fruit Salsa with Cinnamon Crisps

ACTIVE 15 MIN. - TOTAL 20 MIN.

MAKES 4 SERVINGS

- 1 pt. fresh strawberries, chopped
- 1 large banana, chopped
- 1 Red Delicious apple, chopped
- 1 kiwifruit, peeled and chopped
- ¼ cup fresh lemon juice
- ¼ cup, plus 1 Tbsp. granulated sugar, divided
- ¼ tsp. ground nutmeg
- 1¼ tsp. ground cinnamon, divided
- 2 pitas, split

1. Combine strawberries, banana, apple, and kiwifruit in a large bowl. Stir together lemon juice, ¼ cup sugar, the nutmeg, and ½ tsp. of the cinnamon; toss with fruit. Cover and chill.
2. Preheat oven to 350°F. Cut each pita half into eight wedges. Arrange wedges on baking sheets. Lightly coat with cooking spray. Combine remaining ¾ tsp. cinnamon and 1 tablespoon sugar in a small bowl. Sprinkle over wedges.
3. Bake in preheated oven until lightly browned, 6 to 8 minutes. Serve with fruit salsa.

Cuban Black Bean Salsa with Avocado-Lime Dressing

This salsa is loaded with bright flavors and varied textures. You can make this salsa up to a day in advance and refrigerate until serving. Top with the pepitas just before serving to keep them crunchy.

ACTIVE 25 MIN. - TOTAL 25 MIN.

SERVES 8

- 1 ripe avocado
- 3 Tbsp. fresh lime juice (from 2 limes)
- 2 Tbsp. avocado oil
- ¾ tsp. kosher salt
- ¼ tsp. ground cumin
- ⅛ tsp. cayenne pepper
- ⅓ cup chopped fresh cilantro
- ½ cup water
- 1½ (15-oz.) cans black beans, drained and rinsed
- 1 cup halved grape tomatoes
- 1 cup fresh or frozen yellow corn kernels (from 1 ear corn)
- ¾ cup chopped red bell pepper (from 1 bell pepper)
- ⅓ cup finely chopped red onion (from 1 small onion)
- ⅓ cup roasted salted pepitas (pumpkin seeds)
- Tortilla chips, for serving

1. Combine avocado, lime juice, oil, salt, cumin, cayenne, and 3 tablespoons of the cilantro in a food processor. Process until smooth, adding up to ½ cup water, ¼ cup at a time, if necessary to thin the dressing.
2. Combine beans, tomatoes, corn, bell peppers, onion, and 3 tablespoons of the pepitas in a large bowl. Toss with half of the dressing. Top with remaining pepitas, dressing, and cilantro. Serve with tortilla chips.

Baking at High Altitudes

Liquids boil at lower temperatures (below 212°F) and moisture evaporates more quickly at high altitudes. Both of these factors significantly impact the quality of baked goods. Also, leavening gases (air, carbon dioxide, water vapor) expand faster. If you live at 3,000 feet or below, first try a recipe as is. Sometimes few, if any, changes are needed. But the higher you go, the more you'll have to adjust your ingredients and cooking times.

A Few Overall Tips

- Use shiny new baking pans. This seems to help mixtures rise, especially cake batters.
- Use butter, flour, and parchment paper to prep your baking pans for nonstick cooking. At high altitudes, baked goods tend to stick more to pans.
- Be exact in your measurements (once you've figured out what they should be). This is always important in baking, but especially so when you're up so high. Tiny variations in ingredients make a bigger difference at high altitudes than at sea level.
- Boost flavor. Seasonings and extracts tend to be more muted at higher altitudes, so increase them slightly.
- Have patience. You may have to bake your favorite sea-level recipe a few times, making slight adjustments each time, until it's worked out to suit your particular altitude.

Ingredient/Temperature Adjustments

CHANGE	AT 3,000 FEET	AT 5,000 FEET	AT 7,000 FEET
Baking powder or baking soda	Reduce each tsp. called for by up to 1/8 tsp.	Reduce each tsp. called for by 1/8 to 1/4 tsp.	Reduce each tsp. called for by 1/4 to 1/2 tsp.
Sugar	Reduce each cup called for by up to 1 Tbsp.	Reduce each cup called for by up to 2 Tbsp.	Reduce each cup called for by 2 to 3 Tbsp.
Liquid	Increase each cup called for by up to 2 Tbsp.	Increase each cup called for by up to 2 to 4 Tbsp.	Increase each cup called for by up to 3 to 4 Tbsp.
Oven temperature	Increase 3°F to 5°F	Increase 15°F	Increase 21°F to 25°F

Metric Equivalents

The recipes that appear in this cookbook use the standard United States method for measuring liquid and dry or solid ingredients (teaspoons, tablespoons, and cups). The information on this chart is provided to help cooks outside the U.S. successfully use these recipes. All equivalents are approximate.

METRIC EQUIVALENTS FOR DIFFERENT TYPES OF INGREDIENTS

A standard cup measure of a dry or solid ingredient will vary in weight depending on the type of ingredient. A standard cup of liquid is the same volume for any type of liquid. Use the following chart when converting standard cup measures to grams (weight) or milliliters (volume).

Standard Cup	Fine Powder (ex. flour)	Grain (ex. rice)	Granular (ex. sugar)	Liquid Solids (ex. butter)	Liquid (ex. milk)
1	140 g	150 g	190 g	200 g	240 ml
¾	105 g	113 g	143 g	150 g	180 ml
⅔	93 g	100 g	125 g	133 g	160 ml
½	70 g	75 g	95 g	100 g	120 ml
⅓	47 g	50 g	63 g	67 g	80 ml
¼	35 g	38 g	48 g	50 g	60 ml
⅛	18 g	19 g	24 g	25 g	30 ml

USEFUL EQUIVALENTS FOR LIQUID INGREDIENTS BY VOLUME

¼ tsp.						=	1 ml	
½ tsp.						=	2 ml	
1 tsp.						=	5 ml	
3 tsp.	=	1 Tbsp.			=	½ fl oz.	=	15 ml
		2 Tbsp.	=	⅛ cup	=	1 fl oz.	=	30 ml
		4 Tbsp.	=	¼ cup	=	2 fl oz.	=	60 ml
		5⅓ Tbsp.	=	⅓ cup	=	3 fl oz.	=	80 ml
		8 Tbsp.	=	½ cup	=	4 fl oz.	=	120 ml
		10⅔ Tbsp.	=	⅔ cup	=	5 fl oz.	=	160 ml
		12 Tbsp.	=	¾ cup	=	6 fl oz.	=	180 ml
		16 Tbsp.	=	1 cup	=	8 fl oz.	=	240 ml
		1 pt.	=	2 cups	=	16 fl oz.	=	480 ml
		1 qt.	=	4 cups	=	32 fl oz.	=	960 ml
						33 fl oz.	=	1000 ml = 1l

USEFUL EQUIVALENTS FOR DRY INGREDIENTS BY WEIGHT
(To convert ounces to grams, multiply the number of ounces by 30.)

1 oz.	=	1/16 lb.	=	30 g
4 oz.	=	¼ lb.	=	120 g
8 oz.	=	½ lb.	=	240 g
12 oz.	=	¾ lb.	=	360 g
16 oz.	=	1 lb.	=	480 g

USEFUL EQUIVALENTS FOR LENGTH
(To convert inches to centimeters, multiply the number of inches by 2.5.)

1 in.					=		2.5 cm
6 in.	=	½	ft.		=		15 cm
12 in.	=	1	ft.		=		30 cm
36 in.	=	3	ft.	=	1 yd.	=	90 cm

USEFUL EQUIVALENTS FOR COOKING/OVEN TEMPERATURES

	Fahrenheit	Celsius	Gas Mark
Freeze Water	32°F	0°C	
Room Temperature	68°F	20°C	
Boil Water	212°F	100°C	
Bake	325°F	160°C	3
	350°F	180°C	4
	375°F	190°C	5
	400°F	200°C	6
	425°F	220°C	7
	450°F	230°C	8
Broil			Grill

Recipe Title Index

This index alphabetically lists every recipe by exact title

General Recipe Index

This index lists every recipe by food category and/or major ingredient.

MEREDITH CONSUMER MARKETING
Director, Direct Marketing-Books: Daniel Fagan
Marketing Operations Manager: Max Daily
Assistant Marketing Manager: Kylie Dazzo
Marketing Coordinator: Elizabeth Moore
Content Manager: Julie Doll
Senior Production Manager: Liza Ward

WATERBURY PUBLICATIONS, INC.
Editorial Director: Lisa Kingsley
Associate Editor: Tricia Bergman
Associate Editor: Maggie Glisan
Creative Director: Ken Carlson
Associate Design Director: Doug Samuelson
Production Assistant: Mindy Samuelson
Contributing Copy Editor: Peg Smith
Contributing Proofreader: Carrie Truesdell
Contributing Indexer: Mary Williams

Recipe Developers and Testers: Meredith Food Studios

MEREDITH CORPORATION
Executive Chairman: Stephen M. Lacy

Library of Congress Control Number: 2021932672

ISBN: 978-1-4197-5796-9

First Edition 2021
Printed in the United States of America
10 9 8 7 6 5 4 3 2 1
Call 1-800-826-4707 for more information.

Distributed in 2021 by Abrams, an imprint of ABRAMS.
Abrams® is a registered trademark of Harry N. Abrams, Inc.

ABRAMS The Art of Books
195 Broadway, New York, NY 10007
abramsbooks.com

Pictured on front cover:
Eggnog Layer Cake with Bourbon-Vanilla Bean Buttercream Frosting, page 322